The Life of Joy
and Peace

Also by D. Martyn Lloyd-Jones

Faith Tried and Triumphant
I Am Not Ashamed: Advice to Timothy
Love So Amazing: Exposition of Colossians 1
A Nation under Wrath: Studies in Isaiah 5
The Plight of Man and the Power of God

The Life of Joy and Peace

An Exposition of Philippians

D. Martyn Lloyd-Jones

Baker Books

A Division of Baker Book House Co.
Grand Rapids, Michigan 49516

Published by Baker Books
a division of Baker Book House Company
P.O. Box 6287, Grand Rapids, MI 49516-6287
with permission of copyright owner

One-volume paperback edition published 1999

Volume 1 previously published in cloth in Great Britain and by Baker Book House under the title *The Life of Joy.* Volume 2 previously published in cloth in Great Britain and by Baker Book House under the title *The Life of Peace.*

Printed in the United States of America

ISBN 0-8010-5816-3

Readers of Dr. Lloyd-Jones's books will realize that chapters 14, 17, and 18 of volume 2 are also published in *Spiritual Depression* (1971). The reason for this is that he preached those sermons in his Philippians series, but realizing how appropriate they were to the subject of spiritual depression, he included them in that book. However, this volume would clearly be incomplete without those chapters, so with the kind permission of the publisher Marshall Pickering, we have put them again in this series in which they were first preached.

For current information about academic books, resources for Christian leaders, and all new releases available from Baker Book House, visit our web site:
http://www.bakerbooks.com

The Life of Joy

An Exposition of Philippians 1 and 2

Contents

Introduction

Although these sermons were preached in Westminster Chapel between November 1947 and February 1948, they have as powerful a relevance today as they did forty years ago. Firstly, we are no different at heart from those who heard the sermons then. The very core of the Doctor's message is that human beings have always been the same – whether 2,000 years ago in Philippi or today in the twentieth-century West. He proclaimed, he would argue, not his own ideas, but the eternal truths that were set out in God's infallible word. A Jew, awaiting probable execution in a first-century Roman prison, could thus speak to downcast and perplexed Londoners two millennia later. Paul's secret – the inner joy and peace that he had through Christ's presence in his life – is one open to all who look for it today.

This series of sermons was delivered two years after the most terrible war that the world had ever seen. Everyone listening to them had been through that conflict and Westminster Chapel itself had been damaged by bomb blast. By 1947 the Cold War had already begun and indeed the Doctor refers to the possibility of World War Three in his chapter *The Only Way of Peace*. With the development of nuclear technology, we still live in uncertain times. Maybe détente will work – then, maybe not. People of all ages are acutely aware of what will happen if it fails. Resolutions of goodwill can do no ultimate good. Once again, the Doctor points to our one true hope, our Christian gospel. It is only if sinners are born again in Christ that real peace can prevail.

Christopher Catherwood (Editor)
Balsham, October 1988

1

Joy in the Lord

Paul and Timotheus, the servants of Jesus Christ, to all the saints in Christ Jesus which are at Philippi, with the bishops and deacons (Phil. 1:1).

I am calling your attention to this particular verse by way of introduction to the message of this great epistle. It is generally agreed that of all Paul's letters which have been preserved, there are certain qualities belonging to this particular epistle which make it unique. It is the most lyrical, the happiest, letter which the Apostle ever wrote, at least among those which have been preserved. There is in it a note of happiness and joy – not that joy is absent from Paul's other letters, but it is particularly striking here. Although he does give them some warnings, when he wrote this letter Paul seemed to have no reason for reprimanding the church. The relationship between Paul and the Philippians was most cordial; none of the unfortunate or unpleasant things that had taken place, for instance, in Corinth, had happened here, nor did he have to write to them as he wrote to the Colossians. So the situation was particularly happy and harmonious and the Apostle wrote out of a very full and glad heart.

But we come to consider this epistle now, not only because of its own intrinsic merit, but rather as it speaks to us at this present time. That is, of course, one of the most remarkable things, and the unique thing about Scripture. A letter which may have been written for more or less personal reasons has a universal application. That is so, of course,

not only because truth is changeless but also because the
laws of the spiritual life never change either. There are
variations in certain manifestations of the same condition,
but the condition itself never changes at all, which is why the
advice given in these epistles in the New Testament is as
apposite and applicable today as it was when these letters
were first written. That is why the Bible is of such vital
importance in the life of a Christian: every conceivable
experience which the Christian may have to face has already
been met and dealt with somewhere in the Scriptures. There
is no such thing as a new experience in the realm of the
Spirit; you will find everything catered for here. These laws
abide and they are permanent. Therefore what the Apostle
had to say to the church at Philippi so long ago, has a very
urgent and relevant message for us at this present time.

Let us consider first, then, something of the background
to this epistle. Philippi was the first city in which the gospel
of Jesus Christ was ever preached on the continent of
Europe. You will find in Acts 16 the interesting and amazing
account of the vision that Paul had in the night. He saw a
man of Macedonia calling him to come over and help to take
the gospel to Macedonia in Europe. Then we read of how
Paul and Silas went, and how they arrived at Philippi, where
they found a little group of women who had met together
for prayer by the side of the river. We see how they realised
that this was the place to stop; here already was a group of
devout people praying to God. So they expounded and
preached the gospel to them. Then the Lord opened the
heart of Lydia, a seller of purple who was one of them, and
she received the gospel, and so did others with her. They
were the nucleus of the Philippian church and Paul and Silas
went back and fore to that company.

Then comes the account of the poor devil-possessed girl
who followed them and shouted out, 'These men are the
servants of the most high God, which shew unto us the way
of salvation.' And we are told that one day Paul was so disturbed in spirit by the sight of this poor girl, who was being
used by cruel men to make money, that he turned and

rebuked the spirit that was in her and exorcised it. This led to Paul and Silas being put in prison, and that night there was a great earthquake. All the prisoners found themselves loosed from their chains, and the keeper, fearing that they had escaped, had actually drawn his sword to kill himself, when Paul cried out: 'Do thyself no harm ...' Then the man prostrated himself at the feet of Paul and Silas and said, 'Sirs, what must I do to be saved?' and Paul gave that immortal answer: 'Believe on the Lord Jesus Christ, and thou shalt be saved, and thy house.' So the man believed, and his household with him, and they were baptised and began to rejoice in the Lord. Then Paul and Silas, after an interview with the magistrates, left the city.

That, then, was how the church at Philippi, to whom Paul wrote this letter, came to be formed. It is of vital importance also that we should remember that when he wrote this letter Paul was again a prisoner. He was in prison in Rome, which meant that he was probably in a kind of dungeon, chained to a soldier on both hands. We read in Acts of how he got there – how he was arrested and how he had that extraordinary journey to Rome, including the shipwreck on the way. But here he is at last in Rome, a prisoner in chains writing to this church which had come into being perhaps ten years earlier as the result of his preaching of the gospel. He had a special reason for writing this letter. The church at Philippi had sent him a gift, and they had sent it by a man called Epaphroditus, who is mentioned in the second chapter. This man had been taken very ill while in Rome, indeed it had looked as if he was going to die, but he had recovered and now he was going back to the church at Philippi taking Paul's letter with him.

Now that is the context of this epistle and it is indeed from every standpoint an astonishing and remarkable letter. Its theme can be put like this: 'Joy in Christ' or, to put it another way, 'How to rejoice in the Lord'. As you go through the letter you will observe that Paul keeps on saying this; for example, at the beginning of the third chapter he says, 'Rejoice in the Lord', and later, in chapter 4, he says,

'Rejoice in the Lord alway: and again I say, Rejoice' – that
is the word that runs through the letter. Or you may prefer
to look at it from another angle and say that this letter,
perhaps more explicitly than any other, displays to us the
power of the gospel of Jesus Christ. It shows us in a very
concrete and practical manner what the gospel of Jesus
Christ really can do in a life. This is not so much a theoretical treatise as a practical exposition of the gospel. In a way,
Paul is more personal in this letter, right the way through,
than he is in any other letter and yet, though writing about
himself, he is giving this amazing exposition of what the gospel can do in a man's life.

Not only that, he shows very clearly at the same time what
the gospel can do in the life of a community, for as you read
this letter you find that the Apostle is not only describing
himself, he is also describing something of the state of the
church at Philippi. He loved that church because of its state
and condition, because of its harmonious character, because
of the happiness in the life of the people – and all this is due
to the gospel. Think of Paul before his conversion. Try to
imagine that persecuting, foolish Saul of Tarsus, that very
clever, good and religious man. Just think of him 'breathing
out threatenings and slaughter'; think of the spirit of hatred
that animated him, and contrast it with the man who wrote
this letter, and there you will see what the gospel can do.
Then think of the church at Philippi. Look at a man like the
Philippian jailer, a violent sort of man, but now he, and
others probably worse than he, are all members of this
church. Look too at the way Paul loves them and the things
he is able to say about them – all this is just a great manifestation of what the gospel of Jesus Christ can do.

And that, I think, explains clearly why it is important for
us to consider this letter together. Our world is becoming
increasingly like that ancient society in which these people
lived. And the great question that concerns most thinking
people today is, how can harmony and peace be brought
into our relationships? Is there any way of resolving all the
individual animosities and rivalries? Is there anything in the

world that can get rid of the problems and perplexities that are tearing the life of society to shreds and causing such misery in the world and threatening still further calamities? That is what the world is looking for at this time. That is why it is holding its conferences and having its political, its economic and social gatherings.

Now the Christian Church announces, amongst other things, that there is only one way in which such a harmonious society can be brought about. Its claim is that nothing but the power of the gospel of Jesus Christ in individual lives can ever produce that state, either individually or in the corporate life of men and women. It seems to me that as we consider the whole situation of our world today, nothing is of greater value to us than that we should look at the life of this Christian community in Philippi and see these difficulties resolved and the disagreements banished. To put it in still another form, we can say that the themes of this epistle are these: how to triumph over circumstances and how to live happily and harmoniously together.

You will notice, even from a short portion of the first chapter, that triumphing over circumstances is inevitably the central theme. The writer is in prison; in a sense everything is against him, and yet in spite of that he writes this lyrical letter. It is a sheer triumph over circumstances and surroundings. Now there are some people who dislike repetition and who speak scornfully of tautology. But if ever a man was guilty of tautology it was the Apostle Paul: 'Rejoice,' he says, 'and again I say, Rejoice.' In the first chapter he tells us how he is able to triumph over circumstances, then he goes on repeating this, and finally, in the fourth chapter, he concludes by saying, 'I can do all things through Christ which strengtheneth me.' Somebody, I think very aptly and rightly, has described this as the 'tautology of earnestness'. Anyone who believes the gospel is bound to repeat himself; anyone who is really earnest about these things, anyone who sees the state of the world and knows that this is the only truth, must go on repeating and reiterating it. 'To me to say these things,' says the Apostle in chap-

ter 3, 'is not grievous, but for you it is safe', and the other
apostles do exactly the same thing. Peter in a sense half
apologises for saying the same things, but, he says, 'I think
it meet, as long as I am in this tabernacle' – as long as I am
alive – 'to stir you up by putting you in remembrance' (2
Pet. 1:13). Why? Because they are so easily forgotten. If it
were a case of announcing the truth of the gospel to a man
once he had learned it and for ever, there would be no need
of repetition, but, alas, we know ourselves sufficiently well
to realise that we can hear a thing a thousand times and still
forget it. And that is why the Apostle goes on repeating it,
because knowing how to triumph over circumstances is
something very urgent and practical.

I need not remind you of the conditions in which we find
ourselves, we are all painfully aware of them. We do not
know what is going to happen, but I do know, in the name
of the gospel of Christ, that if the fire that worked in Paul
and in the Philippian church worked in us, then we could
face anything that might come. That is not bravado, it is
nothing but Christian experience; it is to know and experience the power of the Lord in our own personal lives. This
is not a mere painting of a beautiful picture, it is the experience of a man in prison. I know, said this man, I have
experienced it and there is no question about it. He had
triumphed, and he knew that so many of them in Philippi
had triumphed too, so he wanted to encourage and help
them to go on with this triumph in Christ and in the gospel.
Therefore he tried to show them how to live happily and
harmoniously together.

Now what really accounts for most of the troubles
between man and man is that there is trouble within man
himself. The man who is arguing with himself generally
wants to argue with everybody else; the man who is
unhappy within, in his own central life, is the man who is ill
at ease and therefore touchy, and because of this, everything in his environment becomes wrong and goes astray.
The secret is to be right within, with God, and then the rest
follows. So it is important for us to consider this subject of

victory in Christ from every conceivable standpoint. We must do it individually, also. Sooner or later in life we all meet untoward circumstances, and find ourselves in some sort of prison. It may be a sick bed, or a hospital; it may be an accident; it may be grief or sorrow. Something puts us there: we are in that prison and we cannot avoid it. The important thing for us is to know, before we get there, the secret of how to overcome it, how to have this joy in the Lord in spite of our circumstances, how to rise above them all; how to conquer and be supreme over them. We need to know this if only for our own peace and joy.

But there is a still more urgent reason. I do not want to minimise that first point, but it is not enough. Even more important is the fact that we are saved to serve – we are saved, in a sense, to be evangelists. Paul makes that plain in the second chapter when emphasising the importance of this perfect harmony of the church: 'That ye may be blameless and harmless, the sons of God, without rebuke, in the midst of a crooked and perverse nation, among whom ye shine as lights in the world.' 'Lights' – that is the point. If ever the world needed the witness and testimony of Christian people it is at this present time. The world is unhappy, it is distracted and frightened, and what it needs is to see stars shining out of the heavens in the midst of the darkness, attracting the world by rebuking that darkness, and by giving it light, showing how it too can live that quality of life. So, apart from our own personal happiness and enjoyment, it is of vital importance that we should understand this epistle and its doctrine and that we should be living and practising it for the sake of the world in which we live; we owe it to the world.

But over and above that, God calls us to that life. He is setting us forth as constellations and lights in the heavens and you cannot shine as a constellation if there is something obscuring the light and preventing it shining out. If the window, as it were, is not clear, or if the reflecting mirror is not as it should be, then the light cannot be seen. That is why it behoves us to consider this together.

That, then, is the theme and purpose of the letter. Let us now look briefly at the Apostle's method of doing all this. According to some of the authorities, his method here is different from that which you find in most of his other epistles. Up to a point I am prepared to agree with that. The Apostle's method, almost invariably, is to start with doctrine and theology and then, after he has worked that out, he shows how he is going to apply it. Most of his epistles can be divided in that way, but Philippians cannot be divided exactly like that. There are some who go so far as to say there is no theology in this epistle, but that is surely a complete error. He here chooses to start with a practical statement but he cannot do that except in terms of his theology. In other words, all the comfort that the Apostle gives is based upon his doctrine, and without that doctrine he really has no comfort to give these people. But though he normally gives first doctrine and then practice, his method here is to mix theology and practical application, they both run right through the epistle, as I am now going to try to show you.

The other thing I want to emphasise is the realism of this letter. He conceals nothing; he faces everything; he is honest. That is why I thank God increasingly for the New Testament – for the sheer realism of the book. I take it that we are all by now sufficiently disillusioned and are no longer willing to listen to men who paint these rosy pictures which have all come to nothing. But when a man becomes a realist the danger is that he may become cynical. There is only one thing that can save a man from such cynicism and that is this glorious gospel expounded in such magnificent terms.

How, then, does the Apostle handle the theme? Here again it is fascinating to observe how different people have divided up this epistle. There are those, for instance, who would say that the whole of the third chapter, where Paul looks back across his life and experience, is a digression. I find myself completely disagreeing with that particular view. Surely there are certain obvious, almost natural divisions there, which correspond to the first chapter. The main theme, let me remind you, is joy in Christ – how to rejoice in the Lord, how to rejoice in tribulation and live this happy buoyant life in Christ. That is what Paul wants to tell them and this is how he does it. He first of all shows how that is possible in spite of adverse circumstances, and continues with this theme immediately in the first chapter where he talks about himself as a prisoner. These loving members of the church at Philippi were very concerned about the fact that Paul was in prison, and so in verse 12 he deals with that and says, 'I would ye should understand, brethren, that the things which happened unto me have fallen out rather unto the furtherance of the gospel …' You can triumph, says Paul, and rejoice, and enjoy this Christian life in spite of adverse circumstances, in spite of being a prisoner.

In addition, he refers to certain people who were preaching Christ out of envy, hoping to add to his troubles, but in spite of that, too, Paul still maintains that this life of joy is possible; this is the great and glorious thing which we must hold in mind at the very beginning. What is offered to us by this gospel is not something contingent, it is an absolute offer. The gospel of Jesus Christ promises to the man who truly loves and believes it that whatever his circumstances and his condition, and whatever anyone else may do, his joy can and shall abide. That is the great theme of chapter 1.

Then I think he shows in the second chapter how all this is possible, even in spite of what I would call the 'weakness of the flesh'. By that I do not mean something purely physical, but rather difficulties and weakness of character – things that belong to us as natural beings. You cannot read that second chapter without seeing that there were, even in the church at Philippi, elements which were tending to produce a certain amount of discord. 'Look not every man on his own things, but every man also on the things of others' (2:4). There is always that tendency, though we are Christians and in Christ. We are tempted to selfishness, to be concerned about nothing and no one but ourselves and our own happiness and prosperity. We are so concerned about ourselves that we forget others and thereby perhaps become

unkind to them; that is an element with which we always
have to deal. Now the Christian gospel does not promise
that if we believe it we will suddenly be taken into a magical
world where there will be no one to upset us. It rather tells
us that we may be surrounded by difficult people, there may
be criticism, there may be jealousy, yet, and this is the
point, this joy of the Lord is something that can survive even
that. In spite of these infirmities and weaknesses, not to say
sins, with which we may be surrounded and afflicted, it is
still possible for us to triumph in and over them all; we need
not be defeated by them. In spite of their presence, the joy
and the harmony should go forward.

That, again, is something that is of vital importance to us.
Let us never think of these New Testament Christians as if
they were living some life apart. Many of them were probably slaves, or ordinary people having to work very hard.
They, like us, knew what it was to be physically tired, they
knew what it was to have frayed nerves, yet, says Paul, if
you have this truth in you and the power of Christ in you,
you can rejoice in spite of everything, you can rise above it;
in the midst of it all the harmony can and will increase.

Then we move on to chapter 3 and to the other things
which tend to rob us of joy and happiness. These were
things of which the Apostle had had a long and deep experience. He went about preaching the gospel and churches
were formed, but they were being upset and the converts'
faith was being shaken by false teaching. The so-called
Judaizers went round after Paul and told these young Christians that belief in Christ was all right so far as it went, but
that if they wanted to be true Christians they must conform
to certain Jewish rites and ceremonies. They put this fatal
plus on to the gospel. They were upsetters of the church and
the life of the Christians, by thus filling their minds with
perplexity. These grievous errors and troubles in the early
Church were drifting into the church at Philippi. Paul saw
that, and in the third chapter he prepared the members
beforehand, answering these arguments once and for ever
by showing how to deal with this false teaching with regard

to the practice of Christianity. False doctrine makes joy in
the Lord impossible. If our faith is not true and right, we can
never experience the blessings of salvation, so we need to
understand the teaching of the Bible with regard to doctrine
and practice.

And then, in the last chapter, he shows how this bliss and
joy can be maintained and increased even in spite of, and in
the midst of, the natural strain of life and living. Paul was
very grateful to the church at Philippi for sending him a par-
cel of food and clothing, and yet he tells them that he knows
how to exist in any state or condition. He knows both 'how
to be abased and how to abound.' He says, 'I have learned,
in whatsoever state I am, therewith to be content.' Is there
not something curiously contemporary about all this? We
are only too well aware of the problems caused by tiredness,
ill-health, old age, the need of food and of clothing, and of
shelter. Yet Paul, even here in the prison, probably suffering a great deal of physical discomfort, now becoming an old
man long before his time because of his incessant labours in
the gospel of Christ, towers above it all and cries out in this
marvellous burst of eloquence that it does not matter, nothing matters, because he knows in whatsoever state he is how
to be content. He has all things because he has Christ.

The strain of life is a very serious thing. He is no friend of
mankind who tries to make light of it. That is where the
superficial psychologists are ultimately our enemies rather
than our friends – they just help us to forget the facts. But
here is a man in the midst of great trials, who glories and
triumphs, and rejoices. Not only that, he is able to impart
something of that joy and triumph, not only to those who
are immediately around him, not only to those who received
the letter from him, but even to us today, almost two
thousand years after he wrote this lyrical letter.

That is the theme, and as we go on to consider this epistle,
these are some of the questions which we shall be facing.
We shall ask, what is life? We shall also ask, what is death?
We are going to see what happened at the incarnation; we
are going to consider the meaning of justification by faith.

We shall consider the doctrine of the resurrection and ask what it means to be glorified. We are going to consider what real prayer means. These are some of the themes. You see, this letter is teeming with central Christian doctrine and yet the whole thing is practical; it is speaking to us today and addressing us in our present critical situation. Thank God that as we find ourselves facing the present situation, one which we may also have to face in the years which lie ahead – we are living in a time when the very foundations seem to be shaking – thank God that we have a message which can assure us that there is something which can not only keep us steady and steadfast, something which can not only give us strength and nerve our wills and prevent us from fainting and collapsing by the wayside, but which will enable us to triumph in it all and rejoice with joy unspeakable and full of glory.

And the secret of it all is, as Paul says in this first verse, that we are saints in Christ.

2

Saints in Christ Jesus

Paul and Timotheus, the servants of Jesus Christ, to all
the saints in Christ Jesus which are at Philippi, with the
bishops and deacons: Grace be unto you, and peace, from
God our Father, and from the Lord Jesus Christ. I thank
my God upon every remembrance of you, always in every
prayer of mine for you all making request with joy, for
your fellowship in the gospel from the first day until now;
being confident of this very thing, that he which hath
begun a good work in you will perform it until the day of
Jesus Christ: even as it is meet for me to think this of you
all, because I have you in my heart; inasmuch as both in
my bonds, and in the defence and confirmation of the gospel, ye all are partakers of my grace (Phil. 1:1–7).

We have seen in our first study how the situation confronting these early Christians was strangely similar to our situation today. The world was then a very difficult place, even
as it is now, and so this letter has a great deal to teach us.
Its great theme is *joy in the Lord, or joy in Christ,* and our
special calling as Christian people is to manifest the kind of
life that is depicted here by the Apostle. That, it seems to
me, is the first call upon every Christian at this present time.
We are to stand out in this modern world, and to show
others how to triumph and how to conquer. That is how we
can persuade people of the error of their ways and attract
them to the Lord Jesus Christ.

To me this is the first step, the royal road. The world
today, as we are all well aware, is not very ready to listen to

us or to preaching. It tells us it has no interest in theology
and dogma, and there may be some truth in that; the world
has become psychological, not to say cynical, and it is not
prepared to listen to what people say. But when it sees a life
which is triumphant, a personality that is clearly victorious,
then it begins to pay attention. The first Christians conquered the ancient world just by being Christian. It was
their love for one another and their type of life that made
such an impact upon that pagan world, and there is no question but that this is the greatest need of the hour – the Christian quality of life being demonstrated among men and
women. That is something to which we are all called and
something which we can all do. And here the Apostle tells
us how to do it, though he does deal with the doctrine at the
same time. This letter gives us incomparable comfort. It tells
both how we can maintain peace and joy, and at the same
time have this great impact and influence upon the world
that is around and about us. That is the great theme of this
epistle and the Apostle deals with it, as we have seen, by
showing us the various difficulties that were confronting him
and the church at Philippi, and then by showing how the
gospel enables us to overcome them.

In a sense he starts doing that in the twelfth verse of this
first chapter, and we must wonder why he does not start on
that at once. Why, instead of his preliminary salutation of
grace and peace, does he not immediately come to the great
comfort he has to give? Now this is, to me, something which
is of real significance and the answer can be put in this way:
what the Apostle has to offer here, as in all his other epistles, is something that is only possible to us on the basis of
certain presuppositions. It is vital that we should understand
that. The amazing thing which the Apostle tells us in this letter, which is true of himself and of the Philippians, and
which is true and possible for all Christians, can only happen
if we are in absolute agreement with what he has to tell us
in these first eleven verses. In other words, this is not a general truth for the world at large; it is a very special piece of
teaching. What the Apostle says in this letter can only be

understood by certain people. To the world in general it is meaningless; it is a comfort and consolation only within certain limits, and unless we are careful to observe those limits, then everything the Apostle has to say to us will be beside the point, and will finally be quite useless. You will find in all these epistles that the practical help and encouragement which is given is always based on doctrine. Paul always gives comfort and consolation by deducing things from certain principles which he has already laid down.

Now that is clearly and of necessity something which is basic and final, and there, surely, we find the explanation of so much that is, alas, true of the Church in general today and also of the world outside. We can compare ourselves with Christians who have lived in times past; we can compare ourselves, for instance, with the Christians during the evangelical awakening of the eighteenth century; we can read something of the works of the Puritans, or we can turn to the Protestant Reformers and read about them; we can consider the Church among certain brethren on the continent of Europe, even before the Protestant Reformation; we can go back to these first Christians, and among all these saints of past ages, we always find this lyrical note, this note of triumph and of joy. We have it in many of our hymns, and when we compare ourselves with that kind of Christian experience, we are at once aware of the striking contrast. Why is this? What is it the Church has lost? Why is it that there is an absence of this quality? Why is there so little assurance, so little rejoicing, so little of this spirit of triumph? To me there is only one answer to these questions: we have forgotten the doctrine, we have not been careful always to base everything upon certain preliminary considerations without which there is no true comfort.

The difficulty with many of us is that we are anxious to obtain the blessings of the gospel, but we are not equally careful to observe the conditions. Everybody wants the blessings, of course; the world today, in a sense, is spending most of its time seeking happiness and joy, because nobody wants to be miserable and unhappy. If an announcement were to be made that there is a theory or a doctrine that can make people happy in spite of everything, the whole world would want to hear it. We want the comfort and the happiness, but we want it on our own terms, we want it easily, we want it simply, we want it by just having *it* and nothing else. Now let me make it clear, before we proceed to any detailed consideration of this great epistle, that what Paul is talking about here can never be obtained on such terms. Unless we accept his foundation, we shall never be able to erect the building that he has constructed; unless we start with his presuppositions we can never draw the right conclusions. Indeed, unless we observe the conditions that are attached to every promise that is made anywhere in the Bible, we shall never experience the blessings of the promises. That is why Paul, of necessity, as a wise teacher, must spend all this time in the first eleven verses before he begins to deal with the detailed situation. Let me put it like this: this epistle was not written to the world at large, but 'to all the saints in Christ Jesus which are at Philippi, with the bishops and deacons'. The New Testament has nothing to say in general to the world which does not believe on the Lord Jesus Christ; it offers no comfort, no consolation, no encouragement whatsoever. It always starts with the gospel and it is only as people have faced that, that they can experience these other things. Paul has not written a general letter to the whole of the Roman Empire announcing the way to happiness and peace. Not at all! It is a special letter to certain special people and it bases its argument upon certain fundamental and primary principles.

Therefore, the first thing we have to consider is this: to whom does Paul offer the wonderful kind of life that he depicts here? Who is it that can be happy in all kinds of states and conditions? Who is the man who can say, 'To me to live is Christ'? Who is the man who can say, 'I have learned in whatsoever state I am, therewith [therein] to be content'? Who can speak like that? And the answer is that it is only the people who can conform to a particular pattern. The Apostle is writing his letter to Christian people, so unless we are perfectly clear in our minds about what constitutes a Christian, we can never derive the benefit that we should from a consideration of this great letter. That is the first thing which we must do. The Apostle himself does this; he takes great pains to define exactly what these people are and what they must continue to be, knowing that if they do not continue, they will never know the benefits which he is anxious for them to have. So the first thing we must do as we approach our study of this epistle is to ask: what is a Christian? We must constantly ask that question, because if we go wrong there, we go wrong everywhere else. People ask, 'Why am I not happy like that? What must I do to get that happiness?' And the answer is that we must be Christian, we must conform to the definition, and if and when we do that, then all these things will follow as the night follows the day.

What, then, are the characteristics of the true Christian? How do we know whether we are Christian or not? The Apostle here tells us three things about the Christian, and the first is that *he is a partaker of the grace of God*. 'Ye all are partakers of my grace' – that is how he puts it in verse 7. Other translations read 'partakers with me of grace', or, 'you are all partners with me in the grace and the favour of God', and that is what it means. Now this is surely one of the most wonderful and remarkable things that can ever be said about the Christian, and it is always the essential, basic New Testament definition – a Christian is someone who is under the grace and the favour of God. And what is grace? Well, in a sense, grace is such a wonderful word that it cannot be defined; but there is no better definition than to describe it as unmerited or undeserved favour. Paul, in writing about these members of the church at Philippi says, you are sharers together with me in this grace, in this favour which God has bestowed upon us together.

What does that tell us, then, about the Christian? It tells us that God, there in heaven surveying this earth, this world and its teeming multitudes of people, all of whom are born in sin and shapen in iniquity, looks with an eye of special

favour upon these people who are known by the name of
Christian. It means that God sees us differently and is concerned about us in a special manner. The Old Testament
sometimes puts this another way – you remember that God,
speaking to the nation of Israel through the prophet Amos,
uses these words, 'You only have I *known* of all the families
of the earth' (Amos 3:2). But this does not mean he was not
aware of the existence of the others, or that he was not
acquainted with the others, for God is omniscient, he knows
all and sees all. It means that he had taken a special interest
in the nation of Israel; he had been unusually favourable to
them, and was concerned about them and their welfare. He
looked upon them with a Father's eye and showered upon
them these special blessings. And Paul says of the Christian
that he is one who is a partaker, or sharer, in this special,
unmerited, undeserved favour and benevolence of God.

This, I say, is a thought which is so tremendous that man's
mind almost boggles at it, it is almost baffling to the imagination – but what comfort and consolation it gives! Before
Paul goes into the details of all he is saying to you and me
that the almighty, absolute God, the everlasting to everlasting, the ruler of heaven and earth, the Father, is looking
upon us and that he has a special interest in us and a concern
about us and is showering his favours and his mercy upon
us. The Psalmist says in Psalm 34: 'The angel of the Lord
encampeth round about them that fear him' (v. 7), and is it
not the teaching of so many of these psalms that the man
who is in the right relationship to God is being watched
over, that God is keeping his eye upon him and is there surrounding him by his love?

Indeed, the whole doctrine of the Bible with regard to
angels comes in at this point. There is a very clear and
specific teaching that there are indeed such beings as guar-
dian angels. Do you remember the words in Matthew 18:10
– 'In heaven their angels do always behold the face of my
Father which is in heaven'? And the author of the epistle to
the Hebrews tells us that angels are all ministering spirits,
'sent forth to minister for them who shall be heirs of salva-

tion' (Heb. 1:14). It is an amazing and an astonishing doctrine, that God in heaven, because of this interest, because of this special, peculiar concern, has these servants of his watching us, protecting us and warning us. If we could only see these things as some of the fathers saw them, it would transform our whole outlook upon life. Like Jacob of old we should realise that we are surrounded by the heavenly hosts, by these unseen ministers of God.

But this is not all. Our Lord put this in another way. In giving this comfort to his followers, he tells them that the very hairs of their head are all numbered. Do not be troubled or alarmed, he says, and do not be perplexed; if only you knew the interest that God the Father takes in you! The very hairs of your head are all numbered: God knows you as intimately as that. He is personally concerned about you. Our Lord made this point on many occasions, so is it not a tragedy that we, as Christian people, fail to realise this and fail to rise to these great and wondrous heights? If only we realised as we should that we are especially in the favour of God. And it is not because we are better than anybody else, for grace is unmerited, undeserved favour. When we deserved nothing but punishment and hell, when we deserved nothing but to reap the fruit of our own sowing, when we were nothing but the children of wrath, God, because of his eternal and everlasting love, and according to his knowledge and wisdom, looked upon us with that eye of favour so that now we are peculiarly under his grace.

Now I need not go into greater detail here. As we go on in our consideration of Paul's definition of a Christian, we shall see that he elaborates this matter, and perhaps we had better delay the details until we come to them. But I must ask the question at this point: do you know that you are enjoying the favour and the grace of God? Do you realise as you should that you are in this special, privileged position? Are you aware, as the prophet puts it in the Old Testament, that 'the eyes of the Lord run to and fro throughout the whole earth' (2 Chron. 16:9) looking for opportunities to bless his people? Now unless we start with this preliminary realisation we shall not be able to follow the Apostle's detailed argument. In a sense we have anticipated the whole argument – if I am in this peculiar position of being in the favour of God, if all that we have been considering is true, the only possible deduction is that whatever may happen to me, wherever I go, whatever may be the circumstances, I am secure. 'If God be for us, who can be against us?' (Rom. 8:31). If I am in this special position as a child of God, a partaker with Paul in God's grace and favour, then I shall know that, come what may, I am protected, I am guarded, I am safe.

② But let me go on with the second point, which is that the Apostle tells us of a Christian that *he is a saint.* 'Paul and Timotheus, the servants of Jesus Christ, to all the saints in Christ Jesus which are at Philippi, with the bishops and deacons.' Now here again is a word that often causes people to stumble. Here are blessings offered to saints, and if that is what I must be before I can enjoy these blessings, then it is obvious that I must be quite clear in my mind as to what a saint is, and whether I am one or not. Let me first of all tell you what being a saint does not mean. It does not mean certain special people only among Christians. That is the error which has been popularised by Roman Catholicism. They talk about 'canonising' certain people, thereby making them saints. They decide to call certain men or women saints – people who have lived perhaps centuries earlier – and they apply certain tests to their lives to decide whether they are to be called saints or not. Certain people, therefore, are saints and the rest of the Christians are not – and that is clearly unscriptural. Notice how Paul puts it here – 'Paul and Timotheus, the servants of Jesus Christ, to *all the saints* in Christ Jesus which are at Philippi, with the bishops and deacons'; and again in the seventh verse – 'inasmuch as both in my bonds, and in the defence and confirmation of the gospel, ye are all partakers of my grace'. The Apostle does not put himself upon a pedestal and say, I am a saint. He says we are all saints together; we are all partakers of the grace of God.

I do not want to waste time with this idea but I am constrained to make this remark in passing: is it not rather sad that people are still giving so much time and attention to these trivialities, and are still arguing whether it is essential to the Church that you should have certain orders? To me there is a divine sarcasm in this first verse – 'to all the saints in Christ Jesus which are at Philippi, with the bishops and deacons'. Paul does not start with the bishops, the great and mighty, not at all! He starts with the saints, then adds, 'with the bishops and deacons', the overseers. There are those who are given certain positions, certainly, but it is a tragedy, when the world is as it is today and this Christian testimony is so needed, that men should still be trying to prove that the bishop is of the very *esse*, or being, of the Church, and that without a bishop there is no Church. After all, what constitutes a Church is the gathering together of the saints, the people in the grace and favour of God, in order to worship God. A saint, then, is not some exceptional Christian, but any Christian, or every Christian. You find the same thing in all Paul's epistles; for example, you read, 'to the saints in Corinth', and to the saints in all the other churches. That, then, is the negative side, but now let me put it positively. The term 'saints' really means the people who are called out, the people who are separated, those who have been set apart. You can translate the word saints as 'holy ones', for when God takes hold of anything and puts it apart for his own purpose, it becomes holy. In the Old Testament, when Moses receives his commission he is referred to as a holy man. You read, too, about the 'holy vessels' of the Temple; it means they have been set apart for use in the Temple. Men and women are dealt with in the same way according to the Bible: the saints are people whom God has taken hold of, and set apart for his own function and purpose. They are people who have been taken hold of by the Spirit of God in this world of time in which they live, and God has separated them and made them different. They are still in the world yet they are different, they are marked men and women, in a category of their own, and they belong to a particular group of people who are under God's special grace and favour, as we have seen. Therefore in the first instance we must not think of saints even in terms of the kind of life they live, because that is something that follows on from this. The essential thing about saints is that they have been called out and separated by God.

Now this is basic to the New Testament idea of the Christian. When Paul was writing to the Galatians he thanked God for his wonderful grace in sending his Son to die for us, and then Paul says – and this is his description of the Christian – 'that he might deliver us from this present evil world' (Gal. 1:4). Though still in the world they have been delivered from it and set apart. He obviously realises that that is true about himself because he goes on to apply the logic, which is that if God has separated me, well, then, I must separate myself. He has separated me for salvation; the world outside is going to be judged and destroyed, but God by his own unmerited favour looked upon me and called me out to save me from that destruction, to save me from that order of life, and to save me for his own kingdom. If I realise that, then I must realise that it is my business to separate myself from the man of the world, and from the behaviour and conduct, and the practices of the world. God has called me for his service, so I must now dedicate myself to that service. Both these things, therefore, are an essential part of what it means to be saints. There is wonderful comfort and consolation in this epistle, yes, but it is for the saints, for those people who are conscious of being separated, and who themselves are anxious to be still further separated; it is for nobody else, only for the holy ones.

I ask again, is not that part of our trouble? We are all so like that false prophet Balaam; we all say that we would like to 'die the death of the righteous' (Num. 23:10), but if we want to die the death of the righteous we had better live the life of the righteous. The trouble is that we want to die like that but we do not want to live like that. We are to live as holy ones, and then we shall know the consolation and the comfort. That is why we enjoy so little of these blessings, it is because we fail to observe the conditions.

But let me add a word on the last heading. You notice the verse does not say, 'to all the saints which are at Philippi', but 'to all the saints in Christ Jesus which are at Philippi', and how vital that is. Someone once said he thought the whole of Paul's doctrine was to be found in the phrase 'in Christ' or 'in Christ Jesus'. Do you know he uses the expression 'in Christ' forty-eight times in his epistles, he talks about being 'in Christ Jesus' thirty-four times, and 'in the Lord' fifty times? But why is this vital? Well, Paul is writing to the 'saints in Christ Jesus', but, you know, there were certain people who had separated themselves before Paul went to Philippi. When you read the story in Acts 16, you find a little company of women led by Lydia who were praying by the side of the river. They were already saints, in a sense; they were saints before Paul preached the gospel, but they were not 'saints in Christ Jesus'. Anyone can be a saint, you find saints among all sorts of people. But that is not what the Apostle says. He says, 'saints in Christ Jesus', and by this he means that we are now members of Christ. Christ is absolutely essential to all that Paul has to say. Did you notice the number of times in these seven verses that he mentions the name of Christ? Paul has no gospel apart from Jesus Christ. The gospel is not some vague general offer, nor is it a mere exhortation to people to live a good life; rather it tells of the things that have happened in Christ, because without Christ there is no salvation. And if Christ is not essential to your position, then according to Paul you are not a Christian. You may be very good, you may even be religious, but you cannot be a Christian. If Christ is not absolutely the core and centre, it is not Christianity, whatever else it may be.

In what other sense are we saints? Let me use a great theological term. The phrase 'saints in Christ Jesus' means we are in Christ federally, or representatively. At the beginning, Adam represented the human race, and when Adam fell, the whole of humanity came under the power and

dominion of Satan. But, thank God, there is another side.
Christ is our representative, and if I am a Christian I know
for certain that when Christ died upon that cross he was representing me, he was receiving the punishment of my sins,
he died for me, and he has risen again for me. If I am in
him, I am already dead to the law, my Representative has
died for me, therefore I have died and I am risen with him
in newness of life and I am justified in the presence of God.
I am in Christ. He is my Representative – it is a federal
union, it is a representative union.

But it does not stop at that point, it means something
even more. To be in Christ means not only a federal union
but a vital union. John 15 shows this clearly: it means a mystical union; it means that the life of Christ is in me and I am
in Christ, and something of the power of Christ flows into
me in this mystical way. It means, in a sense, that my life is
hidden in him. The Apostle asks, What is the Church? The
Church is 'the body of Christ and members in particular' (1
Cor. 12:27) – Christ is the head, we are the body, with the
blood which flows through in this organic vital union. We
are the branches in the vine and the life of the parent tree
flows into us; it is a mystical vital union with Christ – saints
in Christ Jesus.

I have merely given some headings in this study. Each one
of these definitions could take a chapter to itself, so vital are
these things. Do we all, I wonder, view ourselves in that
way? Do we all realise that we are in this amazing favour of
God? Do we know that we are saints? We should not be
afraid to say that we are, there should be no mock modesty
at this point. We are saints if we believe this gospel, we have
been set apart. Do we know that we are in Christ? Do we
know that we have died with him and are risen with him?
Are we in that sense reigning with him? Is his life in us and
are we in him? It is to the saints in Christ Jesus, to those
who are participators in this grace and favour of God, that
these amazing promises are made. If we are in that position
and know it and maintain it, then everything that Paul says
here about the Philippians will be equally true of us.

3

God's Work

Being confident of this very thing, that he which hath begun [or, which began] a good work in you will perform it until the day of Jesus Christ (Phil.1:6).

We have here what may very well be described as the key verse of the entire epistle. It is in this single verse that the Apostle introduces us at once to the whole foundation of his confidence concerning himself and his own future, and the future of the church at Philippi. I think we all agree that this is one of those grand pronouncements which are so characteristic of the writings of Paul. There are people who talk about having favourite verses or texts; I am never quite happy about the theology of such a statement, but if there is such a thing, I would have to confess that this is undoubtedly one of mine. It is one of those magnificent, fundamental, profound statements which leads us to the very depths of Christian doctrine and Christian theology.

It is undoubtedly a remarkable thing that a man situated as Paul was at the time he wrote this letter could ever have uttered these words. He was suffering in prison, you remember, he was being persecuted and attacked by enemies, by people who did their utmost to discredit him and to undo the work that he was doing in their churches. So he knows something about the difficulties surrounding the church at Philippi, and yet, in spite of that, he has this profound confidence both with respect to himself and with respect to them. And he tells us here at once, not only in this verse but also in those that surround it, that there are two main things which create this sense of confidence within him.

The first is that he is aware of the work that is going forward in and among the members of the church at Philippi. He is confident because of the character of the work and because he knows that it is a work which nothing and no one can stop. Secondly, he knows that there are many, indeed, if not all, of the members of the church at Philippi of whom it can be said that this work is going on in them. The two things are important. Paul's confidence is not so much in the members of the church at Philippi, as in the work of God that is going on in them and among them, or, to put it in another way, what really accounts for the Apostle's confidence is his clear grasp of the nature of the Christian life, his understanding of what happens when a man becomes a Christian and of the power and the life that constitute the Christian Church. It is his profound knowledge and understanding of God's plan of salvation that really leads to his confidence. I think we must all admit that it is our apparent failure to understand and to grasp that central, mighty truth, that accounts for so much of our worrying and foreboding, of our unhappiness and of our concern. It is only the person who grasps the plan of salvation, its meaning, its character and its power, who can ever feel as the Apostle felt, and who can ever share his experience.

Now, surely, it is because so many of us fail just there that we are worried, for instance, about ourselves and about our own position and condition. When we look at ourselves and feel our own spiritual pulse we are aware of certain lacks within ourselves and this drives us to worry and introspection, and perhaps even to morbidity and a great deal of unhappiness, and we tend instinctively to think that the Christian life is rather difficult. But I would say that all these moods and states are in a very large measure due to our failure to realise this mighty thing which the Apostle here puts before us.

And in the same way is it not true to say that most of our foreboding concerning the future of the Christian Church arises from the same source? It has become, alas, almost characteristic of Christian people today to speak with a note of moaning and grief and sorrow – 'What is going to happen? Look at the people, look at the indifference!' They paint their doleful picture of the world and even of the Church herself, and they cry, 'Will there be such a thing as organised Christianity at all in twenty or thirty years' time? What does the future hold for us?' There are those, too, who prophesy the end of big Christian meetings and talk about the possibility of small groups of people. Now it is not for me to say they are altogether wrong, but what I am concerned about is that in their talk and conversation one detects a note of profound pessimism concerning the whole future of the Christian Church and of the gospel. And this is due to one thing only, and that is the failure to realise the nature of the Christian life, the failure to grasp this doctrine which confronts us here in this magnificent statement of the Apostle.

Nothing, therefore, is more important for us than that we should be absolutely clear about these things. Paul, as we have seen, has wonderful comfort and encouragement to give in this letter, but it will avail us nothing, it will mean nothing to us, unless we agree with the statement of this sixth verse. For if *it* is not true, then none of the rest is going to be true, it is all wishful thinking; but if this is true, then everything else is certain. You cannot build without a foundation and here again we return to it. In other words, in this verse the Apostle describes to us again the nature of the Christian man, and he describes also the very essence of the Christian process of salvation. He does it in this way: he says that the Christian is a man in whom good work is being done. So we must consider something of what the Apostle tells us here about this good work, and the matter divides itself up, quite naturally, in the following ways.

First and foremost, there is the *author* of the work: 'Being confident of this very thing, that *he* which hath begun a good work in you will perform it [complete it] until the day of Jesus Christ.' Who is he? Who is the one who has begun this

good work in the members of the church at Philippi? Well
of course there is only one answer to the question: it is none
other than God himself. That is the first and fundamental
postulate. It helps, I think, to look at it negatively. Paul
does not refer to the good work that he himself had done at
Philippi. You remember how Paul went over to Macedonia
and preached the gospel to certain women at the riverside;
then he went on preaching to others, and after he was put in
prison he preached to the Philippian jailer. Paul did a great
work at Philippi. It was a grand piece of evangelism; he
established a church there and built it up. Yet when he
comes to write this letter, he does not refer at all to the work
that he had done. No, it was God's work through Paul. Of
course, that was always Paul's method. There is a very
interesting statement at the end of Acts 14, in which we are
given an account of Paul and Barnabas returning to the
church at Antioch after their first missionary journey. We
are not told that they gathered the church together and gave
them an account of all the things they had done – not at all!
We are told they gathered the church together and gave
them an account of 'all that *God* had done with them' (Acts
14:27). 'He who hath begun' – it was not Paul who began it,
but God.

Or let me put it in another negative. Paul does not say
that the Philippians themselves had started something. The
origin of a church is not like that of a society. Men will
sometimes meet together and say, 'Don't you think it would
be a good thing to have such and such a society?' London is
full of them, the Christian Church is full of them, people are
always starting new organisations. They meet together and
they form the society and draw up their rules and regulations – it is what they are going to do. But Paul does not say
that the Philippians started the Philippian church – it was
none other than God's own work. Now the Bible does not
argue about this – we, alas, often do – it just declares it. The
Bible simply tells us that salvation is altogether and entirely
the work of God. It tells us that man in his sinful state is
against God, he does not desire God and would never

return to God. There would never have been a Church at all, nor would there have been salvation, if God had not begun to act. 'He which hath begun a good work in you' – it is all of God.

Of course it is not surprising that Paul, above everybody else, should teach this. He never forgot what he had been himself; he remembered himself as a blasphemer, and a persecutor of the Christian Church and he knew perfectly well that he would have continued in that state were it not that at midday, while he was travelling along the road to Damascus where he intended to persecute a body of Christian people, the Lord suddenly appeared to him. Paul never decided to become a Christian, he never thought about it, he did not initiate the work. It was God who did it in him, and Paul therefore always referred the work to him.

And, of course, not only was that true of Paul himself, it was patently true in the case of the church at Philippi. In order to demonstrate that, we only have to read the story in Acts 16. In verses 6 and 7 we are told that Paul wanted to go somewhere else, but the Spirit did not allow him to do so. That is the first step – he wanted to preach in some place in Asia, that seemed to him to be the right thing to do, but 'the Spirit suffered them not' (Acts 16:7). And then the next thing that happened was that Paul had a vision during the night. He did not create or produce the vision, he did not generate it, he was asleep and it was given to him. Who gave it to him? It was God. A man of Macedonia appeared to him and said, 'Come and help us.' And Paul, you remember, crossed the sea and landed for the first time in Europe, as the result of that vision.

Then, having arrived at this place called Philippi, the Apostle was led to speak to those women who met together regularly by the side of the river for prayer. We are told that the Lord opened the heart of Lydia; we are not told that Lydia was rather impressed and decided to try and take it up. No, the Lord who brought Paul to preach opened her heart and that of her household, and Paul went on preaching from her house. Then the girl with the spirit of divina-

tion came into it; she was delivered by the power of God
and this resulted in a change in her life which led to Paul and
Silas being put in prison. Then came the earthquake – Paul
certainly did not produce that – and the conversion of the
Philippian jailer. That is how the church at Philippi came
into being. The Bible does not argue about this, it states its
doctrine, which is that there is no one and no thing, save
God alone, that can raise man from the depth of sin. 'We,'
says Paul, 'are his workmanship, created in Christ Jesus'
(Eph. 2:10); he is the Master, the Artificer, the Fashioner,
he is the one who has brought us out.

Furthermore, Paul not only tells us here that this is God's
work, but that it is God's work right through from start to
finish. 'He which hath begun a good work in you *will perform it*' – he will go on with it until he has completed and
perfected it, until the final consummation. God does not
merely initiate the work and then leave it, he continues with
it; he leads us on, directing and manipulating our circumstances, restraining us at one time and urging us on at
another. Paul's whole conception of the Church is that it is
a place where God is working in the hearts of men and
women. This is basic and fundamental. Christianity is the
result of God's action and of God's activity. It is not man's
idea, nor man's theory; it is not moral uplift, it is nothing
that man can do – it is God, from the very beginning to the
very end. 'The glory must be his alone' – the great watch-
word of the Protestant Reformation.

And of course the Bible shows us that in this amazing
work the three Persons of the blessed Trinity are involved.
God the Father initiates the work, God the Son performs
and makes it all possible; God the Holy Spirit applies it and
does the work in our very innermost souls. 'He which hath
begun a good work in you' – God, the blessed triune God,
is the author of this good work.

But let me come to the second principle, which is *the
nature of the work* and it seems to me that the key to understanding this is the word 'in' – 'he which hath begun a good
work' – not among but '*in* you'. Now that, again, is vital and

central. What Paul is talking about here is what the New Testament elsewhere describes as the rebirth, or the new creation, or regeneration, or being born again – you are familiar with these terms. What happens to the Christian is not a mere reformation or surface improvement. The gospel is not something that just changes a man and makes him a little bit better, it is not a moral reformation or improvement in a cultural sense. No, it is a vital work which is done by God in and upon the soul, at the very centre and vitals of a man's life and existence. Now this, of course, is the very essence of the Christian gospel. John Wesley's favourite definition of Christianity was that of the Scotsman Henry Scougal who defined it as 'the life of God in the soul of man', and that is virtually what Paul is saying at this point. If the New Testament is true, then Christianity is the most profound and vital change that a person can ever know.

Let me then, summarise this. The first thing that God does is to awaken us to our state and condition. God the Holy Spirit acts on us and makes us see that we are guilty before God; we are lost. He makes us see that we are without life and that we do not know God. He makes us see that even our interest in God is something sinful, because we regard God as a term and do not hesitate to criticise him. The Holy Spirit awakens us to our need. There is a quickening that comes to us; we begin to see ourselves as we really are, and that in turn leads us to a state of repentance and sorrow for sin.

Then the Holy Spirit creates within us a desire for God, a desire for a different order of life, a better life. We realise suddenly that we have been living a small self-centred life outside of God; we see the danger of it, the dread possibilities that will follow such a life, and we begin to long for a knowledge of God. We long to be delivered from this sin that we now see enchaining and fettering us. We try to find God but we discover that we cannot. And then the Holy Spirit does the blessed work of revealing Christ to us in all the perfection of his work. He suddenly opens our eyes to see the real meaning of Christ and his cross; he shows the objective work that was done there once and for ever, and he applies that all to us. He makes us realise that this is not something theoretical, but something that is of momentous concern to us.

And then he does something which is, in a sense, still more wonderful. He forgives us our sins. He brings into being a new life within us; we are aware of a new man, a new nature. He makes us look at ourselves and ask, 'Am I still the same person?' – as Paul said, 'I live; yet not I ...' (Gal. 2:20). We become aware that there is evidence of a new being, a new nature, within us, and we do not like the things we used to like. We begin to like the Bible, we begin to pray and to attend prayer meetings, and it is the Holy Spirit who is doing all this. He is creating us anew, after the pattern and the manner of Christ. That is the good work that God begins in us and continues in us.

Then he goes on to perfect 'the new man', through his word, through other people, through circumstances, or through what we often regard as chance. He is fashioning us by smoothing over our rough edges, by chiselling off this corner and that – this is Paul's conception of what it means to be a Christian, a member of the Christian Church. He uses a most strange analogy in 1 Corinthians 4, where he says that we are God's theatre, the place in which God is acting and doing certain things. Or take another analogy: the Church is God's workshop and Christian people are the articles that God is forming and fashioning. He is working at us; it is not something that happens once and for all when we are converted. God is going on with his work in us and everything that happens is part of this great process. There is, perhaps, a disappointment, we lose our money or our job; we may not see it now, but in the future we will see it as a part of the great process of God going on with the good work which he has already begun in us.

Now, my friends, to be a Christian is nothing less than that: it is to experience this good work of God going on within; it is to be aware of the fact that this is taking place. If you are aware of being manipulated, of being dealt with, then say to yourself: this is God, he is doing something to me. I do not understand it but I know it is God and I thank him even though I cannot fathom it at the moment. The good work, in other words, is that mighty work of God through the Holy Spirit, where the life, death and resurrection of Christ are made real to us and applied to us and we are created anew in his image, 'a new man' in Christ Jesus.

Then we come to the third principle. We have seen that it is God's work, and that it is a good work, so then what is *the purpose of the work*? Paul gives the answer: 'Being confident of this very thing that he which hath begun a good work in you will perform it until the day of Jesus Christ.' That is the grand objective, the end of it all. We are being fashioned and prepared for the day of Jesus Christ. You notice that Paul does not say that we are prepared for the day of our death; no, we are being prepared for the great day to which they were looking forward, the day of Jesus Christ. This, in a sense, is one of the most amazing and astonishing things in the Bible, and it is because of his clear conception of this 'day of Jesus Christ', that Paul is able to do all the other things he tells us.

What, then, is this day? It is the day of the grand consummation, the finishing of the work of salvation. Let me explain it like this. The moment man sinned and fell from God, God began the great process. You remember the promise that was given concerning 'the seed of the woman'? It began there. He went on with that work: he singled out a man called Abraham and made of him a nation; and throughout the whole of the Bible we see the work continuing. But what is it leading up to? Well, the final objective is that this world, which has been cursed because of the sin of man, shall be restored and shall be made absolutely perfect – there shall be 'new heavens and a new earth, wherein dwelleth righteousness' (2 Pet. 3:13) and the Son of God shall return to reign as King. *That* is the day of the Lord. The 'spirits of just men made perfect' shall receive their glorified bodies raised from the dead, and dwell on this new earth, under the new heaven, with Christ, for ever and ever;

it is the glorious day of final emancipation, the ultimate redemption that is coming.

And what Paul tells the members of the church at Philippi at this point is that all is well, and that they will go on, with God working in them, until he has made them absolutely perfect on that great day. Whatever may be happening to me or you, says Paul, it is all right, God is going on with the work, and when Christ returns you will stand before him and receive your reward. You will enter into your inheritance, into that magnificent and amazing consummation, the day of Jesus Christ, the day of his return in triumph to reign. You will be ready for it and you will miss nothing of it. That is the end and the purpose of the great, good work which God had begun and was continuing in the church at Philippi. And, my dear friends, that is to me the profoundest comfort and consolation in the world at this moment. If we are Christians, God is certainly preparing us for that. The world may rob us of much and deny us much, but it cannot touch this inheritance, 'incorruptible, and undefiled, and that fadeth not away...' (1 Pet. 1:4). These are the things which thieves cannot break through and steal, nor moth and rust corrupt, they are safe with God in heaven beyond the reach of man and all his efforts and machinations. If you are a Christian you are being prepared for that day, and being prepared for it by God.

Let me just say a word on *the certainty of this work*. There is no doubt about it, says Paul: 'being confident of this very thing, that he which hath begun a good work in you will perform it until the day of Jesus Christ'. My guarantee is nothing less than the character of God himself. My confidence is based upon the holiness and the righteousness and the power of God. God never starts a work and leaves it unfinished; it would be a contradiction of his very character. God is unlike man; we start things but we do not continue. We have our enthusiasms, but they only last for a week or two. We propose to do a thing, and we begin to do it, but there is no continuance. Thank God, my hope of that day of Jesus Christ and his glory does not rest upon my own will power or upon my own desire or understanding. It rests upon this fact that he would never have started the work if he had not decided to finish it. As Paul puts it to Timothy, 'The foundation of God standeth sure' (2 Tim. 2:19), and when he writes to the Corinthians he says, 'For other foundation can no man lay than that is laid, which is Jesus Christ' (1 Cor. 3:11). God has laid this certain, sure, foundation stone. Two explanations are given to us of this. The first is that 'the Lord knoweth them that are his' (2 Tim. 2:19) and, secondly, this verse in Philippians which assures us that when God starts a work in a soul 'he will perform and complete it until the day of Jesus Christ'. Paul, again, in writing to the Romans says – this is the logic – 'If, when we were enemies, we were reconciled to God by the death of his Son, much more, being reconciled, we shall be saved by his life' (Rom. 5:10). What Paul means is this: if Christ died for you when you were an enemy and a rebel and hated him, if he died for you in that condition, how much more, then, will God keep and sustain and hold you, and finish the work by the love of Christ – it is unanswerable logic. The character of God guarantees the completion of the work.

Let us, then, finish with a practical application. The vital matter for all of us, I think we will all agree, is to know for certain that this work is taking place in us. Has God started this good work in me? Do I know that he is going on with it, and that I am going to be made perfect in the day of Jesus Christ? How can I know this? Paul, in a sense, gives us the answer in this text when he thanks God for the fellowship in the gospel of these Philippian people. What does that mean? It means that they were interested in these things. These people at Philippi would sooner meet together in church and discuss these things than do anything else. They were Roman citizens, they were a cultured people, but once they had seen this, they knew it was the important thing. So they met together and they worked together – this was their fellowship in the gospel. That is a very good sign. If these truths are your first and your greatest interest, I think you can be quite happy that the good work has started in you.

Paul says in verse seven, 'Even as it is meet for me to think this of you all, because I have you in my heart; inasmuch as both in my bonds, and in the defence and confirmation of the gospel, ye all are partakers of my grace.' He means that whenever you hear anybody ridicule this gospel you reply to them and defend it, and if ever you hear anyone speaking unworthily of Christ, you defend the name – the defence of the gospel. All these points, of course, are worthy of a sermon in themselves, I am simply drawing a comprehensive view. If you defend the gospel you can be quite happy that the good work has started in you. And when Paul refers to 'the confirmation of the gospel', he means the spreading of it. We have to defend it and to state it.

What other tests are there? Here are some. Surely, if you have an increasing hatred of sin it means that the good work of God is going on in you – no one else can give you that. If you have an increasing desire after holiness, if you have an increasing concern to please God and to be well-pleasing in his sight, it is a sign that the work is going on. Have you an increasing sense of love and gratitude to God? Are you more and more disposed to say, 'Thanks be unto God for his unspeakable gift', and 'I am what I am by the grace of God'? These are the tests and the signs. If these things are true of us there is only one explanation. It is not the natural man, for the natural man desires none of these things. Whosoever has such desires has them because God has begun and is continuing the good work in him.

God grant that we all, therefore, may be able to join the great Apostle and say, 'Being confident of this very thing, that he which hath begun a good work in us will perform it until the day of Jesus Christ.' Amen.

4

Love, Knowledge and Judgment

And this I pray, that your love may abound yet more and
more in knowledge and in all judgment; that ye may
approve things that are excellent; that ye may be sincere
and without offence till the day of Christ; being filled with
the fruits of righteousness, which are by Jesus Christ, unto
the glory and praise of God (Phil. 1:9–11).

We have in these verses the Apostle's special prayer for the
members of the church at Philippi. Anyone who is at all
familiar with his epistles will realise that Paul's prayers are
always worthy of very careful consideration. They are not
something added in a perfunctory manner; he does not
merely mention them as a matter of course, or as a kind of
aside. Many people feel that these prayers are, rather, some
of the most significant statements in Paul's writings, and we
could well devote a complete study to a consideration of the
characteristics of all of them. But we must go on now to look
in detail at this particular prayer, so the only general obser-
vation I would make is that Paul's prayers are always
characterised by what can best be described as intelligence
or thoughtfulness. The Apostle does not pray merely in
terms of his own feelings. His prayers are always ordered,
and are always in terms of the condition of the people for
whom he prays. He prays in other words, with his mind as
well as his heart. He certainly always offers up his praise and
thanksgiving to God for such people as these Philippians,
and, let me repeat, what characterises his prayers are his
wisdom, his sanity and his ability as a pastor and teacher of

his people – we shall see this as we consider this particular prayer.

Now this prayer, like all the others, is very significant, and we cannot look at it and analyse it without learning a great deal about the whole nature of the Christian life. Paul's prayers, like his teaching, indeed like everything he did, are always based upon certain great principles. His prayers are as theological as all his arguments and discussions. They are full of teaching, of theology and doctrine; he does not know what it means to pray prayers that are moved merely by emotions and sentiment. His prayers are always based upon something foundational; they are always in the light of a certain background and they proceed from it.

Now as we come to this particular prayer we may at first glance be rather surprised. It may occur to us that there is a contradiction here between what the Apostle prays for the church at Philippi, and what he has already said about them. In our last study we were considering this verse: 'Being confident of this very thing, that he which hath begun a good work in you will perform it until the day of Jesus Christ.' That is a statement which people might misinterpret by saying: 'Very well, if that is true, if this is God's work, and if it is work that is certain to be completed because it is God's work, why pray for these people? Why write a letter at all? Why exhort them to anything? Why not just say it is God's work, he has begun it, and is going to finish it because it is based on his character, and therefore it can never fail? Let us relax and allow the work to proceed. All is well.' But here the Apostle seems to pray that the Philippians themselves may do certain things. He wants them to grow in knowledge; he wants their love to abound in understanding and in various other respects. Then he prays that they may be led to do certain things themselves. Thus on the surface there appears to be a kind of contradiction. Indeed, within the very prayer itself there is an apparent contradiction – 'being filled with the fruits of righteousness', then, 'which are by Christ Jesus unto the glory and praise of God.' Paul exhorts them at one point to produce the fruits of righteousness, but then immediately he adds, 'which are by Christ Jesus'.

This is something which you will find constantly, not only in the writings of Paul, but in all the Bible, from beginning to end. We find another example in chapter 2 verses 12 and 13, where the Apostle says, 'Work out your own salvation with fear and trembling. For it is God which worketh in you both to will and to do of his good pleasure.' At one and the same time he seems to be asking us to work something out, and to be saying that it is God who is working. This kind of position has throughout the centuries led not only to much discussion, but also to a great deal of misunderstanding. There are always rival factions who emphasise either one side or the other, and yet Scripture presents the two simultaneously.

The explanation, of course, is that the contradiction is apparent and not real. It is resolved when you understand that this is one of the ways in which God works in us to call forth personal action from us. God, having made it possible for us to do anything at all, then calls upon us to do it. God, by working in us, makes us work; God, by initiating the movement, has decreed and ordered that the movement shall be continued, partly at any rate, by our effort and activity. Thus we discover that what may on the surface appear to be contradictory, is not really so at all. In an ultimate sense, this is a great mystery which we cannot understand, and nothing, it seems to me, is more foolish and fallacious than to attempt to go beyond the work of God and to cross the borderline which separates what is clearly revealed, from our own original presuppositions and deductions. These are the things of which we can be certain: it is God who has initiated this good work in us – salvation is entirely of grace – but once we have received it, then he calls upon us as responsible new men in Christ Jesus to do certain things ourselves. And here we are reminded of some of those things to which he calls us. The Apostle puts it like this. Out of a full heart he has been thanking God for these Philippians and thanking them for the great love which they

have for him and for one another. We have already seen
that there is a lyrical quality about this epistle which, in a
sense, you do not find in any of the others. The relationships
between Paul and this church were peculiarly happy, and
this was also true of the life of the church itself. But Paul is
not satisfied; that is not enough. He prays because he is anxious that they should develop and go on. Paul was never
satisfied with himself. When you read the third chapter of
this epistle you will find him saying: '... forgetting those
things which are behind ... I press toward the mark for the
prize of the high calling of God in Christ Jesus.' He is always
coveting more, and he covets it for his people in exactly the
same way. He is anxious that they should advance and grow
in grace and in the knowledge of our Lord and Saviour Jesus
Christ. And here he shows them exactly how anxious he is
that they should do this.

So, as we come to look at the details of his petition, we
shall be reminded once more of the profound nature of his
teaching. We see here displayed the greatness of his understanding of life and of human nature and of the people with
whom he was concerned. It is important, I think, that we
should remind ourselves again of the context of this prayer.
Paul wants these Philippians to have the same blessings in life
as he is enjoying himself. He is in prison, but he is happy; he
has learned in whatsoever state he is, 'therein', or therewith,
'to be content'. He knows, he tells us, 'both how to be
abased, and how to abound', and he wants them to enjoy the
same things. He knows, too, that it is difficult, that there are
forces which are against all that. The Christian gospel never
merely tells us to cheer up because everything is all right. On
the contrary, it faces life as it is, and then it enables us to
overcome the difficulties. Now the Apostle has all that in the
back of his mind as he offers up this petition. How, then, can
anyone in a world and life like this attain to the experience of
the great Apostle himself? He has already told us certain
basic things of which, as Christians, we must be sure, but, in
addition to that, some other things are necessary and we
must consider what they are.

We can divide the subject up into two main headings which are perfectly simple and direct – all I can hope to do with such a great statement as this is note the words and their meanings, and then leave it to you to work the details out for yourselves. There are, then, two obvious questions. The first is: *What* did Paul pray for the church at Philippi? And the second question is: *Why* did he pray?

First, then, what he prays for is that their love may abound yet more and more in knowledge and in all judgment. That is the petition. There may, however, be some who feel that I ought to go further and include the next verse, but I regard that as one of the reasons *why* he offered the prayer. I do not regard it as part of the petition, but as something to which the petition leads, and in which it results. His prayer is that their love may abound yet more and more in knowledge and in all judgment, and there we are at once reminded of something that is ever one of Paul's outstanding characteristics. It is his balance, his sanity, the perfect way in which he safeguards his own teaching against excess and misunderstanding. He does not, you notice, merely pray that the love of the Philippians may abound yet more and more; no, he wants their love to overflow in knowledge and in all judgment. Nor does he simply pray that their knowledge may increase – you see his balance – rather, he prays that their love may abound yet more and more in knowledge …

Here, surely, is something which must cause us to pause for a minute or two. Is not the failure to observe this balance one of the real difficulties in life today? And are not rival philosophies built upon that very failure? There are those who would have us believe that the whole trouble with people today is that they know too much, or think too much, or reason too much. You are familiar with the school of thought that tells us to 'go back to nature', or with those modern philosophers who maintain that the trouble with man is that he will insist on living purely in terms of his higher centres, instead of his mid-brain. The cause of his misery and unhappiness, they tell us, is that he has become too clever, and that he ought to live more in the realm of the instincts. Man, they say, should not be guided by brain and logic and reason. He should live on that lower level where the more primary things are in control. Then there is the other school which says the exact opposite and which still believes in the power of knowledge and of information.

Now the Apostle lays it down that religion is something that cannot be taught; that is a fundamental postulate. He does not merely pray that my knowledge may increase. In a sense, you must not speak about the place of religion in education. It does not have a place there, because it is apart from education; you can talk of education in the world and yet be utterly ignorant of true religion for it is not something that can be taught, like a subject. Again, the Bible should never be taught like an ordinary textbook; you cannot approach Scripture as you would approach Shakespeare, and if you do, it is a travesty of the whole teaching of the Bible. The Bible is different, it belongs to a different realm altogether. Indeed, the primary, fundamental word, says Paul, is love, and where there is no love there is no life, and there must be life before you can impart knowledge. Paul is afraid of knowledge that is not based upon love, and in the same way he is afraid of love that cannot be controlled and checked by knowledge. He wants their love to increase and abound in knowledge and in all judgment, and the two things must always go together.

There are two temptations which constantly confront us, even in the Christian life. One is the danger of living merely on our experiences and on our feelings. There are so many people who have a dislike of teaching and doctrine and dogma; it is something they cannot understand at all. 'Let's sing,' they say when they lead a meeting. 'Let's enjoy ourselves.' And they work up the meeting merely on feelings. They want to give their experiences and their testimony, they want to be talking about themselves, and they stop there, they never want to go on from that. That is their atmosphere of love; that is something that warms their hearts and draws them together. It is all right, on condition that we do not live on that alone.

But the other danger, of course, is the exact opposite: the danger of becoming interested in doctrine in a purely theoretical and abstract and academic manner, of being concerned about what someone has truly described as the 'aridities of the logomachy of theology'. This means that you just become interested in words, and turn this glorious gospel of love into a mere philosophy or into many philosophies. You display a purely intellectual interest in the Bible and in Christian truth – it is all in the head and it never affects the heart. You can quarrel with men about it, but you may be denying the gospel you are discussing.

Now the way to avoid both those temptations is to observe what the Apostle says: our love is to increase and abound in knowledge and in all judgment. By 'knowledge', here, Paul means spiritual knowledge in its fullest sense. It is a strong word; nothing can be fuller than this knowledge. And this is, as I have already suggested, something that is mainly intellectual, though not entirely so. The Apostle prays that the people at Philippi should have an increasing knowledge of God and of the whole content and nature of the Christian truth and revelation. Peter, in a sense, makes the same point when he says that the people who go wrong and are upset by life are those who are 'unlearned and unstable' (2 Pet. 3:16). And surely this is true in the experience of all of us. The people who are most frequently thrown off balance in their Christian lives are those who are most lacking in knowledge. They are upset by other people and they are upset about the whole condition of the world at the present time. And, according to Paul, the way to avoid these things is to have a greater knowledge of the truth itself and a greater knowledge of God. He says very much the same thing in 1 Corinthians 2:12, where he writes, 'Now we have received, not the spirit of the world, but the Spirit which is of God; that we might know the things that are freely given to us of God.' And that means the whole plan and method of salvation.

Paul, in other words, is anxious that Christian people should know the great eternal decrees of God and how they are being worked out. He wants us to understand the nature of the death of our Lord upon the cross, the power of his resurrection and the application of all that to our lives by the Holy Spirit. He wants us to see that God, from the very beginning, has had this plan which he is certainly working out. Then, as we grasp this more fully, it will increase our love to God, and as we have this growing assurance of our great salvation, so our love will abound yet more and more. In addition, of course, the more we know of that love, the more we shall be able to face the contradictions and the disappointments and the troubles that come to meet us in life. If I know only a love which arises from my sentiments and feelings, I am upset and have nothing to fall back upon; but if I believe the doctrine that what finally saves me is not my feelings, but the finished work of Christ upon the cross, then whatever I may feel like, I know where I stand and I can go forward. If I believe that the very hairs of my head are all numbered, if I believe that all things work together for good to them that love God, if I believe that God has put me through a process which will ultimately be completed and make me perfect; if I believe all this, then I look at things in a new way and I see in any untoward circumstance a part of this 'chiselling' work of his. The great thing is to grasp this truth, and as I do so the greater is my love for God and for those who are with me in this great and glorious process.

But let me go on to the next point in his prayer – 'in knowledge and in all judgment'. Here is understanding, or, as it might be translated, sense – 'that your love may abound more and more in all sense'. But probably the best rendering of the word is 'discernment' or 'discrimination'. Here we see the profound psychology of the Apostle, how he draws a distinction between knowledge and discrimination, or knowledge and discernment, or knowledge and judgment, or knowledge and sense. And what a vital distinction this is. Have we not all discovered by experience, and in contact with others, the difference between these two things? The fact that a man has great knowledge does not of necessity mean that he has wisdom; he may be very knowledgeable but it does not always mean that he has discernment or discrimination or sense. These words are not merely drawn out thoughtlessly by the Apostle, there is a very special meaning attached to each one of them. I want you, he says, to have that knowledge of truth, but if you have not that peculiar faculty which will enable you to love under all conditions and circumstances, it will be no use to you at all. There are men who are learned in particular subjects but they are of very little use, and they fail in practice. There are men who may be very learned in the law, in an abstract and theoretical sense, but who are incapable of handling a case in court. A man may know his medicine thoroughly, he may be able to answer questions on paper, but when confronted by a patient he cannot apply his knowledge. What a difference there is in knowing anything and being able to apply it! And Paul is anxious that these Philippians should not only become expert theologians, he prays that they may also be highly developed in that faculty which will enable them to discriminate between good and evil, between that which is spurious and that which really belongs to the truth.

It was a faculty that was needed in the early Church; fallacies and false teachers arose almost at once, with the work of the Judaists and the Greek religions. The infant Church was surrounded by all these things, and most of the heresies first appeared in the first two or three centuries. There is nothing we need more than the spirit of discrimination, the spirit of discernment. It is very difficult to describe this quality; it is almost something intellectual, but it is also almost something instinctive. You can teach man knowledge, you can impart information to him, but you cannot make him wise. It is one of the most difficult things confronting a teacher, but, thank God, it is something for which we can pray. It is something that the Holy Spirit can give us, and that is why the Apostle prays for it. He desires that the members of the church at Philippi should have this sense which will enable them to differentiate between right and wrong, between good and evil in practice, and in their ordinary departments of life.

And, Christian people, if ever we needed this faculty, we need it today, not only in practice but also in our presentation of the truth; there are so many cults and fallacies, so many professors of the Christian faith. I wonder whether this is the thing that the Church of God needs most at this time, this spirit of discernment of the truth? So many still think that because they are members of a church they are all right. There are some who would not hesitate to say that such and such a man is a Christian because, after all, he is a good man and lives a good life. We do not have discernment and discretion, we are not able to sense between right and wrong, between what is true and what is false in doctrine as well as in practice. Paul prays that the Philippians may have it, because if they accept the false doctrine, then they will not be able to meet the troubles and difficulties of life in terms of their basic faith – that is why this is important. He is considering the happiness of the Philippians in an ultimate sense, and because of that, those are the two things for which he prays.

Then, secondly, *why* does Paul pray these things for them? His answer to that question is that if the Philippians have this knowledge and judgment and discernment, then, he says, they will be able to 'approve things that are excellent'. Here again 'excellent' is an interesting word. Let me give you some alternative translations – that you may approve 'the things that differ', or, perhaps best of all, that you may 'have a sense of what is vital'. That is what Paul is anxious they should have; he wants their knowledge and judgment to increase because that is the only way in which they will be able to develop a sense of that which is vital. The difficulty in life is to know on what we ought to concentrate. The whole art of life, I sometimes think, is the art of knowing what to leave out, what to ignore, what to put on one side. How prone we are to dissipate our energies and to waste our time by forgetting what is vital and giving ourselves to second and third rate issues. Now, says Paul, here you are in the Christian life, you are concerned about difficulties, about oppositions and about the contradictions of life. What you need is just this: the power to concentrate on that which is vital, to leave out everything else, and to keep steadily to the one thing that matters.

And what is that? I think Paul answers that question in the third chapter where he says that he has one great consuming passion and desire: that he may 'know him, and the power of his resurrection, and the fellowship of his sufferings, being made conformable unto his death'. That was the Apostle's one need, the thing which he regarded as vital – that he might know him. Now, says Paul, in this prayer, that is the thing on which you people must concentrate. There will be many other things in your life but make certain that this is always in the centre, for if you 'know him, and the power of his resurrection and the fellowship of his sufferings', whatever else may come to you, whatever may happen to you, you will be safe.

These are the things which are vital and all-important and what a tragedy it is that we should waste so much of our time with organisations and institutions and with all the things that belong to the periphery of the Christian life. I ask again, is not this perhaps one of the central troubles of the Church today? We are so busy with many things that we forget the one thing; we are all so much like Martha that we forget Mary and 'the one thing that is needful' (Luke 10:42). Oh, that we may have this sense of that which is vital and give ourselves to it with a new concentration.

His other desire for them was that they might be pure: 'sincere and without offence till the day of Christ'. I pray that your love may abound yet more and more in knowledge and in all judgment, says Paul, because I am preparing you for the day which is coming, this day of Christ, the day when all will be judged and when those who are outside Christ will be condemned and those who are in Christ will also be judged and, according to their fruits, will receive their corresponding rewards. Our Lord speaks of this in Luke 12; and in 1 Corinthians 3:11–15, Paul writes, 'For other foun-

dation can no man lay than that is laid, which is Jesus Christ.
Now if any man build upon this foundation gold, silver, precious stones, wood, hay, stubble; every man's work shall be
made manifest: for the day shall declare it, because it shall
be revealed by fire; and the fire shall try every man's work
of what sort it is. If any man's work abide which he hath
built thereupon, he shall receive a reward. If any man's
work shall be burned, he shall suffer loss: but he himself
shall be saved; yet so as by fire.' There is going to be a great
judgment of a man's work and that which is approved will
be rewarded, but that which is not approved will be burnt.
The man shall escape, he will be saved – 'yet so as by fire'
– his works will be destroyed.

The day of Christ is coming and we shall stand before
him, and I am anxious, says Paul, that at that day you
should be without offence, you should be pure, that there
should be no stumbling block in your way and that as you
run the race, you will not be tripping and falling and stumbling by the way. I pray that your love may abound in knowledge and in all judgment, in order that, seeing the difference between these things, you may purify yourselves and
lead the Christian life as it should be lived; so that when you
stand before him you will not be ashamed, and he will say,
'Well done, thou good and faithful servant ... enter thou
into the joy of thy lord.' The day of Christ is coming and we
must prepare for it. Yes, but even before we come to that,
our love must grow and abound in knowledge and judgment, in order, says Paul, that we may be 'filled with the
fruits of righteousness, which are by Christ Jesus, unto the
glory and praise of God.'

It is indeed almost insulting to such a great truth to deal
with it so briefly, in this way, at the end of a study, but I just
want to give a composite picture of the prayer. You see,
what Paul says to the Philippians, in effect, is this: 'Even
before you come to the judgment and the day of Christ, I
pray this prayer for you in order that you may be living the
full Christian life as you go on the journey; I want your lives
to overflow with fruit. You see the picture of the Christian

life which Christ himself draws, he compares us to a tree,
Christ is the sap, Christ is the life. Without him we have no
life at all, we have no being, we can bear no fruit. We bear
these fruits of righteousness in Christ Jesus; he is the life,
the energy, the sap; we are the tree. And what do we produce? We produce the fruits of righteousness. But why
should we be anxious to produce these? Unto the glory and
praise of God.'

That is the kind of life Paul is anxious that all Christian
people should lead. We are to live in such a way in this life,
that people coming into contact with us will see these fruits
of the Spirit, the love, joy, peace, long-suffering, kindness,
meekness, temperance, faith. They will see our good deeds,
our good works; they will see that we are altogether different; they will see these fruits but the effect of seeing them
will be that they will glorify God. Our Lord says in the Sermon on the Mount, 'Let your light so shine before men, that
they may see your good works, and glorify your Father
which is in heaven' (Matt. 5:16). And the way to live that
full, abounding life with its fruits of righteousness is to make
certain that our love shall abound yet more and more in
knowledge and in all judgment. How is it done? By reading
the Bible, studying it, meditating upon it, by prayer, by
meditating about the soul and life and God and all these
things; by grasping this doctrine, reading it upon our knees,
not in a theoretical manner, but that we may produce the
fruits of righteousness to the glory of God and ascribe all
praise to our Lord Jesus Christ. That is Paul's recipe, that is
his method of preparing the people for the problems and the
difficulties of life, and any man whose love abounds thus
more and more in knowledge and in all judgment, will know
on what to concentrate; he will know what is vital, and as he
concentrates on it he will not stumble as he goes along, but
he will bear these glorious fruits, these magnificent fruits of
righteousness to the glory of God.

5

The Defence and Confirmation
of the Gospel

What then? notwithstanding, every way, whether in pretence, or in truth, Christ is preached; and I therein do
rejoice, yea, and will rejoice (Phil. 1:18).

We come now to the section which starts with the twelfth
verse, and in a sense, goes on almost to the end of the chapter, certainly to the end of the twenty-sixth verse. The
Apostle, after his words of introduction and salutation, after
the expression of his tender solicitude for the members of
the church of Philippi, now comes to deal with various problems which he knew were confronting that church. His great
desire was that the happiness which these people already
enjoyed should continue, indeed that it should increase, in
order that they might come into a state in which, like the
Apostle himself, they would still be able to rejoice in the
Lord whatever their circumstances or conditions.
This word 'rejoice' is a word which we find running
through the entire epistle, as its main theme and motive,
and here, in verse 12, Paul begins to consider one of the
things which might militate against that state of happiness
and joy. He knew that the members of the church at Philippi
were concerned about the fact that he was in prison, and he
administers comfort to them. That, however, is not our
main theme at the moment, because we must consider a
subsidiary theme which arises from it. The Apostle, in dealing with the whole question that was raised by his being in
prison at all and by his sufferings there, has to deal with
something that was aggravating his sufferings in captivity,

and that was the attitude of certain false brethren. These men were in the church, in a sense, and yet, Paul tells us, they were preaching the gospel of Christ out of envy and out of strife. Now this is an interesting passage in and of itself, but it becomes much more important as we realise that here the Apostle is laying down a great principle which is applicable not only to the state of the Philippians, but also to that of the Christian Church at all times and in all places. Indeed, as we shall see, it has very much to say to us, too, even at this present hour. In dealing with this particular problem, the Apostle adds another touch to the general picture that he has been giving us of a Christian church and of what that church should be like.

Now we have been considering how the Apostle, in the first eleven verses of the chapter, has been telling us a great deal about individual Christians and how they grow in grace and wisdom in Christ Jesus. We have been reminded by him that we are what we are solely by the grace of God; that it is God who has commenced this good work, and who keeps it going, and that it is God who is going to perfect it. We have seen also how Paul was praying for these Philippians, that their love might abound more and more in knowledge and in all judgment, that they might approve and appreciate the things which were vital and that they might be sincere. We have seen him comparing the Christian to a tree in which the life, the sap, is nothing but the life of Christ himself, and so the Christian has to bear fruit. Obviously because of that sap and that life, the fruit which he bears will redound to the glory and praise of God. It has been a wonderful picture, not only of the individual Christian, but of the whole Christian Church. Indeed, the Church consists of a gathering of people of that type, a kind of spiritual orchard where a number of people are to be seen bearing this same fruit as the result of the life and activity of Christ within them, to the glory and praise of God. And we have seen how such a society must of necessity be a happy one; it must be a harmonious society because of these things which they share together.

But the Apostle here takes us a step further. To some degree he has anticipated that step in the seventh verse, where he says, 'Inasmuch as both in my bonds, and in the defence and confirmation of the gospel, ye all are partakers of my grace.' Now there, he has already told us something about the function of the Christian Church. The Philippians, he says, have all been participating with him as partners in that work. So here in this section he returns to that thought and elaborates it. He points out how it is the business of all members of the Christian Church to take part in this great matter of preaching the gospel. He says in verse 17, for instance, that some preach the gospel 'of love, knowing that I am set for the defence of the gospel'. And then in verse 27, he puts it like this: 'Only let your conversation [your conduct] be as it becometh the gospel of Christ ... stand fast in one spirit, with one mind striving together for the faith of the gospel.' There again he expresses exactly the same thing, and here, therefore, is a further picture with regard to the function of the Church.

Let me put it like this. The Church, according to the Apostle, comes into being because a number of people have heard the same message, the same truth, and have believed it. They have accepted the same faith, that is the thing that brings them together. It is thus a very special group and not just a nondescript gathering of all and sundry out of the world. It is not formed on the basis of nationality or continents or anything as general as that; the thing that makes the Church is that all who belong to it have accepted the same faith. That is what brought each one of us into the Church, that is what made us Christians, the whole essence and being of a church has depended upon that fact; we meet together because of that common salvation, that common faith. That is Paul's portrait of the Church, and of each individual church, and, of course, it is the characteristic New Testament picture, too. It is a group of people coming together to consider these things which they hold in common, and to thank God for them.

Now that is good as far as it goes, but unfortunately the

story does not end there. Alas, that community, that church, finds itself in a world and in an environment which in many ways can be inimical to its existence and its real function, and that was the position with the early Church. In a sense, most of these New Testament epistles were written because of that fact. The early Christians were not allowed to meet together quietly in that way and enjoy these things in common. They were being attacked, not so much because of what they were in person, as because of what they believed and what they claimed to preach. You will find reference in Paul's epistles to the fact, that as he went round his circuit of churches, he was followed by Judaizers, people who said in effect, 'You believe the gospel, all right; but if you want to be true Christians you must be circumcised as well.'

Then you will also find in the other epistles that some of those so-called mystery religions, which were common in the Roman Empire at that time, were clearly trying to insinuate themselves into the Church. The world was full of religions. Take the picture we have of Athens in Acts 17; in a sense it was 'too religious', there were temples to the various gods all over the place. Now these other religions were always making their attacks upon the Christian faith. They were for ever either querying the very foundations of Christianity, or suggesting that other things might be added to it. The Christian Church was being attacked by false views and theories, and there were many inside the Church who adopted these suggestions, with the result, as Paul shows us here, that the true faith of the believers was being attacked, not only from the outside but from the inside as well. A wrong idea and false motive came in, even for preaching the gospel, and thus the Christian Church from the beginning has had to fight for her faith.

It is most important to grasp that this is of the very essence of the life of the Christian Church in this world. You cannot read a single New Testament epistle without finding that element in it. All these letters are, as we have seen, polemic, they are all arguing and debating and safeguarding the members from these things, and if one had time to review the great story of the Christian era, it would be a very simple matter to show how this process continued. The ideas of the Greek philosophers have always been applied to any new teaching of the gospel; there has always been the tendency to add certain things to it until in the end it has been so polluted and contaminated that, according to the Apostle, it is no longer the gospel of Christ. This has happened throughout the centuries, and, unfortunately, it is still the position at the present time. Therefore, says the Apostle, you Christian people are called upon to do two main things: you are set for the *defence* and the *confirmation* of the gospel. So Paul thanks God for the members of the church at Philippi because they had done this. They had helped him, they had joined with him, they had stood resolutely by his side, and he appeals to them in verse 27 to 'stand fast in one spirit, with one mind striving together for the faith of the gospel'.

Surely I need hardly emphasise the fact that you and I today are called to this self-same task. And you see how contemporary the Scriptures are; the enemies are not all outside, they are inside also. There are large numbers outside talking about the Christian faith, querying its whole basis and foundation. Attacks from science, from philosophy, from psychology, attacks from the cults, they are all here with us, and they are all assaulting the very foundation of Christianity. And part of our function as Christian people is to stand for the *defence* of the gospel. Now the Greek word which is translated 'defence' means literally what it says. It seems that the original idea was of a man defending himself in a legal action; someone brings a charge against him and the man takes up his defence and answers the judge. That is what Paul means by the defence of the gospel and he uses the same phrase again in verse 17, '… knowing that I am set for the defence of the gospel'. In other words, we are called at a time like this to be able to give 'a reason for the hope that is in us'. We should be in such a position that as these assaults upon the gospel come from various directions, we should be able to meet them. There is an intellectual case for the gospel, apologetics is a valid part of theology and, says the Apostle, every Christian should be active in that. So, as men attack the gospel on these various grounds, we should be able to meet their objections and give our reply. It means activity on our part, it means studying and familiarising ourselves with the facts. Nowhere do I find in the New Testament a picture of the Church as a body of people who spend the whole of their time singing or just relating their experiences and having a so-called good time spiritually. Not at all! They are called to the defence of the gospel; the attack is there and we must say something in reply.

Then, in addition to that, we are set for the *confirmation* of the gospel, which means a positive exposition, an explanation, a setting forth of the truth and, above everything else, it means that we must give the proof which we can supply by our lives and by our daily living.

However, all that leads to this conclusion: is it not perfectly clear and obvious that if we are to do all this, then the bare essential is that we should be absolutely clear and certain as to what this message is? What is this gospel? What am I to defend? What am I to say as I read the attacks at the present time? I see men attacking the deity of Christ, the miracles, attacking the virgin birth, attacking the literal fact of the resurrection. Am I just to say, 'Well, that is his opinion; he is a decent man. It is all right. Every man has a right to his own view, there is no need to become heated about it or say that he is wrong. Let us have a great central organisation and take in all and sundry, irrespective of what they believe. After all, these people are perfectly honest and sincere. Does it really matter what they believe?'

But, surely, as we read these New Testament epistles we must confess that that is an utter travesty of the New Testament picture of the Christian Church! God forbid that any of us should delight in controversy for its own sake or that we should become petty and intolerant; but the way to avoid that is not to become indifferent, or to say that it doesn't matter what a man believes. Rather, it is for us to be certain. If we are called to contend for the faith we must know what the faith is, and it must be something clear and definite.

The Apostle, then, tells us here exactly what it is, and we must notice carefully what he says: 'But I would ye should understand, brethren, that the things which happened unto me have fallen out rather unto the furtherance of the gospel; so that my bonds in Christ are manifest in all the palace, and in all other places; and many of the brethren in the Lord, waxing confident by my bonds, are much more bold to speak the word without fear; some indeed preach Christ even of envy and strife; and some also of good will: the one preach Christ of contention, not sincerely, supposing to add affliction to my bonds: but the other of love, knowing that I am set for the defence of the gospel. What then? notwithstanding, every way, whether in pretence, or in truth, Christ is preached; and I therein do rejoice, yea, and will rejoice.'

Now we can summarise that by putting it in the form of two main propositions. First, *the gospel consists of preaching Christ.* Did you notice how Paul mentions that three times: 'preach Christ' in verse 15; 'preach Christ' in verse 16; and 'Christ is preached' in verse 18? He also talks about 'speaking the word', and about 'the defence of the gospel', but those are just two other words for describing the same thing – the gospel, the word, preaching Christ. Surely it is rather strange that in the twentieth century it is still necessary to say these things, and yet the contemporary situation is such that it insists upon our giving this particular emphasis. What was it that these first Christians preached? That, after all, must be our test and our standard. The Christian Church has come down directly and historically from the apostles, who were the first preachers; therefore, if we want to be clear about the gospel that is to be preached, we must find out what they did. On what was the Church formed and established? What was the original message?

And there can be no doubt whatsoever as to the answer

to these questions. Turn to the book of Acts and you will find the very terms that are used here by the Apostle. Read, for instance, the story of Philip and the Ethiopian eunuch in chapter 8. That man was going back home from the religious festival in Jerusalem. On his journey he was reading Isaiah 53 and trying to understand it, when Philip came up to him and said, 'Understandest thou what thou readest?' Then Philip began to explain the Scriptures to him, and we read he 'preached unto him Jesus' (vv. 30, 35). We are also told that almost immediately after Paul was converted he began to preach Christ to the very people he had been anxious to persecute. Again, there is the story of the Philippian jailer who cried out, 'Sirs, what must I do to be saved?' (Acts 16:30). Paul and Silas gave their reply, 'Believe on the Lord Jesus Christ', and then, we read, they proceeded to preach the word of the Lord to him and to his household. But the most striking incident is to be found in Acts 17:2,3: 'Paul, as his manner was, went in unto them [in the synagogue] and three sabbath days reasoned with them out of the scriptures, opening and alleging, that Christ must needs have suffered, and risen again from the dead; and that this Jesus, whom I preach unto you, is Christ.'

I could go on showing that the preaching of the gospel consists essentially in preaching Christ. That is what the apostles did, and that was what Paul had previously done there in Philippi; that is why he keeps on reminding them about this very thing.

In other words, the message of the Church and of the gospel is definite; it is not a vague message of goodwill, nor a general exhortation to people to live a better life. It is not a mere appeal for morality, or soothing words to a nation which is experiencing economic difficulties. Nor is it a kind of general attempt to raise the morale of the people, and to get more production and things of that kind. All that may come in the future as a result of the gospel, but that is not the thing that confirms the truth; it is preaching Christ. Thus, the test of the message should be: is Christ in the centre? Is Christ essential? Does it all emanate from him?

Does it all revolve about him? Would there be a message if Christ had never lived? That is the test, and I think we must all agree that so much that passes for Christianity, judged by this test, is not Christianity at all; it would all be possible without Christ. There is a great deal of idealism in Greek philosophies, and in Islam. There is much good and moral uplift entirely apart from Christ, but it is not the gospel, it is not the word. The thing that I am anxious about, said Paul, is Christ. I preach Christ. I am set for the defence of the gospel.

And he puts it in this extraordinarily extreme form: he tells us that he even rejoices in the preaching of those people who 'preach Christ even out of envy and strife'. Now you could never find a stronger statement than that. Paul is saying, in effect: 'There are certain people, who, because I am in prison, are taking advantage of my position and are preaching the gospel of Christ largely in order to annoy me. They are anxious to attract a party to themselves, and they are doing so by taking advantage of the fact that I am not able to reply from here. But, you know, it is an extraordinary thing that though they are preaching the gospel and preaching Christ with an utterly wrong motive, with a disgraceful motive, I nevertheless do rejoice and shall rejoice. Why? Because Christ is preached.' What the Apostle means is that, in a sense, he is even prepared to forgive a man whose motive in preaching the gospel is all wrong, as long as he preaches Christ.

Now if you read Paul's other epistles, or even the third chapter of this epistle, you will find that there are certain people whom the apostle is not prepared to forgive or excuse. They are those men who are wrong in doctrine, the Judaizers; he has nothing but condemnation for them. Indeed, you remember his strong language in his letter to the church of the Galatians: 'But though we, or an angel from heaven, preach any other gospel unto you than that which we have preached unto you, let him be accursed' (Gal. 1:8). And he says the same thing in writing to the church at Corinth: 'If any man love not the Lord Jesus

Christ, let him be Anathema Maranatha' (1 Cor. 16:22). That, surely, is the distinction which runs through the New Testament. There must be no arguing about doctrine, says Paul. That must be absolutely right. But as for these other people, in spite of their motives, Christ is being preached and that is the one thing that matters.

But that in turn leads to the second question. What do we mean by preaching Christ? Here again the answer is given abundantly in the New Testament. Turn to the Acts of the Apostles, to the thirteenth chapter, where we have an account of Paul preaching; or to the second chapter, to Peter's sermon in Jerusalem on the Day of Pentecost. Or again, take Peter's sermon to Cornelius in Acts 10; in all these accounts what did the apostles preach? Well – and this is the very essence of the apostolic preaching – they first of all reported the facts, and then they gave the meaning of those facts. In other words, they did something like this: they went round preaching 'Jesus and the resurrection', proclaiming Christ to the people. They said, we are not 'setters forth of strange gods' (see Acts 17:18), we are not like your Greek philosophers. We are here to tell you something that has happened. And then they began to tell the story of Jesus of Nazareth. They told the story which we have in our four Gospels, which were not written at that time; they told the fact of the birth of this babe at Bethlehem, and the extraordinary things that took place at that birth. They told of certain wise men and shepherds who came to see the baby; they told of the things that happened to Mary, and then they went on to describe how he spent those years as a carpenter in Galilee. They reported how at the age of thirty he set out on his public ministry and they spoke of what happened when he was baptised by John in Jordan. They went on to describe his preaching, with his strange message, during those three short years, and they told of the miracles which he worked.

Now the very Gospels which we have were written by such men, the men who had heard these reports, and that is why it seems to me so extraordinary when people say: 'Now don't believe the theology of the Church, but go back and read your Gospels and the words of Jesus. Listen to what he says.' We know nothing of Jesus except what we have in the Gospels; we are absolutely dependent upon the reports of the apostles and of the first Christian people, and they are the very people who tell us that the one who spoke these words, which we have been exhorted to read, also worked miracles. So if I do not believe the account of the miracles, why should I believe the reports and the words he is purported to have uttered? Surely the Gospels are the product of the Christian Church herself? Under the inspiration of the Holy Spirit, these men gave an account of his miracles and of the astonishing things he did.

And then they went on to give the story of his death, of the crucifixion and of how it had seemed to them to be an utter contradiction that he who could raise the dead, should be crucified and die in utter helplessness. They told how his body was taken down and put in a grave, and how they had thought that was the end of it all. Then suddenly they found that he was alive, and they told how they had seen him and how he had entered into a closed room. And all this they reported to the believers. Paul, of course, could not say that he had seen these things, but he could say that he had seen Jesus on the road to Damascus, and how the message that was given to him then corresponded absolutely with the message of the other apostles. This, they all said, is something of what has happened – 'we are his witnesses of these things' (Acts 5:32).

And then they came to the explanation, and this is what they taught. First of all, 'This Jesus whom we preach to you,' they said, 'is none other than the Son of God.' His works, his miracles prove it, and his death and resurrection prove it finally, beyond a doubt. But still more important, in a sense, is the way in which he fully confirms all prophecy. So they quoted the psalms and the prophets, they reasoned and proved throughout that 'he is the Christ, the Son of God'. Then they went on to show that he is the Saviour. In a sense, they said, the problem is this: if he is the Son of

God, then why did he die that strange death in apparent weakness upon the cross? This brought them to the very heart of their gospel. He came, they taught, in order to die like that, because the law must be satisfied before God could forgive. Man has broken the law, and he is under the condemnation of that law of God, and man by all his efforts can never erase his past or undo his guilt. So Christ, the Son of God, came in order that he might be the sin bearer, and he went to the cross and himself bore the sins of man; God punished sin in him 'who knew no sin' (2 Cor. 5:21).

So then the apostles turned to the people and said: That is the good news we have to tell you. If you believe in this Christ, if you say that the Son of God has died for your sins, God forgives you; your biggest guilt is cleared, your sins are removed, you are accepted of God and you have become his child. That is the good news. We preach Christ Jesus as the Saviour of your souls.

And then they went on to preach him as the Lord, as the one who having done all this, had returned to heaven, where he is seated at the right hand of God, waiting until his enemies should be made his footstool. They preached that the day was coming when he would return, not as a humble servant this time, but as the King of kings and Lord of lords who would judge the world in righteousness. There will be a new heaven and a new earth, they said, and those who believe on him shall reign with him. Read any one of the epistles and you will find it all there, as, for example in 1 Thessalonians 1 – Christ as the Son of God, Christ as the Saviour and Lord and finally as Judge. That is what preaching Christ means! We announce him and then we say that the Gospels are facts, that he was born of the Virgin, that he did work the miracles, that he was crucified, and that he did rise in the body from the grave. We preach him in all his fullness as Saviour and as Lord; we contend for that faith; we argue; we debate; we reason; we answer objections; we say that he is fullness and all the parts fit in together.

But above all, according to Paul, if we are truly Christian we rejoice in the preaching of that gospel. 'I therein do rejoice, yea, and will rejoice.' There may be certain people who believe all this, and who preach all this, with sometimes a doubtful and unworthy motive, but, says Paul, what does it matter? Christ is preached. They may not be right in their motive, but thank God, Christ is preached, and Paul rejoices because of that, because of the glory of his person, because of the magnificence of the truth, because of what it all means to him. It is because of what Christ has done that I am a Christian, says Paul. I would still be blaspheming and persecuting but for that.

That, then, is the Apostle's picture of the Christian Church; a body of men and women who believe, and who therefore defend the preaching of Christ and encourage it; a body of people who rejoice, who are sensitive to the criticisms and the attacks upon the gospel, but who have a large charity in their hearts to all who really believe in spite of their imperfection. That, it seems to me, is the great call to us today. There are attacks from without and attacks from within; let us earnestly contend for the faith, the glorious faith, and let us individually preach Christ. Let us pray that the whole Church may preach Christ, let us above all plead with God to send his Spirit in mighty revival and reawakening, that Christ may be preached and glorified and magnified among the nations.

6

More Than Conquerors

But I would ye should understand, brethren, that the
things which happened unto me have fallen out rather
unto the furtherance of the gospel. (Phil. 1:12)

In this study we shall be considering what Paul has to say in
verses 12, 13, 14, 19 and 20, but the real key to the passage
is that statement in verse 12. The Apostle here comes to
deal with one of the particular problems which engage his
attention in the course of this great letter. He was writing in
prison, and he wanted to let these people know that though
in captivity, he was triumphant and rejoicing; he was happy,
and he wanted them to have the same experience. He was
not quite sure, when he wrote this letter, whether he would
ever be at liberty again. There were many indications which
seemed to point to the fact that he was likely to be put to
death, so he was particularly anxious that before that happened the Philippians should have such a firm grasp of the
truth that whatever might be their lot or fate in the future,
they, having the same faith as he had, would be able to
triumph even as he was triumphing.

So here he takes up this point. He knew that the members
of the church at Philippi were troubled by the fact that he
was in prison. They loved him, they were concerned about
him, and they had expressed all this in the messages they
had sent to him through Epaphroditus. Now here the
Apostle replies, and this is how he puts it to them: 'I would
ye should understand, brethren, that the things which happened unto me have fallen out rather unto the furtherance

71

of the gospel.' You seem to think, he says, that this is a tragedy, that the gospel is being crippled, and that I am wretched and unhappy, but it is not like that at all. It is, indeed, quite the reverse and I am anxious that you should have a right view of this whole question.

As we come to consider what the Apostle has to say, it is indeed important that we should remember the precise conditions in which he found himself when he wrote these words. As we have seen, he was not only in prison but, according to the custom of that time, was chained to soldiers, quite possibly to one on each side. In other words, he was not only confined to a particular cell or room, but his liberty was encroached upon in that way. He was never by himself, never left to himself even for a second. There was a constant relay of soldiers, who took their turn to be chained to him, one after another, as each period of duty was finished. He was not able to live privately in any sense of the term. There was a complete absence of everything that makes life comfortable, and a complete denial of all the customary amenities. Now it is difficult for us to imagine how trying and galling that must have been, especially in view of what some of these soldiers might be like – rough, uncouth men, probably the very antithesis of Paul himself with his refined, cultured, sensitive and spiritual mind. One can imagine such men with their oaths and blasphemies and cursing, and there was Paul constantly in their presence. That is the kind of trial he was enduring. And here, in this sentence, we really have what you might call the Christian philosophy with respect to adversity. This is one of the classic passages of the New Testament with regard to this whole question.

Many countries of the world have a day which they observe as a Day of Remembrance.* It is a day which should and does inevitably remind people of the trials of life. We cannot use the term 'Remembrance' without being

*This sermon was preached on Remembrance Sunday, November 9th, 1947.

reminded of all that. Whether we like it or not, we are
reminded of the fact that the world has suffered and
endured two great wars within a quarter of a century. We
remember the horrible period between the wars, one of
utter futility and of 'make believe' that ended so disastrously
in 1939. We are reminded of the whole state of the world,
the difficulties, the problems, the trouble, those are the
thoughts that come back to us. The world is a place of trial
and of trouble; there are wars going on, dear ones are killed
and taken away, and there is sorrow and tribulation.

All that, of course, inevitably reminds us of something
else. This whole question of the troubles and trials of life is
something which often causes people to stumble. You are
familiar with the kind of statement that people so often
make. They say that they cannot reconcile a world like this
with a God of love. 'How does God allow these things?'
they ask. 'Why should these things happen?' There are
people who are confounded; their dear ones have been killed or wounded or lost, and they cannot understand these
things. So many, alas, have become embittered and soured;
many during the first world war turned their backs upon the
Church and upon organised Christianity. They felt that they
were justified in doing so, and that problem is still with us.
What do we make of these things? Why do they happen?
What are we going to do about them? What is the answer of
the Christian gospel to the world as it is today?

Now that is the theme which the Apostle deals with in this
phrase that we are considering together. Let me put it like
this: the Bible does not answer these questions of ours
directly. We must not think that it is the kind of book which
has a simple answer to all problems, and that when somebody asks a question you just turn up the index and find the
appropriate page and there is your immediate solution. The
Bible does not regard us, or treat us, as children. It gives us
principles; it lays down postulates and then it tells us: 'There
is the truth, now apply it.' That is its method. No direct,
immediate answer, no yes or no. The whole question is too
big for that, and the problem is too involved. Indeed, I can

go further and say that in this life and world there are certain questions which are not answered, though, thank God, he gives us sufficient to enable us to go through. But there are some problems which we shall not be able to solve: God, in his wisdom, has decided that we shall go through life uncertain about some things.

I have no doubt myself but that this is because of our sin and our unworthiness. It is part of our discipline, sometimes to be kept in ignorance, to be shown that we are finite, to be reminded that we are not gods. We cannot understand everything and though we have a knowledge of good and evil, we do not know everything. After all, in that sense, these things are sent to try us and to humble us, and to remind us that we are but creatures under the hand of our almighty Maker. But, thank God, it does not stop at that. There is a doctrine which is given to us and it is more than enough; and the doctrine, if you want it in one principle, can be put in this way: the vital matter in life is not so much what happens to us as our *attitude* to what happens to us. And that, I think, is the answer to the whole situation. These things will happen in life, they are inescapable, but the teaching of the Bible is that the things themselves do not matter; what matters is the way in which you and I look at them.

Now we must not stay with this preliminary point, but it is important. There is a tag that is often quoted, and yet it contains the essence of truth:

> Two men looked out through the same bars:
> One sees the mud, and the other stars.
> *F. Langbridge*

Here is another: 'Beauty is in the eye of the beholder.'

There is a type of man of whom you can say:
> A primrose by a river's brim
> A yellow primrose was to him,
> And it was nothing more.
> *W. Wordsworth*

That is all he sees. But another man can say:

> To me the meanest flower that blows can give
> Thoughts that do often lie too deep for tears.
>
> *W. Wordsworth*

It is our attitude that counts, and that is the great principle that is taught in the Bible.

And the Bible's next principle is that the only true and right attitude towards these things is the one which it teaches. In other words, it is our attitude to the gospel. That, of course, is something that comes out in almost every one of these statements made by Paul: 'I would ye should understand, brethren, that the things which happened unto me' – the chains and the soldiers and the insults and the blasphemy and all these things that are happening – 'have fallen out rather unto the furtherance of the gospel; so that my bonds in Christ are manifest in all the palace, and in all other places. And many of the brethren in the Lord, waxing confident by my bonds, are much more bold to speak the word without fear.' He is thinking of the whole thing in terms of the gospel, or the word, or the preaching of Christ. That is the principle. The way to look at all these hard things is in terms of the gospel and its teaching.

Let me put it like this: the only people in this world who are able to face 'the slings and arrows of outrageous fortune' in the way the Apostle could are those who believe what the Apostle believed. The gospel of Jesus Christ has no comfort whatsoever to give to people who do not believe it. It has nothing to say at all to men and women who are not in Christ, except that they are lost and that therefore every-thing must be wrong to them. The whole secret is that we start in the right place, that we have the right view, and perspective and that we look at things through eyes that have been illumined by the Holy Spirit himself. We can, therefore, go on to say that there is perhaps no more thorough test of our profession of the Christian faith than this very test of our reaction to circumstances. I suppose that in the last analysis this is what tells whether we are truly

Christian or not. What is our reaction to the things that happen to us in this life and world? Have you been bereaved? Are you sorrowful? Has something happened to you which has affected you at some very vital spot in your life? How are you reacting to it? That is the test. Are you like Paul or are you not? It is one or the other.

Let us, then, consider how this worked out in detail in the life of the Apostle. Here was a man in the position I have described. You cannot imagine anything much worse; a man who was so active, who so delighted in travelling and preaching the gospel, now in prison, chained to soldiers, suffering the indignities and all the horrors of such a prison life. And yet that is what he says. What is his secret? Let me put it still more generally. What should always characterise the Christian's reaction to a time of adversity? That is what we are anxious about at the present time, and in this passage the matter divides itself very conveniently into two sections. First of all, there is a negative aspect. Let us look at Paul in prison, and draw the following lessons from what he says. The first thing we find is that Paul does not grumble or complain, nor does he express a single query with respect to God and God's ways. There is an entire absence of that. You may read this epistle right through, search it and examine it microscopically, and you will not find the slightest hint that he ever did that. Now this is very significant. Conjure up again a picture of what he was enduring, yet not a word of complaint. How do you explain it?

Well, Paul lets us into the secret. The first answer is that he was right in his attitude towards God. This is primary and fundamental in its importance. Paul was so completely right in his view of God, in his reaction to God, and in his relationship to God, that, in a sense, it was quite impossible for him to grumble or to complain. There was one thing about which Paul was absolutely certain, and that was the love of God. He just lays that down as something which is sure, absolute and immovable. When he found himself in trouble or enduring tribulation, the devil undoubtedly tempted him to begin to ask questions about God and his love, but Paul says, in effect, 'No, I am certain of that one thing, and I stand by it.' He does not admit such a thought because he is so sure of the love of God. So he reasons and argues like this: 'Whatever else,' says Paul to himself, 'may be or may not be the explanation of all these things that are happening to me, they are not, in any way, to be explained by the fact that God does not love me, or that God is acting in a manner that is inconsistent with that love. And that is the thing that matters.'

And there, I really think, you have the whole Christian philosophy of life. That is the thing which determines whether we do stand up to these things and emerge as conquerors, or whether we do not. If once you query the love of God you will go wrong; that is something a Christian should never do. Paul argued like this (and how valuable is this man's Christian logic): 'He that spared not his own Son, but delivered him up for us all, how shall he not with him also freely give us all things?' (Rom. 8:32). Now that is logic, and yet it is essential Christian truth. His argument is this: is it possible that God who sent his only begotten Son from heaven to earth, and even sent him to death on the cross in order that I might be saved and redeemed and made an heir of God, is it possible that that God does not love and is not concerned about me and has allowed me to be handled anyhow by life? No, it is impossible, it is unthinkable, and therefore I rule it out.

He has also put that same argument in Romans 5:10: 'If, when we were enemies, we were reconciled to God by the death of his Son, much more, being reconciled, we shall be saved by his life.' If when we were enemies the Son of God gave his life and died for us that we might be rescued and redeemed, then, surely, by his life now in heaven he is going to sustain us and perfect the work. Obviously it is inevitable. That is what I mean by saying that Paul was absolutely certain about God; his attitude towards God was right, not for a second can he admit any doubt about that, it was impossible, it was a denial of the whole of his gospel.

Christian people, I wonder whether we apply this logic? I

wonder whether we always reason like that? Or do we listen
to that dastardly thought which tends to come in like this: 'I
am a Christian trying to live the Christian life, yet look what
happens to me! But look at that unbeliever, see how he is
enjoying life.' But the moment you stand and face this
mighty postulate – 'God has so loved me that he sent his
only begotten Son to the death on that cross for me and my
salvation' – you will be put right about the love of God. Paul
does not grumble or query God's will or God's way because
he is absolutely certain of that love, he knows that 'neither
death, nor life, nor angels, nor principalities, nor powers,
nor things present, nor things to come, nor height, nor
depth, nor any other creature, shall be able to separate us
from the love of God, which is in Christ Jesus our Lord'
(Rom. 8:38, 39). You see, it is not his love to God he banks
on, it is God's love to him; he relies on that and he is safe.

But there is a second answer as well. Paul does not grumble and complain, not only because his attitude to God is
right, but also because he has the right attitude to himself,
and that is second in importance only to the first. Here, of
course, Paul, once and for ever, shows what that attitude
was. He did not think of himself just as himself, he was not
interested in himself, as such. There was a time when he
was, and he kept a very careful record of all that he did. He
could tell you exactly what he had done – he put it all in his
diary – but once he had become a Christian he stopped
doing that. This is how he puts it: 'According to my earnest
expectation and my hope, that in nothing I shall be
ashamed, but that with all boldness, as always, so now also
Christ shall be magnified in my body, whether it be by life,
or by death'. I do not want to stop with this now, because I
hope to take it up in detail later, but it tells us that Paul's
secret was that he was in love with Christ to such an extent
that he had forgotten himself altogether. Paul in prison does
not say, Why does this happen to me? He says, How does it
affect the gospel?

We all, surely, know exactly what I mean. Even
psychologists are aware of this fact and, indeed, it is a part

of their stock in trade. The whole business of psychological treatment is to make men and women forget themselves, to become interested in something else, to transfer this self-interest to something else. It is this morbid, pathetic interest in self that makes us so miserable. That is why we break down in life; that is why we fall when tribulation comes – self-pity. 'Why should this be happening to me?' I ask. I am looking to myself all the time and because of that everything is exaggerated. Now Paul does not do that because he is looking for Christ and the glory of Christ and the gospel is what he is concerned about. It is not, 'Why am I chained to these men?' or, 'What I am suffering or enduring!' His one concern is '... that with all boldness, as always, so now also Christ shall be magnified in my body, whether it be by life, or by death.'

Clearly, the man has lost himself and therefore there can be no self-pity, no sympathising with himself, no feeling sorry for himself and going down hopelessly before it all. No, he has a healthy attitude towards himself. He says, I am in Christ, I am a citizen of the kingdom and it is not self that matters, it is the kingdom, it is the King. He is so concerned about this that he is emancipated out of this whole vortex of morbidity and unhappiness that is such a curse in life at the present time.

My beloved friend, shall I again ask you that simple question? Have you suffered one of these trials? How have you come through it all? You know what has happened to you – the heart knoweth its own bitterness – but I ask you, are you like Paul? Are you free from this grumbling and querying the love of God? Are you sure of God and are you right in your attitude towards yourself? Have you become lost in Christ, which is the secret of it all?

Now let us turn to the positive side of the picture. These are the things that Paul did in his tribulation and trouble, and which we should all do. First, he seeks for signs and indications of God's over-ruling of his circumstances – that is in verse 12. The old commentator, Matthew Henry, uses a very good expression on this point. 'Contemplate this,' he says, 'here is an explanation of divine chemistry, which I would almost describe as Divine Alchemy.' It is as if something bad were placed into the crucible and you wonder what is going to happen to it, and because of this divine alchemy it becomes very good; God has over-ruled it. Paul says to the Philippians, Do not think that my preaching is at an end because I am in prison; nor that because I am a prisoner I cannot preach the gospel; because my being in prison has turned out in an extraordinary manner and some amazing things are happening. 'So that,' says Paul, 'my bonds in Christ are manifested in all the palace,' – or as you will find it in the Revised and other translations, 'throughout the whole praetorian guard' – 'and in all other places.'

Do you know, he says, that the main result of my imprisonment has been that it has been the means of talking about the gospel to people who probably would never otherwise have heard of it? The soldiers in charge of him were the members of the Praetorian Guards and Paul was chained to these men, spending his hours with them. He says, in effect, 'These men have discovered that I am not a common criminal; they have found that I am here because of Christ; they have asked what it is all about and I have had an opportunity of telling them. These soldiers would probably never have heard it had I not been a prisoner, but now, when they go off duty and when they go to their homes, the gospel of Jesus Christ has become one of the greatest topics of conversation in the whole of the palace.' At first you might have thought Paul's imprisonment was the end of all, but God with his chemistry came in and turned it to the furtherance of the gospel.

Now that, you will find, is a very common theme in the Bible. In Genesis 50 we read what Joseph said to his brothers, after their father Jacob had died in Egypt. They were afraid that he would now take revenge on them because of their cruelty to him, but Joseph said to them, 'Ye thought evil against me, but God meant it unto good.' You did it because you were jealous of me but God sent me down before you to prepare for the famine and to save you from death. What you did, you meant for one thing but God meant it for another – God came in and over-ruled the entire circumstance in order to prepare us.

Then you will find that the Psalmist in Psalm 119 puts it like this: 'Before I was afflicted I went astray: but now have I kept thy word.' And again, he says, 'It is good for me that I have been afflicted; that I might learn thy statutes' (vv. 67, 71). I could not see clearly what was happening, says the Psalmist, or the meaning of these untoward circumstances, but God came in and used them; God over-ruled.

Now that is the Christian's certainty. When, then, we find ourselves facing this adversity, this trial or this tribulation in life, having first put ourselves right on the love of God, the next thing to ask is, I wonder what God is doing in this? What is his purpose? I wonder how God is going to make use of it? What is the set purpose of the Divine Chemist at the back of all this? I am now going to watch this amazing experiment, and I am going to see what the Divine Alchemist is going to work in this situation; God is going to make something out of this. And the moment you look at it like that, you have already conquered it, you have beaten the temptation down. You are seeing something that God is going to use to the furtherance of his gospel and his kingdom.

The second thing is that the Christian in this situation always grasps the opportunity afforded for witnessing. That is what Paul was doing here. He tells us, as we have seen, that the main effect of his imprisonment was that the Praetorian Guard and others had heard about the gospel. Not only that, he tells us that many of the brethren in the Lord, 'waxing confident by my bonds, are much more bold to speak the word without fear.' So these were two main things that happened as a result of Paul's conduct of himself in prison. There he was, suffering acutely physically, suffering these indignities, suffering as only a sensitive, cultured man like Paul could suffer under such conditions, and yet he bore it in such a way that the soldiers began to look at him, and began to talk about him in such words as these: We have never seen a man behave like this before. What is it that enables him to put up with the insults without even a second's impatience? What is the meaning of his calmness and his equanimity? So they say to him, 'You look as if you are enjoying it. You are not behaving like an ordinary prisoner.' And then Paul gave them the gospel. He was living in prison, but all the time he was witnessing for Christ to the prison guard and to others in the palace.

But not only that; there were also weaker brethren in the church at Rome who were equally being affected by him. It was a very difficult time to be a Christian. They were being persecuted because of their faith, and threatened with still worse things, so that some of the weaker Christians were beginning to forget 'the hope of their calling'. But when they heard of Paul in prison, how that true man of God was conducting himself, and how he was standing for Christ in the face of death, then their courage began to revive. That is what happened – they were fainting, but Paul was beginning to preach and testify. Ah, my dear friend, no man lives to himself in this world. What you and I do in the time of adversity and trouble is going to affect many others. Is not this the one way to face life and its troubles and tribulations – to see in it an opportunity of witnessing for Christ? When the blow descends, say to yourself, here is a grand opportunity. There will be people who are going to watch me, they know I am a church member and that I call myself a Christian, so they will look and say, 'Let's see how he stands up to this. Let's watch her, let's listen to their words.' And there is your opportunity to testify to the gospel.

And then, says Paul, remember those who are weaker than yourself: Christian people who have become a little bit doubtful and hesitant. You must live in such a way that after they have seen you they will say, 'Yes, it is quite true after all, he went through it; she stood up to it, without any change, without any flinching, without any apology at all.' Thus, the weaker Christians will see that the gospel is true and that the promises are sure. See in it an opportunity for witnessing and if you face it like that, whatever it may be, you will conquer it.

But let me just comment briefly on the last thing. Paul saw in all this nothing but a part of God's process of perfecting. That is the nineteenth verse: 'For I know that this shall turn to my salvation through your prayer, and the supply of the Spirit of Jesus Christ.' Salvation there does not mean deliverance from prison, because in the next verse he says he does not know whether he is going to live or die. It means salvation in the fullest sense. In effect, what Paul is saying is, 'There are aspects of this trial of mine which I do not quite understand, but I am perfectly sure of this, that it is a part of my sanctification, it is a part of God's process of perfecting me. I am still very imperfect, and God is perfecting me through this. He is doing certain things to me here which in a sense cannot be done anywhere else and I am coming out of all this a better man than I was before.'

So it works like this: these trials and tribulations come to give us a right view of life. Some of us stop thinking when things go well. Sometimes all we care about is making money. Then some calamity comes and we lose our business and this makes us begin to think seriously about life. Such things are good for us; anything that makes us think truly about life is good for us. It makes us think more of the next world and it makes us prepare the ground for it. How prone we are to forget and to live only for the present.

Then it makes us realise our own sinfulness and unworthiness, and it reminds us of our own weakness and inability. But above all, it sends us back to him and anything that makes us rely upon him and desire to know him better is an excellent thing. It is a part of the process of perfecting, of sanctification. My dear friends, in the economy and wisdom of God, so many of these things happen to us in life because God loves us. 'Whom the Lord loveth he chasteneth' (Heb. 12:6) – that is it. It is a part of God's process of bringing his children into ultimate perfection. I am sure, says Paul, that this is turning out unto my full, final and complete salvation in Jesus Christ.

There, then, we have seen the Apostle's prescription, or recipe for facing the trials and tribulations of life.

Remember the negative, the complete absence of grumbling and complaining, based upon a right view of God, and a right view of self and of life. Then remember the positive things; look for the divine chemistry, seize the opportunity for witnessing, submit yourself to the process of perfecting, of sanctifying, and realise that it is the loving hand of God bringing his work to its final consummation. Thank God for a gospel that can meet life at its worst and enable us to emerge more than conquerors through him that loved us.

7

He and He Alone

For to me to live [or living] is Christ. (Phil. 1:21)

We stand here face to face with one of the sublimest and
greatest statements ever made, even by this mighty Apostle
of our Lord and Saviour Jesus Christ. There is a sense in
which anyone who faces this verse must feel that he stands
on very sacred ground. Indeed, I am ready to admit that I
would almost regard it as sacrilege to approach a verse like
this in an unworthy manner. Here we have not only the
statement of an experience which was true, which was a fact
and a reality, but at the same time, and for that reason, we
also find ourselves face to face with a standard of judgment.
Any God-given experience is sacred, and nothing is further
removed from the spirit of the New Testament than
approaching a statement like this in a purely objective manner, handling it with our rough hands, bringing our critical
or dissecting apparatus to bear upon it. There is something
so sublime about it, so delicate and pure, that one is – as
always with such verses – confronted with a kind of
dilemma. On the one hand, one is afraid of handling it in a
detached, so-called scientific manner yet, on the other hand,
of course, there is also the danger that, if we do not analyse
it up to a point, we fail to realise its inner meaning and its
true purpose. One is compelled to do both – to analyse it
and try to understand it, while always remembering that it
is a living experience and a statement of fact which puts us
under judgment.

Now Paul, as we have seen, is comforting the Philippians who were concerned and troubled about him. He has told them how this imprisonment of his has turned out 'rather unto the furtherance of the gospel', and added, you remember, that it was his earnest expectation and hope 'that in nothing I shall be ashamed, but that with all boldness, as always, so now also Christ shall be magnified in my body, whether it be by life, or by death.' That is the background of the statement. Paul means that as far as he is concerned, it is immaterial whether he is to be put to death, or whether he is to go on living. The two possibilities are there and he does not know which it is going to be, but, he says, it is all right. He is not concerned and they need not be either, for, 'to me to live is Christ and to die is gain'. And then he proceeds to work it out a little further, for he says that if he were to express his own personal preference, it would be to depart, yet for their sakes it is better for him to remain. At this point, however, we are concerned with this particular statement that the Apostle makes with respect to life and to the meaning of living.

In these words we are surely brought face to face with the most important questions that can ever confront us – What is life? What is living? What does it mean to us? What is it all about? Is it not one of the major tragedies of life, indeed, is it not the greatest of all tragedies, that amid all our concerns about life, all our intellectual activity, all our discussions, the one thing which men and women are never concerned to face is the first and most obvious thing of all, namely life itself, and living. Not only is this a most important question in itself, but I want to go further and point out (and this, indeed, is especially the burden of this study) that here we stand face to face with the most thorough test we can ever encounter of our profession of the Christian faith. Because, of course, this is a word which is more or less meaningless to someone who is not a Christian. It speaks especially to those who claim to be Christians, and that is why I am so anxious not to deal with this subject in an objective manner.

The temptation at this point, of course, is to look at it as Paul's experience only, but, my dear friends, we are speaking about ourselves, not just about Paul. It is true of Paul first and foremost, but what is true about Paul should be true of every other Christian. The last man to recognise any essential difference between himself and every other Christian was the Apostle Paul. He never claimed that there was one kind of Christianity for him and another kind for everybody else. To me, one of the most subtle dangers confronting most of us is that for some extraordinary reason, though we have been Protestants and have rejoiced in Protestantism for 400 years, we still seem to appropriate some of those false Roman Catholic distinctions between Christians and non-Christians. We have seen how they draw an essential difference between saints and ordinary Christians. The saints, they say, are special people, or 'spiritual Christians', as opposed to 'worldly Christians', and that is why they ask these worldly Christians to pray to the saints. But that is a distinction which is never recognised in the New Testament; indeed, it is a distinction which it denounces.

Of course, we recognise that there are differences in gifts and in offices; you see that in 1 Corinthians 12 and Ephesians 4 and in other places in Scripture. But while there are differences in the ministries that are given to Christians by the Holy Spirit, as children of God, through Jesus Christ, we are all the same and all our lives must show this. That is why the Apostle talks so constantly about 'we'. What is true of him is true of others, and here in this statement we are faced with the most searching and thorough test which we can ever apply to ourselves. Can we say honestly with this man that to us living means Christ? Is that true of us? I have no doubt at all but that the greatest thing in the Church and therefore in the world today is that Christian people should be able to say that. It is when they have spoken like this that they have counted in this world; it is when they have been consumed by this passion for their Lord that their very lives are radiant and the whole world has known that something has happened to them.

So let us look at these words first in terms of the Apostle's own experience, and then let us apply them to ourselves. There Paul is in prison and he raises this problem. 'I may live another twenty years,' he says in effect, 'or I may be put to death tomorrow. But you know,' he continues, 'I find myself in such a state and condition that really it is immaterial to me, because if I am going to live another twenty years that means Christ, and if I am going to be put to death at once, it still means Christ; whichever it is to be, it comes to the same thing. Christ means living, living means Christ.' I repeat, the vital question for us all is whether we can say the same. Paul here makes a vital, fundamental distinction between those who are Christians and those who are not and the thing that characterises the Christian is that to him living means Christ.

What, then, is life? What is living? Perhaps the best way of approaching this is to consider some of the answers that have been given to this question. Now there are, of course, large numbers of people who never think at all about the meaning of life. Life to them just means existence, a kind of animal condition, or a state almost like that of a plant or flower. There are many people who have no philosophy whatever. Here they are in this amazing thing called life; they have this astounding gift of being, and yet they go through without contemplating it. They never stop to ask what it means, they just go on from day to day, eating and drinking, without any such thoughts at all.

Then there is what we might well call the Epicurean view of life, which can best be summed up by the phrase: 'Let us eat, drink and be merry.' The Epicurean attitude to life was very familiar in the time of Paul, as, indeed, it is today. It centres on the living rather than on the life; it means pleasure: eating, drinking, dancing, or whatever it may be. Now there is a very definite philosophy which covers that kind of life and there are people who really believe in it. I do not want to tarry with these preliminary considerations but it is amazing to notice the numbers of people who, if they answered honestly, would have to say that to them that is life – that round of one pleasure after another. It is tragic, but it is true. How often have we heard of people leaving the provinces and going to live in the big cities because they want to see 'life'. They pity the people whom they have left behind because life to them means an opportunity for pleasure.

But there is another view which we may describe as the Stoic's view of life. It is more intelligent than the Epicurean's and it expresses itself like this: life is something which has to be endured. The Stoic does not keep a perpetual grin on his face and say: 'Isn't everything wonderful?' He is sufficiently intelligent to see that that is far from true. He has come to realise that this world can often be filled with tears; he sees the harshness and the wretchedness, the suffering and the torment, and he decides that living means putting up with it, going on with it, going through with it, taking yourself in hand and carrying on, whatever may come. His attitude to life and living means hard endurance, a determination to hold on. And, alas, there are large numbers, who, if you were to ask them what living is all about, would have to say that it is a battle with circumstance and chance; a standing up to the 'slings and arrows of outrageous fortune'; an everlasting and endless struggle.

And then today, and always in times like this, when life is particularly difficult, there is the cynic's view of life. Perhaps one of the best expressions of this is the speech that Shakespeare puts into the mouth of Macbeth:

> Out, out brief candle!
> Life's but a walking shadow; a poor player,
> That struts and frets his hour upon the stage,
> And then is heard no more; it is a tale
> Told by an idiot, full of sound and fury,
> Signifying nothing.

That is what I mean by the cynic's view of life, and how many there are who take that view today! It is perhaps a peculiar temptation in a time like this, when so much idealism has been falsified and so many bright hopes have been dashed to the ground. The typical comment of men today is: What is the use of anything? Nothing.

Then, to advance up the scale, there is the view that may be described as the mystic's view of life. It is important that we should understand this, because oftentimes the Christian view has been mistaken for what I am describing as that of the mystic. There is, of course, such a thing as Christian mysticism, and it is important that this should always be qualified by the word 'Christian', to make it clear. The typical mystic's view is that life and all its ills are ultimately due to the flesh, and that salvation is to be found by going out of the flesh and not being identified with it. Consequently, the mystic spends his time in trying to mortify the flesh; he tries to live in a passive manner, not allowing the world to influence or affect him. That is his outlook, a kind of dying to the world and adopting a purely passive attitude.

But let me now go on to what I would describe as the average man's view of life and this is where the word of the Apostle tests us so profoundly. Christian people, members of Christian churches, if we were asked, 'What is living to you? What really constitutes life to you? What is the thing of all things to which you hold?' is it not true that many of us would have to admit and confess that it means our families, our homes, our work, our occupations, our activities in life? Does not living often mean to many of us the companionship and love of our loved ones, the home life and circle? What precious things these are, yes, but they often become *the* thing in life, and when they are taken from us, our life, our world, collapses and we have nothing left. I always feel one of the most difficult tasks that we ever have to do is write a letter of sympathy when a dear one has been taken from a family which we know is not Christian. They are good people perhaps, nice people, living a perfectly moral and very happy life, but when one of them is taken you know that the whole basis of their life has gone.

But let me go on. There is the humanist's view. To the humanist living means an opportunity of doing good, of improving the world and uplifting the state of society. Now there are large numbers of people who have that idealistic view of life, and if you ask them what they mean by living, they say, 'It is an opportunity of changing and improving the life of mankind, and of elevating it.'

Then let us go on to what we may call the religious view of life, and I am putting it like this to differentiate it from the Christian view. There are some people, who, if you ask them, 'What is life?' are bound to say that it means being religious and performing religious duties. Let us examine ourselves, my dear friends. One of the greatest dangers facing preachers is the danger that they will live on their own activity: speaking, preaching, being engaged in church work, being very active about their religion. There is a danger of living on all this until suddenly, when the activity is gone, one is left empty-handed. Have you not seen that? To me, it is one of the great tragedies of life. Sometimes, I have to talk to men and women who have led very active lives in church circles and who, when they have been taken ill, seem to have nothing left to them. They have been living on their own activity and interests, and there is a danger of substituting these things for this about which Paul speaks.

Shall I go further and put it like this: living, to the Christian does not even mean God. Is that irreverent, or extreme? Is that going too far? I suggest it is not. A Jew or a Muslim can say quite honestly that life to him means God, and there are many in the world who can say that God is the centre of their lives. So that in this statement of Paul's it is the specific Christian language, that is the distinguishing mark of the Christian. 'To me, to live is' – what? – '*Christ*'. Not God even, not God the Father, but Christ the Son; not my religious interests, not my religious activities, not any of the things I have mentioned: to me, says Paul, living is Christ.

What, then, does he mean by life? In a sense, I have already been defining it – it is love. He means the supreme thing in life, the thing for which and by which he lives, the thing without which life would to him be pointless and meaningless. He means the thing that controls the whole of his life. Perhaps the best way of putting it is like this: the thing that Paul is really saying about himself is that he is in love with Christ. He loves him and, as is always true of love, that love dominates his life and controls it. That is what I live for, he says, that is the nature and object of it all.

Now let me analyse that just a little further in order that I may bring home to us just what Paul means when he says that Christ controls the whole of his life. What is life? One good classification is that life consists of what we do. Let us put it like this. The Apostle there in prison says to himself, I may live another twenty years; but what if I do? What is it going to mean? What am I going to do during those twenty years? To us it may mean ten, twenty, thirty, or forty years, perhaps, ahead of us, and what are we going to do with them? What is life going to mean to us? That is the first thing.

And this, again, is something that can be sub-divided. Life consists of what I think and the realm of my interests. Life does not just mean eating and drinking and sleeping and rising and doing my work or job in life. That is not what Paul means by life. He means a purpose in life, the things that give it real meaning. He is referring to how I spend most of my time when I have my leisure, what I read and what I think about. That is a very good test. It is, of course, a characteristic of love that it is always thinking about the object of its love, and, whether we like it or not, that is true of every one of us. That is why this text comes as such a test, 'Where your treasure is, there will your heart be also' (Matt. 6:21). What do we think about? What are our real interests? What is the thing that we are anxious about more and more? Well, with Paul it was Christ: it was always Christ in the centre.

And there is more. Love consists of this – expressing our feelings, expressing our emotions and giving vent to the desires that are within us. And you remember how Paul tells us so clearly that his one desire was to know Christ better and to love him more. That, he tells us in chapter 3, is what he longs for: 'That I may know him, and the power of his resurrection and the fellowship of his sufferings'; that, above everything else. He has this feeling, this impulse, this emotion and it is all centred in Christ. 'To me to live', in the matter of feeling and emotion, 'is Christ.'

And then it means activity, action. And here again the Apostle tells us what that means to him. He has spent his time in spreading the glory of Christ, so that Christ may be preached, whether by him or by someone else. That is why he is willing to stay with the Philippians – in order that he may tell them more about Christ. If I remain another twenty years, he says, what am I going to do? Well, as far as I am concerned, I am just going to preach Christ. I am going to tell people about him and try to get them to believe on him; I am going to do everything to make his name great and grand and glorious. Living is activity, in that sense.

But the other thing that is true about living is that things happen to us in life. If I live another twenty years I am going to do certain things, and certain things are going to happen to me; it is a part of life. And here again Paul says that in that respect also, that to him life means Christ. Has he not already been saying that? Was that not what he said in verses 12–30? These people are trying to add to my bonds by preaching Christ of envy, but it is all right, Christ covers that too. Paul sees even a thing like that in terms of, and in the light of, Christ. What he means is that in Christ he has been delivered from the thraldom of things that happen. He is no longer a victim of circumstance and chance. He goes on in the last chapter to say, 'I have learned in whatsoever state I am, therein to be content.' Christ has delivered him from the tyranny of what might happen to him.

And the other thing, of course, about love and life is that we all desire satisfaction. There are certain demands I make of life, there are certain things I am looking for. I am looking for peace and joy, I am looking for happiness, and Christ completely satisfies Paul in every respect. I have intellect: Christ satisfies it, says Paul; I have feelings and desires which need satisfaction: Christ is my all and in all. Every demand that I make of life is more than fully satisfied in Christ. That is what he means by saying that living to him is Christ. The action, reaction if you like, to things that happen and all the demands of his nature and his personality are fully satisfied and filled. My dear friend, can you say the same thing? I am sorely tempted just to stop at this point and go on asking that question. This, to me, is the very essence of the Christian position. The thing that makes a person a Christian is Christ. Christ is always central, he is everything to me. 'Living' to Paul meant Christ in all that full sense.

Let me ask another question. What was it that made Paul feel this? I think he gives us the answer in the various epistles he has written. I am quite sure that the first thing was the glory of the Person. In Acts 9 we read the story of his going down to Damascus, breathing out threatenings and slaughter. Paul said within himself, I ought to do many things contrary to the name of Jesus of Nazareth. He did not know him, but then he saw him, and, if I may use such an expression, Paul fell in love with him, he never forgot the face or the sight. Once he had seen him, everything else receded. Everything else paled into insignificance beside the face of Christ, the glory of the person, the blessed one. Ah, if we have ever seen him, even by the eye of faith, for a second, it must lead to this consuming passion! Paul had seen him and therefore inevitably loved him. Thomas, you remember, saw him, but you remember what our Lord said to him: 'Thomas, because thou hast seen me thou hast believed, blessed are they that have not seen, and yet have believed' (John 20:29). You may say to yourself, 'If I had the vision that Paul had on the road to Damascus, I might be able to say that I love him in exactly the same way, but I have never seen him.' But that is foolish – 'Whom having not seen, ye love' says Peter in 1 Peter 1:8. Read some of the great hymns, read the lives of the saints, they loved him. They have seen him with the eye of faith and we have their testimonies to that. The glory of the person of Jesus is the main cause of love. The tragedy is that we stop so much at the benefits of the Christian life. We are so anxious for blessings, that we forget the one who gives them. Paul did not; he saw that that blessed one had actually given his life and had gone to the cross for his sins – 'The Son of God, who loved me' – even me – 'and gave himself for me' (Gal. 2:20). It is the glory and wonder of the cross. He gave all his life's blood for such a wretched sinner.

Next Paul had come to see and to know that apart from Christ there is no such thing as true life. In chapter 3 he uses that strong expression, 'and do count them but dung': refuse, worthless. Without Christ no one lives, it is only existence. Life, as we have seen, is meant to be full orbed, the intellect satisfied, the feelings satisfied, the whole life enveloped, the whole man taken up by this complete, rounded life.

And, lastly, he felt and said it because of the new view of life which he had thus obtained. Paul had now been given to see that life in this world is really but a preparation for the great life that is coming. That does not mean to depreciate this world, nor does it mean scepticism or mysticism. If ever anyone lived an active life it was Paul: no, he did not die passively to the world in that sense, but rather to the sin of the world. For Paul had come to see that the world is in a great state of conflict between the kingdom of heaven and evil. He knew a day was coming when the King would return and rout the forces of evil and set up his kingdom. Now, said Paul, I am destined for that; I am going to be in that. I may spend twenty years longer in this world, but think of the glory that awaits me, think of the life that is coming, the real life when the King shall reign and I shall be with him! And that, too, made him live for Christ.

So, then, I end with my question: is living to us, Christ? I wonder whether we can make that statement that was made by Count Zinzendorf, the Moravian leader who helped John Wesley both before and after his conversion. He had never had the vision that Paul had on the road to Damascus, but to him, too, Christ was in the centre. Can we make his motto our own? 'I have one passion, it is he and he alone.' 'To me living is Christ.' Oh that we all might have this passion! I believe we could transform our land in a day, I believe a great revival would come, if only we had this passion. He and he alone! Let us dwell upon him; let us meditate upon him; let us ask the Holy Spirit to reveal him to us. Let us pray for it; let us spend time with it; let us absorb it; let it take the central place; let us do all we can to get to know him better, for to know him is to love him.

I have one passion – it is he and he alone.

8

'To Dwell with Him Forevermore'

For to me to live is Christ, and to die is gain. But if I live
in the flesh, this is the fruit of my labour: yet what I shall
choose I wot not. For I am in a strait betwixt two, having
a desire to depart, and to be with Christ; which is far better:
Nevertheless to abide in the flesh is more needful for you.
(Phil. 1:21–24)

We come now to the second statement in the twenty-first
verse: 'to die is gain'. In our last study we followed Paul as
he considers the possibility of remaining in life, and we saw
how he says so magnificently that for him 'to live is Christ'.
But now we look at him as he faces the other possibility,
death. And immediately, before giving any reasons at all, he
says that for him to die is gain. So here, again, he makes one
of those challenging and thrilling statements which are so
characteristic of his letters.

The Apostle thus brings us face to face with what I would
call the second great question of life, one that every thinking, thoughtful person should of necessity be pondering constantly. The first question which we considered in the last
study, is, what is life? And the man who does not face that
problem is, in the philosophical sense of the word, a fool.
But now we come to this second question, what is death?
What is it going to mean to us? What is our attitude to it?
Now here again I am constrained to say that surely there is
nothing that is quite so extraordinary about men and women

97

as the way in which they not only evade this question, but
dislike it. There is no need to seek proof for that. You start
talking about death to anybody, and immediately they will
charge you with being morbid. The argument is that it will
come soon enough in any case and you need not go to meet
it. To talk about death is not popular; nor is preaching about
it – it is very rarely done these days. The whole concern of
life seems to be to help people to forget the fact of death
and to postpone it as long as possible. Of course, that is very
different from the attitude of our forefathers, and especially
of the Puritans of the seventeenth century with their great
tradition; a time, let me remind you, when the real foundations of the greatness of this country were laid. Those men
thought perpetually of life in terms of death, but this has all
become unusual and strange. People dislike it, and regard it
as unhealthy.

But this is an attitude which, apart from being quite
ridiculous and senseless, is utterly inconsistent with what we
do in so many other respects. We never get annoyed with
the man who persuades us to take out a health or a life
insurance policy, that is admitted to be the height of wisdom. 'Surely,' one man says, 'you are not going to take
these risks, your house may be burnt down.' Or another
says, 'Can't you see how wise it is to make provision for
these possibilities?' The thing on which modern man prides
himself so much is that he is making provision, and he covers himself in every respect. And yet, when it comes to this,
the most certain and the most vital and the most important
fact and event of all, he completely reverses the process and
even becomes annoyed with anyone who impresses upon
him the duty and the importance of facing it and of making
some provision for it.

Now that, to me, is such an interesting attitude. It is so
utterly inconsistent that it does seem to affirm the biblical
teaching with respect to man and his attitude towards death.
There is only one way of explaining this modern reaction
towards the subject and that is that modern man, in spite of
his apparently blasé attitude towards death, is simply in the

position that is described in Hebrews 2:15, where we are told that men in sin, 'through fear of death, were all their lifetime subject to bondage.' That is the cause of the annoyance, and of this disinclination to face and to consider the subject. That is why men feel you are insulting them when you ask them if they are ready to die; if this were not true, they would not react so strongly.

But here we have a statement by a man who immediately makes us see that there is an entirely different attitude towards death. Paul says, I am facing it, I have looked at it, and I say with respect to it, 'to die is gain'. Now of all the achievements of the gospel there is none, perhaps, which is quite so striking as the way in which it has entirely changed the attitude of mankind towards death. If you consider death apart from the New Testament gospel, you will see at once what I mean. Take even the Old Testament. In its view of death the Old Testament rises higher than any pagan philosophy or teaching, yet, when you read it, you find that there is still an element of uncertainty. It sometimes has a hope, the writer of a psalm seems to rise to a higher level and almost gets hold of the fact of the resurrection, yet it is shadowy and uncertain. You even find psalms in which the Psalmist complains that when a man dies, he dies altogether – 'In the grave who shall give thee thanks?' (Ps. 6:5).

It is only with our Lord and Saviour Jesus Christ that we find the new attitude to this question of death. As Paul puts it to Timothy, it is Christ who has brought life and incorruption, or immortality, to light through the gospel (2 Tim. 1:10). The moment you come to the New Testament, and especially when you read the Gospels, you find an entirely new outlook upon death, something new and strange which the world has never known before. Of course, in the last analysis it is due to the resurrection; it was there that the final proof was given that death could be, and has been conquered. By rising from the dead our Lord made it perfectly clear to his disciples that he had conquered death and the grave. And it was because of that great and glorious fact that Peter and all the apostles and all the first Christians had this completely new view of death, and could face it with a smile, and could say 'to die is gain'.

And also, of course, in the light of the resurrection they were reminded of many promises that had been made by our Lord himself in the days of his flesh. They remembered how he had said, 'Let not your heart be troubled: ye believe in God, believe also in me. In my Father's house are many mansions ... I go to prepare a place for you. And if I go and prepare a place for you, I will come again, and receive you unto myself; that where I am, there ye may be also' (John 14:1–3). And in the light of the resurrection that becomes the glorious possibility. Thus, it was because of the teaching of our Lord and especially because of the resurrection, that the Apostle was able to write this glowing, challenging, magnificent statement to the church at Philippi.

Yet, once more, as we look at it, we are not merely looking at an objective statement, we are really examining ourselves. This is a statement that is meant to be true, not only for Paul, but for every Christian. Paul, as I have pointed out, never claimed uniqueness for himself in that respect; in our Christian experience we are all meant to be the same, and if Paul can face death like this, I ought to be able to as well. But can I really do so? Am I facing death in this particular way? I think we must agree that this again is one of those deep, thorough-going searching analyses of our very profession of the Christian faith. If you were asked which was the most difficult and searching test – to say, 'to me to live is Christ', or to say, 'to die is gain' – I wonder what your reply would be? For myself, I have no hesitation in saying that the former is the more difficult test. I do not feel that the second statement is as difficult to say as the first and I will tell you why. The fact and the question of my death and eternal destiny, thank God, is determined by Christ. If I believe at all in Jesus of Nazareth as the Son of God, and in his death on Calvary, and in his resurrection, then whatever may happen to me, 'to die is gain'. I know it is right, it must be right. But when I am asked to say, 'to me to live is Christ', then it is not so much something that he does for me, as something that I myself have to do and in that sense living is more difficult than dying.

Perhaps there is little point in comparing the two, and yet I think it is important. To be able to say, 'to die is gain' is a very thorough test. It may not be as difficult and as searching as the other and, yet, how vital it is. In other words, it comes to us like this: do I feel as I face the fact of death that it is going to be gain to me? Can I look at it as the Apostle looked at it? Now in order to help us in this self-examination let me remind you of some of the ways in which people do look at death, so that we may see to which of these groups we belong. So often when we come to a practical test like this we seem to belong to other categories instead of to the Christian. What, then, are some of the common, characteristic views of death at the present time? First, there is a fear or a hatred of death. Death is the last enemy, that haggard person that comes ever nearer and nearer, and we have a horror of it. Another attitude is that of resignation. It has got to come and I have to face it, so it is no use worrying or being annoyed about it. Then a third view, which men have tried to make popular in the last hundred years or so, is that we must have courage, we must stand up to it and refuse to be frightened; not resignation but a kind of defiance.

And then, lastly, there is the Christian's attitude.

I think perhaps the best way of putting these different views is to put them in the form of three quotations of poetry which I found once in a book and which seem to me to put this whole case very well. They certainly express the fear, and the defiant courage, and the Christian's view of death. But before I come to these, let me give you what I consider to be the best description of resignation; it is given by Walter Savage Landor.

> I strove with none;
> for none was worth my strife;
> Nature I loved and next to Nature, Art;
> I warmed both hands before the fire of life;
> It sinks, and I am ready to depart.

Resignation! The fire is going out in the grate; it sinks and I am ready to depart.

But now, bearing that in mind, let me remind you of the other three attitudes that have here been put together in a most interesting manner. One idea at the back of these three quotations is of death as drinking the 'stirrup cup'. There was an old custom that when cavalrymen set out upon their exploits they drank from the stirrup cup and that idea is reflected here and so too is the apocalyptic symbol in Revelation 6 of death as the pale horse.

There was once a man called the Hon. John Hay who was at one time Secretary of State in the United States, and this is how he expresses the fear and horror of death:

> My short and happy day is done,
> The long and lonely night comes on,
> And at my door the pale horse stands
> To bear me forth to unknown lands.
>
> His whirring shrill, his pawing hoof
> Sound dreadful as the gathering storm,
> And must I leave this sheltering roof
> And joys of life, so soft and warm?
>
> Oh, joys of life, so soft and warm,
> Kind friends so faithful and so true,
> My rosy children and my wife
> So sweet to kiss, so fair to view.
>
> So sweet to kiss, so fair to view,
> The night comes on, the light burns blue,
> And at my door the pale horse stands
> To bear me forth to unknown lands.

When General E. P. Alexander read that, he felt that it expressed nothing but the fear of death: a strange adventure, terrifying and horrid but unavoidable. He felt that this was not good enough, and he wanted to express in dauntless, unfaltering language the way in which he would face death, so he wrote these lines in the light of that first poem:

> But storm and gloom and mystery
> Shall only nerve my courage high;
> Who through life's scenes hath borne his part
> May face its close with tranquil heart.
> No trembling hand will grasp the rein
> This life has not been mine in vain;
> In unknown lands I'll seek my place,
> I'll drain the cup and boldly face
> The heritage of the human race
> Whose birthright is to pierce the gloom
> And solve the mystery of the tomb.
> I follow some, and others lead
> From whom my soul would ne'er divide
> One fate for all. Where moves the great
> Procession, there let me abide.

Now both these poems came into the hands of James Powis Smith, a distinguished minister from the State of Virginia, someone who had fought with Stonewall Jackson, and had ridden with him through many a valley of the shadow of death. He felt that the fear of death as expressed by the Hon. John Hay was not good enough and that General Alexander, too, had failed in his attempt at courage; so he, as a Christian, wrote this:

> The pale horse stands and will not bide,
> The night has come and I must ride;
> But not alone to unknown lands,
> My Friend goes with me holding hands.
> I've fought the fight; I've run the race,
> I now shall see him face to face,
> Who called me to him long ago
> And bade me trust and follow.
> The joys of life have been his gift,
> My friends I'll find when clouds shall lift;
> I leave my home and all its store

To dwell with him for evermore.
What does he give? His cup of love
Until with him I rest above;
I'll mount and ride, no more to roam,
The pale horse bears me to my home.

You see the difference – not fear, not mere resignation, not an attempt at boldness and courage, but triumph; he smiles at it, he is confident, he is certain. Now that is the characteristic expression of the Christian's attitude towards death, and that is what Paul says in one phrase in this magnificent statement – 'to die is gain'.

Now Paul, here, is not talking so much about the act of dying as about the state in which the Christian finds himself after death; though in a way he does give us a hint about the dying in the surrounding verses and that is why we must read them with this phrase. In verse 23, he uses the word to *depart*. The authorities are not quite agreed as to the exact meaning of this word. There are two possible translations, but no one can prove which is really correct; in a sense, they both say the same thing. The first is the idea of lifting the anchor. There is the ship in harbour, the anchor is raised and the ship sets out upon her voyage. Death, therefore, means passing from this land across a narrow sea and entering another harbour, or crossing the narrow sea from this world to the next and then living in the land of pure delight. That is one suggestion; to depart means boarding the ship, crossing the sea and arriving at your ultimate destination.

The other possible meaning for this word is striking the tent, breaking up the camp and going on with the journey. Now you can choose whichever you prefer, but for myself I have no hesitation in accepting the second, because it seems to be the characteristic Jewish view of life. Paul writes in 2 Corinthians 5:1, 'For we know that if our earthly house of this tabernacle were dissolved...' That is the idea. Peter, too, in his second epistle tells the Christians that as long as he is 'in this tabernacle' or tent, he is going to go on reminding them of certain things, 'knowing that shortly I must put off this my tabernacle even as our Lord Jesus Christ hath shewed me' (2 Pet. 1:13–14). That was the typical Jewish view. The idea was that this is a temporary world where you live in tents; there are no permanent buildings here. Death means breaking up the camp, striking the tent, moving on to the permanent residence which is awaiting you. That is how Paul views the act of death – just a moving from this world to the next.

But, you remember, and we must surely note it as we deal with this subject, the beautiful statement with regard to the fear of dying that was made by our Lord himself in his story of Lazarus and Dives: 'It came to pass that the beggar died and was carried by the angels into Abraham's bosom.' And what a glorious statement that is. You know, my friends, we do not understand these things, but we believe this on the authority of the Son of God himself. If you and I are in Christ when the last act comes, the final crossing, we shall be carried by angels. That is death to the Christian.

But, as I say, Paul was really concerned here, not with the act, but with the state and condition of the Christian after death. 'It is gain,' he says and because of this he adds in verse 23, 'I am in a strait betwixt two, having a desire to depart, and to be with Christ; which is far better.' Indeed, we ought to translate it like this: '... which is very far better.' And what more could he say than that?

So then, the question for us is, why is it far better to die and to be with Christ? Let me suggest some of the answers. The author of the epistle to the Hebrews helps us by putting it like this: 'For they that say such things declare plainly that they seek a country. And truly, if they had been mindful of that country from whence they came out, they might have had opportunity to have returned. But now they desire a better country, that is, an heavenly...' (Heb. 11:14–16). He has already said that they were ultimately seeking for 'a city which hath foundations', not a tent, or an encampment, but an immovable, unshakeable city 'whose builder and maker is God'. That is 'much better' because it is a permanent place. To put it in a slightly different way, it means going to

a life which is not transitory but is never ending. Again, as
the author of Hebrews says in chapter 13, verse 14, 'For
here we have no continuing [or abiding] city, but we seek
one to come.' It is a continuing, everlasting and changeless
condition, an abiding life which is far better, for that reason;
it is not contingent and transitory like this one.

But then I must mention this other idea, the idea of death
as just a going home. Paul, in effect, puts it like this: 'If I
consult my own longing I should desire to dissolve this
earthly tabernacle and to go home to Christ.' Can you think
of anything more beautiful than that – to go home to Christ?
I am certain that is what Paul meant. You note at the end of
Philippians 3 that the words in the Authorised Version are
'our conversation [citizenship] is in heaven.' Someone once
described Christians as 'a colony of heaven, waiting for the
homeland'. We have been sent here to colonise this particular place but we really belong there; there is the homeland,
that is the place to which we belong. And that is what Paul
seems to think. I am a stranger here, a pilgrim, a sojourner,
heaven is my home; death means going home: it is far better.

Let me suggest another reason to you why to die is gain.
In Christ and his resurrection I shall get rid of 'the body of
this death', the desire, the lust, the things that remain of the
old man and all that is sinful and imperfect. Christ assures
me of an ultimate glorification when I shall be entirely free
from sin, not only from its guilt and power but also from its
pollution. The day will come when none of the elements of
sin will be left in us, we shall be utterly and absolutely free
from it all.

What else? Well, to know fully and finally, and to understand, and see, things as they are. Paul writes in 1 Corinthians 13, 'Now we see through a glass, darkly'; thank God for
the little that we do see in life, life would be impossible if we
did not see that much, but even at its best it is only 'in a glass
darkly', and then it will be 'face to face'. We shall see things
clearly then, the whole sweep of the great plan of salvation.

Oh, to see God and the wonder and the glory of it, to know and to understand without limit or hindrance!

But we must end in this way. What really makes death gain, says Paul, is that it means to be with Christ. That is the great, the positive thing; the others I have mentioned have, in a sense, been negative. This is what makes Paul say, If I had the power to choose, I would choose death, for this reason – to see him as he is. I put it again as I did earlier: Paul had had that glimpse of Christ on the road to Damascus. He had seen the face and never had he forgotten it, and this is what dying meant to Paul – to go on and see him always, to spend the whole of eternity looking at him. To be with Christ, just to look into his face, that is heaven, that is eternal bliss, that is what Paul longed for and lived for; and then to enjoy perfect communion with him for ever, without any hindrance, without any interference, without any intermission.

Thank God for the experiences we have in this world from time to time when we feel that Christ is with us and speaking to us, but, alas, it is not a permanent condition. There are days when the soul seems lifeless and Christ seems far away, and the communion is broken, but, as Paul says, we walk by faith and not by sight; in spite of our feelings, and all the things that seem to be against us, we just go on by faith. But *there* the communion is unbroken, there is never an intermission and we shall enjoy his companionship for ever and for ever.

Well, these are some of the things, surely, that make Paul say that to die is gain. Let me add just a footnote. People have often asked me why we are not told more in the New Testament about life beyond the grave. I have two answers to give. The first is this and I am sure that it is right: we are not told more because there is a sense in which we cannot be told more. Everything in this world is sinful, even our language. I do not hesitate to assert, therefore, that if the New Testament had given us a detailed description of heaven and of being with Christ our language would misrepresent it. Our language is not pure enough, the thing is so wonderful that all the vocabularies of the universe are not adequate to describe it. It is so glorious and wonderful that we need to be qualified and perfected before we can take the description or are capable of understanding it. I am sure that is the first answer.

The other answer is that we are deliberately not told, in order that we may think of it only as Paul thought of it. Paul only put it in one way. It is not just to be rid of the things I have mentioned, they are for my perfecting. The only reason for wanting to go to heaven is that I may be with Christ, that I may see him. That is why the little word 'and' is so important – 'to me to live is Christ *and* to die is gain'. The only man who is really happy about death, the only one who can say confidently, 'to die is gain', is the man who has said, 'to me to live is Christ'. You remember the prophet Balaam who said, 'Let me die the death of the righteous' (Num. 23:10). But he forgot that if you want to die the death of the righteous you have to live the life of the righteous. If I want to be able to say with certainty 'to die is gain', I must be able to say here and now 'to me to live is Christ'. That is what enabled Paul to say it. Christ was the consuming passion of his life: to know him, to dwell with him, that is the thing, said Paul, that is my life, and therefore to die must be gain; to go home, to be with Christ, is very far better.

God grant, my beloved friends, that as we examine ourselves in the light of life and death we may be able to join the Apostle in his glorious affirmation.

9

Citizens of Heaven

Only let your conversation be as it becometh the gospel of
Christ. (Phil. 1:27)

We find here a transition in this letter, from a description of
Paul himself and his condition, to an appeal to the members
of the church at Philippi, yet, like all these movements of
thought which are so characteristic of the writings of this
great Apostle, there is no sudden break, no abrupt difference; everything always follows with a strange and wonderful logical sequence. But Paul comes here to a practical
exhortation and it is interesting to observe exactly how he
does so.

Paul, you remember, has been reassuring the Philippians
who are concerned and grieved about his being in prison.
He has shown them that what appeared to be so bad at first
has turned out, under God's blessing, to be something wonderful. His imprisonment has encouraged the preaching of
Christ, and in this he rejoices. Then we have been considering his philosophy of life and death – 'To me to live is
Christ, and to die is gain' – and we have seen that he really
does not know which of the two to choose. If pressed, his
own personal preference would be to say that he would
desire to depart and to be with Christ because it is 'far better'. Yet he knows that for the sake of the members of the
church at Philippi it is preferable that he should remain in
order that he may help them to understand the gospel still
better, and that he may further their joy and faith: 'that

your rejoicing may be more abundant in Jesus Christ for me by my coming to you again'.

And then, in the light of all that, the next thing, and in a sense the inevitable thing for him to say, is, in effect, 'Only, whether I go or do not go, whether I am put to death or whether I am to live for a number of years, whatever may be my immediate future, whatever may happen to me, whatever may happen to you, there is only one thing that matters; whatever,' says Paul 'you may remember or forget, hold on to this, and see that this is always true – 'only let your conversation be as it becometh the gospel of Christ.'

So here we come to the realm of the practical, but we can never reiterate enough that these practical exhortations in Paul's writings always come after a preliminary announcement of doctrine. He never starts on the level of conduct, there is always an introduction, a preliminary salutation. He insists on painting in the background before he comes to the detail of his picture, and he never makes an appeal like this without basing it firmly and solidly upon the truth. And here is something very characteristic of him. He has not only been describing his own view, he has also been suggesting to the Philippians that this should be their view of life and of death too. As we have seen, he does not claim that only he can say, 'To me to live is Christ, and to die is gain'; it is the normal standard of the Christian, and it should be true of us all. Then, having said that, he goes on, 'Only' – therefore, that is the real force of the word, in view of all this – 'let your conversation be as it becometh the gospel of Christ.' Having told them what their view of life and death should be, he now tells them how to live in the meantime. As Christian people we are not meant to be spending all our time in contemplation of these exalted and glorious views. That is essential and we must do it, but we do not stop there. We realise that having done that we now go on to apply it in practice and in daily operation.

So here we have a perfect illustration of the New Testament teaching with regard to conduct, and of the whole New Testament outlook upon our behaviour in this world. And it always seems to me that the vital aspect of this matter is that we should clearly understand the setting, and the order in which it is put. Paul's concern is still about the gospel. That is the basis for the appeal which he makes to these people, and, of course, his reason for doing so is that he knows full well that there is nothing that so thoroughly recommends the gospel of Jesus Christ as a practical demonstration of Christian living. That was true in the early days, and it is still true today. There can be no doubt at all but that it was the behaviour and the life lived by individual Christians that was most responsible for the spread of Christianity in the first centuries.

We get accounts of that in the book of Acts. We are told, there, that as a result of certain persecutions Christian people were scattered abroad, and that wherever they went, they spread the good news of the gospel by their lives and testimony. And even secular and pagan historians bear eloquent testimony to the fact that nothing more influenced the ancient world than the quality of life which was being lived by these people. What John Wesley said of his early Methodists could also be said of the first Christians: they not only 'died well', they lived well also; and others observing all this were impressed and constrained to ask questions. The fortitude of the early Christians face to face with persecution and death was something that made a profound impression upon that ancient world and they began to ask, 'What is it these people have? What is it that enables them thus to live and die?' And by enquiring they were given the answer and thereby the gospel was spread.

It has been the same throughout the centuries and, surely, if it was ever true, it is true at the present time. People are constantly telling us that they have ceased to be interested in abstract teaching, and mere theory. They tell us they have no time for theology and dogma and all these things, but they are interested in life and in living. They are facing problems and troubles themselves, and there is a unique opportunity at this present time for Christian people to spread and preach the good news of this gospel and to act as

witnesses. And the most effective manner of doing that is
just to live the Christian life, for it is obvious that other
ideas and philosophies are breaking down around us. Men
and women are most certainly unhappy, and there are those
who would have us believe that at the present time there
seems to be a wistful turning back to the Church and a looking at the gospel in sheer desperation. People are asking
whether that old gospel has, after all, something to offer us,
and whether it is, perhaps, the way out of our troubles.
Well, if that is true, then surely there is nothing more important than that we should so represent the gospel as to make
it attractive to others and win them from their present
opposition; and the way, above all others, in which to do
that, is to obey this exhortation of the Apostle.

Let us, then, see how he approaches it. This is his
method. First, he puts conduct second to doctrine: conduct
is the outcome of certain things that have been believed.
The New Testament, in other words, is never interested in
conduct and behaviour in itself. I can go further and say that
the New Testament does not make an appeal for good
behaviour to anybody but to Christian people. The New
Testament is not interested, as such, in the morality of the
world. It tells us quite plainly that you can expect nothing
from the world but sin, and that in its fallen condition it is
incapable of anything else. In Titus 3:3 Paul tells us that we
were all once like that: 'For we ourselves were sometimes
foolish, disobedient, deceived, serving divers lusts and plea-
sures, living in malice and envy, hateful, and hating one
another.' As the Psalmist says, we were 'shapen in iniquity'
(Ps. 51:5); this is true of every natural person. Thus there is
nothing, according to the New Testament, that is so fatuous
and so utterly futile, as to turn to such people and appeal to
them to live the Christian life. They cannot do it, the Christian life is impossible to the non-Christian and the New Testament announces that everywhere. The truth is that it only
has one message for people like that – the message of repentance. The New Testament approaches such people and
shows them that they are under the wrath of God, and

makes them see themselves condemned and in a desperately hopeless condition. It then offers them the gospel of salvation and, when they have believed it, it indicates to them the kind of life they should live. It is no use approaching a man and saying to him, 'Only let your conversation be as it becometh the Gospel of Jesus Christ', unless such a man believes the gospel of Jesus Christ; that is why Paul has told the Christian view of life and death before he comes to this exhortation. That, then, is the first principle. Christian conduct and behaviour are only possible on the basis of Christian doctrine.

Let me now put it in the form of some other negatives in order to make my meaning plain. There is nothing quite so foreign to the New Testament teaching as to regard the Christian appeal for ethics and conduct as a catalogue of negative prohibitions. I sometimes think there is nothing that does such grievous harm to the gospel as those people who give the impression that the Christian life is merely a collection of prohibitions, restrictions and restraints. That impression has been given far too often and we have known people who have watched the lives of certain Christians and then have described Christianity, and Christian men and women, as the people who do not do certain things. Now there is an element of truth in this, but if we give the impression that we are merely people who refrain from certain actions, we are being false to this exhortation of the Apostle.

Let me go further and say that it is not merely a moral code or law. The New Testament appeal for ethics and conduct has that essential point of difference from the Ten Commandments and the moral laws that were given in the Old Testament. Do not misunderstand me. I am not saying that the Christian gospel has abrogated the Ten Commandments, but that it puts them in a different way. The Ten Commandments were a law, a moral code. The Children of Israel were told, thou shalt and thou shalt not. This is the characteristic of law; it does not so much reason with us as just tell us what or what not to do.

The New Testament, however, puts the whole appeal on the very highest plane. If I may use such a term, the New Testament's appeal for conduct is a more intelligent appeal. It makes it inevitable, it does not merely legislate and command. It makes a series of statements, it lays down its doctrine, and then says, 'In the light of that...'; 'Therefore...'; 'Only...'. There is nothing, let me emphasise again, that is further removed from the New Testament method than to be interested in conduct as something in and of itself. The New Testament never isolates conduct, and it is never interested in it for its own sake. Conduct, according to the New Testament, is the outcome of life, and it must never be thought of as something which we can separate from the action of life.

There is, furthermore, something else which to me is tremendously important, especially at a time like this. The New Testament on the whole does not give us a detailed list of rules and regulations. Rather, it gives us a great principle and asks us to apply and live it. Now that is, in a sense, the difference between the Old and the New. 'But,' someone may ask, 'are there not particular injunctions laid down in the New Testament epistles? Don't the epistles tell the members of the churches not to steal, not to purloin and to avoid being jealous and envious?' Yes, but I think it is important that we should observe the way in which the Apostle does that. He never does it in the form of a series of rules and regulations, that is the Old Testament way; what the Apostle does is to give his principle and then put the whole question in the light of his great doctrine. In the light of all this, or in view of this, he says, can you not see how utterly incompatible it is for you to lie, or steal, or rob? It is the *principle* that he enforces, and he asks us as intelligent people to grasp that and to put it into practice.

And this is precisely what he does in our present text. Whether I come to you again or not, says the Apostle, whatever may be the immediate future, whatever may lie ahead of me, this is the one thing I ask you to remember – 'Only let your conversation be as it becometh the gospel of Jesus

Christ.' Now in a sense the whole of the New Testament appeal for conduct and behaviour is in that phrase. And we can also put it like this: our conduct is to be something that is worthy of the gospel. If I want to know what I am to do as a Christian, well I do not face a daily list of rules and regulations, which I can carry about and tick off one after another. Not at all! It is rather a general appeal to me to be worthy of the gospel, to live in conformity with the gospel, to live a life that matches the gospel.

Now it is generally agreed that the translation in the Authorised Version is not the best, and yet there is something about this word 'becometh' that surely does suggest a very profound truth to us. The word is one that would be used of dress and clothing. In the matter of clothing, there are certain things which are becoming and certain things which are not. There are certain things, for instance, which are very becoming in a young person, but which are not becoming in someone older. That is the sort of idea the Apostle has in mind. There are also certain things that are not becoming with other things, they don't match, and if we want to be dressed in an appropriate manner we must make sure that our dress, as well as being good and beautiful in and of itself, also conforms to the overall effect. In a sense that is what the Apostle means here. Beloved Philippians, he says to them, let your conduct be such that it is fitting, that it is becoming to the character that you claim for yourselves as Christian people; let it match the thing that you are claiming for yourselves. Let it suit the designation you have taken upon yourselves, let it conform to the kind of person that you say you are, and that other people think you are.

There, then, is the general principle. But the Apostle divides this up into two sections and I really only want to give you headings at this point.

'How, then, am I to live as a Christian?' asks someone. Well, the Apostle answers first of all by saying this: behave as colonists, or as citizens of heaven. Now the Authorised translation, 'conversation', is certainly not the best here. Today we use the word conversation to mean talk, or speech, and only that, but when the Authorised translation was made in the seventeenth century the word meant general behaviour. So the Apostle is really saying, let your whole life and behaviour be as becomes the gospel of Jesus Christ. But this word goes even further than that, and here the authorities are agreed that perhaps the best way of translating the phrase would be, 'Behave worthily as citizens of the gospel of Jesus Christ'; or alternatively, 'Act your part as citizens in a manner worthy of the gospel of Jesus Christ'; 'Perform your duty as citizens'. It does not matter which of these you choose; this is certainly the idea that was in the mind of the Apostle. As Christians we have to realise that we are citizens of a different kingdom. I suppose it was natural that the Apostle should use that figure in writing here to the members of the Philippian church. Philippi was a Roman colony. The centre and seat of government was in Rome, it was the capital city. But the Emperor had planted a number of colonies throughout that ancient world and Philippi was one of them. There were people living in Philippi who were Roman citizens, who claimed the privileges of a Roman citizen, and who were not under the local law, but under that of Rome. In Acts 16, you remember, Paul claims his right as a citizen of Rome.

And so he makes that appeal as a basis for his ethic for behaviour. Christian people, he says, you must regard yourselves in this world as but colonists. You are here in this world, it is true, but you are citizens of the kingdom of heaven, just as the Romans in Philippi are living in Philippi while belonging to Rome. The colonist does not really belong to the colony in which he lives, he belongs to the land from which he has gone forth, that is his homeland and country. He just lives in the colony for the time being and he is doing certain things there. Now that is how the Apostle would have us view the whole question of conduct in this world of time. We are to regard ourselves as citizens of a heavenly kingdom; we do not belong to this world and to its order. The first thing we must remember is that we are a unique, distinct and separate people. In writing to Titus,

Paul says that our Lord died in order 'that he might ... purify unto himself a peculiar people, zealous of good works' (Tit. 2:14). Purify unto himself, draw out unto himself, set apart for himself; we are his special people.

Again, in writing to the Galatians, Paul refers to the death of Christ as something which has delivered us out of 'this present evil world' (1:4). Indeed, this idea runs everywhere throughout the New Testament. It would have us see that to become Christians means that we have been put into a separate position and that we are now distinct from the world that does not believe in Christ. Now this is surely the very best definition of the Christian life. The Christian is not a man of the world who just adds something on to his life or tries to make himself a little bit different. The first thing about him, according to this doctrine, is that he is separated and essentially different. He is a colonist in a strange land, he belongs to a particular order, and to a different society. Indeed, he is a man who is under an entirely different jurisdiction.

Now you see the great appeal that this makes to us in the matter of conduct. As citizens of our own countries, we surely know something about this. We know what it is to go to other lands and to take a pride in our country and to feel that the honour of that country perhaps rests upon us; and that is the kind of appeal that the Apostle is making to the church at Philippi. You remember the great word that was sent out by Lord Nelson on the morning of Trafalgar – 'England expects every man will do his duty.' He did not so much give detailed rules and regulations as say, in effect, 'The one thing you have to remember throughout this day is that England is expecting certain things of you. Let that guide and rule you, and then you will never falter or fail, for you will do all for the honour of your country.' And that is exactly what the Apostle says at this point. Let your citizenship be something that governs you, rules you and controls you.

In other words, we are to realise, as Christian people, that the honour of the homeland is in our hands, so that when we ask the questions: 'What am I to do as a Christian? How am

I to live as a Christian?', we do not want to be given a list of rules and regulations. The name of God, the name of Christ, the very reputation of heaven, as it were, is in our hands. Therefore we must live a life as citizens that is always mindful of that fact. The Apostle Peter puts it still more explicitly. In 1 Peter 2:11–12, he makes the same appeal to the people to whom he wrote: 'Dearly beloved, I beseech you as strangers and pilgrims, abstain from fleshly lusts, which war against the soul; having your conversation honest among the Gentiles: that, whereas they speak against you as evildoers, they may by your good works, which they shall behold, glorify God in the day of visitation.'

That is the same idea, '*strangers and pilgrims*' – you do not belong to this life and world now you have become Christians. There was a time when you were not a people of God but that is what you are now. You used to be a kind of rabble, but you are now citizens of a new kingdom, and therefore, because of that, this world is a strange world to you. You are in it but not of it, you belong to that other realm, and you are to live in this world as strangers and pilgrims.

So, says Paul in this passage, exercise your citizenship, remember that you belong to the kingdom of heaven. Do not regard yourself as belonging to this world, do not be ruled by its outlook, do not be governed by its tastes and interests. Of course, this is the most difficult thing of all to do with the newspapers, the radio and the films and all these things around us. The world is influencing us on all sides, but the call to you and to me is to remind ourselves every day of our lives: 'I do not belong to it. I am a stranger. I belong to another kingdom, I am a citizen of the kingdom of God.'

Paul's second appeal is for me to exercise my citizenship in a manner which is worthy of the gospel. 'Only let your conversation be as it becometh the gospel of Christ.' This means that I am to live in a way which will make everybody who sees me know whose is the doctrine which I hold, and what this doctrine is. It is the gospel that has enabled me to understand the sinfulness, the hatefulness, and the evil of sin. That is the first difference between a Christian and a non-Christian. The non-Christian is not aware that there is much wrong with him. He may sometimes think he is a fool when he does something that causes him pain, but he does not see anything essentially wrong in the way of the world, and he is enjoying it for that reason. But the man who believes the gospel sees that the whole world is 'lying under the wicked one'. It is the Christian alone who sees that the whole world is desperately wicked, and under the wrath and condemnation of God. He believes that God made the world perfect so he asks, 'Why is it that the world is as it is?' And he sees that the only answer is that sin has come in, and he hates this thing that has ruined life and the world and insulted God – the sinfulness of sin. How am I to live in this world? Well, first, I am to do so realising that I am sinful, seeing the ugliness, the foulness and the enormity of sin.

The next thing Christians believe is that in spite of sin and man's rebellion and unworthiness, God, with his great and everlasting love, sent his only begotten Son into this world. They believe that the Son came and endured so much, indeed even staggered with that cross upon his holy shoulders, was nailed to it and suffered agonies, and died in shame and ignominy. And why did he do all this? The answer comes back from a thousand places in the New Testament – that we might be forgiven and that we might be redeemed and rescued. And not only that we might be forgiven but also that he might separate unto himself 'a peculiar [special] people'. I believe that Christ died to make atonement for my sin. I see that it is the only way I can be delivered out of the condemnation in which this world is involved: sin is so terrible that nothing but death could deliver me. I see that in order that I may become a citizen of the kingdom and a child of God, he had to suffer. And if I believe all that, I am to live in such a way that I proclaim it. My conduct is to match the doctrine of the cross and the atonement.

What else? The Christian also believes the doctrine of the

rebirth and the new nature, which tells me that by the power of God, through the Holy Spirit, in Christ I become 'a new man'; I have a new life; 'old things are passed away; behold, all things are become new' (2 Cor. 5:17). If I claim that, then I must live as one who has a new nature, altogether different from the other, with a different outlook, different tastes, different interests and desires. So 'let your conversation be as becometh' the doctrine that preaches regeneration and the new birth.

Then Christians believe, too, in the power and the teaching of the Holy Spirit. Paul puts it like this: 'For I am not ashamed of the gospel of Christ' – Why? – 'For it is the power of God unto salvation' (Rom. 1:16). It is not only the power that can deliver us from the guilt of sin, but that which can also deliver us from the power of sin, so that I claim that as a Christian I have a power which enables me to overcome sin, to live above it and to defy it. Only 'let your conversation be as becometh' a Christian that preaches a doctrine like that. Peter tells us that all things that appertain unto life and godliness are given us (2 Pet. 1:3), and we are to exemplify that in our lives.

But, lastly, the gospel teaches me about the kingdom which cannot be moved and shaken. The gospel, as we have seen in these studies, holds before me a blessed hope. It makes me say, 'For to me to live is Christ, and to die is gain.' This means, to be with him, to enter into that kingdom; it means that there is a glory awaiting me. If I say I believe all that, then how am I to live as a Christian? 'Every man,' says John, 'that hath this hope in him purifieth himself, even as he is pure' (1 John 3:3).

Now that is the way the New Testament appeals to us to live the Christian life. It does not put us under rules and regulations, or merely say that we ought to be living this kind of life because it is better than any other. Rather, it comes with its own inevitable logic and reasons. You say you are a Christian, you say you believe the gospel of Christ, very well, all I ask of you, is to live your life in the way that is becoming to that gospel. All I say is, if you believe in the fact of sin, show that you hate it; if you believe in the death of Christ, then demonstrate it. If you believe in the rebirth and the power of the Holy Spirit, let it be evident to all that this is a fact; if you really say you believe in that glory that is to come, well do you not think that it is only reasonable and logical that you should be setting your affection there and not here, and that you should be gazing on those things rather than on these? Should you not rather be hasting on to it and purifying yourself and doing your utmost to be ready for it? Only exercise your citizenship in a manner that shall be worthy of the gospel of Christ.

My dear friends, I say again that this is our unique opportunity at this time. That is what we stand for in a world that is so largely non-Christian. The way to convince the world of the truth of that gospel is to let them see that it makes a difference, that it is a power, that we are not mere theorists and philosophers but that we preach the power of God. And we prove that there is a power in the gospel by showing what we are in work, in business, in profession and in the home. Wherever we are, whatever we are, only let our citizenship be worthy of the gospel of Jesus Christ.

10

Standing for the Truth

Only let your conversation be as it becometh the gospel of
Christ: that whether I come and see you, or else be
absent, I may hear of your affairs, that ye stand fast in one
spirit, with one mind striving together for the faith of the
gospel; and in nothing terrified by your adversaries: which
is to them an evident token of perdition, but to you of salvation, and that of God. For unto you it is given in the
behalf of Christ, not only to believe on him, but also to
suffer for his sake; having the same conflict which ye saw
in me, and now hear to be in me. (Phil. 1:27–30)

We continue now with our study of Paul's practical exhortation in these verses. As we considered the first phrase in the
twenty-seventh verse – 'Only let your conversation be as it
becometh the gospel of Christ' – we saw that we must realise
that we are citizens of the kingdom of heaven and that our
whole conduct is to be governed and determined by the gospel of Jesus Christ. But the Apostle is not content with just
leaving it like that, in the form of a general exhortation, and
he comes now, as is his custom, to the particular. His division of the Christian life is twofold. We find one half of it
here in this section at which we are now looking, and the
other section is to be found in the first verses of the next
chapter. The division of the chapters here is a little unfortunate, because it does tend to break up a theme which is
clearly meant to be continuous. The Apostle deals first of all
with the external aspect of our Christian life, and then with
the internal aspect. According to Paul, as Christians in this

life, we must all wage a war with forces outside ourselves and, too, we have a fight with forces that are within. So here he goes on to deal with both of those aspects.

But it is very important that we should realise the essential nature of this particular sub-division. What the Apostle says is true of the Church in general, but it is equally true of the individual Christian. Here we are, set in a world like this, either as individuals, or as a body of Christians, and, says the Apostle, we will inevitably find that we have to watch these two things; certain things will be happening from the outside and others from the inside. Now that is true of the Church which has to fight a battle against those that are without, and also has to be aware of subtle foes that are within the body of the Church herself. Or take it in terms of the individual, who thus has to fight with forces that are outside himself, and, in exactly the same way, has to be aware of these subtle foes and enemies that reside within himself. And here, having laid down his general principle which covers everything, the Apostle now proceeds to deal with the life of the Christian in this twofold aspect.

Taking the two things together helps us to see something of the paradoxical nature of the Christian life. Indeed, if a man were not a Christian, he could not write a passage like this without feeling, in a sense, that the whole thing is contradictory, because on the one hand we are told to be very strong, and yet on the other hand we are told to be humble. We have to do these two things at one and the same time; we have to adopt an aggressive bold attitude and also this amazing and strange humility. Yet, of course, from the Christian standpoint there is not the slightest contradiction between the two. There is all the difference in the world between this fight with the enemy outside and the fight against the enemy that is within.

So, then, this is the position with which the Apostle confronts us, and at this point I want to consider only the first aspect of that fight. These verses at the end of the first chapter give us one of those extraordinary pictures, which are found so frequently in the writings of the Apostle, of the

Christian, the Church, and the individuals within the Church engaged in a battle. Paul uses quite a number of different pictures. There is the one at the end of Ephesians 6, for instance, where the exhortation is to 'put on the whole armour of God'. He encourages the Colossians, in exactly the same way, to stand shoulder to shoulder. The Apostle was very fond of drawing his pictures in that way from the Roman and other armies. Here, in Philippians, the picture is probably taken more from the athletic contests, an image which the Apostle often uses. He tells us in verse 27 that we must 'stand fast in one spirit, with one mind striving together for the faith of the gospel.' Elsewhere he writes about men running in a race, or striving as gladiators in a contest. The actual picture, of course, does not matter so much, the important thing is to realise that to which the Apostle is exhorting us.

This idea is very characteristic of all Paul's letters, indeed, you cannot read a single New Testament epistle without finding in it an exhortation to courage, to strength and to fortitude; an exhortation to stand and to fight. No one can read the New Testament without getting the impression that the Christian Church is a kind of army, or that it is involved in a great contest, a test of endurance, a striving for a prize from the enemies; this whole idea of a struggle, a fight, a contention is an essential part of all the teaching. It would be so easy to give you quotations from almost every epistle. Think, for instance, how Paul puts it in writing to the church at Corinth. It comes out almost like the crack of a whip: 'Watch ye, stand fast in the faith, quit you like men, be strong.' Followed by – 'Let all your things be done with charity' (1 Cor. 16:13–14). It is the same idea, and as you go through the New Testament and come finally to the book of Revelation, you will find the same thing: this exhortation to steadfastness.

Now, surely, the thing that is important for us is to realise that this is not only something that was meant to be true of the early Church, it is also something, according to the New Testament teaching, which is inevitably a part of the Christian life in a world like ours today. Our danger, is it not, is to say that of course we can understand the early Church having problems. Christianity was just beginning, it was a new religion, and it came into the ancient world among its mystery religions and paganism, causing a good deal of turmoil. It was offensive to Judaism, and it was equally offensive to the various religions in the Roman Empire; but, of course, times have changed. That is our tendency, I think we must all agree, and yet the New Testament denies that, and makes some very striking and explicit statements. Our Lord said that as the world had hated him, so it would hate his disciples, because they were his followers. Or again, Paul says to Timothy, 'Yea, and all that will live godly in Christ Jesus shall suffer persecution' (2 Tim. 3:12) – it is something that is going to happen, it is laid down as a universal rule, and the New Testament puts it as strongly as that. The gospel is such a complete contradiction to everything for which the world stands, that it must of necessity lead to conflict with the world. It cannot but happen, and that, therefore, is the inevitable result of true Christian living; the Church is bound in some shape or form to experience and endure this conflict with the world that is outside.

So then I would suggest, once more, that a very good test of our whole position is our attitude towards such an exhortation as this. Does it seem to us to be something very theoretical and academic, something remote from us, just a very interesting thing to consider in the case of the Philippians who lived two thousand years ago, but clearly not for us as modern Christians? In the light of New Testament teaching, this becomes a profound test. For if it is true to say that all who love our Lord shall suffer persecution in some shape or form, then the question is, do we know anything about this persecution? Is it happening to us? The New Testament teaches that the Christian Church, and individual Christians, are set in a world that is opposed to Christianity, a world that is inimical, and fighting against it, and the business of Christians is to hold their ground, to stand firm: '... that whether I come and see you, or else be absent, I may hear of your affairs, that ye stand fast [firm] in one spirit, with one mind striving together for the faith of the gospel; and in nothing terrified by your adversaries: which is to them an evident token of perdition, but to you of salvation, and that of God. For unto you it is given in the behalf of Christ, not only to believe on him, but also to suffer for his sake; having the same conflict which ye saw in me, and now hear to be in me.'

Let us, then, consider this magnificent exhortation, first of all in general. What does he mean by telling us to hold our ground and to stand fast, to stand firm? In general it means that we must realise that there is a fight, and we must realise, too, something of the nature of that fight. Now I am prepared to argue that in a sense this message was never more true than it is at this present moment. And I am not at all sure that one of the greatest tragedies in the modern world is that on the whole the Church does not realise the nature of the fight. It is a battle that has been going on ever since the Church was founded, and it is still going on. I am not here to indulge in forebodings of evil; I am not going to be foolish enough to attempt to forecast the future, or to prophesy, but I would like to contend that the days may well come when we shall know what we read of in the New Testament in a literal and in a physical sense. I wonder whether we are truly aware of the nature of the conflict which is actually going on?

Let me remind you of some of the implications of it. Think of the intellectual, or the philosophical, or the so-called scientific attacks that have been made upon the Church and upon the gospel, and upon the whole of this view of life, of God and of salvation. I wonder whether there has ever been such an attack upon the Church and her truth since those very early days. Just try and consider the attacks and the criticisms that have been made during these last hundred years. It even happens every Sunday when men who are supposed to be advocating the gospel are criticising it and trying to undermine its authority. This has been going on for the past century or so – the so-called higher criticism of the Scriptures by those authorities who say that they can tell us what is true and what is not; who divide the Bible up into sections and say, 'Believe this, and don't believe that'; who claim that unless you happen to be learned in Greek and Hebrew, you do not know what is true, and you have to sit and listen at the feet of these great authorities who, though never unanimous even amongst themselves, are undermining the very foundations of the truth itself.

Then there is the so-called scientific attack. Never has this attack been hotter than it is today; it has been going on for many years and it is still going on. I do not want to weary you with these things unduly, but I must try to paint a full picture.

And then think of the attack from the standpoint of world-liness; it is the whole story of human life: 'the lust of the flesh, and the lust of the eyes, and the pride of life', and all these things that the Apostle John speaks of in his first epistle.

Again, there has been a very subtle attack, which is still continuing, which lies in the way that polite people scoff at the gospel, and say, 'It is all right as far as it goes.' Consider the way in which some of the central doctrines of the New Testament itself have thus been attacked by these critics. 'Oh yes,' they say, 'it is all right to preach religion in general, but, you should not be talking about conversion and about rebirth, and regeneration and things like that – that is almost indecent.' This is a subtle attack that strikes at the very foundation and essentials of the whole of the gospel and dismisses it.

Then there is persecution in its various forms. Is not persecution as active and rife today as it has ever been? What happens to the man who becomes converted? What happens to him when he gets into his office, or sometimes into his own home, or it may be in his college or in his profession? There is the subtle persecution, the ostracising, the looks and the glances as he comes into the company, the suggestion that he has lost control of his reason; indeed, sometimes it can even affect a man's livelihood by threatening his prospect of promotion. These things are happening in the modern world, there is a conspiracy against the gospel. And then think of the power of fear and the power of ridicule. Think of how men and women would even try to frighten us out of our allegiance to Christ, even as they were doing in the case of the Philippians, as Paul here reminds us.

So, then, this great conflict is going on. The whole outlook and attitude of the world, and the so-called scholarship of the world confirms this. There are the intellectual, the philosophical and the scientific arguments – you are familiar with the discussions on the radio – and these attacks on faith are being made in a very fearful and subtle manner. So the first thing we have to do is to realise that this attack is happening, we must be awake and alert to the situation.

But that leads us to the second point under this general heading. According to Paul, not only must we realise that the fight is going on, we must make it our fight. He puts it like this: 'with one mind striving together for the faith of the gospel'. Paul did not say, 'Look here, Philippians, you go and enjoy the meetings, I will do the fighting for you. Leave it to me, I will fight and contend for the faith, and you enjoy your church life.' Not at all! He exhorts every one to make this his own personal fight and we must not contend just with a cold-blooded acquiescence in the Christian faith and its glorious message. No, we must exert ourselves, and rouse ourselves, and enter into the fight. You remember the kind of race these people engaged in – we would call it a relay race – one man ran with a torch, and as he flagged, another stepped in and took his place; they were agonising and striving, with all their might and main. And you and I are called to such a contest at the present time.

Let me put this in the form of a question. We are aware, I think, in general, of the importance to us of this struggle that is taking place. We know of the way in which the world scoffs at it all and dismisses it; we know of these various attacks that are being made, and so the question that comes to us is this: what are we doing about it? Have we done anything about it? Are we content to sit and listen and allow people to blaspheme the name of Christ and God, and in their subtle jocular manner pour out their scorn and sarcasm? Do we just acquiesce? Do we take it lying down? Are we more concerned about our own personal reputation than the reputation of Christ and the gospel? That is the kind of thing the Apostle means by striving for the faith. It means that we do not allow these things, we defend the gospel and repel these attacks and stand as men for this glorious faith that has been transmitted to us.

I will go one step further – we are, according to the Apostle, to be prepared to suffer anything for its sake. Do you know how they had to do that in the early days? The ordeal confronting most of these first Christians was this. They were taken to the courts and were asked to say that Caesar was Lord, and they were told that if they did not say that, they would be put to death. That was the test and those who believed that Christ alone is Lord did not want to say those words. They knew that if they refused they would be killed, but they readily and gladly refused and went to their death. And Paul tells us that if we are to be Christians worthy of the name, and if the choice should ever come, we must stand for this. If it is a choice between our allegiance to Christ and our work, or position, or job, or anything else, there must be no hesitation. If it is a question of standing for this or going to prison, then I am to go to prison; if it is a matter of standing four square to this, and being loyal to it, or even giving up my life, I must gladly die for him. These people did it, and they conquered the world by so doing. Our fathers have done it throughout the centuries; thank God for the Reformers and the Puritans and others. And this is the succession to which we belong.

That, then, is the general call. We must now look briefly at the particular aspects of this. Paul tells us to stand fast, so now I need to know how I am to do it. Let me give you some headings. The first thing I must do if I am to stand in this way, is to realise there is such a thing as *the faith*. 'Whether I come and see you, or else be absent, I may hear of your affairs, that ye stand fast in one spirit, with one mind striving together for the faith of the gospel.' Now this needs no demonstration. I cannot earnestly contend for the faith unless I know that there is such a thing. Paul does not say that I am to stand fast for *a* faith but for *the* faith of the gospel. There are those who would have us believe that religion is not something that is taught but something that is caught. But the Christian faith is taught; it is a body of doctrine, a substance to believe. It is a spirit that enters into man – the faith – it is something for which I can contend, something which I can defend.

Or, to put in another way, there are so many who think that to be a Christian means that one sets out in a great search after truth. Or, again, some think that the Christian faith is just one among many religions. There are so many today who are talking in this way. They say, 'You know the trouble with you Christians is that you are too narrow; you say your faith is right and that everything else is wrong.' Many say: 'I believe in taking out what is good in all religions, I believe in taking the best out of Hinduism, Buddhism, Confucianism and Mohammedanism, and too, out of the Christian faith and the vague cults like Christian Science, and then putting them all together and saying, 'Now this must be Truth.' But that is not what the Apostle says; we are earnestly to contend for *the* faith, the deposit that is enshrined in these documents. There is such a thing as *the* faith, and if we do not realise that, how can we possibly stand firm in it and defend it?

That leads me on to the second point. I must know exactly the nature of the truth which is taught. There must be no doubt about that, and there is today a body of doctrine which has been agreed by Christians throughout the centuries as being the Christian faith. What, then, is it? This is not the place for a comprehensive definition, but there are certain truths which I would say are the irreducible minimum of our belief. I believe in the unique deity of the Lord Jesus Christ; if I do not I am not a Christian. I may be a good man, I may have a wonderful natural spirit in me, but I am not a Christian. The unique deity of Christ, the miraculous and the supernatural, the atonement, Christ's death, the literal rising of his Body on the third day, the ascent into heaven, the personality of the Holy Spirit, his descent on the Day of Pentecost: these are the minimum. I suggest to you that the exhortation of the Apostle is that I should contend for that faith, that I should stand for it, defend it, and repel the attacks made upon it; and that I should not allow anyone to take from the glory of my Lord in any sense, or from the wonder of his perfect, finished work. I must fight for this truth and be sure of it.

Another good way, I think, of fighting for the truth is to examine the alternatives, and perhaps we as Christians are a little negligent in this respect. Listen to some of those scientific gentlemen who are opposed to the Christian faith, and what have they to say? They may sound clever, but when you turn to them and ask, 'What do you believe yourself? What is your view of life and morals? What kind of belief do you outline for us?' – and then examine what they say, you will find that of all men they are the profoundest pessimists. They really have nothing to say to us except much negative criticism; they have no positive philosophy to offer. Examine the lives of some of the so-called intellectuals, examine their morals. How easy it is to talk cleverly, but it is the life that counts. As you look at those who oppose the Christian faith, it will strengthen you and enable you to stand.

Then finally, we must always refuse to be frightened by our adversaries. They will try to frighten us in various ways, but here we just take hold of the word spoken by our Lord when he said, 'Be not afraid of them that kill the body, and after that have no more that they can do. But I will forewarn you whom ye shall fear: Fear him, which after he hath killed hath power to cast into hell' (Luke 12:4,5). What a wonderful thing it is to remember that! We do not know what may be awaiting us, but we know this for certain – and to me it is wonderful – man can only destroy my body, my soul is beyond his reach. With all this atomic power and everything else, he cannot touch my soul, let him do what he will; there is that in me which is imperishable and beyond the reach of harm. 'In nothing [be] terrified by your adversaries,' says Paul to the Philippians, there is a limit to what they can do. They can pour forth their venom, their sarcasm and their scorn, they can ruin your life and your career, perhaps, but they leave you uninjured in everything that is vital and eternal.

There, then, is just a brief indication of how to stand fast. The next question is *why* should we stand? And the answer is that we should do so because of the nature of the truth. Is there anything else that is worth standing for? Look at the zeal and the enthusiasm of the politicians as they stand for their party and see how they will work and argue with people, but what have they to offer and to stand for by comparison with this truth? What a glorious truth! The truth that God has given his own Son, his only begotten Son, and that there is a grand redemption possible to all, one which suffices in this world, and for the next, and to all eternity. What a mighty, glorious truth, what food for the mind, what a stimulus for the heart, what a magnificent truth! Do you need any other exhortation? Truth itself, its very character and nature, is worthy of our standing on the defensive.

But beyond that, we must stand for it for Christ's sake, for his honour and his glory – yes, stand for it even for the sake of the poor world which is attacking it. That is what you and I are called upon to do. The world is attacking the truth and yet it is the only thing that can save them, and even for their sakes we must stand for it, because nothing else will suffice for them.

But we must stand for it even for our own sakes. I have already used the comparison to an army, and if you have no other reason for standing for the truth let me commend this to you: there is a day coming when the Commander in Chief is going to review the troops, and we shall be standing there in the ranks. I see the Son of God walking up and down the ranks looking at us one by one at the grand final review, and if you do not want to feel you are a cad, if you do not want to feel terribly ashamed on the morning of that great review, stand as a man now, hold fast, be firm, never let an attack come but that you repel it. Stand for the truth and the faith, even for your own sake.

And lastly, let me give you a word of encouragement. Paul says to the Philippians, I am exhorting you to do nothing but what I am doing myself – 'having the same conflict which ye saw in me', when I was with you, 'and now hear to be in me' in prison, in Rome. Do you know we are in a wonderful succession? If there is anybody who is facing this conflict because he is a Christian, if there is anyone being persecuted or misunderstood, let me remind you that you are simply being subjected to that to which Paul himself was subjected – you are in a grand succession. Let me go higher and say, do you know that when you are suffering like that because you are a Christian, you are simply enduring what Christ had to endure? The world hated and crucified him. Do you know that you are in that great company: Paul, the apostles, the martyrs and the people of God everywhere, and at the head of them all, the Lord Jesus Christ himself? What an honour!

But there is something more wonderful still. He says '...in nothing terrified by your adversaries: which is to them an evident token of perdition, but to you of salvation, and that of God.' This means that if you are being persecuted and attacked for Christ's sake, it is a proof that you are a Christian. This only happens to Christians and the very fact that you are being attacked is proof to you of salvation. But let me take you still a step higher to the summit of the mountain. Is there anything more wonderful than this: 'Unto you it is given in the behalf of Christ, not only to believe on him, but also to suffer for his sake.' Let me interpret that. It means that suffering for Christ's sake is a very special boon and blessing that is given by Christ to his own. Had you thought of that? When you are suffering for Christ's sake, you must turn to him and say, 'Thank you, thank you that I have been counted worthy to receive this supreme blessing.' You know, it is told us of those first Christians that they generally agreed among themselves that the ultimate blessing was that of martyrdom; and that was why, when they were thrown to the lions in the arena, they always thanked God. They said, 'At last we have this, the ultimate boon and blessing.' It is given; as faith is a gift, so suffering for Christ's sake is likewise a gift. That is why I say now, <u>blessed are you if you are suffering for Christ's sake</u>, he has given you that assurance that you belong to him. As James says in his epistle, 'My brethren, count it all joy when ye fall into divers temptations' (Jas. 1:2). God grant to us this spirit, the spirit of the first Christians, the martyrs and the saints. God grant that we shall stand fast and strive with all our might for the faith of the gospel of Christ.

11

The Only Way of Peace

If there be therefore any consolation in Christ, if any comfort of love, if any fellowship of the Spirit, if any bowels and mercies, fulfil ye my joy, that ye be like-minded, having the same love, being of one accord, of one mind. Let nothing be done through strife or vain-glory; but in lowliness of mind let each esteem other better than themselves. Look not every man on his own things, but every man also on the things of others. Let this mind be in you, which was also in Christ Jesus.
(Phil. 2:1–5)

It is essential that we should take these verses together because obviously a common thought runs through all of them. The Apostle here is making his great appeal for unity in the church at Philippi, and, surely, it is commonly agreed that these verses contain perhaps the classic statement of the New Testament on the whole subject of concord and peace.

Paul has assured the Philippians that no external conditions can rob him of his joy. 'Therefore,' he says in effect to the members of the church, 'if you really are anxious that I should continue to be happy, and that, indeed, my joy may be fulfilled and overflowing, then, it rests with you to see that that may happen. As far as I myself am concerned, all is well; the one thing that really can add to this condition is that all should be well with you.' And so he introduces this great theme of the importance of unity amongst Christians.

Now I call your attention to this subject because it does

seem to me that this is one of the most urgent problems facing us at the present time. As we consider the whole situation in which we find ourselves, not only as Christian people, but as citizens of the world, as we contemplate the tragic state of the world, then surely the one thing that we are all supremely concerned about is that there should be a state of peace and concord and happiness amongst men. But, alas, we are looking out upon a situation which is the very antithesis of that. It is right to face facts as they are, and as we do so, we see a world that is torn asunder. In spite of two world wars in a quarter of a century, in spite even of our hope at one time that these wars were going to put an end to war, and were going to bring mankind together as one big family, we find ourselves in a state of acute uncertainty, with suspicion abroad between nation and nation. We see the threat of a world divided into two sections, fully armed, still increasing their armaments, and preparing for further hostilities. And added to that, there is the dread question of atomic power and all the fateful possibilities that lie in that direction. You cannot look at the international scene without at once being made aware of the fact that there is discord, disunity, trouble and suspicion, with thoughts of war and rumours of war. Indeed, you find wars actually still taking place in many countries. That is the kind of world which we see as we think of the international situation.*

But unfortunately when we come to look at it even from the standpoint of individual nations we see very much the same thing. Within the nations there is this self-same discord: strikes, quarrels, disagreements, suspicion, the tendency to divide up into sections and into groups, each one concerned only about itself and its own rights and demands. In every nation there is this same tendency to quarrelling and to disunity, and furthermore, when you come down to even still smaller units you find exactly the same thing. Nothing is so tragically true of the modern world as the fact

* This sermon was preached on December 28th, 1947.

of the break up of certain of the fundamental units in life, such as the home, the married state, and the family, which used to be so stable and steadfast; even there this spirit of disunity and discord has entered in.

It is the tendency for men and women to be in a constant state of confusion and quarrelling. The whole world is in a turmoil. There is a tragic and pathetic absence of peace, and everywhere there is an absence of the concord and unity of which the Apostle is speaking in this section. And the questions that arise at once are: what has the Christian Church to say about all this? What is the message of the Church? What is the message of the gospel? What exactly and precisely have we, who claim to be Christians, to say in this special situation?

There are many, who, at this point, say something that we need to examine carefully in the light of the Apostle's teaching. I suppose that one of the commonest of all ideas is that the main business of the Church, face to face with such a situation, is to utter vague and general appeals for brotherhood and understanding and concord. Many who are inside the Church hold that view, as do the majority, I would say, of those who are outside. The Church is conceived of as some kind of institution or organisation whose task is to remind us of certain idealistic conditions; that, it seems to me, is almost invariably what is expected from her. People feel that she should look out upon the political and social, the economic and international discord, and call for brotherhood and peace, for friendship, and for give and take. And they think that if she addresses this general appeal to the world, then the world is likely to respond. That is why there are many outside the Church who tend to blame her for the present state of affairs. They consider that the Church is not making this appeal for understanding and brotherhood with sufficient force and power. Again, according to them, the one great business of the Church is to appeal to the world to disarm, to cease quarrelling and fighting, and to urge that all should be brothers and be happy and friendly together. It has often been put in terms of the 'Fatherhood of God and the brotherhood of man' and, according to these people, the Church is the institution above all others which is designed to propagate such teaching.

Now I want to consider the whole idea with you in the light of what the Apostle tells us in these verses in Philippians. Before we come to the detailed consideration of the matter, let me introduce the subject by putting to you three general propositions.

The first is that surely it is a very remarkable thing that men and women are still capable of speaking like that, in spite of the facts with which they are confronted. Is it not surprising that there is still anyone left in the world who really believes that all that is needed today is a general appeal for friendship, goodwill and brotherhood? I ask my question because surely that appeal has constantly been made for many years past; indeed, we can go further back and say that there has scarcely ever been a time in the history of the world when such an appeal has not been made. It was made by the philosophers before Christ was born. They were anxious to find peace and that was the whole idea behind the concept of Utopia. For many years the appeal has been made in books, in journals, and in sermons; it has been made, too, on the radio – this call upon men to cease quarrelling, and to come together. And yet, in spite of all this, the world is as it is today. It is astonishing to me that anyone can still believe, in spite of the facts of this present century alone, that all you have to do is to appeal to men and women to live together peaceably, and they will immediately proceed to do so.

But that leads me to the second proposition, which is that this fatal optimism with respect to man, is hopelessly superficial. It is only those who hold such a superficial view of the cause of disunity who can possibly believe that an appeal for unity is, in and of itself, going to be sufficient. In other words, the tragedy of this fatal, sanguine optimism, that still satisfies so many people, is that it has failed to understand the biblical doctrine of sin and the message of the New Testament. It is in their diagnosis of the cause of our troubles that such people are in error; and because their view of the cause of the trouble is superficial, their suggested solution to it is equally so.

Now these are days when it is necessary that we should be realistic, though sometimes, when we are, people say that we are depressing. Yet surely it is the business of anyone who attempts to explain the New Testament message or to preach it, to give it exactly as it is. And the New Testament nowhere tells us that by nature man is so good that you only have to point out to him the right and the true, and he will rise to it. Indeed, the New Testament says clearly that this world will never know a state of peace, until certain mighty and dramatic events have taken place. From the standpoint of the optimism of the world, the New Testament is a profoundly pessimistic book; it takes a realistic view of man and his condition, and it tells us that any solution that is merely superficial can never adequately meet the position with which we are confronted.

So, bearing those general propositions in mind, let us see exactly what the Apostle has to say with regard to this question of peace and unity. The matter divides itself up quite simply. The first thing we have to consider is the cause of the disunity. Why is it that the world is as it is today? The Apostle answers that, in a sense, by putting it in two words. He says, 'Let nothing be done through strife or vainglory.' Now there is the cause of the trouble. Let us observe that the problem is as great and as deep as this. There is something in man, says the Apostle, which is so profoundly wrong that it tends to lead to trouble and discord, not only in the world, but even in the Church herself. As we have seen, the Apostle has a very high conception of the Church. It is not merely a gathering of people, it is not just a society of men and women. Paul says, 'He which hath begun a good work in you will perform it until the day of Jesus Christ' (1:6). The Church, Paul tells us, is something formed by God: it consists of new men and women who have been regenerated. Yet, according to the Apostle, there is something so radically wrong in man that there is even the danger of this wrong principle entering into the life of the Church. We have agreed that there is no more lyrical epistle in the New Testament than this epistle to the Philippians. Paul has less cause to criticise the church there than any other single church. The only thing that seemed to be wrong in Philippi, the one thing that threatened the life of that church, was the tendency for a spirit of disunity to enter and you will find that Paul mentions this in almost every chapter.

What is it, then, in human nature that tends to divide and cause suspicion and discord? According to the Apostle, it can be put under these two main headings. The first is '*strife*', or a better translation perhaps is 'the spirit of faction'. I am afraid that we are all probably familiar with what is meant by this phrase. It is much in evidence in the world at the present hour: a kind of party spirit, a group mentality, the tendency to think solely in terms of certain prejudices. You see it between nations. There can be no doubt that one of the greatest causes of war is the spirit produced by the idea of national sovereignty. 'My country,' says one, but, '*My* country', says another. It is something quite unreasonable and unreasoning, it is not governed by thought or understanding; it is prejudice, something which overpowers our reasoning. A man does not ask, 'Is my country right or wrong?' he says, 'My country is right', and the other man says the same thing – hence war.

You see this not only in terms of country, you see it in almost every division of society. You have your so-called social groupings and distinctions, with one group despising another, and one envying another. There is a pathetic tendency for people to divide themselves up into groups according to birth, status and position. They do not stop to think; it is not something rational. There is a kind of unwritten law and code which governs their behaviour: people belong to these different groups, and so they do certain things. Surely we have to recognise that this is one of the great dangers at the present time. It is the class spirit, and it is equally true of whichever class you may belong to. It always leads to discord and misunderstanding and strife.

Indeed, it may well be that in the years that lie ahead, this self-same spirit of faction will divide the world into great groups, and may be the genesis of another terrible world war. You meet the same thing, of course, even in industry and commerce; you have it in terms of money; and in all these areas, the important thing for us to consider is the spirit that is involved.

Perhaps there is an even better illustration of this in Paul's first epistle to the Corinthians. You remember the foolish Christians who divided themselves up according to certain people: 'I am of Paul; and I of Apollos; and I of Cephas; and I of Christ' (1 Cor. 1:12). The whole church in Corinth was divided into these sections and factors, in terms of persons, and the tragedy was that they did not meet together to consider the truth, and discuss their understanding of the truth. They were fighting for these respective men; one man said Paul was the best, another said Apollos, another Cephas, and there they were, all governed solely by prejudice. Now that is the spirit that always leads to trouble and discord. This is why it is a very rare thing indeed for people to be able to have a political discussion without losing their tempers. They are not governed by reason but by this spirit of faction; the whole discussion is not conducted in terms of what is right or wrong or beneficial, but of 'my group', 'my party', the lot to which I happen to belong.

But, alas, there is something still more serious behind the spirit of faction and strife, and that is what Paul calls '*vainglory*'. This is just another term, of course, for pride, man's conceit, and, according to the Bible, that is the ultimate source of discord and of all these troubles. The Bible puts that doctrine like this: God made man, and mankind was meant to live in subservience to God; as long as man did obey God, there was peace. So why should there be discord? The biblical answer is that man in sin sets himself up as his own supreme authority. He says that his own will is to be supreme and that he is entitled to what he wants and desires. Every man, in his pride and arrogance, sets himself up like this, as god, and, obviously, with a number of such gods there must inevitably be a clash, for everyone is thinking of and is concerned about himself.

Is not this the tragic cause of all our troubles? Is there anything so sad and pathetic in the world as this unutterable selfishness and self-concern, which is so much in evidence? 'I demand my rights, why should I not live my life as I choose?' – that is the argument. It is all self in control, looking at everything from the standpoint of what *I* deserve, what *I* am entitled to, *my* rights. That is the cause of all the disunity and trouble in the world: the spirit of faction, rival groups, and then within the groups, individuals with their pride and vainglory.

So, according to the Bible, that is the way to understand the situation. The trouble of the world is not something just on the surface; it is not that man is insufficiently cultured, or has not the right outlook upon life. No, there is that within his nature which is twisted and perverted, which has turned all the qualities that were put into man by God in the wrong direction. There is this foul canker in his very elements and vitals; it is the heart of man that is desperately wicked and deceitful; it is something radical and fundamental.

If, then, that is the cause of the trouble, we can now face, in a more realistic manner, the only way with which to deal with the trouble. Paul tells us that there are two things which are absolutely essential before there can be real peace and unity. The first is that there should be a common allegiance: 'Fulfil ye my joy, that ye be likeminded, having the same love, being of one accord, of one mind.' According to the Apostle, the only way in which men and women can get rid of this spirit of faction and vainglory is by being linked together in a common object, or interest, a common allegiance. Now this is something which I think we can prove quite easily as a perfectly sound psychological principle. How often during that last war were we told of the extraordinary scenes in air-raid shelters; how different people belonging to different classes, there, in the common need to shelter from the bombs and death, forgot all the differences between them and became one. This was because in the common interest they forgot the divisions and the distinctions. That is why you always tend to have a coalition government during a war; in periods of crises and common need all distinctions are forgotten and we suddenly become united.

Now that is the very thing that the Apostle is teaching here. It is no use just asking men and women to forget their differences and distinctions and be kind and friendly, that is not the New Testament teaching. The New Testament knows that this is hopelessly inadequate. The world believes in that kind of thing, and has its own reasons for doing so. By drugging itself in various ways it can produce a spirit of good cheer and friendship and understanding, but it is merely the result of drugs. The New Testament says that before you can get that real unity and concord, that peace and amity among men, there must be a common allegiance, and it must be a common allegiance to God and to our Lord and Saviour Jesus Christ. The only hope for peace among men is that men be brought off their throne, that they be humbled and together bow their knees to God. One touch of nature in that sense, makes the whole world kin. It is only as we all realise together that we belong to God and not to ourselves, that we shall be one, because of our common allegiance to him.

But you must go even further than that, says Paul. In addition to this common allegiance – for they had that in the church at Philippi – there must be another principle, which is that of humility. 'Look not every man on his own things, but every man also on the things of others.' If only everyone, men and women, implemented that one verse, what a different world we should have! 'In lowliness of mind let each esteem other better than themselves.' That is the secret, says the Apostle. This 'lowliness of mind', this humility, is the absolute essential, and it expresses itself in that way: every man esteems the other better than himself. 'But does this mean,' asks someone, 'that the Christian gospel asks every single individual to think of every other single individual before himself? Is a man to regard a drunkard in the gutter as better than himself?' No, that is not what the Apostle is teaching, that is to make it too extreme. What he is saying is that apart from major distinctions like that, where in practice there is a very clear difference between man and man, apart from that, we are all to hold such a view of ourselves and our condition, that <u>we esteem others better than ourselv</u>es. This is the Apostle's way of saying that if we only knew ourselves as we really are, we should inevitably behave like that.

And, furthermore, I am to think not only of my 'own things', but also of 'the things of others'. I am not simply to ask, 'What are my rights? What demands can I make? What do I deserve?' But rather, 'What is the best for everybody? What about the other person?' Instead of always starting with myself and ending with myself, I am to look upon the other man. When I say I am suffering and having a hard time, I am to think of people in other countries and in worse conditions. We in this country are not only to think about our own problems, we must also think of people who have no home and no shelter or clothing. And in the same way we are to apply this in our own personal lives. Think of all the quarrels and the discord and the unhappiness in every circle in life, does it not all tend to arise from the failure to implement this principle? If only we were to stop and think of others and the position of others, before we assert our rights and make our demands, would it not smooth out life in every realm and in every department? That is the secret, says Paul, the humility that manifests itself in that way.

So that is the programme. <u>Let me end with what is perhaps the most vital question of all. What is it that is going to enable men and women to do this</u>? In the light of all that I have been saying, someone may ask, 'Are you not doing the very thing you denounced at the beginning? Are you not just telling us to be humble and to think of others in their needs and demands and desires? Are you not just making a general appeal once more, but this time in the way in which the Apostle made it?'

No, what I am saying is that Paul tells us here that there

is only one way in which this can be done: 'If there be any consolation in Christ, if any comfort of love, if any fellowship of the Spirit, if any bowels and mercies ...'* Let me put it again, quite bluntly. The programme which is outlined here by the Apostle is only possible to the Christian, it is useless for the world outside. There is nothing that is so utterly idiotic as to ask men and women who are spiritually dead because of sin, to be humble and to think of others before themselves. They are incapable of such an action because before they can implement the Apostle's teaching, they must be born again. This is the way in which the Apostle makes the appeal and it is the only ground on which the appeal can be made – 'If there be therefore any consolation in Christ ...' But let me give you a better translation: 'If there is any *exhortation* in Christ ...' What Paul means is this: 'Philippians,' he says in effect, 'I am going to appeal to you to live your life in a certain way. How can I best make my appeal? I will put it like this. If your experience of Christ has any exhortation for you, or any argument with you, then live like this. That is the position. If love, and the spirit of love, that you have received from Christ can likewise exhort and plead and argue with you, then let each esteem other better than themselves. If there is any such thing as fellowship and companionship of the Holy Spirit, well show it in this way. If,' says Paul, 'there are any bowels and mercies; if anything of the very life of God has been planted in you, well then proceed to live that life. This is something that is only possible to the Christian.'

Let me put it in this way. I am told that I am to esteem others better than myself, and there is only one thing that can make me do that – and thank God, it does make me do it – it is this. When I read the Bible I see the sinful nature that is in me; I see my failures, I see my shortcomings. But even then there is a tendency in me to defend them. There is only one thing I know of that crushes me to the ground,

---

* Translated in the NIV as tenderness and compassion. (Ed.)

and humiliates me to the dust, and that is to look at the Son of God, and especially to contemplate the cross.

> When I survey the wondrous cross
> On which the Prince of Glory died,
> My richest gain I count but loss,
> And pour contempt on all my pride.
> *Isaac Watts*

Nothing else can do it. When I see that I am a sinner, or feel lost, or condemned or helpless, and that nothing but the Son of God on the cross can save me, I am humbled to the dust. I say that no one can be worse than I am; I am 'the chief of sinners', and anyone must be better than I am. But it is only the cross that makes me feel that. Nothing but the cross can make a man esteem other better than himself. Nothing but the cross of Christ can give us this spirit of humility. We need to see this truth, we need to receive the Holy Spirit. It is only when the love of God is shed abroad in our hearts that we will be able to love and have this tenderness and compassion towards others.

Surely this is the whole argument of the New Testament. Men and women must be humbled; they must be reduced; self must be crucified; and it is only at the cross that this happens. As Paul writes to the church at Ephesus, it is only there that 'the middle wall of partition' is broken down; it is only there that one new man can be made out of the two, thus making peace. That is the only basis for unity, the only hope of the world. Now Paul puts it in a phrase like this, 'Let this mind be in you which was also in Christ Jesus ...' and then he goes on, 'who, being in the form of God, thought it not robbery to be equal with God: but made himself of no reputation, and took upon him the form of a servant, and was made in the likeness of men: and being found in fashion as a man, he humbled himself, and became obedient unto death, even the death of the cross.' It means that Christ left the courts of heaven and was born as a babe in the manger. He lived here on earth, and endured the contradiction of sinners and even died on the cross – why? Because he did not consider himself; because he was not concerned only about his own enjoyment of that glory, which he had shared there in eternity with the Father; because he looked upon you and me; because he 'looked upon the things of others'. It was because he implemented this that he came and saved us, and what the Apostle says is that we are to be like that, and we can only be like that when we receive his nature; when we are born again, when we are regenerated; when the Holy Spirit has worked the miracle upon us, and we are indeed partakers of the divine nature. That is the only hope of unity and peace and concord. Self must be crucified and got rid of, and the new self, the new nature given by the Son of God, must be received. 'Let this mind be in you which was also in Christ Jesus ...'

12

Jesus the Lord

Let this mind be in you, which was also in Christ Jesus: who, being in the form of God, thought it not robbery to be equal with God: but made himself of no reputation, and took upon him the form of a servant, and was made in the likeness of men: and being found in fashion as a man, he humbled himself, and became obedient unto death, even the death of the cross. Wherefore God also hath highly exalted him, and given him a name which is above every name: that at the name of Jesus every knee should bow, of things in heaven, and things in earth, and things under the earth; and that every tongue should confess that Jesus Christ is Lord, to the glory of God the Father (Phil. 2:5–11)

I am sure we will all agree that this entire passage is one of the most magnificent in the whole Bible. We looked a little at the earlier verses in our last study and now in verses 9, 10 and 11 we see how the Apostle brings to a great climax this extraordinary review which he here gives us of the whole course of the earthly life of our Lord. Paul starts in heaven and he ends there, and in these few, brief, pregnant words he summarises perfectly what was involved in our Lord's coming, what happened when he came, and what has resulted from his coming. We must remind ourselves again, if we are to catch the full force of this great statement, that the Apostle's purpose was to exhort the Philippian church members to dwell in a state of unity and amity and concord with one another. That is how he came to introduce this great passage. 'Look not every man on his own things, but every man also on the things of others.' Then suddenly he says, 'Let this mind be in you, which was also in Christ Jesus', and then there follows the whole of this tremendous statement. Now here, in other words, we are reminded of something that is of supreme importance for us. It is very characteristic of this Apostle's method, as it is indeed of the whole of the New Testament, for it is always calling our attention in some way or another to our Lord and Saviour Jesus Christ.

We are living in an uncertain world. No one knows the future, not even those who are always ready to express their opinion (in spite of the fact that their prophecies are so constantly being falsified) for the future is full of uncertainty and strange possibilities. The New Testament does not tell us very much in exact detail, of what lies ahead of us. People have often tried to identify the future in terms and statements from the Bible, but, alas, as I say, they are proved to be more frequently wrong than right. That is not the New Testament method, which is, rather, to tell us that whatever the future may hold, whatever may await us in the days and the months that lie ahead, if all is well between us and God in Christ Jesus, then there is a sense in which it is true to say that it does not matter at all what may or may not happen. In other words, the New Testament constantly tells us that the most important thing in life and in this world is our relationship to Jesus Christ, and that is the theme which is worked out here by the Apostle in these three verses which we are now considering.

Paul's contention is that as the result of Christ's coming from heaven, as the result of his incarnation and his humiliation of himself, Jesus Christ has been made the centre of all things, and therefore must be central. We are told that because of what he has done, 'God also hath highly exalted him, and given him a name which is above every name', the purpose being, 'that at the name of Jesus every knee should bow, of things in heaven, and things in earth, and things under the earth ...' This word introduced here in the Authorised Version, as 'things', is probably a little misleading. It means, rather, 'beings' and includes the angelic beings of every order and character. Paul tells us that 'beings' in heaven and in earth should bow, and that 'every tongue should confess that Jesus Christ is Lord to the glory of God the Father'.

Now we can do nothing better than to remind ourselves of this. Jesus Christ is to be at the very centre of our lives and at the very centre of our thoughts. Let us not misunderstand a statement like this. We are reminded here that it is not enough to believe in God, or to have a thesis, nor is it enough to say we believe in a Supreme Being and that we recognise the Person of God. That is not the particular thing that makes us Christian. As the result of all that has taken place, Paul tells us, God himself has appointed Christ to be the centre, and therefore we must say with Martin Luther that we know of no other God save Jesus Christ. He is the only way in which we can know God and therefore he is to be central. And our thinking about God and all our relationship to God must be in terms of our Lord and Saviour Jesus Christ, and the exhortation is that we should all bow the knee to him.

Let us observe, as the learned authorities all very rightly point out in this connection, that there has surely been no greater travesty of Scripture anywhere than the way in which certain sections of the Christian Church have interpreted this to mean that every time the name of Jesus Christ is mentioned we should bow our heads, an act that is regarded by them as a mark of exceptional devotion. But how far short that falls of what we are told in the text! We are to bow the knee, not merely bow the head! Paul says, in effect, that we are to surrender ourselves, to make obeisance. This is an act of acknowledgment, of giving ourselves. We are to bow the knee to him, because he is Lord, and, according to the Apostle here, God has given him such a name that the whole universe, beings in heaven and in earth and under the earth, are thus made subject unto him, and are to acknowledge him, and every tongue everywhere will confess 'that Jesus Christ is Lord, to the glory of God the Father'.

There is no contradiction here between worshipping God and worshipping the Lord Jesus Christ. We are to worship God by worshipping the Lord Jesus Christ. You will remember how on several occasions in his own earthly ministry our Lord himself made exactly the same point. He said: 'He that honoureth not the Son honoureth not the Father which hath sent him' (John 5:23). Thus in his teaching, this is made perfectly clear and beyond peradventure, exactly as we have it here repeated by the Apostle Paul. It is impossible truly to worship God, and bow the knee to him, and live the life he would have us live, except in and through our Lord and Saviour Jesus Christ. Now there is the great starting point. You see, Paul puts him here in the centre of the universe; he is at the centre of life, and if he is not there in our lives and experience, then, according to our gospel, not only are we not Christian, but our worship of God is valueless. God has appointed him, God has exalted him, and God is calling upon us all to bow the knee to him, to surrender to him, to acknowledge him and to confess him with the whole of our life.

Let us therefore try, just briefly, to analyse what this confession means. First of all, let us look at it as regards his Person – the confession we are called upon to make about the Person of Jesus Christ. And here the terms themselves really say everything that can be said. We are told that 'Jesus Christ is Lord'. That is the confession, and you notice how carefully the Apostle uses the terms. When he gives this great description of the incarnation in verses 6–8, he points out to us how that man, the one who was called Jesus, was none other than God in the flesh. While still in the form of God, he took the form of a servant. He did not hold on to his divine prerogatives, but considered others, he saw their need and so he humbled himself, not ceasing to be God but taking on human nature and appearing in the likeness of man; and 'in fashion as a man, he humbled himself and became obedient unto death, even the death of the cross'. Jesus, Jesus of Nazareth.

Now the Apostle directs attention to that Person, and he

puts it here in this wonderful way in the tenth verse. It is at the name of *Jesus* that every knee should bow; it is the same Jesus who was here on earth, who is now in the glorified state. In other words, Paul is here again emphasising the glorious nature of the Person. We must not forget that the eternal Son of God became man, took on to himself humanity and was known as Jesus. We must always remember that the Lord Jesus Christ, whom we worship and confess, is the very Person who walked the face of this earth. Let us never lose him, in his teaching; let us never lose sight of him in any philosophy that can be elaborated from him and from his teaching. God forbid that we should ever turn him into a mere collection of ideas and thoughts. No, Paul holds us to the Person, by bringing in the word Jesus; that Person whom we can read about in the pages of the four Gospels.

But then we have the next word, Christ – Jesus Christ – which means, of course, that he was peculiarly and specially the one who was anointed by God and set apart to do a certain work. He is the Messiah, which means 'anointed one'. Whenever anyone, or anything, was anointed in the Old Testament it meant that he was set apart for some particular purpose. The High Priest and the other priests were anointed because they were set apart to carry out those specific functions of worshipping God in the manner he had indicated. Now here is Christ, supreme above all others, who was anointed or set apart to do this special work, about which Paul has already told us. He set himself apart, and he was set apart by God, in order to perform that work that he alone could do. As we have seen, he humbled himself and took upon himself the form of a servant; he went still further, and became obedient unto death, even the death of the cross. That was the thing that he was set apart for.

He came into this world, in other words, not merely to give us his incomparable teaching, or to provide us with an example, perfect and glorious though it is, but the work he came to do was to taste death for every man. That is why he went to the cross, that is why there was the agony in the Garden of Gethsemane, before he went to die; it was this, ultimately, that God had called upon him to do; it was the only way by which man could be delivered –

> 'There was no other good enough
> To pay the price of sin.'
>
> *C. F. Alexander*

And there on the cross he became a sin offering. At one and the same time he was the priest and the offering, for he offered himself and his own shed blood to God the Father as the expiation for sin. Jesus Christ. Not merely the peasant of Galilee, or the Teacher and Instructor, not merely the Exemplar, but over and above that, this Anointed One, this Priest, this everything; the Christ, the Messiah, the Deliverer, the one who makes an atonement and opens up the way of salvation.

So what you confess is that Jesus Christ is Lord, which of course simply means that Jesus Christ is God. The word translated here as 'Lord' is the word that is so often used by God of himself in the Old Testament. You remember that the Jews avoided the pronouncement of the name of God; they regarded it as so holy and sacred that they very rarely used it. They adopted various symbols to express the idea, and one of the common words they used instead of using the name Jehovah was this word 'Lord'. So that when they spoke of 'the Lord', they meant God, and when Paul says that the Christian confession is that Jesus Christ is Lord, he means God, the supreme, one with the Father, who has been set in this position of sovereignty in the whole of God's economy. Every knee should bow at the name of Jesus, because he is Lord, he is God. And that is the tremendous and startling statement which the Apostle here makes with respect to the Person. And that, of course, is the thing of which we remind ourselves now, before we go any further.

We can, perhaps, consider it best of all by looking at it in the form of a question. What is Jesus Christ to us? Where does he come into our scheme of things? What do we believe concerning him? Have we bowed the knee to him, have we surrendered to him, do we make this confession concerning him? Do we say that Jesus of Nazareth, that man who walked about the face of this earth, is Lord, the anointed of God, the one who was set apart to bear the sins of man, including our own? Do we say that it is there alone, in that death, that we find salvation and all that it means, and by which we are reconciled to God? Do we confess that to us he is God and that we worship him to the glory of God the Father? That is the confession.

Am I returning to this too frequently? I wonder if that is possible! My plea is that I find it everywhere in the New Testament and that there has surely never been a greater need of this re-emphasis than there is at the present time. How easy it is to turn the New Testament into a philosophy or a set of rules and regulations and a scheme for life and living, a general outlook. No, the central point everywhere, the whole emphasis here, is that it is my personal relationship to him that matters. I do not accept the Christian philosophy primarily; I accept *him*. I believe on him, I bow my knee to him, the Person. I make a statement about the individual: Jesus Christ is Lord, he is my Lord; it is a personal relationship, and a personal confession. And that is the primary thing in the whole Christian position – our relationship to him. There is no true knowledge of God apart from him, and to know him is to know God. Jesus said, 'He that hath seen me hath seen the Father' (John 14:9) – that is it. The centrality of Christ.

That, then, is the Person. Let us now consider what Paul has to tell us about his present position. He not only directs attention to the glory of the Person, but tells us some amazing things about the present position of this Person, and I think we will all agree that there is no greater consolation to be found anywhere than we find here. There is nothing so good and comforting, as we face life, than to realise the present position of this glorious Person whom we confess to be God. The first thing we are told about him is that he has already triumphed. You notice how Paul puts it: he 'made himself of no reputation, and took upon him the form of a servant, and was made in the likeness of men: and being found in fashion as a man, he humbled himself, and became obedient unto death, even the death of the cross.' But that is not the end. The next word is 'Wherefore' – don't you see the whole of the gospel there? Don't you see things happening? Don't you see the sun peeping through amidst the darkness? Wherefore! It does not end with the humiliation of the cross and the shame and the agony of it all: 'Wherefore God also hath highly exalted him.' We are reminded here that Christ has already triumphed.

Let us look at it like this. He came into this world in which you and I live, and it was exactly the same then as it is now. The world is a place dominated by the god of this world, Satan, or the devil. It is a place of sin, and of evil, a place of foulness and of everything that is inimical to God and opposed to his holy law; a sinful world, ruled and controlled and governed by sin; a world which, because of that, is a place of sorrow, of grief and of unhappiness. Nothing is so characteristic of it as death and the grave. That is the world into which he came, a world which fought and strove against him, even as it does against us. Now what Paul asserts is that he humbled himself, he came into that world, and all the forces of evil and sin and hell arrayed themselves against him. You remember how the author of the epistle to the Hebrews put it – he 'was in all points tempted like as we are, yet without sin' (Heb. 4:15). This means that there has never been anyone in this world who has been so tempted as our Lord and Saviour Jesus Christ. Satan met him in person. It is clear from the teaching of the Bible that Satan does not always meet us in person. He has his underlings, principalities and powers and the rulers of the darkness of this world, and all the others in that evil spiritual hierarchy, which are more than sufficient to attack us. But in the case of the Son of God, Satan appeared in all his might and was able to offer him the kingdoms of this world and all their legions. Never was anyone tried and tempted as he was. He came into it, he humbled himself and he faced it all; it did its worst and its utmost against him. But what the Apostle tells us is that though his deliverance of us did involve the shame and death of the cross, nevertheless even there he was spoiling the principalities and powers, and was triumphing over them. Paul says, 'Wherefore God hath highly exalted him'. He has conquered sin and Satan and death and the grave; he has been highly exalted, and a name has been given to him which is above every name. It is because of what he has done, it is a consequence of his incarnation and humiliation and especially of his death upon the cross. He, by doing that, has redeemed the universe and God has placed him in control. What a glorious thought to have in our minds as we face life in this world. Sin is still there and we shall be tempted, we shall be tried; Satan in his various ways will attack us, but oh, I beseech you, look above it to him who is there glorified and exalted because he has conquered. That is the Person we confess, the one who has already triumphed over all, the last enemy included; he has already risen, he has vanquished death and the grave. Satan, having tried him to the uttermost, has been repelled, he has been robbed of his power, he has received a mortal wound and the day is coming when he shall be finally destroyed. Wherefore God hath also highly exalted the Lord – he has triumphed.

The second thing we are told is that he is therefore, and of necessity, in control. The teaching of the New Testament, in so many places, is that God has handed over the control and the government of the world to him. He said once to his disciples, 'All power is given unto me in heaven and in earth' (Matt. 28:18), and if you read 1 Corinthians 15 you will find that God has committed the kingdom to him until it is absolutely perfect, and then he will hand it back to God the Father. This means that at the present time the Lord Jesus Christ is in control of the universe. Now, my friends, can there be anything more comforting and encouraging than that! We are all aware of the state of the world, we know about the materialism and the godlessness and the immorality, we see all the confusion and threat of war, and there are some people who sometimes ask whether Christianity is going to end. 'Is this the finish of it?' they say. 'Is evil going to triumph?' And the answer is this: Christ is in

control. He is sitting at the right hand of God until his
enemies shall be made his footstool. He is the one who is
opening the seals of the Book; he is behind human history.
It is very difficult to understand this at times, and yet if you
take the long view of history you will see it perfectly clearly.
We should not look at history from day to day, or even from
year to year, or decade to decade, rather, we should look
back across the centuries. How often have people thought
that Christianity was defeated! When you look back you will
see that people have said, 'This is the end.' Then a revival
has come. He is controlling everything and the promise of
the New Testament is that he will continue to do so until the
time has arrived for him to wind up world history and all its
affairs.

This leads on to the third element in Christ's present position, which is that he will be visibly triumphant over all. He
is now in the place at which every knee should bow and
every tongue should confess, but, alas, that is not being
done. There are men who, in their foolishness, stand arrog-
antly in defiance of him. They laugh and ridicule him; they
refuse to bow the knee; they will not confess with the lip and
the tongue that Jesus Christ is Lord. They deny him, yes,
but it says in the New Testament that he who has been
exalted will appear, not in the form of a servant this time,
not in the likeness of man, not in the fashion of a man. He
will come on the clouds as King of kings, and Lord of lords.
He will come attended by the heavenly hosts and will finally
rout his every enemy. At that time every knee *shall* bow to
him, while those who pierced him will see him, and the sight
of him in glory, and the sight of his holiness, will subdue
them, and he will consign them to their punishment. Then
reluctantly and with shame, but nevertheless with awe, they
will have to confess that Jesus Christ is Lord; that the lowly,
despised Jesus was none other than the Son of God; that the
death on the cross at which they laughed, and which they
regarded as a sign of weakness, was the work of the Messiah, the anointed one who has removed the guilt of sin from
those who believe on him. They will have to confess that he

is the eternal Son of God. He is there in the position of authority and power. He has already had his victory, and he will finally manifest himself beyond any doubt or question in the sight of the whole world. Then you see where Paul's imagery comes in; things in heaven, things in earth, things under the earth, angels, spirits, fallen beings, all, everywhere, throughout the entire universe will acknowledge him. Read right through the book of Revelation, and especially the fourth and fifth chapters, and you will see that everything will have been subjugated and he will be confessed as the God he is.

That, then, is the confession which we make. Let me give a few reasons as to why we should make this confession. Firstly, we should confess that Jesus Christ is Lord because it is a fact, and that is sufficient in and of itself. Whether we like it or not, the fact is that Jesus Christ is Lord, he is God. Jesus is God, and we know no God apart from him; he is also the Christ.

The second reason for making this confession is that it is a confession of God, and it glorifies him. If you say you believe in God and want to glorify him, acknowledge the Son.

And surely we are to make this confession because of the consequences that follow the making of it, or the refusal to make it. To make this confession means that we have passed from death to life, from judgment to security, that we have become the children of God, and citizens of a kingdom which can never be destroyed. If we make this confession it means that we are in such a relationship to God that whatever may happen nothing can separate us from his love. If you refuse to make this confession and acknowledgment, it means you belong to those people who at the end finally confess against their will, who will have to recognise him and acknowledge him, and make their confession in spite of themselves.

But, lastly, let me point out to you the comfort of the doctrine, and the first thing I see here is the faithfulness of God. After all, the Apostle is exhorting these Philippian Christians to humble themselves and to obey God implicitly. In his epistle, James says, 'If you humble yourself, God will highly exalt you' (Jas. 4:10). That is the argument – Christ humbled himself, 'Wherefore God also hath highly exalted him'. If we humble ourselves God in his faithfulness will exalt us also.

And then the other thing, and this perhaps is the supreme comfort, it is Jesus whom we worship, whom we acknowledge, and to whom we pray. He is the one who has lived life on this earth, even as we are doing. It is at the name of Jesus that every knee shall bow. You remember how the author of the epistle to the Hebrews put it – we have a High Priest who has been touched with the feeling of our infirmities. He knows about our weakness, he ever sympathises with our ignorance, so that as we face the uncertain future, and as we feel weak and small in this great difficult world, that is the consolation. Jesus is our High Priest. It is this Person, of whom we know these things, who is there addressing us. Jesus is the Christ and the Lord, and it is at the name of Jesus we bow. It is to him we make our confession and our acknowledgment, and we remember as we do so that there is nothing which can possibly afflict us but that he has known it, and has experienced it, and is therefore able to sympathise with us. What a glorious doctrine! There before us is the future, unknown and uncertain, but we are not left alone, we are walking with Jesus, the one who has been through it all and who has triumphed over it all. And we look to him, the glorified Lord, who has all power, and who can hold us with his powerful hand.

13

God's Initiative

> Wherefore, my beloved, as ye have always obeyed, not as
> in my presence only, but now much more in my absence,
> work out your own salvation with fear and trembling. For
> it is God which worketh in you both to will and to do of
> his good pleasure. (Phil. 2:12–13)

I suppose there has been no statement, even by the Apostle
Paul, which has been so frequently the battleground of discussion and of disputation as these two verses. This is something which must be so because of the profundity of the
statement itself. It is not only great and interesting because
historically it has provoked so much discussion and disputation, but it is also a statement which is great in itself,
because, I venture to put it to you, it is perhaps one of the
most perfect summaries of the Christian life to be found
anywhere. It is one of those perfect pictures which we tend
to find so frequently in the writings of this Apostle. He was
very fond of stating the whole thing over and over again; he
liked to give a summary of the Christian life, and here is one
of the most pregnant statements which even he himself ever
made.

It merits our study because it brings us face to face with
some of the great practical questions of the Christian life.
But, above all, our reason for considering it is that, if we rightly
understand it, this mighty declaration must, surely, bring us
great encouragement and consolation in our Christian life and
warfare. I feel, therefore, that it is but right that we should look
at it more or less along all those various lines.

160

I am not suggesting that we should approach it merely because it has been a famous battleground and we delight in discussion in and of itself. But I feel it is a good and right thing that we should grapple with these great statements that have occupied the attention and thought of the Church so much during her long history. I freely confess that for myself I approach a statement like this with what I would call a sanctified sense of excited anticipation. There are few things, surely, in this life which can be and which ought to be so thrilling to Christian people as to exercise their minds on some of these mighty and resounding statements. Is it not, I wonder, the final criticism, not only of our age in general, but of the Christian Church in particular, that she seems to have lost her taste for these things. Is it not a tragedy that we have become disinclined to face the theological problems, and that we have come to regard the business of preaching as something merely to soothe and encourage us, or to talk to us in a material, psychological manner? Our fathers, when they came to two verses like this, would have been agog with excitement; they would have looked forward to discussing it, and they would have revelled in these things. But there is always a danger of going from one extreme to the other and it is sad that today we rather tend to avoid these great matters, simply because there is, of necessity, a controversial element in them.

Let us, then, look together as best we can at this great statement. It seems that there are three main ways of approaching it. These verses can be approached generally, theologically and practically. Now it is quite impossible to deal with these three approaches in one study, and I have been compelled to divide my attempt at an exposition of these two verses into two main sections. First, we shall look at them generally and also theologically, and then, in the next study, we shall go on to consider their practical application.

So, then, let us look at this subject generally. We can take a kind of synoptic view of it, and look at it as a whole, before we come to our analysis, and there is a sense in which we are bound to do that, if we are to be honest in our exposition. The very word 'wherefore' at the commencement of verse 12 compels us to take this statement in its context, because it links the verse with what has gone before. And that reminds us at once that the Apostle, when he wrote these words, was really not concerned primarily to make a theological definition or statement. I am going to show you, I trust, that they are packed full of theology, but at this point, Paul was still making his practical appeal to the Philippians to live the Christian life in the way that it should be lived.

Paul really starts his practical exhortation at the end of the previous chapter, where he tells the Philippians that nothing should be done by strife or vainglory. He wants the church at Philippi to live harmoniously, in a state of amity and concord, and he is making this appeal to them especially in terms of the glorious example of our Lord himself, basing it on the whole doctrine of the incarnation and the resurrection. Here, in these verses, he is still going on with this, and his appeal to them is that they should live this Christian life in all its fullness.

Paul reminds the Philippians that there is a very special, personal relationship between the church at Philippi and himself. He loves these people and they love him, and he knows, as we have already seen in discussing the first chapter, that they are all very dejected by the fact that he is in prison. Some of them are beginning to feel that without Paul they cannot live this Christian life, and it is particularly in view of that fact that the Apostle makes his appeal: 'Wherefore, beloved, as ye have always obeyed, not as in my presence only, but now much more in my absence, work out your own salvation with fear and trembling. For it is God which worketh in you both to will and to do of his good pleasure.'

What Paul is saying in general is this: Don't for a moment imagine that my presence or my freedom is essential to your living the Christian life. In the mercy of God I was given the privilege of bearing the gospel to you in the first instance, and I was able to teach you and set you on your feet and, in a sense, establish your goings. But you must not think of this new life into which you have come in terms of me, as if I were essential to it. You must not feel that the whole thing is going to end because I am in prison and cannot come and preach to you. Neither must you think of it as a human thing; it is not any idea of mine or some theory that I have evolved. It is not as if it were my special and peculiar idea of life and living to which I am therefore essential.

Not at all, says Paul, you must realise that you yourself have been given the gift of salvation; you have it as much as I have it, and I want you to work that out, that gift which you now have, that life which you have received – 'work out your own salvation with fear and trembling'. Indeed, says Paul, far from my presence being essential, I would remind you that the one who is essential to you is with you; 'it is God that worketh in you', and not I. It is not Paul, but God. That, then, is the general meaning of this statement: Paul tells them that they must not feel that all is lost because he is not there. It is God who matters and God is there; it is God who is working in them 'both to will and to do'.

Now there, I think, is something which is of primary importance, not only in our understanding of this letter as it applied to the church at Philippi, but as it applies to all of us, even at the present time. The Apostle was making a general statement: teachers and preachers may be of help and of value but they are not essential. The Christian life is something that we have as a possession within us, and though every teacher and preacher were silenced, and every instructor banished, it would not ultimately matter. This has, of course, often been true and, as I have suggested, it has been of fundamental importance in the life and history of the Church and of Christian people. There have been days of persecution when teachers and preachers have been silenced, when they have been prohibited, but, thank God, the Christian gospel has gone on. There have been times when all leaders have been killed or destroyed, but because Christianity is of the love of God within the soul, because it

is a personal possession of every true believer, it has gone
on. It is God that works and he can do it, in a sense, apart
from his servants.

God grant that we may all have this understanding of the
elements of the Christian life, that it is a personal possession
– your *own* salvation – and, therefore, there is a sense in
which we are gloriously independent of all men, even of
teachers within the Church itself. That, obviously, is not to
detract from the value of teachers, but to say that we are not
finally dependent upon them. I must not enlarge on this, but
I am constrained to point out that far too often one has met,
amongst Christian people, almost the exact opposite. There
is often a kind of slavish dependence upon men, a kind of
personal attachment; and, of course, when the teacher goes,
the person dependent upon the teacher tends to collapse.
How often, in our ignorance and our failure to understand
doctrine, have we become over-dependent upon persons
and have thereby robbed ourselves of some of the greatest
benefits of the Christian life.

Moving on from a general approach to the subject, we
come to something which is more difficult, namely the
theological or the doctrinal aspect of this great statement.
And here we divide our subject up, quite obviously and
inevitably, into some three main sections. I only note them
here.

First of all, let us see what Paul says about salvation itself;
and here the point we must make is that the Apostle was not
exhorting the members of the church at Philippi to produce
their own salvation, or to arrive at it, but rather to work out
the salvation that they already possessed. I put it in that
negative form because even this statement has been misinterpreted in that way. People have taken it to mean that if
you do your best to work out your own salvation, and do all
you can, you will be given the gift of salvation. But that,
patently, is a complete travesty and denial of what the
Apostle is actually teaching. He has already been reminding
the Philippians, in the first chapter, that they have received
the gift of salvation, so he is certainly not telling them here:

'Now you live a good life, and then you will become a good
Christian and receive this gift.' No, he is writing to people
whom he says have already received it and he thanks God
for their fellowship in the gospel from the first day until
now; his whole argument is that they *are*, and not that they
are going to become, Christians. This is, then, not an exhortation for them to do certain things in order to arrive at a
given position, rather, Paul is saying, 'Because you have
started, now continue.'

Let me put it like this: nowhere does the New Testament
represent the Christian life and salvation as something
which we achieve as the result of our own efforts and striving and our own endeavour. Paul has put that quite clearly
in the sixth verse of the first chapter where he says, '... he
which hath begun a good work in you will perform it [con-
tinue it] until the day of Jesus Christ.' This is something
which is quite basic and fundamental. The whole postulate
of the New Testament is that you and I, by nature, can do
nothing which will entitle us, or enable us to merit, salvation, because salvation, according to the Bible, is the gift of
God. It is something which is given to us and until we have
been given that 'something' we can do nothing.

Perhaps we will see it more clearly if we remind ourselves
of the ways in which the New Testament speaks of salvation.
The New Testament talks about justification, sanctification
and glorification; those are the divisions of the term salvation. The New Testament talks about people being justified
before God, which means that God regards these people in
Christ as guiltless; he forgives them in Christ; they are justified by faith. However, sanctification is not that, but something different. It is that process which is going on within us,
and which is making us perfect. Sanctification is continuous,
whereas justification is God once and for all regarding us as
sinless; it is God clothing us with the righteousness of Christ
and thereby regarding us as free from guilt. Sanctification is
Christ being formed in us, our nature being purged and
purified and cleansed and perfected. And then the ultimate
state is that of glorification, the state in which you and I, and

all Christian people, will be when, beyond this life and death and the grave, we shall stand face to face with God with a perfect resurrected body, entirely free from sin and evil and pollution. There we shall be glorified.

Now salvation really includes those three things. If you prefer to consider this from a different aspect, we can look at it like this: there is a sense in which we can say that as Christians we are already saved; there is a sense in which we are being saved; and another in which we shall be ultimately saved. It is vitally important that we should have that kind of classification in our minds, because what the Apostle is talking about here is not justification, but sanctification; he is not exhorting these people to earn their salvation – that is, to do something in order that their sins may be forgiven and that God may smile upon them, or in order that they may be free from guilt. Because you are justified, he says, work out your salvation. It is not their standing in the presence of God that he is considering here, it is this process of cleansing and purification and perfecting, which is ultimately going to lead to their glorification. It is important that we should realise this, because if we regard it as a matter of justification we shall not only be falsifying the Apostle's teaching, we shall also be false to the New Testament teaching from beginning to end. What the Apostle is concerned about here is the working out of the life which we have received, not our arriving at it. It is practising it because we have been given it.

And, of course, the interesting thing to observe is that the word which the Apostle uses in this connection is the word 'work out'. In other words, our sanctification is something in which you and I are active. Here, you see, there is a great doctrine involved. There are those who think that sanctification is something in which you and I are quite passive. There are people who teach that as you have been justified by just believing and doing nothing, so you must receive your sanctification in exactly the same way. They say that you are justified by faith, and that the big mistake that most Christian people make is that they strive and endeavour to improve and perfect themselves. That, they say, is an error; you have nothing to do but to stop and give in and receive this sanctification and then you will be held to be perfect. They put it sometimes in a phrase like this – 'Let go and let God', and they have based it upon this word that we are considering together. You have nothing to do but to let go and wait upon God and then you receive. And yet the answer is found in the Apostle's words here, which are an active commandment: '*work out*', do something, 'work out your own salvation, with fear and trembling'.

Now that is where the confusion of doctrine comes in. By all my efforts and working and striving I can never make myself a Christian, but because, and only by the grace of God, I have become a Christian, then I must work with all my might and with all the energy and effort that I can command. Once having been made a Christian I am in a position to work, and so the exhortation to me is to work out my salvation. Paul, then, exhorts us to work and to labour and to strive and fight the good fight of faith. He says in Romans 6:11 that we must reckon ourselves to be 'dead indeed unto sin, but alive unto God'. Therefore, it does seem to me to be entirely contrary to the Apostle's doctrine to teach that we are to be sanctified in a passive manner and that we should do nothing but wait for God to do everything for us.

The second point, of course, is perhaps the most controversial of all, and yet it is one which I think I can show you is full of comfort and encouragement and exhortation. The second great matter is that of God's part and our part in all this – 'Work out your own salvation with fear and trembling. For it is God which worketh in you ...' There is the problem at once. This is the point at which the argument has always been keenest, and I think there have been reasons for that. The danger is to approach the text in a party spirit – saying we are in this camp, or that. Instead of approaching the gospel and its message and statements with a mind which is as free from prejudice as possible, we are all concerned to prove our point of view; we do not enter into the discussion in the spirit which makes a true understanding possible. The other danger is that of pressing our own logic beyond the precise statement of Scripture. In other words, the trouble, I feel, has often arisen simply because men are not willing to admit that they cannot understand certain matters. But as long as we are in this life there are certain things which ultimately we cannot reconcile.

Now I believe that this is for our good and our ultimate sanctification. There are certain statements in the New Testament which appear to be contradictory, and yet are not contradictory at all; it is just that our finite minds are incapable of reconciling them logically. Here we have an example of that very thing. Let us approach it like this: our business is to submit ourselves to the revelation of what Scripture teaches us. No one can dispute that all the initiative in this matter of salvation is always with God. 'It is *God* which worketh in you both to will and to do of his good pleasure.'

We can summarise this great doctrine in this way. According to the Bible, man by nature is dead in trespasses and sins. If we read Ephesians 2 we see the background of this doctrine. According to the teaching of the Bible everywhere man by nature is spiritually dead, and can do nothing. We are told in Romans 8:7 that the natural mind is 'enmity against God: for it is not subject to the law of God, neither indeed can be.' And not only can man do nothing, he does not want to do anything. He is alienated in his mind against God; he cannot please God, nor does he want to. So why are we now at all interested in these things? Why are we not spending our time, and living our whole life, in utter unconcern about God? What has happened to us? What has made the difference? The answer of the Bible is this: '*But God* ... for his great love wherewith he loved us ...' (Eph. 2:4). Our salvation was God's initiating; it was God that did something.

Now, my friend, let me put it in terms of your own experience. Look into your own life, face yourself quite honestly, and ask yourself, 'Why am I what I am? Why am I interested and concerned about these matters? Why am I not like so many people, perfectly honest and decent and

good people, but people who are just not interested? They
are not concerned about these things and if you mention
them, they smile kindly and just dismiss it. What has made
the difference?' – and you find the answer in the Word of
God. It is something that has happened to you, to make you
face yourself and your life like this. It is God working, God
the Holy Spirit who came to you and arrested you and pulled you up and made you think and ask questions, and gave
you certain views of yourself and your life, and of himself.
It was God who came and convicted you of your sin. It is
God who quickens, God who awakens, God who gives us
the gift of life – let me remind you again of how Paul puts it
in the first chapter of this epistle. Even when you were
unconcerned, he began to interfere with your life, he came
after you, and he disturbed you. God's initiating!

But the Apostle goes on to say something still more striking. God does not merely start this, he goes on with it, and
continues it. This statement we are considering is one of the
most striking that is to be found even in Scripture itself with
regard to this matter. 'It is God,' says Paul, 'which worketh
in you.' He does not merely present certain things to you
from the outside. God, in Christ, in the New Testament
doctrine of salvation, is doing something right within our
nature. In us – we must not whittle down the meaning, it
really does mean inside – in the vital depths of our being,
God by the Holy Spirit is doing something. And what is he
doing? This is how Paul puts it: he energises us, he works in
us, 'both to will and to do of his good pleasure'. Can anything be more radical than that? It means that every good
desire, every Christian thought and aspiration which I have
is something which has been produced in me by God. God
controls my willing, it is God who energises my very desires
and hopes and aspirations and thoughts, he stimulates it all.

Now I wonder whether we always realise that as we
should; that these desires for a fuller and better and more
perfect Christian life are not self-generated or self-pro-
duced. When you have a desire to do something good, or a
desire to pray, it is God who energises it in your will, God

working in us both to will and to do. But it affects not only the will. He is the energy and the power also in our breathing, in our ability to live this life. That is the Apostle's statement which he not only makes here, but in many other places also. The initiative is his from beginning to end. It is God who began, it is he who keeps it going and it is he who is making it perfect.

And yet you and I are told to work it out, we are told to do something. Is this a contradiction? I suggest that it is not and we can put it like this. God carries on this work within us by placing these desires and powers in us. In other words, God is perfecting us, he is bringing his great purpose to pass in our Christian life, not by acting upon us in a passive state or condition, but by controlling our will, our desires, our thoughts and aspirations and everything. It is God who starts it and he makes us do it. I do not say that God forces our will. Rather, God does something more gracious: he persuades our will, and gives us holy desires, so that we will those things, and our desire and ambition is to work it out because it is 'God which worketh in us'. There is no essential contradiction in this, indeed there is not ultimately any contradiction at all, it is God's initiative.

Let me show you how Paul puts it: why has God started this work, why is he working in us both to will and to do? He has done it all *of his own good pleasure*. Is that not one of the most amazing statements in Scripture! Let us not misunderstand the verse. It was in spite of your sin and mine that God has done it. Is this not the glorious doctrine of the New Testament? Though we were sinners and rebels, though we were deserving nothing but punishment, God, of his own good pleasure, in his grace, began the work and is going on with it. I ask myself, why are you what you are? I say it is all the grace of God, and yet I feel responsible. I feel my will and energy come in and I am told to work it out and I am anxious to do this. It is God that makes me anxious to work it out, but that does not lessen my responsibility.

Let me say a final word on the whole question of my perseverance in this life; and here I must make two remarks.

Do you not see that this doctrine guarantees our persever-ance in this life? As long as God is controlling my will I must go on. People seem to fail because they do not will and desire the right thing, but it is God that is working in you and he will make you will the right things so that you can go on doing them. And, thank God, it does not stop at that. I might have a will to live this wonderful Christian life, but I am weak, I have no energy or power or spiritual dynamic. It is all right, says Paul, he will also give you the energy to carry it out. 'It is God which worketh in you both to will *and to do.*' In other words you will have the desire and you will be given the power, and by those two things your Christian life is guaranteed and God who started the process will con-tinue it.

'But what about the fear and trembling?' asks someone. Yes, I hope to deal with that in our next study. Yet you can see, at this point, that it does not mean fear about your ulti-mate salvation; it means a kind of reverence and godly fear. The guarantee is there in the fact that it is God who is work-ing in you.

So now, we have looked hurriedly at this glorious doc-trine. Shall I end by putting a single question – and it is the most important thing of all? Are you aware of God working in you? You know that that is the proof that we are Chris-tians: not that we hold certain views about life and living, nor that we have a moral code, or anything like that. This is the fundamental thing – am I aware of God working in me? Am I aware of something I cannot explain except in terms of God's mighty action? Can I say that God is working in me both to will and to do? Am I aware of his interference in my life and of that disturbing, that persuading, that interrupt-ing, that whole movement of God that makes me feel that I have felt 'the Presence that disturbs me with the joy of ele-vated thought'. Have I felt the hand of my Maker upon my soul remaking, remoulding me? That is the truth about every Christian. God is working in you. Thank God for such a doctrine that assures me that in spite of my sin and all my unworthiness, God, who made the whole universe and who sustains everything that he has made, is fashioning this life of mine until, ultimately, he will produce a perfect product, and I shall stand and see him face to face.

14

Working Out Our Own Salvation

> Wherefore, my beloved, as ye have always obeyed, not as
> in my presence only, but now much more in my absence,
> work out your own salvation with fear and trembling. For
> it is God which worketh in you both to will and to do of
> his good pleasure. (Phil. 2:12–13)

We are considering these two verses for the second time
because we have found that it is impossible to deal with
them adequately in just one study. I have suggested that
perhaps the best way of dividing up this statement would be
to look at it in three ways: first of all, generally: then
theologically, and lastly practically, and in our previous
study we dealt with the first two headings.

We also saw that the Apostle's object in writing the words
was not to give a disquisition on theology, but rather to
make a practical appeal. Yet, as is his custom, he cannot
make a practical appeal without putting it in terms of doctrine. That is where the New Testament way of life differs
from a merely ethical system. Any appeal to the world to
live a Christian life before it has become Christian, is, as we
have seen, a negation of Christian teaching. We have here a
perfect illustration of the Apostle's method. But it is true
also of all the New Testament writers; it is the characteristic
way of making an appeal for conduct and Christian
behaviour. We are not put under a law but an appeal is
made to us. There is a great law of life in the New Testament, but it is what the New Testament calls 'the perfect law
of liberty'. This does not mean that the Christian is living a

lawless life, but that he has a higher kind of liberty. The New Testament always lays down its doctrine first, and then, having done so, says, 'If you believe that, cannot you see that this is inevitable?' It is an appeal to equity, to fair play. It does not confront us with a way of life, and say, 'Go and live it.' It first of all tells us of certain things that have been done for us, and then says, 'Now then ...' As you make the transition from doctrine to practice in the epistles, there is always a 'wherefore' or a 'therefore', and I am at pains to point out that the essential approach is to be found in such a connecting word. Without that, there is no appeal, but because of that, there is a very definite appeal to reason and to commonsense.

Perhaps, I can put it like this: is there anything that so thoroughly tests our whole profession of the Christian faith as our reaction to it when it calls upon us to live a certain kind of life? I put it like that for this good reason: do we not all know something in our experience about this unnatural and artificial dichotomy? We may like to hear the gospel with its grand good news and all that it has to offer, but we do not always feel quite so pleased when it goes on to call us to live in a particular way. There are people who say, 'But it is so narrow.' When it outlines a 'straight and narrow way', they say, 'Narrowness again!' Because of the 'wherefore', because of this indissoluble connection between doctrine and practice, because, too, of this inevitable logical sequence from doctrine to behaviour, our attitude towards the appeal tells us a great deal about our ultimate attitude to the doctrine. The New Testament says that these things are really inevitable, they are linked together, so if I object to doing them, it surely implies that there is at any rate something wrong with my view of the doctrine.

There is, then, no better test of my whole position, than my reaction when I am confronted with this amazing call of the New Testament to deny myself and take up the cross and follow Christ, to mortify my 'flesh', 'the deeds of the body', and 'my members which are upon the earth' – and all those other New Testament ways of putting it. Now, the

Apostle is doing something like that here, so let us try to see what he teaches us, as we approach it from the purely practical standpoint. To assist us in our consideration, I am going to ask three obvious questions. First, what does 'work out' mean? Secondly, how, or in what manner, should I work out my salvation? And thirdly, why should I do so?

What, therefore, does working out our salvation mean? The best answer is to define our terms, and if we discover the answer to the first two questions, I think we shall automatically find out the answer to the last. So let us try to do this. The Apostle tells us to work out our own salvation, and, as he tells us here, and as we are told in every other epistle, salvation is the very essential message of the New Testament itself. It means that I have come to see my own sinfulness and to understand something of the nature of sin. The Philippians had realised that they were sinners, and they had seen themselves as under the wrath of God. They had seen that they were condemned by the law of God and that, therefore, they were guilty in the sight of God. They had come to see that every effort they might make themselves would, in the last analysis, avail them nothing. Paul says the same thing in greater detail in the third chapter. He describes how he was a Jew and a Pharisee, how he had been circumcised, and so on, and yet, says Paul, I came to see that it was all refuse, worthless and useless.

Now these Philippian Christians had come to see that, too, and they had realised that they were really helpless to deliver themselves out of it. But then they had heard and believed this amazing good news of the gospel, that God had sent his only begotten Son to die on the cross in order to make atonement for them. God was giving them salvation as a free gift, saying to them, 'I have punished your sins there; I see you no more as sinners, but as righteous people. I am giving you a gift.' They had seen that they were given a new nature, that they had undergone a new birth. They had received the Holy Spirit and he was imparting to them this new life. They had a new outlook and understanding – they really were new people. Furthermore, they were conscious of a new strength and power which was delivering them, conscious of a sense of emancipation. They had become children of God and citizens of heaven – 'our conversation is in heaven', which means our citizenship is there. These people had now come to see that in this life they were travellers, sojourners, pilgrims; they had an entirely new view of life.

So that is the essential meaning of salvation, and what Paul's appeal tells them to do is to work out that salvation. And working out means perfecting, bringing to pass, leading to a full result, or finishing something which has already been commenced.

And that is the practical exhortation of the New Testament gospel to us today. I must now perfect this thing which has been given to me. The seed has been planted; I have been given it in embryo. My business is to allow and to encourage this gift to grow and develop, until it comes to its final perfection and full maturity. I have got the gift: I need not be worried lest God is not present and not with me. God is working in me and I must develop it all I can.

Now I am anxious that we should all be convinced of the utter inevitability of this appeal. If I believe what we have just seen about the nature of salvation, then is it not inevitable that I should do these things? In view of the fact that I have received this salvation, what am I to do? Well, first of all I must submit myself entirely to God. The Apostle puts it here in terms of the amazing account that he gives us of the earthly life of our Lord in verses 5–11. Now that, says Paul, is the very thing that God is demanding of you. He wants you to manifest that same obedience which was to be seen in our Lord and Saviour Jesus Christ – an utter and absolute submission to the will of God. Though he came as a man, our Lord went even further, even to the death of the cross. Whatever God asked him to do, he did it; and that is the first part of the working out of our own salvation. It is to see that in view of this amazing gift that God has given us, he has the right to demand of us this utter submission of our wills. Before I begin to do anything, I must say to myself, 'In

view of what God has done for me, in this world I must
desire to please him in all things. I must make my will, his.
My one concern must be to live to his honour and his glory.'
I do not think that that needs any proof. If I believe that
God has done this astounding thing for me, is it not inevita-
ble?

Clearly the next step is that I must avoid everything that
is opposed to God, what the New Testament calls 'the
world': 'Love not the world, neither the things that are in
the world' (1 John 2:15). The New Testament tells us that
man cannot love God and the world at the same time. It
puts this to our common sense and reason. It is perfectly evident that the outlook of life and organisation in this world is
opposed to God. We have only to read our newspapers. The
world is godless, ready to make fun of God and religion. It
is not interested in God; it panders to the flesh, and ridicules
everything that is connected with God. But the New Testament says that working out my salvation means avoidance of
everything that is opposed to God.

There is no limit to that. I must in no way be concerned
with those things, or be interested in them, or allow them to
appeal to me or to attract me. I must avoid everything that
is opposed to my own best interests. If I believe that this
world is a very dangerous place to me, that temptation and
sin are all round and about me, and that the whole world is
doing its utmost to drag me down, if I see that it leads me to
hell and destruction, but that God has delivered me from it
all, am I not being contradictory if I go on doing worldly
things and enjoy doing them? It is an appeal to commonsense. It is surely ridiculous to say, 'I want to go to God and
I thank God I have been delivered', and yet to work in the
opposite direction. 'Work out your own salvation'; perfect
it. God has delivered you by this amazing act of self-sac-
rifice; you have been given a new start and nature, salvation
is set before you. Turn your back upon the other once and
for ever. If we really believe that, there is no need to argue;
it is inevitable.

We can summarise it like this. The best way is to consult

the textbook on this subject. Here it is perfectly clear: the more I read the Bible and see the picture of the Christian man, the more I understand the nature of sin and life in this world, and what God has done for me in Christ, then the more I shall desire the things of God and hate the other. So I suggest that the best practical step is to read God's word, and to be thoroughly soaked in it. There is a very simple, practical test that one can apply at this point. I wonder what the result would be if we all kept a chart for one week and put down on paper the amount of time which we spent in reading God's word and things which help us to understand it, and the time we spent reading newspapers and novels or watching films? Now I am just asking the question. We say we believe in salvation. We believe God has given us this gift, so then, I ask, what are the relative amounts of time that we give to these things? Working out our own salvation means that we do everything we can to feed this life, to stimulate it, to enable it to extend and develop and grow.

And the other thing, clearly, is prayer: prayer for an increasing knowledge of God, for a greater measure of the Holy Spirit and for a greater understanding of this word; prayer for guidance, for leading and for understanding. If I believe in God and that he has done this for me, why do I spend so little time with him? Why do I not long for him more and more? That is how we work it out and I must follow and obey every prompting and leading that I am conscious of in this direction. The fathers used to regard the Christian life as a whole-time occupation. They used to spend their time with it and, I feel, it is one of the greatest condemnations of us today that we are guilty of not working out this amazing salvation that God has given to us.

But, then, what is the manner in which we do this? The Apostle says that we are to do it 'with fear and trembling'. Here again we must define our terms. He does not mean that we must do it in fear of losing our salvation. You will find that in the New Testament these words never carry that implication. When Paul wrote to the Corinthians 'I was with you … in fear, and in much trembling' (1 Cor 2:3), he did not mean that he was afraid that he would lose his soul. Neither is it a kind of craven fear, one of self torment. It means humility and a holy reverence, or, if you like, a holy vigilance and circumspection. It means that as I work out my salvation, I should realise the tremendous seriousness of what I am doing.

I wonder whether this is not the thing which needs to be emphasised most at the present time, not least in the ranks of evangelical people? I wonder why it is that the whole idea of the godly man has somehow or other got lost amongst us? Why is it that Christian people are not described as 'god-fearing' people? Why is it that there is such a difference between us and the Christian of a hundred or two hundred years ago, or the Puritan of the seventeenth century? They were truly Christian. 'Methodist', too, was a kind of nickname given to people because of their methodical life. I wonder why it is that somehow or other we have lost this particular sense of the Christian life? I have no doubt but that the explanation is that it is an over-reaction on our part from the pure legalism that was so common at the turn of the century when many people had lost the true spirit of the New Testament. They imposed a certain kind of life upon themselves and upon their children; they laid down rules and regulations; and people then reacted and said, 'That is pure legalism, not Christianity.' But now we are so much like everybody else because we have forgotten this about 'fear and trembling', vigilance and circumspection. Some-times I am afraid we have been so anxious not to give the impression that to be Christian means being miserable, that we have imagined that we must be smiling and laughing all the time and we have believed in this so-called 'muscular' Christianity.

Now I suggest that that is somewhat of a denial of what is taught here. The Christian must of necessity be a serious and sober man. 'With fear and trembling' means a holy reverence and awe of God. I must realise that the God with whom I am concerned is 'the Father of lights, with whom is no variableness, neither shadow of turning' (Jas. 1:17), that

'God is light, and in him is no darkness at all' (1 John 1:5). If he is in the light, I must walk in the light (v.7). Also, I should have a fear of the world in the sense that I realise that the world is opposed to me, that it is there to drag me down and away from God. I should have a healthy respect for it.

I should also fear myself. A man who knows his own heart is a man who cannot be light and carefree and flippant. He knows that in his flesh there 'dwelleth no good thing'. The Christian is one who works out his own salvation with fear and trembling; fear lest he should fail or falter, lest he should not discern the subtlety of the world, the power of sin and his own weakness, and the holiness of God. So he walks with gravity lest he should be unworthy of this great salvation.

So, then, we have seen what it means to work out our own salvation, and how we are to do it, and now, lastly, why should we do it? First of all, as we saw earlier, we should do this because it is exactly and precisely what our Lord and Saviour Jesus Christ did. He submitted himself to God; he said, 'For I came down from heaven, not to do mine own will, but the will of him that sent me' (John 6:38). Is there anything higher for us than to imitate and emulate his example?

The second reason is because of what he has done for us; we believe that Christ shed his blood and allowed his body to be broken that we might be delivered. As Paul wrote to Titus, 'Who gave himself for us, that he might redeem us from all iniquity, and purify unto himself a peculiar [a special] people, zealous of good works' (Tit. 2:14). It was the reason why he came and went to the death of the cross. It was in order that we might do this.

Then I must work out my own salvation because of his honour and his glory. The world judges him by his people. In that sense his glory and his honour are in my hands. I am dishonouring Christ if I fail. Another reason is that there are others who are watching me. Even the world itself is doing so, and I must so live that I attract them to Christ, warning

them of their sinful and terrible condition and trying my
utmost to bring them to know him.

And then there is another, powerful reason: if I really
believe that I am going to heaven, that I am a citizen of the
kingdom of God and that when I come to die I enter this
amazing inheritance, then, 'Every man that hath this hope
in him purifieth himself, even as he is pure' (1 John 3:3).
God is absolutely pure and perfect, and if I say I am going
on to him, have I then a moment to waste? I must prepare
myself, there is not a second to lose.

And, lastly, I must work out my salvation with fear and
trembling, for this good reason: the New Testament teaches
me that if I fail to do so myself, then I must not be surprised
if God begins to do certain things to me. Do you remember
the teaching of Hebrews 12? 'Whom the Lord loveth he
chasteneth, and scourgeth every son whom he receiveth.' It
is put still more strikingly in 1 Corinthians 11, where Paul
says that there were many in the church at Corinth who
were sick, and there were even some, he said, who were
dead, and he tells us that the reason for that was that they
had not examined themselves before partaking of the Lord's
Supper, and were partaking unworthily. Such a man, Paul
said, 'eateth and drinketh damnation to himself, not dis-
cerning the Lord's body' (1 Cor. 11:29).

The doctrine of the New Testament can be put into this
form: if God has called you and given you his salvation, he
destines you for salvation and he is going to perfect you. His
method is to put promptings within us. He energises our
mind and whole outlook, but if we fail to practise these
things, then God, in his very love to us, is going to chasten
us – a sickness, an illness, a disappointment, a loss, a sorrow. These are ways which God uses because of our failure
and our recalcitrance. 'It is a fearful thing to fall into the
hands of the living God' (Heb. 10:31). The love of God is as
great as that. The Christian man who is not doing his utmost
to live the Christian life is a fool, and he must not be surprised if certain things begin to happen to him. If you are a
child of God, he is going to bring about your perfection and

if you do not do it yourself to please him in this way, then, I say, you may well find that God will do it to you in one of these other ways. That is a very wonderful thing. I am not saying that every Christian who suffers is being chastised, but I do say that God does do that, and if we fail to respond to his appeal, then we must not be surprised if we experience his chastening.

Therefore, my beloved, 'work out your own salvation with fear and trembling. For it is God which worketh in you both to will and to do of his good pleasure.'

15

God's Special Concern for His People

> Do all things without murmurings and disputings: that ye
> may be blameless and harmless, the sons of God, without
> rebuke, in the midst of a crooked and perverse nation,
> among whom ye shine as lights in the world; holding forth
> the word of life. (Phil. 2:14–16a)

The Apostle here continues the theme that has been occupy-
ing his attention in this entire section. He is appealing to the
members of the church at Philippi to live the Christian life
in all its fullness and he obviously has a scheme in his mind.
He reminds them first of all of the very nature of the Christian life, and we saw that when we considered those familiar
words, 'Work out your own salvation with fear and trembling. For it is God which worketh in you both to will and to
do of his good pleasure.' God has done something to you,
says Paul. He has made you what you are and he is still
working in you, energising even your thinking and willing as
well as your actions. Therefore, work it out, give it full
scope, bring it to perfection, finish it. And we saw that he
emphasises that in various ways.

But Paul is not content even with that. He is so concerned
about the state of these people because he was the one
whom God had used to bring them into the faith in the first
place; he has such a pride in them that he is anxious that
they should arrive at a complete state. As a wise teacher, he
knows the importance of a negative. He realises that it is not
enough just to tell them what they have to do in a general
manner, he also has to tell them what to avoid and beware

of. He knows that as there are certain things that are likely
to attack them, he must warn them beforehand, and thereby
prepare them for the day of trial. Therefore he elaborates
this appeal for Christian living and conduct, and selects certain things which are, of course, of primary importance. He
has already put it all in one great statement when he told
them to work out their own salvation 'with fear and trembling', but they must be given reasons, perhaps, for the use of
this phrase.

Why, then, is this 'fear and trembling' necessary? The
reason, he tells them here, is because of certain things which
are likely to attack them. Paul is not only a profound Christian psychologist, he is also familiar with his Old Testament
Scriptures, and with certain major, basic warnings which are
to be found in the story of the Children of Israel. The Apostle also knew something of those dangers in his own life, and
he had already had many experiences with several of the
churches; and all these things together made him anxious for
his beloved church at Philippi. So he writes to warn them,
to forearm and safeguard them against some of these subtle
enemies of the soul. And that is what he is doing at this
point, as he again paints us one of those great, inimitable
pictures of the Christian man and of the Christian life.

The Apostle Paul seems to be quite incapable of merely
making an exhortation, as such. As we have seen, he never
just gives people a number of rules and regulations – do this
or do that – he always puts his warnings in terms of the
whole. Paul's immediate purpose here is to exhort them to
do all things, to work out their salvation, without murmurings and disputings. But he puts it all in terms of their status
and position as children of God. That is the central thing in
this exhortation. The appeal is couched in that manner
because they are children of God, and it is addressed to
them as such. The implication is: because you are that, these
are the things you must now remember and put into practice. In this way we are once more reminded that the Apostle Paul is never interested in ethics *qua* ethics; his interest
is always theological, and of course it must be, because the

Christian is not only a good and ethical man, he is more than that.

And this is vitally important, because we are living in an age when, surely, we ought to be seeing, with clearer eyes than men have ever seen before, the utter impossibility of a Christian ethics and morality divorced from the only basis from which that ethics and morality derive. The tragedy of this particular generation is that we are living on the capital of the past. Our fathers fondly imagined that they could shed the gospel and still maintain the Christian life; they thought, too, that they could deny the basic principles of the Christian faith but still retain what they considered was good in it, namely its ethics and morality. But by today we surely must be seeing very clearly that that is an utter impossibility, and if our fathers had only read these epistles more carefully they would never have imagined such folly. Our text reveals a perfect understanding of the whole thing; when the Apostle wants to show the Philippians that they must not murmur, he says, 'Now, as children of God you must not murmur.' How different it is when it is put like that! Here you have a mighty appeal and if we forget this, then we must not be surprised if there is a grave failure in ethics and morality.

Let me put this in the form of an illustration; it is an illustration used by Professor Emil Brunner to show the difference between truly Christian conduct, which is the outcome of the Christian life, and this attempt merely to incorporate Christian ethics and morality into daily life and living. He says it is the difference between cut flowers in a vase and flowers growing out of the ground. You can take those cut flowers, you can put them into your vase and for a while they will flourish, but they will soon die. However, if you had left them in the ground, they would have continued to live – that is the difference. To think you can maintain Christian ethics and morality without Christian doctrine, is exactly like that. You can enjoy the beauty and scent of those cut flowers for a night, but they cannot last, because the life flow has been severed. The Apostle forewarns us against all such error and once more shows us that you must never make any appeal in the Christian realm except in terms of the whole of your doctrine.

Perhaps the best way to consider the matter, and the best way to summarise the message of these two and a half verses which we are now studying, is to look at it first of all in terms of the description which Paul gives of the Christian, and then in terms of its inevitable implications. Let us start with the description itself. 'Do all things without murmurings and disputings: that ye may be [or become] blameless and harmless, the sons of God,' as the Authorised Version has it, or 'children of God' as the Revised puts it, 'without rebuke ...' Now there are many ways of describing the Christian but I suppose that this is the characteristic New Testament description, and it certainly is the best and the most significant. Christians, Paul reminds us again, are children of God.

The first point we surely have to make in this connection is that this is something which is true only of Christians, and yet it is not enough just to make a dogmatic assertion like that. There has been a great deal of talk, especially in the last fifty years or so, about the so-called 'universal fatherhood of God and the universal brotherhood of man' and it has been a very popular theory that all people are children of God. It is not, of course, surprising that this theory came into vogue as Christian doctrine was being stripped of its essential meaning. The whole idea was to dispute the old teaching that only Christian people are children of God. No, said this new teaching, you must not emphasise your doctrine and dogma like that; *all* people are God's children whether they believe in Christ or not. The universal fatherhood of God and the brotherhood of man was so emphasised that the need for Christian truth disappeared, and the gospel was regarded as some kind of general vague appeal for people to be nice to one another and to live a good life. That kind of thinking has been very popular during this century. So let us examine it, because the whole of the Apostle's argument here, I think I can show you, is dependent upon the fact that only those who are Christians are children of God.

Now there are those who would say that the statements made in Acts 17 are a confirmation of this idea of the universal fatherhood of God, because Paul, in preaching at Athens, says that, 'we are the offspring of God', and he says that God 'hath made of one blood all nations of men ...' (Acts 17:29, 26). Now clearly what the Apostle was teaching was that ultimately we all derive from God, in the sense that we are all made by him. We are all descendants of Adam, and Adam, in the ultimate sense, is described as a 'son of God', which means that he was made by God. God is our Creator and Maker and that is true of everybody living.

But we have other evidence which is still more striking than that. You remember what our Lord and Saviour Jesus Christ said one afternoon concerning certain people who were arguing with him and wrangling against him? He said, 'Ye are of your father the devil, and the lusts of your father ye will do' (John 8:44). You call yourselves the seed of Abraham, he says, but you are not Abraham's children, for if you were you would believe on me – you are all of your father the devil. Then, also, the Apostle Peter says to the Christian people to whom he was writing, 'Which in time past were not a people, but are now the people of God' (1 Pet. 2:10); 'Before', he says in effect, 'you were just a rabble, but you are now the people of God, so, dearly beloved, I beseech you ...' It is the same argument that we find here.

Then let me give you the positive statement which we have, confirming this doctrine. In the prologue to John's gospel we find these significant and important words – 'But as many as received him, to them gave he power [or authority] to become the sons of God.' By nature they were not the children of God, sin had broken that relationship. Then Paul himself, in Ephesians 2, where he is writing to Gentile believers, reminds them of the fact that they had been 'aliens from the commonwealth of Israel, strangers from the covenants of promise, having no hope, and without God in the world.' But now in Christ, says Paul, they have been brought nigh. They were outside the family, and were not members of the household, but in Christ they have been brought into the household and into the family of God. They have become his children.

Again, in Romans 8:15, Paul writes '... ye have not received the spirit of bondage again to fear; but ye have received the Spirit of adoption, whereby we cry, Abba, Father.' Formerly we were not children, but now we are, because we have received this spirit that makes us children, the spirit of adoption, and we cry, 'Abba, Father'. Now surely, all these statements, and there are others that we can adduce, should make it abundantly clear that the term 'children of God' is a limiting term and only applies to those who are Christians. In a sense we need not have gone any further than the words we are considering together, because the whole emphasis here is that Christians are different, they are lights in the world, luminaries, set apart. They are separate because they are, as he says, the children of God. The others are not, hence the difference, and also the reason why they must be different.

Here, therefore, is something which is quite basic and fundamental. The New Testament is always at great pains to show that to be a Christian is to be entirely different from the man who is not. We cannot reiterate that too frequently. It is not a difference in degree, but in kind; it is not a difference in certain things we do in life, something quantitative, it is a qualitative difference. It is a vital one, the difference between belonging to a family and not belonging – it is a blood relationship. That is the point made here, and I am emphasising it because the Apostle's appeal is based upon this difference, so that if we are not right and clear about it, the appeal will fall upon deaf ears.

But having established that fact, we must now go on to consider what it means and what it implies and tells us about ourselves. These are some of the things that the New Testament tells us. We have, as the Apostle has reminded us in writing to the Romans, been adopted into the family of God. This is a great New Testament conception. We were, as it were, waifs and strays, outside, with no one to care for and look after us, or be vitally interested in us. But God in

Christ has taken hold of us and adopted us. He has taken us into the family. He regards us as children; he has done it in a legal manner, making it absolutely right.

But we do not stop at that, because, according to the New Testament, in addition to being adopted into the family of God, we are also partakers of the divine nature. This is a great mystery, a doctrine which we cannot hope to understand in this life and world, and yet it is here in the Bible: we read all these statements about being born of the Spirit, receiving the Spirit, being regenerated, being born again, and being created anew – those are the terms. So in addition to being taken hold of and adopted into the family, a vital change is wrought within us; we receive something of the divine nature. Now we must be careful not to think of that in terms of a material process, as something that is injected into us. Yet it is a reality and we do receive of God's own nature. By the Holy Spirit dwelling in us we are partakers of that divine nature itself, so that it is not merely a legal adoption, there is a transaction accompanying it.

Then, of course, the other things that are true of us as children of God are that we become the special objects of God's care and favour; that is inseparable from this idea of being children. The children, of course, are always the special concern of the parent; that is why there are families, that is God's provision in this world into which we are born. God has seen to it that there are two persons who love us in a special manner, we are their children, they are going to watch over and look after us; in the same way, Christians are told 'ye are children of God'. And the result of this, of course, is that we are in a very privileged position. We have been separated, called out and set apart. We are in this privileged position of being the special objects of God's solicitude and concern. 'Yes,' says the Apostle, in effect, 'and because of that, I would have you see that there are special responsibilities that devolve upon us.' And it is that which he has in mind: 'Because you are the children of God, because of that, therefore ...' Now, says the Apostle, in view of this special relationship of ours to God, we are to be what he asks us to be, and we are to do what he calls upon us to do.

There, then, we have taken a hurried glance at the general picture of the Christian that Paul presents to us. Now, secondly, we must go on to consider the way in which we are to live and conduct ourselves as children of God. To start with, let us look at what the Apostle has to tell us about our essential character as God's children. The first thing is that we are to 'Do all things without murmurings and disputings'. Now the 'all things' means everything connected with our salvation, and that takes us back to the exhortation in verse 12: 'Wherefore, my beloved, as ye have always obeyed, not as in my presence only, but now much more in my absence, work out your own salvation with fear and trembling.' The 'all things' has reference to this realm of salvation in which we live and about which we are concerned. All the things he has asked us to do, this living of the Christian life, must be done without murmuring and disputing.

Now this is a striking statement, and we must analyse it together. There can be no doubt at all but that at this point the Apostle Paul has something very definite in his mind – the ancient story of the Children of Israel. Read, for instance, Psalm 106 because it is such a perfect and wonderful account of those people. God singled out that nation, amongst all the nations of the world. He called them his own chosen people, and led them out and showered blessings upon them. You remember the long story of their being called out of Egypt and bondage? They were destined for the glorious and wonderful land of Canaan; but then what happened? They murmured against God in their tents and they constantly complained and argued. Yes, they acknowledged that God had brought them out, but what was the point of it all? Why should they not go back to Egypt? Had God called them out to destroy them in this wilderness? And they longed for the 'leeks and the garlic and the onions' of Egypt. You find it all in the book of Numbers especially, and also in other parts of the Old Testament; they murmured and that was their trouble.

So the Apostle has that in mind when he writes to the members of the church at Philippi, and the way to learn from it is this. 'Now,' said Paul, in effect, to the Philippians, 'I have already reminded you that God is working in you, and so I want you to look at the Christian life as a great pilgrimage. The initial step, of course, was that step of conversion where you came out of the world into this realm. But God has not finished with you. He is leading you out, exactly as he led the Children of Israel of old, and there is Canaan, the haven of eternal bliss, in the future; but you have to get from here to there. God, I am reminding you,' says Paul, 'is leading you; it is God who is working in you both to will and to do – God is there at the very spring and source of the fountain of life. He puts desires, thoughts and suggestions into your mind, and you will find that he will lead you on; he will put you in certain positions and situations. God is going to do many things to you,' says Paul, 'exactly as he did to the Children of Israel.

'But this is the question. You must be very careful that you do not fall into their error and follow their evil example, and murmur. For you know,' Paul continues, 'you will find, as the Children of Israel did, that God will sometimes put you in places you do not like. There will be days when you will seem not to have any water to quench your thirst; there will be days when the food will not seem to be interesting, and there will be days when the enemy will confront you; but you will find that it is God that is *working in you, both to will and to do.* He is leading you and is perfecting his process. You will find that there will be occasions when you will say, "Why this? Why has God brought me to this? God says he loves me and he is my Father, so why is this happening?" And there,' says Paul, 'the temptation will be to murmur and to have these disputings in your mind. But wherever you find yourself, wherever you are situated in this Christian process through which God is taking and leading you, do everything without murmuring and disputing.'

Let us now analyse these words. Murmurings, of course, are undoubtedly the result of a stubborn spirit and will.

They are indicative of moral rebellion, or, to put it still more forcibly, murmurings are always the outcome of a lack of love. You see here that the Apostle does not use his words thoughtlessly; he puts murmurings before disputings and what a profound psychologist he is! I suppose most of us would have thought that disputings should have come before murmurings, that you start by doubting and then you murmur. Not at all! It is the other way round in the Christian life. The first thing that goes wrong with the Christian is that he begins to doubt God's love, and disputings are the result of intellectual rebellion. As murmurings are indicative of a lack of love, so disputings are always indicative of a lack of faith.

That is the order, and this is how it works. The Christian finds himself in a certain situation, and his first thought is, 'Why has God done this?' The querying of the love comes before anything else. Then, having got into that state in which you lose your love for God, you cease to believe in God's love for you, and you begin to ask questions. 'Is there anything in it?' you ask, and so disputings follow doubts. When people come and would have us believe that their difficulties are entirely intellectual, they are not speaking the truth. It is a lack of love, it is moral lack, that leads to trouble in the realm of faith – murmurings and then disputings.

These two things go together, of course. If once we begin to doubt God's love, then we begin to doubt everything. We begin to doubt the facts; we begin to doubt the whole principle; we will be worried about miracles and all sorts of things – that is the order. You love first, then you understand, and if you do not have that fundamental confidence, you cannot hope to have faith – that again is the order. And, of course, that is what is illustrated so perfectly in the case of the Children of Israel. They had seen God's wonders, they had absolute proof of his power, and while all went well, as the psalm reminds us, they believed. Then something happened and they began to turn against God, and to query his love. When you have lost confidence in God, you cannot believe

anything; when you love God you can be afraid of nothing –
these things always go together and the murmurings lead to
the disputings.

There is nothing that leads to such havoc in the Christian
life, there is nothing that so ruins life, as this spirit of murmuring and disputing. It ruined the whole story of the
ancient people, it has ruined the Christian life and experience of many a Christian in this world. It makes you ill at
ease; you become despondent; you do not understand anything; you feel your lot is the only difficult one in the world.
It leads not only to that, but to a poor testimony; it brings
disgrace and disrepute upon the Christian name. That is why
the Apostle urges the Philippians to avoid it at all costs, and
to consider that glaring illustration of the ancient Children
of Israel.

But let me put it in other terms. 'How can I implement
this Apostle's exhortation?' someone may ask. 'It is all very
well for Paul to say, "do all things without murmurings and
disputings," and it is all very well for preachers to stand in
the pulpit and say the same thing, but if you were in my position what would you do? If you just knew the things I am
faced with! How can I go on without murmuring and disputing?' Let me suggest to you some of the answers we find in
the Bible itself. This is the antidote to the tendency and the
terrible danger of giving way to this harmful spirit. Start first
of all by reminding yourself of the character of God. God is
holy and just. He is absolutely righteous. God neither
tempts any man with evil nor can be tempted, says the
Apostle James. Whatever else may be wrong, of this we can
be certain, and it must never be examined or queried. God
is incapable of doing anything unkind or unfair. His character is absolute. Therefore, when you begin to feel like
grumbling and murmuring and complaining against God,
just remind yourself of that absolute character of his nature.

Then, next, the Apostle emphasises here the fatherhood
of God. If you are a Christian, my friend, then God is your
Father and he is a Father who loves you and is concerned
about you. When you were an enemy of his, he sent his only

begotten Son to the cruel death on the cross for you. It is
God who initiated this whole movement of salvation so that
you might be forgiven, and that you might be saved and
redeemed. So whatever your position, and however little
you can understand it, remind yourself that that Holy God
is your Father. Whatever may be happening, say to yourself,
I am a child of God, and God loves me and is concerned
about me. He is specially interested in me, and is watching
over me.

Then, thirdly, remind yourself of the greatness of God,
and your own smallness, and especially the smallness of
your mind and your understanding. I sometimes think that
this is the key to the whole situation. I take it that the final
sin is that we want to understand God. Was that not the
trouble in the Garden of Eden at the beginning? 'Why
should you not be as gods?' – that was the suggestion put to
them. And their cry was: 'Why should we be prohibited
from eating of the fruit of the garden? We are big enough to
understand the mind of God! We want to be able to understand the mind of God!'

But you and I have such pigmy little minds, and God is
infinite and absolute and illimitable. I am increasingly coming to think of faith in that way. Faith means that I should
be content with the revelation that is given me, that I should
be content not to ask questions, that I should not even
desire to know more, that I should say, 'I am satisfied with
what you have given me to understand.' We cannot understand the working of the mind of God; it is such a great
mind and my little mind is so small. I may not understand
the process, but the fact that I cannot understand does not
mean that the mind of God is wrong or unkind or cruel. You
cannot measure your mind against the mind of God.

The next thing is that we should always remember that
God's chief concern for us is our sanctification. It is he that
'worketh in you both to will and to do ...' and the will of
God is our sanctification. God's concern about you and me
is not just that we should have a good time in this life and
world; that is not the first thing in his mind for us. His will is

that we should one day be perfect even as the Lord Jesus Christ is perfect; that we should attain unto the measure of the stature of the fullness of Christ. God is not concerned that we should be prosperous in this life. He is concerned about your soul and mine, and he is going to bring that soul to a state of perfection, when it shall be blameless, spotless, and absolutely pure and holy. That is what God wants and he is so intent upon that, that because of our sinfulness and stupidity, he sometimes has to do things to us in this life which we do not like, because by nature you and I would prefer to enjoy life in this world at the expense of the soul. We would like to go on just as we are, but God puts the soul first. He is so concerned about your spirit that he may have to strip you of earthly things that are quite all right in themselves, but that you have allowed them to come between you and God. He does it in love, because he wants your soul to arrive at ultimate glory.

That explains most of the things that make us murmur and complain. God is concerned about our sanctification, and the ultimate goal is glorification, therefore chastisement is necessary in this life. When you ask, 'Why has this happened to me?' are you quite sure that you were not allowing that thing to come between you and God? It may be the death of a dear one, it may be financial loss – I do not care what it is – are you sure that that was not monopolising the place of God? Let me repeat what I said at the end of the last study: God so loves us, and is so concerned about us, that sometimes he strikes us with illness, we may even die, in order that the ultimate good may be safeguarded. And this is a repetition of that same doctrine. If we allow these things to come between us and God's purpose, then we must not be surprised and disappointed if we find God dealing with us. My dear friends, put this first and never lose your hold of it: if you are a child of God, other things will have to go. He is holding on to you, and he will go on working in you, until you have arrived at that state for which he has destined you. If you are convinced of that, you will not murmur and complain, but in the midst of your loss and heartbreak you will rather turn to God and say, 'God forgive me, I thank you even for this, because I now see your purpose.'

Let me sum it all up by putting it like this: what the Apostle is asking of us is simply that we do what the Lord Jesus Christ himself did. You remember that he came from heaven (you find it all there in verses 5–8 of this same chapter). He put himself into the hands of God, and then he allowed God to use him. And God led him through some strange places. He was led into the wilderness to be tempted but he did not grumble or complain – you remember the whole story. Look at him, supremely, in the Garden of Gethsemane. There he saw that the time had come when those sins that he had taken upon himself were going to stand between him and God, but he did not murmur or complain even there. He asked, If there is any other way, let this cup pass from me, nevertheless not my will but thine be done.

Even though God led him to Gethsemane, he never murmured, he never complained. Let this mind be in you which was also in Christ Jesus. Wherever God may lead you, wherever this process of sanctification may land you, never give way to this spirit of murmuring and of disputing, and avoid it all by reminding yourself of these things concerning God and his gracious purpose with respect to you.

16

Essentially Different

> Do all things without murmurings and disputings: that ye
> may be blameless and harmless, the sons of God, without
> rebuke, in the midst of a crooked and perverse nation,
> among whom ye shine as lights in the world; holding forth
> the word of life. (Phil. 2:14–16a)

I would remind you that we are still considering the exhortation of the Apostle to the church at Philippi, in which he urges them to work out their salvation with fear and trembling because it is God who is working in them both to will and to do of his good pleasure. That is his general exhortation and here in these verses he gives the Philippian Christians instructions and teaching as to how they are to do this. We have seen that the key to the understanding of the exhortation is that the Apostle puts his appeal to them in terms of the fact that they are children of God. That is the basis of the appeal: 'that ye may be blameless and harmless, the sons of God, without rebuke'. They are to do everything realising that they are the children of God: and in our last study we considered together the meaning of that term. We saw something of what is meant by that designation, and we began to consider the appeal which the Apostle makes in terms of this filial relationship to God.

Now the appeal which he makes is threefold: as children of God we are to consider ourselves, first of all, in our relationship to the Father; secondly, we are to consider our nature as children of God; and thirdly, we are to consider ourselves in our relationship to the world that is around and about us. That is the division of this exhortation in verses 14, 15 and the first part of verse 16. In our last study we considered the first of these subsidiary appeals – the child of God in his relationship to his Father, and Paul's exhortation to us was that we should 'do all things without murmurings and disputings'. Let there be no cloud of our own making between us and the face of God; let us always be confident and sure of his holy love with respect to us.

But we must come next to the second plane the Christian in and of himself or, if you like, in his relationship to himself. The Apostle puts the subject in terms of three words – 'blameless, harmless, without rebuke'. Now here we are looking at something of the essential nature of the Christian as a child of God. In the light, then, of our relationship to God, what do these terms mean?

The first thing the Apostle tells us is that we must be *blameless*. This is a term that, in a sense, explains itself. It means that we should be unblameable; that there should be nothing to blame in us, nothing at all at which anyone can point a critical finger. Perhaps the best way of putting it is to say that 'blameless' is a description of – or has reference to – moral integrity manifesting itself externally. In other words, this term is one which calls us so to live that those who are around us, looking at us and observing us, will never be able to see or find anything in us which is worthy of blame, or of criticism, or of reprimand. The emphasis here is not so much on what I should be in myself, in my inward nature, as on my appearance amongst others who are observing me.

This is something which is really so self-evident that it needs no elaboration at all. We surely must realise, at a time like this, that as Christian people we are being carefully scrutinised and watched in every relationship in life. It may be a trite thing to say, but the world always judges not only Christianity, but our Lord himself, and even God, by what it sees in us who name his name and profess to be Christians. Therefore, says the Apostle, at all times and in all places, and in every conceivable circumstance, whether in your personal life, your moral life, your home life, your business or professional life, or wherever you may chance to be, see to it that there shall be nothing which anyone can criticise. There must be no evidence of sin or failure, you must be blameless.

Again, the pattern is that of our Lord and Saviour Jesus Christ himself. You remember how he was able to turn upon his accusers one day and say to them, 'Which of you convinceth me of sin?' (John 8:46). His life was blameless; no one could point the finger at him, there was nothing reprehensible. As men looked at him and his life, and all that he was and did, they could find nothing to criticise morally, and the Apostle's exhortation to us is that we should be men and women like that, that our life should be beyond the reach of criticism. It is elementary and it is simple, and yet I think that most of us would agree that it is one of the things that we tend to forget. Above all, and especially at a time like this, the call is obvious. We are children of God, and as a parent sending out the child to a party or to school, says, 'Now, mind you behave. Remember to whom you belong', so God, in a sense, is saying that to us. We are his children and we are to live in such a way that no disrepute is ever brought to his holy name through us. By our lives we are to indicate that we belong to him, and in our lives there should be nothing worthy of rebuke.

Then the second word is *harmless*. Now this does not mean that you do not do harm to others – the word is a little misleading. A better way of translating it would be innocent, unmixed, simple, pure, or unadulterated. As 'blameless' was a description of moral integrity manifesting itself externally, so 'harmless' is moral integrity manifesting itself inwardly or internally. With this word, we are considering not so much what I am as I appear to others in my conduct and behaviour, but what I really am in and of myself, in those hidden recesses of my being, which are not visible to anybody outside. The Apostle says I should be harmless; I should be innocent, removed altogether from that which is sinful; I must be pure and unadulterated – there should be no admixture.

You see how the Apostle is proceeding in a logical order? As a Christian man I stand first of all in a world that is looking at the outside, and he puts that first. But if I want to be quite sure that my external conduct and behaviour are always going to be right, then I must of necessity pay attention to those inner springs of conduct. What I am and do is, in a sense, the result of what I really am, and that is why the Apostle brings in that word harmless. In other words, we must not only not do things which are wrong, we must not even think them.

There is a perfect illustration of what I am trying to say in the Sermon on the Mount where our Lord gives the position of the ancient law on this. Our Lord said that the commandment, 'Thou shalt not commit adultery' really includes this: 'Whosoever looketh on a woman to lust after her hath committed adultery with her already in his heart' (Matt. 5:27, 28). To lust or desire is, in the kingdom of God, as damnable as the deed; to covet is as reprehensible as to steal. Not only must my action be beyond blame and criticism, but my thought, the springs of action, the motive of these things, must also be utterly free from that which is evil and sinful. We must be blameless and harmless, the children of a God who 'cannot be tempted with evil, neither tempteth he any man' (Jas. 1:13); and who is, 'The Father of lights, with whom is no variableness, neither shadow of turning' (Jas. 1:17). There is no darkness in him; he is purity and utter absolute holiness, unadulterated with any evil. That is the ultimate standard for Christian people; blameless, yes, but also harmless. That is to be our essential nature.

Then Paul uses still another term in order to complete his description — 'without rebuke' which is a summary of the other two, for it means with no blemish at all. There should be nothing in the Christian which in any way can mar this perfect specimen. There should be no speck or spot, no indication of disease. That is the standard, or pattern, which is set for the Christian in the New Testament, that is the goal to which we should be striving and the position we should be seeking to attain. And the ultimate reason for all this is that we are the children of God and there is nothing too good for us. We are to be more and more like our Father. Thank God there is a promise there in the New Testament that one day we shall be blameless, spotless and without rebuke. For there is one who 'is able to keep you from falling', and who will 'present you faultless before the presence of his glory with exceeding joy' (Jude 24), and in the meantime our business is to be striving after these things. My goal for myself, my standard for my whole life should be that – to become blameless and harmless and without any blemish whatsoever.

But now you observe that the Apostle exhorts us to all this not only because he is concerned about us, nor simply because all these things matter, but because he is so concerned about the Christian in his relationship to the world that is around and about him. We have seen our relationship to our Father, we have considered ourselves as children of God, and now we come to the third of these three main divisions – the Christian in his relationship to the world. This is always the motive which we find impressed upon us in the New Testament exhortation to holiness. There is never a suggestion that we should become monks, or hermits or acolytes, in order that we might become holy. No, we are called to be blameless, the sons of God, partly because of our status and position, but also because of the world in which we live, and because of what God has said we should do to that world and in that world; it is a highly practical reason.

Here again, of course, we are face to face with one of the great exhortations of the Bible, this appeal to Christian people to consider themselves in their relationship to the world that is around them. It is not confined to the New Testament, you find it in the Old quite as definitely. God chose the Children of Israel to be his people, and all those rules and regulations which you find in the books of Exodus, Leviticus, Numbers and Deuteronomy, are nothing but a great elaboration of this appeal that we are considering together here. God said to the Children of Israel, You are my people, and because you are my people you must live a different kind of life, you must separate yourselves from all those other nations: 'Ye shall be holy; for I am holy' (Lev. 11:45) – that is the great appeal.

And how urgently this appeal is needed by Christian people at this present hour! We are a small and dwindling company, but we are concerned about the world, and the first thing we must realise is our relationship to that world, our responsibility with respect to it, and that to which God calls us in view of this relationship. Never, perhaps, has this problem been more urgent and never, perhaps, has it been more difficult than it is today; that is why we should take our time as we consider the terms of the Apostle's appeal.

Now what do I mean exactly when I talk about the Christian's relationship to the world? Well 'the world' here really means the mentality and the mode of life of those who are not Christians. I do not mean the world in a material or physical sense, but in the sense of 'cosmos'; the outlook and the way of looking at things that characterises those who are not the children of God. So then, we shall consider the Christian in his relationship to the world, in that particular sense, and the first thing that Paul tells us is that the Christian is to be essentially different from the world. The very words and terms employed by the Apostle – blameless, harmless, without rebuke – make this abundantly clear.

These terms are especially significant when I contrast them with the words that the Apostle uses to describe the world itself. The world, he tells us, is crooked and perverse. Let us stop for a moment to look at these words also. The word 'crooked' means that which is dishonest, that which manifests itself externally as being perverted and twisted. It is crookedness in action, in demeanour and behaviour. Perverse, on the other hand, describes an inward quality. It means an inward, distorted nature. So you see the perfect balance that is observed here. Blameless, says the Apostle, is the opposite to crooked, while harmless is the opposite to perverseness. It is in that way that Paul enforces upon us this great principle that as Christian people, children of God, we are to be altogether and essentially different from those who are not Christian. A non-Christian is crooked, not straight; you look at him and you see a twist and turn in all his conduct and action. But Christian behaviour is to be without twist and turn, it is a blameless life.

And if you look at the two persons in an internal sense, you will find the same principle. The Christian is to be innocent, harmless, pure and unadulterated, there are to be no twists or pleats in his nature and character, while the essential characteristic of the ungodly, and of the non-Christian, is that he is perverse, twisted and perverted. His very nature is crooked, in addition to his actions, for the action arises out of the nature. So there we see that the child of God, obviously and of necessity, is to be essentially different from someone who is not a Christian.

But perhaps the Apostle brings out this contrast most of all in the next phrase he employs, in which he tells us that we are to appear, or shine, as *lights in the world*. Lights really means luminaries. It is the term that is generally used for the moon and for the stars in the heavens. So that the Christian in this world, says the Apostle, is to be similar to the moon and to the stars shining in the night. Now the first thing that we are taught there, again, is that the Christian is to be absolutely and essentially different, as the moon and the stars differ from the darkness not only in appearance, but in their essential nature. The nature of light is essentially different from the nature of darkness, and Paul says that we are to be what the light is to the darkness, what the stars and the moon are to the darkness of the night. Our holiness is represented as standing out in this striking contrast to the darkness and the night of sin and of evil in this world in which we live.

But perhaps all these terms which are used by the Apostle are quite unnecessary; there is a sense in which the whole thing has already been put by the very phrase, 'sons of God'. There is a saying that 'breeding tells' or that 'family counts' and there is a way in which that is perfectly true. You can tell a great deal about the parents if you know the children. Very often the children are a reflection of their own parents, and by observing the child, and its conduct, you discover a great deal about the parents and the home in which the child has been brought up. Now, Paul says, we are children of God. This, as we saw, is only true of Christian people and the world is divided into those who are Christian and those who are not. So, does it not follow, of necessity, that there must be a striking difference between the two groups? Can we say that we are partakers of the divine nature, that God is our Father, that we have been schooled and taught by God through the Holy Spirit, while we lack this quality of being in an entirely different position by birth and nature and training and everything else? The tragedy is that being conscious of the divine nature within us, we do not long to show that we are essentially different.

Am I being unfair when I suggest that perhaps the greatest contrast between the Christian of the present century, especially of the last twenty years or so, and the Christian of the Puritan era and of the eighteenth century (and, indeed, many of the Christians of the last century too), is that of their attitude towards being essentially different from the non-Christian world? I suppose the first world war was very largely responsible for this, when there was the kind of Chaplain in the Army who made himself very popular, and was looked upon as a very fine Christian, because he was so remarkably like everybody else. He did everything that everybody else did – 'What a fine Christian,' people said. Now that is not the New Testament way of describing a Christian. Christians are not people who are remarkably like everybody else though they are Christians. They are children of God and not children of the world or of the devil and they are to be entirely different from everybody else.

Shame on us so-called Christian people for having this unworthy desire to be so like the world, and for having this fear of standing out in contrast. I can put it like this – because the Old Testament puts so perfectly everything that I am trying to say – the Christian is to be a man like Moses. When Moses went up to the Mount for an interview with God, the result of that interview and of his communion and fellowship with God was that his face began to shine, and when he came down from the Mountain to the plain his face was radiant, still reflecting something of the holiness of God. The Children of Israel saw it and were overawed, and he had to put a veil over his face while he spoke to them. You and I are to be people like that; something of the radiance of God is to be on our face and in the whole of our personality, so that, of necessity, we stand out in society as lights in the world, as luminaries in the heavens.

But let me go on to the second point. In our relationship to the world as Christian people, we are to rebuke and to warn the world. Once more the term which the Apostle employs makes these things perfectly clear: we are to live as lights in the world. Consider what Scripture says about this in John 3:20, 'For every one that doeth evil hateth the light, neither cometh to the light, lest his deeds should be reproved.' Or again: 'But all things that are reproved are made manifest by the light: for whatsoever doth make manifest is light,' says Paul in Ephesians 5:13. One of the functions of light is to reprove and to make manifest the works of darkness.

Now you and I, as Christian people, as children of God, are to be as lights in the world. It means that because we are what we are, and who we are, we are to reprove, we are to unmask, we are to expose, the hidden works of darkness that are around and about us. Our business in society at this present time is to make men and women see the kind of life they are living, and the way for us to do that is to live a life which is the exact opposite of theirs. We are to make the world see what it has become, as the result of sin and evil, by being lights ourselves and exposing these works. Let me, then, suggest some of the ways in which we are to do that at a time like this, how we are to present this striking contrast in this muddled, immoral world.

First of all there is the matter of appearance. I suggest to you that the world is becoming loud in its appearance, bold, arrogant and aggressive. How often does one see a person today whom one feels an instinctive inclination to describe as being humble? There is a boldness, an aggressiveness, a high-mindedness, which manifests itself in the external appearance. I do not hesitate to suggest that at a time like this Christian people should be reproving the hidden works of darkness even in their dress, with all the suggestiveness and the insinuations of sin that are to be found in the very dress and clothing. I wonder, Christian people, whether we consider these things as we ought? Is it not evident that the whole organisation of these things is of the devil and of the flesh and of that which is unworthy? So I suggest that our very appearance should be different, it should be a rebuke to the loudness and the insinuations of sin.

Let me give you another example. In our speech we should rebuke the hidden works of darkness. Have you noticed the appalling increase in swearing, in cursing and in oaths, how this has become almost current in the language of most people? As Christian people we are to present this contrast, and we are to rebuke the foulness of language and expression.

Then there is the importance of truth and of accuracy of speech and statement. The lying and the falsehood which are current around and about us are appalling, alarming and frightening. Christian people, by just speaking the truth, we shall rebuke the works of evil and shall convict the world of its sin.

Let me mention another very important matter, the question of honesty. Is there anything more alarming than the petty pilfering and thieving, the robbery and the dishonesty that is becoming increasingly characteristic of life in this country? Christian people, we are to present a contrast by being scrupulously honest. This is not just so that we may be seen to be different, but that we may bring men and women to see the wrongness of their lives; and it is our business to convict them.

Then there is our attitude towards work. One of the great problems of today is the attitude of the average man towards work. His idea is that you do the minimum and obtain the maximum. Work is being regarded as a nuisance;

men think that they ought to be entitled to live in a constant round of pleasure and, therefore, when they do work they do the minimum. This attitude is common to every single class of society and it is altogether wrong. I feel that this is where you and I can bear a particularly striking testimony. If you are in an office or profession, be all out at your work, be honest, work with all your might, do the best job you are capable of doing, and thereby show the world that is around and about you what it means to be a Christian, and the essential sinfulness of this false attitude towards work and labour. Let us earn the money that we receive; let us be scrupulous in our attitude towards work.

And then I cannot but mention the whole question of marriage, and the marriage relationship. We are all aware of the breakdown of marriage on all sides. What a wonderful opportunity we have of testifying for Christ by just showing the difference which being a Christian makes to the married state. Let us, therefore, in our married relationships show how Christ binds together two persons in holy love. Let our married life stand out in contrast in today's world, as stars in the heavens stand out in the night, or as the moon in her shining. Let our conception of marriage and home be a rebuke to the world; let us so live in this relationship that people of the world looking at us shall say, 'Would to God we could live like that; would to God we were as happy as they are; would to God our homes were as those Christian ones!' Is there this contrast, this difference? That is what Paul is calling us to, indeed it applies to the whole of life. The world is selfish and self-centred. It thinks of itself and its own interests, and does not consider anybody else. We have in a sense already been considering this in the first part of the chapter where Paul says, 'Look not every man on his own things, but every man also on the things of others.'

And so, that is the Apostle's exhortation, and the question to us is, how do you react to it? Do you feel that I have been rather narrow in coming down to details? Do you feel like saying, 'Ah, but that is the old Puritan life, so narrow and cramped and confined'? My friend, my reply to you is, it is the New Testament! It is just asking you to be as different from the world that is around and about you as the Lord Jesus Christ himself was; to be harmless and blameless, to be without rebuke. If you are a child of God and say that you love your Father and want to honour and bring glory to his name, then this is the appeal. We must expose and unmask the licentiousness and the evil, the arrogance and the loudness, the horror of the immorality of the modern world. We are to bring it all to light by flashing the light of holiness upon it. And, as I have already said, we are not only to rebuke it in that way, we are also to warn the world. As the lighthouse warns the ship against submerged rocks that are going to wreck it, so you and I are called, in this age and generation, to warn men and women who are around and about us that their works not only lead to moral muddle now, but that they are going to lead to further failures also. This moral failure may ruin the country, it may destroy the whole commonwealth of nations to which we belong, as it destroyed ancient Rome. Rome fell because of moral rot at the centre, and that always leads to destruction in every sense. We are to warn them of this, and we are to warn them that ahead lies death, the judgment of God, and everlasting destruction.

In the next study, we must go on to consider the positive part of the appeal, which is that we should be holding forth the word of life. But we finish now with this negative exhortation; we are to live in such a way that the world will be convicted by us. By being lights we shall expose the hidden, submerged, things of darkness. By being what we are, we shall solemnly warn this crooked and twisted, perverse, immoral generation of its terrible and alarming danger, and of the certain nemesis and doom and ultimate final judgment that will descend upon it, unless it repents and turns to the Lord.

Oh, blessed privilege of being a child of God, oh, dread responsibility of representing such a Father in such an age and at such a time.

17

The Word of Life

Do all things without murmurings and disputings: that ye
may be blameless and harmless, the sons of God, without
rebuke, in the midst of a crooked and perverse nation,
among whom ye shine as lights in the world; holding forth
the word of life. (Phil. 2:14–16a)

We are now completing our consideration of the description
which is given here of the Christian in this world, as a child
of God. We have seen that Christians are meant to be
entirely different, a complete contrast to the world around
them. As lights in the world, they are meant to stand out in
society, to expose the hidden things of darkness and to warn
people against certain consequences which will happen
unless they pay heed and give attention to the Christian
message. But I ended the last study by saying that that is not
all. There is still one other thing about Christians as children
of God, especially as 'lights', and the Apostle here tells us
what it is. In the sixteenth verse he says: 'holding forth
the word of life'. We do not finish our witness by just exposing
the other type of life, and by warning of the consequences
which are certain to follow. Light has a positive function: it
is to impart knowledge and to give instruction. This is something, again, which is really quite self-evident. We have certain terms in current use in our language which really say
everything that we are talking about. We talk about the 'enlightenment' of a person – you enlighten him about the state
of his health or his business; in other words, you throw light
on to it. You not only expose certain dangers, but also, in

209

order to help and instruct him, you enlighten him as to the way in which he should conduct himself or the way in which he should live and walk. The eighteenth century is generally described as 'the Enlightenment', and that was particularly true in Germany, where you have the origin of the great school of philosophy which proudly gave itself that name. It claimed that whereas mankind hitherto had been left in a state of semi-darkness as the result of ignorance, it had discovered the light and the truth, and was thus in a position to teach the people and the nations.

Now this is an essential part of the work of light. Light is here to throw its beams upon the road, upon the way; it is a kind of headlamp which shows us the direction we are to go. Light not only helps us to avoid certain things, it also indicates the route. And that is the last thing which the Apostle tells us here about the function of Christians in their relationship to the world. They are to enlighten and teach it; they are, in other words, to hold forth this word of life, which is, of course, but another term for the gospel of our Lord and Saviour Jesus Christ.

Now I regard this as being of such crucial importance that it did seem to me to be very wrong just to rush this and include it at the end of the last study. The Apostle himself gives great prominence to it, and I think that there are various reasons which behove us to concentrate upon it. For the Apostle is here writing, not to ministers, and church leaders only, but to the whole church, indeed to the individual members of the church at Philippi. This is something, which, according to Paul, every church member should be doing, and when, for instance, we sing our hymns about the Church holding forth the word of life, we must realise that that means every single one of us. There is a constant danger of thinking of the Church only in terms of its preachers or ministers or clergymen, and the idea that every single member of the Church is to be 'holding forth the word of life', has somehow or other fallen into the background.

Yet, if I understand the current scene at all, nothing can be a greater mistake at the present time. We are all, I think, aware of the fact that it is no longer the habit or fashion for people to attend a place of worship, as they did a hundred years ago. Then, it was the custom for people to listen to the preaching of the word of God, and there was a sense in which it could be rightly said that the business of holding forth the word of life devolved mainly upon the minister. But everybody knows that that is not the case today. There was never a time when the individual church member was more important than today, and if God's word is to be propagated and spread, it must be done by individuals in their daily contacts.

It was like that in the early period of the Church. We often bemoan our present state, but I sometimes think we have one very great advantage over those who lived in the last century, in that our world today is so remarkably like that of the early Church. There is a sense, therefore, in which we can understand this gospel better than they could. Think of the mid-Victorian era with its affluence, and its success and comfort, with no major wars in the world, and everything at peace. It must have been very difficult for them to understand the background to the New Testament, with its sense of doom and urgency. I imagine that in certain respects those Victorians must have found the New Testament a very strange book.

We, with all our troubles, have, at any rate, the means of understanding the Bible in a way that they had not, and I have no doubt it was that which accounted so often for the fact that they quite unconsciously began to wander away from the true emphasis of the New Testament. They assumed that this country was Christian and, therefore, they ceased to preach a gospel which was evangelistic, assuming that every one born in this land was Christian, and only needed to be taught in the gospel. We, however, living in an age when the foundations are shaking, do, I think, understand the background of the New Testament – why the world is as it is. We know what doom and disaster mean, we know something of the urgency of the times and the uncertainty of the whole situation. We know what it is to experience the Church as just a little handful of people in a great mass of society that is pagan in its very essence, a society that does not understand the Church and is not interested in it.

Now in a situation like that we must realise that certain duties devolve upon us as individual Christians and this is one of them – the propagation of the gospel. This is not only something that you and I must do, we are the only people who can do it, and if we do not hold forth this word of life, then the world is going to remain in ignorance and in darkness. It is an appeal to every single Christian, and it brings home to us the tremendous responsibility that rests upon us at this present hour.

Let us consider first of all what this exhortation of the Apostle tells us about ourselves. We are to realise that all our behaviour and all our conduct is to lead to this, namely, the holding forth of the word of life. As we saw in our last study, the Apostle has told us that we are to be blameless and harmless, and without rebuke. Yes, but we must also be clear as to *why* we are to be like that, and why we are to live this kind of life. According to Paul, it is all designed to enable us, ultimately, to hold forth this word of life. Let me put it like this. The appeal to the Christian is not only an appeal to us to be moral, it is that, of course, but it is more than that; it is not only a negative appeal, it is a positive one too.

Now there are many good people in the world who by life and good living are exposing the hidden things of darkness. Any man who conducts his business in an honest and true way is doing that; so are people who have a moral code and live up to it. There are people in professions, in business, in various walks of life who, because they are upright, moral and good and because they have their standards, expose, in that way, the hidden things of darkness. They are recognised in the circles in which they turn, as being people on whom you may rely. 'You do not need any guarantee from them,' others say of them, 'their word is as good as their bond. They are upright people whom you can trust'. Such people expose the hidden things of darkness, and are a warning to those who are going the wrong way, but they stop at that. Their whole position is a negative one and that is not to be so of the Christian. Our morality and ethics are but an introduction to our gospel. We are to be blameless, harmless sons of God, that we may hold forth the word of life.

In other words, all that I am as a Christian, all that I do and say, and all that I refrain from doing, is nothing but a kind of introduction to my soul. It is the background to my picture, the condition in which I live. It is a pointer to what is true about me; it is an indication of something which is still more vital. Now that, I think, is a very important principle. We are not *just* to be different, nor are we simply to live a good life for the sake of that in and of itself. The Christian, in this world and life, is in an essentially positive position. He does not merely rebuke that which is wrong, he is able to point out that which is right. He does not just expose the hidden things of darkness, he shows the true things, he has something positive to give and contribute.

The second thing, therefore, that this exhortation tells us about ourselves is that it must always be perfectly clear to the world that you and I, as Christians, are what we are because of the gospel. There must be no uncertainty whatsoever as to the motive, and the spring, and the origin, of all that we do and are. It must be perfectly plain and clear to everybody, that the thing that is responsible for us is this gospel, this word of life, about which the Apostle is speaking. This, again, is a very important principle. You look at a man, and you see that he is living a good life; he is the kind of moral, ethical person whom I have just described. You see that he is different from the vast majority and that there is much about him that you admire. But you somehow get the impression that he is like that because he happens to have been born that way. He was born with that nice nature, and there is something about him which almost makes it impossible to think of him being anything else. And you say to yourself, 'Well, I wish I could be like that man, but I seem to have been born different.'

But that is not the impression the Christian makes. As Christians we should always be giving the impression that we would not be what we are were it not for this gospel. All our conduct and conversation, our behaviour, our every activity, should always be pointing to the gospel of Jesus Christ as the only explanation of what we are doing, as the only adequate motivation for our conduct. We are to be blameless and harmless, the children of God without rebuke, in the midst of a crooked and perverse generation, among whom we shine as lights in the world, holding forth the word of life, by our being what we are as well as by our speaking.

We can put it like this. When others see us, they should be asking these questions: 'What is the secret of these people? Why are they as they are? What is the explanation of their conduct? Why do they stand out like that? Why do they seem to be so different?' You are so to live, says Paul, that when men ask those questions, they are bound to get this as the only answer: 'These people are what they are because they are Christians; they are like that because of this gospel which they believe. They have been made what they are by that word of life, about which they are always speaking.' The whole of our conduct and behaviour is to be a prelude to the gospel.

And that brings me to the third and last point on the subject of what this exhortation tells us about the Christian. It is quite obvious, is it not, that the Christian is a man who has life – 'holding forth the word of life'. There should never be anything mechanical about the Christian, never anything set and formal. That is the trouble with the mere moralist. He is very complete and perfect, he is a paragon of all the virtues, but it is a machine-like morality; he seems to be living according to rules and regulations. There is something almost horribly exacting about him – the perfection of the machine. He is not alive like a flower or a plant; there is no life there; it is man-made perfection; how perfect, yet how cold! He is lacking something essential, something living and vital. Now that is never true about the Christian. The

Christian is a man who is alive, and that is why he is interested in the word of life.

There, then, are some of the things that the exhortation tells us about ourselves. But let me go on to the second matter, and look at this exhortation from the standpoint of what it tells us about the gospel. You and I are called to hold it forth, and here Paul describes it in this most fascinating and picturesque manner. He calls it 'the word of life', and what a wonderful description it is of the gospel! You will find it often repeated by the preachers of the centuries and by the writers of the hymns; for example:

> We love the word of Life
> The Word that tells of peace.
> *William Bullock*
> *Henry Williams Baker*

– and that is one reason why we like coming to the house of God. So what exactly does the Apostle mean by this description of the gospel? Why should we always remind ourselves when we preach it, or talk to people about it, that it is the word of life? Let me suggest some reasons. First, and above everything else, we must always guard against the terrible danger of turning the gospel into a philosophy. The Apostle Paul was aware of this danger: 'Beware lest any man spoil you through philosophy,' he said to the Colossians (2:8), and he told the Corinthians that he did not use 'wisdom of words, lest the cross of Christ should be made of none effect' (1 Cor. 1:17).

Of course, it is the simplest thing in the world to turn the gospel into a philosophy by thinking of it as a collection of thoughts and ideas, and as a philosophical outlook. There are various ways of looking at life, people say. There are subdivisions of philosophy: the purely materialistic view, the idealistic, the pessimistic, and so on, and then, amongst others, there is this Christian view. And it is very fascinating to think of it as just a philosophy and as a number of thoughts and ideas. When Paul preached in Athens, we are told that that was the first impression that he apparently made upon the people. 'What will this babbler say?' they said; they were so interested in philosophy. And people still often say things like – 'I find Christianity frightfully interesting, what a fascinating view of life it is!' Or they say about the Bible, 'What an interesting book to study!' My dear friends, when you only find the Bible 'interesting' it means you are regarding it as a philosophy. The Bible is a terrifying book if it is read through, because it gets beneath the realm of ideas and thoughts and concepts. It is a living word, it is able to pierce 'to the dividing asunder of soul and spirit, and of the joints and marrow' (Heb. 4:12).

Now that is the kind of thing the Apostle is saying here. The gospel is not a philosophy; we are not here simply to put forth ideas, or thoughts, to the world. No, it is the word of life, the word that does things. It is the word that is full of power, and which is mighty and active. 'Is not my word,' says the Lord to Jeremiah, 'like a hammer that breaketh the rocks in pieces?' (23:29) – the gospel of Christ which is 'the power of God unto salvation to everyone that believeth' (Rom. 1:16). It is alive, it is not merely a theory, an idea, a philosophy, a point of view, something to be considered, something to be interested in, something to analyse, as if it were a crossword puzzle. No, it is alive, it is the word of life.

But why is it called the word of life? Let me suggest some answers. It is first and foremost *the word that tells us about life*, and this is something that I must sub-divide still further. The first thing it does is to tell us that we are dead. That is always the first statement of the word of life, it is a word about death. The first thing that it tells us is that, by nature, we are all dead in trespasses and sins. Man goes on living in this state in the world until this word comes to him, and then he discovers that he is spiritually dead. The word makes him see that he has been living life on the level of the flesh and of the animal. It tells him that there is another kind of life, and that we are meant to live in communion with God – 'And this is life eternal, that they might know thee the only true God, and Jesus Christ, whom thou has sent' (John 17:3).

We see that we have been living on a number of assumptions. We have been so concerned and occupied about doing business, and making contacts with other people, that we have never considered that 'something else' which is called the spiritual. We have never thought of the fact that there is another realm altogether, a realm that has been right outside our whole life and conduct. We have been spiritually dead, 'dead in trespasses and sins'. We have had nothing but the horizontal view of life, and have forgotten the vertical; we have been living on the lower level and have forgotten the heights above; we have been dead to certain unseen spiritual realities, which are the only true realities. And this word comes to us and makes us see that we are dead; it is the word of life that speaks about death and exposes our whole natural condition.

But, of course, and thank God for this, it does not stop at that. Having made us see that we are utterly lifeless, it then begins to tell us about this other kind of life. It does not just tell us to pull ourselves together and to live a better life, it does something infinitely greater than that: it tells us that another order of life is possible for us. We find this put so clearly in those words our Lord spoke to Nicodemus. Nicodemus was a very able man, a master and teacher in Israel; he knew all about the law and he was a highly moral man. He had been watching our Lord, and then one night he went to him and said, 'Rabbi, we know that thou art a teacher come from God: for no man can do these miracles that thou doest, except God be with him' (John 3:2). 'Now,' said Nicodemus in effect, 'I can see something about you that I have not got; you have got something extra, what is it?' You remember the answer that came flashing back? 'Verily, verily I say unto thee, Except a man be born of water and the Spirit, he cannot enter into the kingdom of God ... Ye must be born again' (vv. 5, 7). You need a new life, a new birth. You cannot get it by thinking about it, you cannot get it by working for it. It is something that comes to you from God, it is being 'born from above', being 'born of the Spirit'.

The gospel tells us about this whole order of life. It tells us that even in this life and world we can enter, as it were, into an entirely new life, where God becomes not a term or a proposition, but a reality, where we know him. 'This is life eternal, *that they might know thee ...*' (John 17:3). It tells us about a fellowship that is possible with God and with our Lord Jesus Christ through the Holy Spirit – 'our fellowship is with the Father, and with his Son Jesus Christ' (1 John 1:3). We write unto you, said John, in his first epistle, that you may also have this life and fellowship. It tells us that whatever we may be by nature, and however much wrong we may have done in life, we can be given a new life, and be made 'new men'. We can be surprised at ourselves. It tells us that however weak our wills may be, we can receive strength and power that will lift us out of the pit and vortex of evil, and enable us to walk on a new and higher level.

It tells us about this wonderful spiritual life that is possible to us even in the world of flesh, and it goes further and says how that life is to be obtained. It tells us that we are so dead in trespasses and sins that we can never raise ourselves out of that grave. But, thank God, it tells us that Jesus of Nazareth was none other than the only begotten Son of God, and that he came all the way from heaven and its glory, and imposed those limits upon himself, in order that he might come down to earth. Not only that, he went down into the pit, he took upon himself your guilt and mine and he made atonement for it. He has taken away the barrier between us and God – the thing that had blinded our eyes – and has raised us up. He has taken hold of us by identifying himself with us; he gives us his own nature, and there we receive this life. He sends the Holy Spirit and we receive power and understanding and development. All these things are given us by Christ, the Word of life.

That is the word that you and I are to hold before men and women at a time like this. Our business is to tell them that their main trouble is that they are spiritually dead. We are to have a great heart of compassion for them – which is why I never denounce the way in which people are living. I mention it, but I trust I mention it with a heart that is partly broken. They cannot help living as they do; they are dead, without spiritual life, and we are to show them their condition, and tell them about this other life that is possible to them; we are to show them how it becomes possible in Christ. This gospel is the word that tells about life.

But it is also *the word that gives life*. James puts it like this: 'Of his own will begat he us with the word of truth, that we should be kind of firstfruits of his creatures' (Jas. 1:18). We have been begotten by the word of truth. Or, again, Peter says, 'Being born again, not of corruptible seed, but of incorruptible, by the word of God ...' (1 Pet. 1:23). It is this word that gives men the re-birth, the second birth, new life. When this word of truth, this seed of life, has been implanted and engrafted into the souls of men, it gives the life. What a wonderful word!

Yes, but I must mention still another thing it does. It is *the word that supports life*, that feeds it, and sustains it. Listen again to Peter: 'As newborn babes, desire the sincere', or unadulterated, 'milk of the word' – why? – 'that ye may grow thereby' (1 Pet. 2:2). This word is full of spiritual vitamins; it is not one of those synthetic foods that may just give a limited amount of nutriment; rather it is a word which gives life. If you want to grow you must drink this milk, it has life-imparting, life-sustaining qualities. If you take it, it will build you up, you will grow and develop, your muscles will be strengthened and your whole quality of life will increase.

And, lastly, it is *the word that shows us how to live this life* which we have been given, and we have already considered. This is the word which is the lamp and the light that shows us how to walk; it exposes to us the ills and the dangers, it shows us our relationship to God and the life he would have us live.

The gospel is the word of life in all these various respects, and here, according to the Apostle, is the call to us, especially at a time like this. We are to hold forth this word of life. How do we do it? I have to some extent already answered that question. We do it first by being what we are. We do it by being blameless, harmless, without rebuke. We do it by showing that we have life in us, so that men and women looking at us say, 'What is it that they have got? How can they keep so calm? What is it about them?' We must live in the way that a man like D. L. Moody lived. I read recently a story told by President Woodrow Wilson of how he was in a barber's shop one day, when suddenly a man came in. He was rather a stoutish man, nothing to look at, and yet the moment he came in everything changed in that barber's saloon; conversation changed; there was an obvious and evident difference. When this stoutish man had gone out, Woodrow Wilson asked the barber, 'Who was that man?' And he received the reply, 'That was Dwight L. Moody.' Moody did not preach in that barber's saloon, he was just being the Christian he was; there had been a radiance about him, and, by being himself, he was holding forth the word of life.

And, thank God, that is not confined to people like D. L. Moody. It is still happening among quite ordinary people whom the world will never know or hear about. I was, for example, told of a Christian young man who had gone into the Air Force. He was being badly handled one night by some of his mates who had been drinking, and the very way in which he took it, his manliness, his refusal to grumble, his just being what he was, so affected the ringleader of that crowd that he began to take an interest in Christian things. He wondered what it was that this young man had. He felt he would rather like to be like that, and he began to take an interest in that young man and in the gospel of Jesus Christ. I know there are many who have had the same experience and that is the sort of thing I am speaking about – the holding forth of the word of life. If you do that men will see and will ask, 'What is this?' and they will come and talk and so give you the opportunity to tell them. We hold forth the word of life by being what we are, but we must know the gospel exactly; we must be able to explain it; we must be able to help a soul in agony; we must be able to tell people how they become Christians and to explain what it means. We must hold forth this word of life that is able to give men the very life of God himself and to prepare them for eternity in his holy presence.

Beloved Christian people, let us be up and doing; let us take the torch of the word of God, and wave it abroad, so that the darkness of the world may be illumined, and men and women may be translated from the kingdom of darkness to the kingdom of Light, to the kingdom of God's dear Son. What a privilege we have to be lights, to be light bearers, at this dark and difficult hour in the history of the world.

18

Even unto Death

… holding forth the word of life; that I may rejoice in the day of Christ, that I have not run in vain, neither laboured in vain. Yea, and if I be offered upon the sacrifice and service of your faith, I joy, and rejoice with you all. For the same cause also do ye joy, and rejoice with me. But I trust in the Lord Jesus to send Timotheus shortly unto you, that I also may be of good comfort, when I know your state. For I have no man likeminded, who will naturally care for your state. For all seek their own, not the things which are Jesus Christ's. But ye know the proof of him, that, as a son with the father, he hath served with me in the gospel. Him therefore I hope to send presently, so soon as I shall see how it will go with me. But I trust in the Lord that I also myself shall come shortly. Yet I supposed it necessary to send to you Epaphroditus, my brother, and companion in labour, and fellowsoldier, but your messenger, and he that ministered to my wants. For he longed after you all, and was full of heaviness, because that ye had heard that he had been sick. For indeed he was sick nigh unto death: but God had mercy on him; and not on him only, but on me also, lest I should have sorrow upon sorrow. I sent him therefore the more carefully, that, when ye see him again, ye may rejoice, and that I may be the less sorrowful. Receive him therefore in the Lord with all gladness; and hold such in reputation: because for the work of Christ he was nigh unto death, not regarding his life, to supply your lack of service toward me. (Phil. 2:16–30)

In our studies of this epistle of Paul to the Philippians, we come now to consider the section which is to be found in the second chapter from verse 16 to the end of the chapter. Departing from our customary method, which rather tends to be microscopic, we are going to take what might be termed the telescopic view. There is, you notice, a kind of break in the Apostle's argument half way through the first half of the sixteenth verse. He has been speaking very high doctrine, that of the incarnation and of the essential nature of the Christian life, as it is worked in us by God and as we are thus exhorted to work it out. Great doctrinal questions were raised for us by that statement alone. But, now, suddenly, the Apostle seems to turn to personal matters. He talks about himself; he tells them how he is hoping to be able to send Timothy to them in order that he may have a first-hand report of their state and condition, and in order that Timothy may likewise help and strengthen them. Furthermore, even before he can send Timothy, he is proposing to send Epaphroditus at once (probably, Epaphroditus carried this letter with him). Paul goes into detail, explaining how Epaphroditus had been desperately ill, almost on the very point of death itself, but how God had had mercy upon him and delivered him so that now Paul is able to send him back.

At first sight, this is really a very striking contrast to what we have been looking at together for so many studies. We have been considering heaven and the coming thence of the only begotten Son. Then, from these 'infinities and immensities' as Carlyle called them, we suddenly come down to ordinary, mundane, human family matters, the question of visits and illness, and things of that kind. It seems to be a complete break, yet all I want to try to do, as we take a hurried, composite view of this entire section of some fifteen verses, is to show you that in reality, of course, there is not a break at all. The Apostle is dealing with practical matters, and yet I think I shall be able to show you very easily that even in doing that, he is being thoroughly doctrinal and, in

a sense, is expounding the truth quite as much as he has
expounded it in the more specific and obviously doctrinal
and theological statements.

For the fact of the matter is, as we have seen, the Apostle
Paul cannot write about anything without being doctrinal.
There are no departments in this man's life – it is a whole.
He does not say, as it were, 'Here I am writing as a Christian, now I am writing as a man', because he has no room
for doctrinal dichotomy. The Christian is a man who cannot
say, 'I say this as a Christian, but I do this as something
else.' He is one, he is a whole, and the presence of any of
those artificial distinctions in our lives is a proclamation of
the fact that we are not Christian. Our Christianity is to
affect every part and portion of our activity. We are to act
as a whole, as one, as a unit, and this is why, if you take the
trouble to look, you will find that when the Apostle is dealing with the most ordinary matters conceivable, they are all
based upon doctrine. He cannot speak of man without
describing him in doctrinal terms and he cannot express his
own feelings in prison without doing exactly the same thing.

Here, therefore, we have something which we can put like
this. In this section we have a practical manifestation and
demonstration of what the Apostle has already been laying
down. Starting at verse 12 and going on to verse 16, he has
been giving this wonderful description of the Christian man.
He says: You are children of God, and as children of God
you must remember your relationship to him, in all your
conduct, in what you are in and of yourself and in your
relationship to the world outside; you are to work out this
great salvation with fear and trembling. Then in this practical section, it seems to me, he gives a demonstration of all
that, as it did actually work itself out in his life, in that of
Timothy and of Epaphroditus, and in the life of the members of the church at Philippi.

Now to me a very interesting question for discussion is to
which of these two types of teaching is ultimately of the greater value? I suppose, though, that is a foolish question, for
they are both valuable and they should never be compared;
it depends very largely upon our state and condition. There
are days and times when we feel physically, mentally and

spiritually fit and well, and we like doctrine, plain and unvarnished, in its pure unadulterated form. We can grapple with it and struggle with it, and it stimulates and comforts us. But there are times when we perhaps feel tired and weary in every respect, and, thank God, the Bible seems to know all that about us, and so it reminds us of this same doctrine in this practical form. We see it in action. It does not require great mental effort – we just see it. There is a charm about it, and we say, 'What a wonderful thing the Christian life is! I cannot today grapple with the doctrine of the incarnation, but I can admire people like Paul, and the church at Philippi.' In other words, there are mountains and valleys in the Scriptures; there is a glorious and wonderful variety, so that whatever our change of mood and state, there is always something here to help us. We are given this choice, as it were, but we are still doing the same thing in a slightly different manner. After the hard grappling and the studying in this spiritual university, we are taken on a little vacation and we have left our learning behind.

That, it seems to me, is the way to approach this truly interesting and fascinating section which we are now considering together. It is one of those charming (I do not hesitate to use the word) portrayals of the nature of the Christian life, which are to be found in the New Testament; a very wonderful picture of the life of a church. It is church life like this that really conquers the world, as it did the ancient world. Men and women saw something in the Christian society that they had never seen anywhere else. We get glimpses of it here, but just imagine its effect on any township or village or country district! And this has been repeated many times in history; every revival reproduces this kind of thing, and this, it seems to me, is the thing that is greatly needed in the world at the present time.

We can best summarise it in this way. Let us look for a moment at the character and nature of the Christian life as it is pictured here in general; and here there are two main comments. The first thing I observe is that it is a life which is dominated by the Lord Jesus Christ. You cannot read this section without seeing that. There are two verses in particular that bring this out: verses 19 and 24. 'But I trust in the Lord Jesus to send Timotheus shortly unto you, that I also may be of good comfort when I know your state' (19); 'But I trust in the Lord that I also myself shall come shortly' (24). Paul is incapable of thinking apart from Christ; he does not arrive at any decision except in terms of Christ. It was Christ who controlled the whole of his life and it is the Lord Jesus Christ who is going to decide whether or not he should send Timothy.

We can put this best perhaps by putting it negatively. Let me remind you of the position in which he was situated when he wrote these words. There he is in prison in Rome – the Emperor at that time seems to have been Nero – and yet the interesting thing is that Paul does not consider possibilities in terms of Nero; that is not what governs his life. You would have thought that he would have said, 'Well, of course, I am a prisoner. I do not quite know what the Emperor is going to do; he is a man of whims and may suddenly become irritated and say that every Christian is to be put to death – it all depends on what Nero says.' Not at all! No, he is a prisoner of Nero, but he describes himself as being a bond slave of the Lord Jesus Christ, and although he is chained to Nero's soldiers, he says that what is really going to determine whether he can send Timothy or not, or whether he can come himself or not, is the Lord Jesus Christ.

Now that is the great characteristic of this Christian life: it is a controlled life, it is bound together and surrendered, and governed by the will of the Lord Jesus Christ. Paul was in such a state of communion with him, in such a state of communication, that he knew his will, and he was not going to act apart from that will; indeed, the whole of his outlook was covered and dominated by it. Paul desired only to please him and he was conscious in the things which he did that he was being definitely led and directed by him. Surely that, therefore, is the call which comes to us at this point. Our danger is it not, is that we decide what to do – there are so many things in life which we regard from the standpoint of mere commonsense. But while that has its place, it must be a commonsense which is ultimately subject to the will of the Lord Jesus Christ himself. Our every action and move must have a relationship to our central relationship to him, dominated by him, and recognising that he is actually in control.

So here is an illustration of what we saw earlier. You remember how Paul told us in the doctrinal section that 'every knee should bow, of things in heaven, and things in earth, and things under the earth; and that every tongue should confess that Jesus Christ is Lord, to the glory of God the Father'? Here Paul is putting that in its practical form. He says in effect, 'Now do not be terrified by Nero. Caesar, though he has such great power, is even now under the domination of the Lord Jesus Christ, and the very decisions of Nero are finally over-ruled by the Lord Jesus Christ and his decisions. The will of Christ covers everything.' And, of course, if you read history in that light, you will see how often this has been proved to be true. Look at it in the Old Testament: think of how the word of the Lord came to those kings and potentates, how they were governed and controlled by God. We find exactly the same in the New Testament and in the subsequent history of the Christian Church. Oh that we could recapture this very idea! Oh that we knew at this moment, in spite of everything that might be seen or not seen in the history of the world, that ultimately it is all under the hand of the Lord Jesus Christ! He can open gaols, he can change the minds of rulers – there is nothing which he cannot do. It is his will that matters and ultimately nothing can frustrate it. That is the first principle.

That leads us on to the second statement which again, at first sight, sounds as if it were a contradiction. While it is a very exalted and high life, this Christian life, yet what a natural life it is, how human it can be. If ever there was a section of Scripture that finally explodes everything that lies behind the whole idea of monasticism, it is surely this. It shows the fallacy of the idea that if you are to be a true

Christian you have to become a supernatural person, who
has no human feelings. It corrects the idea that the Christian
has to be an unnatural person, that the opposite of 'natural'
is 'unnatural', instead of realising that the opposite of
natural is spiritual, and the spiritual man is not unnatural.
Let me show it in this section. Notice, for instance, what the
Apostle tells us in verse 19: 'I trust in the Lord Jesus to send
Timotheus shortly unto you, that I also may be of good comfort, when I know your state.' You see, Paul was anxious
about the people at Philippi. This Apostle is a wonderful
man of faith; he can say, 'to me to live is Christ, and to die
is gain'; he lives in the heavenlies with Christ, in a sense,
and yet he says, I am longing to send Timothy to you in
order that I may be comforted by a first-hand report. How
natural and human!

Let me take you on to verse 26 where we read this about
Epaphroditus: 'For he longed after you all and was full of
heaviness, because that ye had heard that he had been sick.'
Now a better translation of that would be: 'For he was
homesick after you all and so full of heaviness because you
had heard that he had been sick.' Here is a wonderful servant of the Lord, this man Epaphroditus, a man whom Paul
describes as brother, fellow-labourer and fellow-servant; a
man who was such a fine Christian that he risked his very life
in the work of Christ. 'Well, you know,' the Apostle says in
effect, 'the man was homesick, he longed to be back in
Philippi with his friends and relatives, especially when he
had been told that they were anxious and worried about him
because of his very serious sickness there in Rome.' This
wonderful Christian suffers from homesickness!

There is, alas, a school of thought that seems to think that
we are only Christian when we have lost all natural feeling,
but all that is contradicted and denounced, in a sense, by
this practical section. You may be called to the foreign mission field and you may be finding it a little bit difficult,
because you wonder how you can stand that break with your
father and mother. You must not think that you are the
poorer Christian because of that; do not think that you will

only become a perfect Christian when you no longer know what it is to be homesick. Think of this mighty servant of God who knew what it was to be homesick, to be heavy-hearted, and who longed to see his friends face to face once more.

Let me give you some further instances of the same thing. In verse 27 the Apostle says, 'For indeed he was sick nigh unto death: but God had mercy on him, and not on him only, but on me also, lest I should have sorrow upon sorrow.' Some people, perhaps, while away a few hours in reading novels, or in paying attention to things that are considered to be moving and affecting, but I defy you, whatever your literature or form of entertainment, to find anything that is more grand and moving, and that can rouse one so much in the depths of one's feeling and emotion, as that statement of this great man. Here is a man who says, 'to me to live is Christ, and to die is gain', a man who was ready to sacrifice everything for the sake of Christ, yet who says, This dear brother of mine was desperately ill, I thought he was going to die, but God not only had mercy upon him, he had mercy on me, too, to spare me, lest I should have sorrow upon sorrow. He would have felt it grievously, it would have hurt him, he would have known what it was to feel a temporary sense of desolation. Oh, let me emphasise this doctrine once more, the Christian is never meant to be unnatural. 'Mortifying our members' here in this world does not mean mortifying, or trying to kill, these things which have been implanted in us by God. He made us human beings: it is the perverse things that are sin; things that are noble and true all have their legitimate place in the Christian life. Paul knew what it was to be anxious about his dear brother who was so desperately ill and he thanked God when his life was spared. 'He spared me sorrow upon sorrow', says Paul – he knew this wonderful consolation of the Lord Jesus Christ.

And then verse 28: 'I sent him therefore the more carefully, that, when ye see him again, ye may rejoice, and that I may be the less sorrowful.' You see the human touch again? 'You know,' says Paul in effect, 'I am sending Epaphroditus back to you, because I know that when he arrives back in Philippi, and when you see him, you are all going to be so happy. And the fact that you are going to be so happy is also going to make me less sorrowful; as I think of you and your happiness when you look into the face of Epaphroditus, it will make me forget everything, and I shall rejoice as a man who rejoices in the Lord.' I need add no more – I have said enough to show you that this amazing life which is so dominated by Christ, and so dwells in the realm of the heavenlies, is also perfectly natural. This is a supreme example of the kind of thing that Wordsworth speaks about in his poem, the 'Skylark'.

> Type of the wise, who soar, but never roam
> True to the kindred points of Heaven and Home!

There is no contradiction between the two – Paul is able to soar to realms unseen and yet always with his feet upon the ground. We have here none of that false asceticism, none of those unnatural monstrosities, who think that to crucify the flesh, is to crucify all feelings and gifts. No, the Christian life is always true to the 'kindred points of Heaven and Home'. Oh that we might see that in our ordinary, humdrum, daily lives we can thus manifest and show forth something of the beauty, as well as the glory, of the Lord.

There is another sense in which this natural element is shown. You observe that this Apostle Paul, who had been enabled by the power of God to work such mighty miracles, was clearly not able to heal Epaphroditus miraculously. There is, you know, much false teaching on this subject at the present time. There are those who would have us believe that whatever illness we may suffer from, if we only have faith, we can be healed. Epaphroditus was not healed – Paul was not able to heal him. No, miraculous healing is possible, thank God for it, we believe it with the whole of our being, but miracle healing is not possible just whenever you and I think it ought to take place. It is under the hand of the Lord Jesus Christ, either he wills it or he does not will it. Epaphroditus was at death's door, and Paul could not heal him, and he could not heal himself by prayer, but God had mercy upon him.

Let us bear that in mind. There is an apparent, but not an actual, contradiction here. All these matters are governed by this rule: every gift of the Holy Spirit is under the sovereignty and the Lordship of the Holy Spirit. Therefore, when a man says, 'I am going to be healed miraculously at such and such a time', he is denying scriptural doctrine and he has no right to say it. The Spirit dispenses the gifts; he decides to heal one miraculously, and the other not; some are even allowed to die. God forbid that we should say that anyone who is not miraculously healed is therefore lacking in faith, or that if a man dies as a result of illness, it is because he is lacking in faith. It is all under the sovereignty of the Lord Jesus Christ; what he decides is that which is to take place.

Now let me just give you headings of the other part of the wonderful teaching in this section. Let us look at this life in detail. I think you will find it in the three words to be found in verse 25, the words that Paul uses about Epaphroditus primarily, but which are equally true for every Christian: 'I supposed it necessary to send to you Epaphroditus, my brother, and companion in labour, and fellowsoldier, but your messenger, and he that ministered to my wants.' Now there is a perfect description, in detail, of the Christian. We are first and foremost *brothers*. This means that we are all children of God. We are not just the sort of diverse collection of people that you find in a political meeting, or a cultural meeting, where you get different types giving their different experiences, held together by a common interest in the matter in hand, but separated from each other the moment they get out. That is not true of Christians. We are brothers because we are, as he has already told us in his doctrine, children of God.

Now this brotherhood is something which is manifested in many ways, as is shown here in this section. I am almost tempted to put it like this: the way to show we are Christian people is not merely to be constantly addressing one another as 'brother'; it does not mean just a mechanical use of the term in that way, it is, rather, a manifestation of love. In your family relationships you do not always address your brother as brother, you call him by his name; the family and the brotherly relationship is something which is manifested in action. You see it all perfectly in this section. Look at their concern for one another. The Philippians had sent Epaphroditus to Paul to attend to his wants while he was in prison – that is the manifestation of the brotherly spirit. Though they loved Epaphroditus very dearly, they sent him all the way over to Paul to minister to the needs of the great Apostle – loving brotherly concern. Timothy, too, says Paul, served him as a son with his father. And then you notice Paul's concern for these people at Philippi. There in Rome, Epaphroditus was of great value and help to him, and yet because Paul knew of their need of Epaphroditus, he sent him back; their need was Paul's only consideration. That is what is meant by brotherly relationship: this sense of blood relationship, this great concern for one another which shows itself in action.

Secondly, Paul also calls him his *companion in labour*, which we might translate as fellow-worker, and that is a perfect description of all of us together who are Christians. The Apostle says that the first thing we must realise about the work that concerns us is whose work it is. He tells us of Epaphroditus, that *for the work of Christ* he was sick and nigh unto death. He says in verse 21, 'For all seek their own, not the things which are Jesus Christ's.' We are fellow labourers – Why? Because it is *his* work. We are working together for the same Master, and we must never forget it. This, as we have already considered in the doctrinal section, is 'holding forth the word of life', just telling people about their dangerous position, and leading them into the Christian life.

Note, too, the spirit and the way in which the work is to be performed. Again, let me start with the negative, in verses 20 and 21. Paul says he is going to send Timothy to them for this reason: 'I have no man likeminded, who will naturally care for your state. For all seek their own, not the things which are Jesus Christ's.' 'The trouble for me here in Rome,' Paul says in effect, 'is that though I am surrounded by these Christian people, the only man I can send to you is Timothy, for, alas,' he says about the others, 'I admit that they are Christians, they are good people in many ways, but they are more concerned about themselves and their own things, than the things of Jesus Christ.' Now that is especially sad in the Church, but, alas, it is so true of many of us at this present time. The way to work for Christ is just this; we must realise that he must come first; we must not consider ourselves and our own comforts and our own benefits, it is he, and not our own things. This again is a practical application, for Paul said, right away at the beginning of the chapter, 'Look not every man on his own things, but every man also on the things of others.' That is the rule, and that is exactly what Paul did. Though he needed Epaphroditus, he sent him back to Philippi. We must put ourselves, and our concern for ourselves, on one side and work for him.

Then Paul describes the characteristic of the work in verses 16 and 17. He says, 'Holding forth the word of life; that I may rejoice in the day of Christ, that I have not run in vain, neither laboured in vain. Yea, and if I be offered upon the sacrifice and service of your faith, I joy and rejoice with you all.' This means that he regards the Christian life and service as a sacrifice which is offered to God. You remember how the Jews in their sacrifices would take an animal, and then a drink was poured upon it, a kind of libation, a drink offering on the top of the sacrificial offering. And that is how Paul pictured himself and the people at Philippi. He says, in effect, 'You are offering yourselves and all you are doing as service to God, and if my life blood is to be shed, well, I rejoice, and regard it as a kind of drink offering upon your sacrifice of praise.' What a tremendous conception of our activity in this world and life.

Then we are *fellow soldiers* This means that you and I are

in the army of the living God. We are fighting principalities and powers and the rulers of the darkness of this world, and spiritual wickedness in high places. Do you know that there are forces of evil in this world today, striving against man, trying to get him down, to ruin the soul, battling against God and heaven – these mighty, unseen spiritual forces? And you and I have the privilege of fighting as soldiers against them. We are also fighting against false doctrine, against error in the Church as well as outside the Church. Paul, as we saw earlier, says that in the first chapter where he talks about 'striving together for the faith', and you and I are to be fighting that battle. We are to ensure a purity of doctrine and we are to contend earnestly for the faith once and for ever delivered to the saints.

But above everything else we are to be fellow soldiers in the sense that we are animated by this glorious spirit that is to be found in Paul and Timothy and Epaphroditus. Paul says that for Christ's sake he is perfectly ready, if necessary, to be put to death. Timothy, he says, does not consider himself at all, he is the one man Paul can rely upon; he considers first the things of Jesus Christ. And what about Epaphroditus? Well, for the work of Christ he was nigh unto death, not regarding his life. Surely that is it. Is that not the spirit of the soldier who is commended in the war, a man who leaves all, and is willing to lay down his life for his king and country? To me, the tragedy of this generation is that whereas we all readily exalt the man who manifests this spirit in terms of nations, we do not see the same spirit when we talk about the everlasting, glorious kingdom of our God and of his Christ. Men are exhorted, in times of war, to lay down their lives for king and country – that is all right – but are we not called, to an infinitely greater degree and extent, to be prepared to do that for Christ's sake? And yet we are a little afraid of the sneers of our colleagues and of the meaningful looks of the club room as we enter it, because we have become Christians. We are afraid of the slightest degree of persecution.

Oh, shame on us Christian brothers, let us rather be like

these three mighty servants of God, Paul, Timothy and Epaphroditus, who were ready to risk their lives for the sake of Christ and for his work. The battle is on and the fight is keen and hot. Let us all be certain that as fellow soldiers we keep rank, we never falter or fail, and whatever the demands may be, whatever the cost, we shall be ready at any moment, yea even unto death, to stand and to fight for our glorious King, the Lord Jesus Christ.

The Life of Peace

An Exposition of Philippians 3 and 4

Contents

1

True Rejoicing

Finally, my brethren, rejoice in the Lord (Phil. 3:1).

There can be no question but that in these words we come
to a point of transition, or a turning point, in this letter written to the church at Philippi. From the very earliest days of
the Christian Church there has been much discussion and
disagreement about just what this injunction means. We need
not enter into that in detail here, but it is interesting, from the
standpoint of a study of the Scriptures, to attempt, by
analysis, to arrive at the precise idea that was in the Apostle's
mind. There are those who think that Paul was about to end
his letter here, that he really had said everything he had set
out to say, but that as he was writing the words, 'Finally, my
brethren, rejoice in the Lord,' he suddenly thought of something else he wanted to say. So he went on to say it, and
hence the whole of chapter 3 and the first part of chapter 4,
for you notice that in the fourth verse of that chapter he
returns to the same theme and says, 'Rejoice in the Lord
alway: and again I say, Rejoice.' These interpreters, therefore, would regard the entire argument of chapter 3, and the
first part of chapter 4, as a kind of afterthought which Paul
incorporated in the letter instead of making it a postscript.

Well, it is not necessary for us to discuss that question, for
ultimately, of course, it really does not matter; the
mechanics of this letter, while they have their interest, are
the least important part of it. But for myself, I find it difficult to accept that analysis as an explanation of what the

Apostle says at this point. It seems to me, rather, that Paul is merely resuming here the theme we tried to indicate in our introductory study* when we took a general view of the whole epistle. Paul wrote this letter in order to teach the Philippian people how to rejoice in the Lord – that is the theme, that is the message. And because he is such a practical man, he talks about various things which are likely to rob them of that joy; he deals with the difficulties one by one, and shows how they are to be surmounted. You remember how, in the first chapter, he talks about his imprisonment. This was tending to depress the people at Philippi and he puts them right about it, by dealing with various facts about his own state. He says, You need not worry about me, 'to me to live is Christ and to die is gain'; it was immaterial to him whether he be put to death or not.

Then Paul talks about the trouble which was caused by certain false brethren, and he says that in spite of that the Philippians can rejoice, for, although the false brethren preach Christ with the wrong motives, Paul will still rejoice because Christ is preached. He goes on next to talk about the persecutions which they were experiencing, and he shows them how to deal with these, too, still in order to maintain their joy. Then there was the tendency, perhaps, for the Philippian Christians to experience a certain amount of jealousy and envy with respect to one another, and Paul deals with this at the beginning of the second chapter, where he produces that amazing antidote, giving his wonderful description of the incarnation. He says, 'Let this mind be in you . . .', for if that mind is in them, then their joy will be maintained. Then he takes up once more the question of his absence from them, and points out that they need not be dejected or troubled because of this; he knows that the work will go on, because 'it is God which worketh in you both to will and to do of his good pleasure' (2:13); and he shows them how to work that out. And, lastly, he comforts them over the illness of Epaphroditus, and he says: I am sending

* See chapter 1 in Volume 1, *The Life of Joy* (Hodder & Stoughton).

him back to you, and not only that, I am hoping to send Timothy too.

All along, then, in various ways Paul is showing these people how to maintain their joy and now here in verse 1 of chapter 3 he comes to the end: 'Finally' – or, if you prefer it, you can translate it, 'For the rest' – 'Finally, my brethren, rejoice in the Lord. To write the same things to you, to me indeed is not grievous, but for you it is safe.' He has something else to bring to their remembrance, and, like the excellent teacher, the profound psychologist that he is, he thus reminds them, in passing, about the joy, and we are back again with the great theme of rejoicing in the Lord. It is as if he were saying, 'Now that we have dealt with these matters, let us continue; the big thing is to rejoice' – and then he talks about the things which were tending to cause trouble, namely, the work of the Judaisers and those false teachers who followed him around and caused intellectual and theological confusion in the infant Christian churches.

That, it seems to me, is the most natural way of regarding this point of transition in the epistle. It is merely a continuation and a reminder of the same central theme. We can illustrate this from the realm of music. In a symphony, for example, there is one predominant theme, and again and again the composer just throws in that theme; he may wander off in his variations, and it would seem that he has forgotten it, but he always comes back to it. That is what you find Paul doing in this, the most lyrical of all his epistles. So here once more he is reminding us of the major theme in the light of which all these other particular matters must always be considered.

That, then, is the setting, and it is important for us to bear it in mind. But I am also anxious now to concentrate on the positive exhortation itself. All along Paul has been inclined to suggest it; it has been there in different forms, but here he puts it explicitly. It is an exhortation, a command – 'Finally, my brethren, rejoice in the Lord . . .' I suggest that the obvious way to approach this is to divide it into three parts. First of all we must consider what it means to rejoice in the Lord. Then we must ask the second obvious question: why should we rejoice in the Lord? And thirdly: how are we to do this?

Now as we look at that first question and ask what it means 'to rejoice in the Lord', the first thing that strikes us is that it is, as we have said, a command. It is not a description of the state in which we find ourselves so much as something which we are exhorted to do. The tendency is always to think of joy as some subjective state or condition, and, of course, ultimately it is, and yet the very fact that Paul commands us or calls us to rejoice is proof positive that it is not something which we experience in a purely passive or subjective manner. We are not to sit down, trusting and hoping that we shall suddenly begin to rejoice! No, we have to do something in order that we may rejoice and it is something that we are capable of doing. These words are not just an intimation that we should passively expect or hope that something will happen or take place in us and that then we shall suddenly feel tremendously happy.

This whole question of joy in the Christian life has often caused a great deal of confusion. If I may so put it, many Christian people are unhappy because they are not experiencing joy. Their whole idea is that joy is the result of things that happen to us. They believe that we have no control over it, that we are not capable of making ourselves rejoice, that joy and rejoicing are the end result of the interaction and inter-operation of a number of forces and factors, most of them without, but some of them within ourselves. And, they say, as a result of all this, we are either happy or we are not. But that, it seems to me, is an error which is constantly exposed and denounced in these New Testament epistles, and here it is exposed by the very fact we are given a commandment – we are to rejoice, it is something we can do.

But having said that, I must again point out that two dangers arise immediately. The first is the danger of trying to produce this state of rejoicing by making a direct attack upon the emotions. I need not elaborate this, it is perfectly obvious, is it not? Some people will say that as rejoicing and happiness belong to the realm of the emotions, then, if we are commanded to rejoice, we must begin to do things to ourselves emotionally in order that we may get into this happy state. And, of course, we are familiar with the various methods that people will persist in employing to this end. For instance, in a public meeting, or in a public act of worship, think how often something like this happens: the leader of the meeting, or someone else, says, 'Well now, the first thing is to get this congregation or gathering into a good mood. Let's put on hymns or tunes or choruses of a certain type – we must get them happy, we must get them to rejoice. They have come in cold and miserable, let's get them into a good, happy state.' So, they put on bright, cheerful hymns to get the people to rejoice. That is what I mean by a direct attack upon the emotions, an attempt to produce joy by doing things to our emotional life which are calculated to lead to that result.

Now I want to show you that that is not the teaching of the Apostle here, as it is not the teaching of the New Testament anywhere. Indeed, I think I can demonstrate that such a direct attack upon the emotions is, according to the New Testament, one of the most dangerous things that we can ever do; that it is the high road to false teaching and the various cults. There are many ways in which people can make themselves feel happy: by taking drugs, by manipulating circumstances, or by groping in the realm of make-believe, fancy and fantasy, for example. There is an almost endless variety of ways, and, from the Christian standpoint, that is the major trouble of the world today. The world is full of troubles and unhappiness, terrible things are threatening life today, but instead of facing these things realistically and adopting the Christian way of surmounting them, people deliberately turn their back upon the troubles and, in their search for joy, happiness and peace, create an artificial sense of happiness and pleasure. And if that is wrong for the world, it is wrong also for us as Christian people. The principle is that we must never try to become happy and be full of rejoicing by doing something immediately and directly to our emotional nature.

The other danger which we must avoid is the pose of being bright, happy and cheerful Christian people. I think there are a number of people who have rightly seen and understood that Christians are meant to be men and women who rejoice. There is a type of Christian – a type that was perhaps far too common in the last century – who gives the impression that being a Christian means being mournful and miserable. This is the sort of person described by Milton as one who 'scorned delights and lives laborious days'. But people have now seen that that is a false representation of Christianity and of New Testament teaching, and that really the Christian is the only one who can know true happiness in a world like this. So, because of that, they adopt a bright and cheerful pose, and are always trying to give the impression that it is a wonderful thing to be a Christian.

That, it seems to me, is the second form that this error of the direct approach tends to take. I do not know what your experience is, but, speaking for myself, the most depressing people I think I have ever met are those who try to give the impression that they are always cheerful and happy. Is there not all the difference in the world between a person who is trying to give that impression and the one who really is happy? If a person is truly happy everybody can see it, it needs no explanation because you cannot help noticing. But you never feel that about these other people; you feel they are playing at being happy, it is the thing to do and therefore they are trying to do it. You see through them. You feel their joy is only skin deep, for it lacks some vital and essential quality.

But we are not exhorted by Paul to be exponents of what we may call 'mechanical' Christianity. No, it is unbelievable that the Apostle Paul was ever like that himself or would teach anybody else to be like that. He was a man who knew a joy greater than most people have been privileged to know in this world, and yet, at the same time, he said, 'We that are in this tabernacle do groan, being burdened' (2 Cor.

5:4); and that element must never be absent.

So when we are told to rejoice in the Lord, we must avoid the error of trying to do so by a direct attack upon our emotional nature. How, then, is it to be done? Well, first of all, our rejoicing is always something that results from a realisation of our position in Christ. My joy is the product, almost the by-product, of my concentration upon my relationship to God in Jesus Christ. That will become more clear as we work out these other points. Let me sum up this first point by saying that we do see very clearly that as Christian people we should rejoice; and I suppose that there has scarcely ever been a time in the history of the Church and of the world when this exhortation has been more important than it is today. The world, in spite of outward appearances and the various drugs with which it is drugging itself in an attempt to be happy, is profoundly unhappy, and what it is looking for is the secret which will bring it to this position of rejoicing. Now our whole case is that no one but the Christian can truly rejoice, and it is here, therefore, that we can bear the most striking witness at this present time. Are we giving the impression in practice that the words which our Lord spoke to his disciples are literally true: 'In the world ye shall have tribulation, but be of good cheer [rejoice]; I have overcome the world' (John 16:33)? And we are called to show that we do believe that to be true in our experience, that we do overcome the world.

The Apostle Paul expressed exactly the same thing on many occasions. He said to the Roman Christians, 'I am persuaded, that neither death, nor life, nor angels, nor principalities, nor powers, nor things present, nor things to come, nor height, nor depth, nor any other creature, shall be able to separate us from the love of God, which is in Christ Jesus our Lord' (Rom. 8:38–39) – that is the position, and you and I are called to it. We are commanded to this and it is our privilege just to shock the world, to convict the world and to lead the world to Christ by showing that even as things are today and in spite of everything, we still rejoice. But if that is true, it is also true to say that this is a

very thorough-going test of our profession of faith. Are we
rejoicing? We claim to be Christians – well this is one of the
results of being a Christian, this is one of the things to which
the Christian is inevitably exhorted. The Christian is actually commanded to rejoice – are we experiencing joy and is
this great statement true of us?

But let us leave it at that and go on to my second question. Why should we rejoice in the Lord? And here again
the Apostle gives us abundant answers to the question.
There are many reasons why we should rejoice in the Lord.
The first is the one we have already considered – that we
have been commanded to rejoice. But that is not all. We
should also rejoice in the Lord for the Lord's sake. This
great salvation, that is in this world in the person of our
Lord Jesus Christ, is something that has been worked out by
God, it is God's plan, God's scheme, and he has sent his Son
into this world. We are told that even the angels in heaven
are looking out over the parapet, as it were, to see how this
work of God is being conducted in this world. If you read
Ephesians 3:10 you will find Paul's description of this: 'To
the intent that now unto the principalities and powers in
heavenly places might be known by the church, the manifold
wisdom of God.' The principalities which appear in
heavenly places are given an insight into the manifold wisdom of God by what they see in the Church; salvation is
God's handiwork; salvation, the whole Christian gospel, is
something that God has sent into life and into the world.

And so, since it is God's action, this is the greatest reason
why you and I should be rejoicing. What credit to God is a
miserable Christian? What credit to God and his great salvation in Christ are people who seem to be always apologising
for their faith – does that manifest the manifold wisdom of
God? There is the reason for rejoicing – for God's sake. In
1 Peter 2, Peter says the same thing when he tells us that
God has called us out of darkness into his marvellous light
that we may show forth his praise and his glory – that is the
object. You and I have this inestimable privilege, therefore,
of manifesting the glory of God, and the way we do so,

supremely, is by showing that this Christian life of ours is one that enables us to overcome this world and rejoice even in the midst of tribulation. That is the second reason.

The third reason is obvious. It is for the sake of others. I have already dealt with this so I do not need to stay with it,* but it is our bounden duty at a time like this to rejoice in the Lord for the sake of the men and women who are around us, in their misery and unhappiness, seeking and searching for an answer, going from disappointment to disappointment, sometimes even contemplating going out of life through that back door that should never be opened. For the sake of others, then, who are defeated and frustrated by life, it is our business to stand out and radiate this new life, this different life that calls for rejoicing, so that they, seeing it, may say, 'There is hope for me after all.'

But let me show you also how the Apostle shows us that even for our own sake we ought to rejoice in the Lord; and that, in a sense, is the one big theme of this epistle. He has already been emphasising the point so I need only summarise it. There are two reasons why I must rejoice for my own sake. Do you know that rejoicing in the Lord is one of the greatest safeguards against most of the dangers that confront us? 'The joy of the Lord is your strength,' says Nehemiah (Neh. 8:10), and that is an obvious, psychological principle. When we are happy we can do our work very much better than when we are unhappy; the happier you are the more easily you can do things and that is equally true in the Christian life. The Christian who really rejoices in the Lord has many fewer difficulties in this world and life than the one who does not, because, if you are not centrally right, you already have problems before you begin to deal with other people. So that the way to live the Christian life smoothly and freely is to be right at the very foundation.

But not only that; look at the various dangers with which the Apostle has already dealt in his letter. To rejoice in the Lord is the greatest safeguard, says the Apostle, against

*See Volume 1, *The Life of Joy.*

those brethren who are preaching Christ falsely. If I were rejoicing in myself and my own preaching, says Paul, their attacks upon me would be very hurtful; but thank God I do not preach for my own sake or reputation, I do it for his sake, so that though they are trying to hurt me they are not touching me at all. I rejoice in the Lord, therefore I cannot be attacked at that point. Is it not obvious that what makes us all so sensitive is our self-consciousness and our self-esteem? And it is these things that make us vulnerable to the attacks that are made upon us. The one thing needed is to rejoice in the Lord, just to forget yourself; you are not working for yourself, you are working for him. Paul talks about it in the second chapter: 'Let nothing be done through strife or vainglory; but in lowliness of mind let each esteem other better than themselves. Look not every man on his own things, but every man also on the things of others' (vv. 3–4), and if you only do that, says Paul, even if you lose all things, you will not be dejected because you have already been regarding yourself as a steward. He says, I am holding them in trust for the Lord, they are not mine, therefore if I lose all, I have not lost anything in that personal sense.

To rejoice is a safeguard against something else, too. The Philippians, you remember, were unhappy and wondering how they were going to do without Paul; they were tending to look a little too much to Paul as their guide and instructor. So Paul says in effect, 'Don't rejoice in me, rejoice in the Lord; and then, whether I am alive or dead, it does not matter, the Lord is always with you.' True rejoicing is a safeguard against such a danger, and as we go on to deal with the third chapter, you will see another very great reason. The Judaisers were boasting about their nationality and about the fact that they had been circumcised. They were boasting about their morality and various other things, and the result was, ultimately, that they had arrived at a state of wretchedness and misery and the only cure was to rejoice in the Lord. True rejoicing is a safeguard from the attacks that come from every direction.

The fifth great reason for rejoicing in the Lord is that it is the only joy that can never fail us. That is literally true. Whatever else you and I may try to base our joy and happiness upon will finally fail us, whether it be ourselves, our success, our ability, our worldly learning, our home, or our children. It does not matter what it is, every one of these things is finally going to be removed and we shall all be left in isolation. A moment will come when we will find ourselves going out of life, and out of the world, and we will realise that there are things which we cannot take with us. Then our souls will be suddenly stripped and made bare, and we will awaken to the fact that we have been depending upon things that cannot go with us across the river of death – that is the loneliness of death.

In John 16:32 our Lord says, 'Behold, the hour cometh, yea, is now come, that ye shall be scattered, every man to his own, and shall leave me alone: and yet I am not alone, because the Father is with me.' Ultimately, we are all coming to this. The test will come when we find ourselves stripped of all the world offers, then we will find that this joy is the only joy that abides – that it will never fail us or leave us. His promise is: 'I will never leave thee, nor forsake thee' (Heb. 13:5), so if my rejoicing is in him I am in an invulnerable position, for nothing can come between me and the love of God which is in Christ Jesus our Lord. They could throw Paul into prison, but they could not rob him of his Christian joy. They could persecute and strip him and malign him; they could try to rob him of his character and of everything else, but it did not matter. Here is something that can never be touched, that is beyond the reach of man and all his machinations and efforts to destroy; it is a joy that never fails and of which we can never be despoiled.

How, then, are we to rejoice in the Lord? That is the most practical point of all and yet it is perfectly simple. Let me put the answer in three propositions. The way to rejoice in the Lord, as we are commanded to do here, is, first and foremost, to be able to control every other source of joy. That is a negative proposition but it is essential. If I find that my joy is dependent upon anything which can be taken from me, I must correct it. As a Christian I am in this life and world, but though I must be in it, I am not of it; I must ride loosely to it, and to all that it can give. I must be very careful that I am not brought under the power of any one of these things. They are quite permissible and legitimate in their place, many of them have been ordained by God, but I must look at the very centre of my joy, and must always be watching and correcting it. I must expose it to myself and realise the danger, and I must refuse to build the whole of my energies upon any insecure foundations.

The next aspect, a positive one, is this: I am to meditate upon him. You cannot rejoice in the Lord without thinking about him. I must deliberately turn my eyes from the other things that tend to charm and fascinate me and I must dwell on him. Is that not the great reply of the author of the epistle to the Hebrews: '. . . let us lay aside every weight, and the sin which doth so easily beset us, and let us run with patience the race that is set before us, looking unto Jesus . . .' (Heb. 12:1–2). Contemplate him, keep your eyes fixed upon him. You have to look at him before you can rejoice in him.

And then the third and last thing is this: we must consider and meditate upon what he has done for us – his great, his marvellous, his glorious work. We must go back and look at the cross; we must see all the suffering that led to the cross, and contemplate the meaning of the cross to him. As we read the Bible, we must say, 'This is not a philosophy, this is not an idea, or a fable.' We must go right over the whole story of how he left the courts of heaven and humbled himself, of how he staggered up Golgotha and went to the cross. We must consider all that he endured, and we must say, 'He did all that for me.' That is the way to rejoice in him. We must contemplate what he has done for us, and then go on to remember what he is doing for us now. Paul has already told us that he works in us 'both to will and to do' (Phil. 2:13). He has not only started this work, he is continuing it – 'he which hath begun a good work in you will perform it unto the day of Jesus Christ' (Phil. 1:6).

My dear friends, is it not amazing and wonderful, the way he comes into your life, changes your circumstances and raises hope and assurance in you? These are the ways in which he is working and continuing to work by the Holy Spirit, and the more you realise it, the more you rejoice. Then you look forward to the end and see the final consummation of it all. You take a grand view of history and see the world in all its confusion, its chaos and trouble, the warring factions and all the muddle of it all. Then you suddenly remind yourself that his work is going on and that he is working towards a goal. There is to be a final, grand consummation when Christ will come and rout all his enemies and set up his kingdom. Then there will be the glorious 'new heavens and a new earth, wherein dwelleth righteousness' (2 Pet. 3:13), and we who believe on him and rejoice in him shall reign with him for ever.

Is that not the way to rejoice – to contemplate that? That is what is meant by this exhortation. You do not sit down and hope you are going to feel joyful; you do not try to work up these feelings by some artificial stimulus. The way to rejoice in the Lord is to meditate upon the Lord and upon his salvation; it is to see what he has done and is doing and is going to do. If you truly see this, you cannot but rejoice. He will raise you to your feet; he will enable you to smile at the world and all its troubles; he will enable you to smile even in the face of death, because death will be nothing but the opening of that little door which will lead you into glory and into the presence of your beloved Lord. 'Finally, my brethren, rejoice in the Lord.'

2

True Worship

For we are the circumcision, which worship God in the spirit, and rejoice in Christ Jesus, and have no confidence in the flesh (Phil. 3:3).

In this verse the Apostle gives us one of the many definitions of the Christian which are to be found scattered so freely throughout his various letters. He found it necessary to give such definitions constantly. The people to whom he was writing had heard and believed the gospel; they had been converted and were made members of the Christian Church, but that did not necessarily mean that they perfectly understood the teaching and the doctrine. Most of the heresies that subsequently troubled the Church arose during its first years. Throughout the remainder of his career, the Apostle had to fight a great battle against heresy and that was why he had to keep on repeating these definitions of the Christian. In effect, he was constantly saying, 'If you believe this, or if you do that, then, of course, you are not a Christian: to be a Christian is this' – and then he gave a definition. And that is just what he does at this point.

I think you will find that every time you get one of these definitions in the Apostle's writings, it is always a matter of great interest and profound instruction to note the exact way in which he came to give the definition. In this verse, his reason for giving a definition of the Christian is that he is concerned about the joy and the happiness of these Philippian people. When we dealt in chapter 1 with Philippians 3:1 – 'Finally, my brethren, rejoice in the Lord' – we

pointed out that that is the theme of the whole epistle and
that Paul wrote this letter in order to help the Philippians
not only to have this joy, but to hold on to it and to maintain
it. He has been dealing, as we have seen, with the various
problems that were attacking them and threatening their
happiness and here he takes up another trouble which was
tending to interfere with the joy of the church at Philippi.

This time the problem was not something that was happening to him, or to them, it was the devastating false teaching and error which must be attributed to the people who
are called Judaisers. Here were people who were going
round those early Christian churches presenting a teaching
and doctrine in the name of Christ which the Apostle goes
on to show is entirely and utterly subversive of everything
that constitutes true Christianity, and that is why Paul takes
up this matter with such vigour. Let me make it plain that
his primary interest is not mere controversy – Paul was
never interested in controversy qua controversy, he did not
delight in argument for its own sake, and he never argued,
unless something of great importance was at stake. He takes
up this point here because, in his view, if the members of the
church at Philippi were to believe this other doctrine that
was being offered to them, then their whole standing in
Christ would be destroyed.

You notice how he shows us the all-importance of this
subject. He does so in at least four different ways. First, he
tells the Philippians that he is going to repeat something that
he has already told them: 'To write the same things to you,
to me indeed is not grievous . . .' Now the learned commen-
tators exercise themselves very much over that statement.
What does Paul mean by it? Has he written another letter
which has been lost? Is he referring to something he has
written in two or three other letters? Theologians show their
learning in trying to settle that question.

But to me the obvious explanation seems to be that Paul
is referring to something he had already told them while he
was with them; it is, indeed, something that he is always
repeating, you find it in almost every one of these letters.

'Therefore,' he says, in effect, to these people, 'I am going to tell you again something you have heard from me many times before, but I make no apology for repeating myself because "for you it is safe". This thing is so important and vital that at the expense of repeating myself I must say it again.' And that is something which displays Paul as a profound and wise teacher. There is no more subtle temptation for Christian people than the temptation to imagine that they are perfectly right and clear in the fundamentals of the faith. In one of his other epistles Paul said he was writing because the people were not certain of their principles. They seemed to be perfectly sound in their beliefs, but their behaviour revealed very plainly that they were wrong about some primary things. And there are people still who say, 'Oh yes, of course, I have been a Christian now for years, I understand the message of justification by faith and all that,' and yet it is at that very point that they have gone hopelessly astray. Let us never assume that we have arrived at a position in the Christian life where we do not need to be frequently reminded of the first principles of the gospel of Jesus Christ. This repetition is necessary; there is always the danger of slipping away from the truth and of assuming that we are right on fundamentals when sometimes we are not. Paul repeats himself and he makes no apology for doing so.

Then the second way in which he emphasises the great importance of this subject is by the repetition, three times over, of the word 'beware': 'Beware of dogs, beware of evil workers, beware of the concision.' Now this is not just undue exaggeration on the part of the Apostle. This matter is so vital that no pains are too great for him to take in his attempt to rouse these people to an awareness of their terrible danger. So Paul puts up this placard, this notice – beware, beware, beware – and by repetition impresses it upon their minds.

And then the next way in which he does it is by the violence of language with respect to these false teachers. Now by nature Paul was not a violent man. When you read his speeches in the Acts of the Apostles you see what a gentlemanly man he was, how unfailingly courteous in his addresses; he was not a man who would easily abuse others, and when he uses strong language, as he does here, there must be a very good reason. Because he sees the terrible danger of what was being taught by these false teachers, he calls them 'dogs'. They had claimed that they were preaching the true gospel and that Paul was not, and they had referred to all others as dogs, so Paul is saying that they are the dogs; they are behaving like dogs, tearing and destroying with this kind of talk.

And then he calls them 'evil workers', men who are doing evil things, upsetting churches, upsetting Christian people and causing schisms and divisions. It is evil work, says Paul. That is his estimate of the doctrine which they were preaching. Then, finally, he calls them 'the concision'. That is almost a pun. These men are talking about the circumcision, but what they really mean, what they are really interested in, is the concision: some mutilation of the body. But, Paul says, we, by contrast, are the circumcision. The violence of this language is again striking proof that the Apostle regards this matter as of the greatest importance.

And then, fourthly, Paul impresses this upon us by the way he gives his positive statement as to what does constitute a Christian, and here we come back to the point I was making earlier. Paul is writing to Christians; he is writing to people to whom he has said the noble and wonderful things that are to be found in chapter 1:4–10 and in the second chapter, too. Yet this man is such an expert in the spiritual life that he knows the subtleties of these teachers; so, once more, he says to the Philippians, Let me tell you what a real Christian is. Then he gives his three-fold definition.

There, then, we have seen the all-importance of this subject. Let me summarise it like this. According to the Apostle, our whole position in time and in eternity depends upon our clear understanding of what constitutes the Christian – of what are the basic elements of the Christian position. And Paul is so concerned about this, because, according to his teaching, if we are wrong about this, our whole future in eternity will suffer. How vital it is, then, that we should avoid those false teachings which are always ready to lead us astray.

But there is a second reason, and that is the one that Paul is so concerned about here. True joy in the Christian life also depends upon a correct understanding of doctrine. I know of nothing that so tends to rob us of our joy as Christians as uncertainty about doctrine. Alas, how many people there are who truly believe they are Christians but have never known the joy of the Lord about which Paul is speaking, simply because the teaching they have received has been false. There are those who think that it is almost sinful to rejoice as Christians. They think that the Christian walks with his head down, and goes mourning through life, and this in spite of the exhortations to joy which we find in such profusion in the New Testament. Such people are looking at themselves so much that they forget to look at the Lord; they have not understood the foundation. And that is why I maintain that it is so important for us to be perfectly clear and certain about this matter; it is the only way really to rejoice in the Lord and to have the full benefit of all that is offered us in Christ.

How urgently important this is for us! We are living in a world that is full of uncertainty. Many Christian people today do not worship in peace and safety and liberty; they are in circumstances where they seem to have been bereft of everything on which they have depended in the past, and the one thing that matters to them now is to know God and to be able to pray. And if you want to be able to do that you must be certain about your position. If, when you get on your knees, you begin to ask yourself whether you are a Christian, or whether you have any right to pray, if you are there querying the foundation, how can you build the superstructure? In a time of crisis one has no time to be thinking about these things, one must be able to presume or assume them, and go immediately to God. That is why Paul is so concerned about this. 'If you are right about this first matter,' he is saying in effect to these Philippians, 'then, whatever may happen to you, all will be well between you and God, and nothing can come between you. So make certain of where you stand.'

And I suggest to you that this is something which comes with force to us also. It is not for me to prophesy – who can prophesy in days like these? But are there not many signs in the world at this time which seem to point to the fact that you and I may have to face a period in which nothing will matter but this and the one thing that will count is that we know God? That is why I say that there is nothing more important than that we should know exactly what it means to be a Christian. So that with the Apostle Paul I make no apology for calling your attention to this subject, so that you may be very familiar with it, because for all of us 'it is safe' that I should do so.

Now the Apostle puts his case, as I have reminded you, in terms of the Judaisers. They went around teaching that it was not enough to believe in Christ. 'You must be a Jew,' they said; 'you must be circumcised.' And they went to the new Gentile churches with that message. 'Ah, yes,' they continued, 'you believe the gospel as preached by Paul, but he did not go far enough. If you want to be a true Christian you must be circumcised. You must know something about temple worship. You cannot do away with all those sacrifices, they are still essential – it must be Christ-plus.' That was their message and that is the message that Paul counters in his three-fold reply.

Of course, you and I do not meet teaching in that precise form but the principle which underlies it is still with us, and as we proceed to study the Apostle's definition I think you will see very clearly that we are not doing something that is merely of academic interest. That may be the case in times when the world is at ease, as, for example, in the days of the Victorian era, but we are looking at things which are relevant today, and are as threatening to us as they were to the Philippians. That is why we must be so careful truly to understand Paul's three-fold definition of the Christian.

The first characteristic which Paul gives of Christian

people is that they 'worship God in the spirit'; or, to give an alternative translation (it is impossible to decide which is correct), 'We are the circumcision who worship by the Spirit of God.' Either may be right, it does not matter, because essentially both these translations are saying the same thing. In other words, the first thing we have to face if we are anxious to know whether we are truly Christian or not, is the whole question of worship. What is our idea or definition of worship? What do we really mean when we say that we worship God? 'Surely,' says someone, 'you are not asking us to consider something so elementary?' But I ask it because the Apostle shows us very clearly that the mere fact that we think we are worshipping does not prove that we really do worship.

There is, then, a false way of worship which is opposite to the true. The Apostle, you see, puts it in a form which contradicts the false teaching of the Judaisers. 'They talk about "the circumcision"', he says, in effect, to the Philippians, 'these other teachers, who are trying to impress upon you that they are right. They are always telling you that you must be circumcised and go back to the Jewish ceremonials and rituals and temple worship, but I tell you that you cannot worship by doing things that way. We are the circumcision which worship God in the spirit.' What does that mean? Well, in the first instance, the Christian is one who worships God in the spirit and knows that these other things are no longer necessary. There is a new way to God, another method, which is now the right one; the other has been done away with. It is not that it was wrong in itself, but when you become a Christian it is not necessary, and to go back to it is to deny Christ. That is Paul's message.

This is surely a subject that is still relevant at the present time. There has been a great deal of talk in recent years about worship, and there are sections of the Church that put very great emphasis upon it. I once attended a conference at which an excellent man, who happened to belong to the Anglican Church, was speaking, and without any desire to be offensive, he said: 'Of course, the real difference between those of us who are Anglican, and others who are nonconformist is that we emphasise worship.' And it fell to my lot to suggest that he clearly was not able to differentiate between liturgy and true worship. He meant that they paid more attention to form and ceremony than to preaching and proclaiming the word, and he forgot that every part of the service is worship of God.

Now I use that merely as an illustration to show you what I mean. It is very interesting, as you look back across the history of the last fifty years or so, to see certain tendencies that are coming into the Church. I am concerned about these because of the state of the Church at the present time. We all, I am sure, bemoan the fact that the number of Christians in this country is so small. There are some who love to say that all is well, and that the country is almost full of Christians, but I imagine that most of us would not want to argue like that. We see that Christians do not count, that the Church does not count, and that the spiritual life of the nation is going down. So the question that arises is: Why? Well, to me it is not without significance that there has been an increasing tendency during past years to return to a more elaborate form of service, to the use of written prayers and of liturgy. There is a tendency to exalt buildings, especially ornate buildings, and a tendency to go back to mechanical forms of Christian life and of worship.

It seems to me that this has been a marked tendency recently in nonconformity as well as in Anglicanism, and it is something, therefore, which surely we ought to face together, because it is based upon a certain idea of worship. There is a tendency to exaggerate, and impress upon us the form and the dignity of worship, and to laugh at our forefathers who worshipped with greater liberty, and prayed so freely, and praised God so freely; there is a tendency to look down upon their worship and feel that it was somehow lacking in solemnity. Today, so-called worship has been reverting to a form, and people have believed that that is true worship. To me it has always been so pathetic to hear a service in some great church, when they have merely meant the effect upon them of a particular kind of building. The way to test whether or not people are truly worshipping is to observe their behaviour. Worship has nothing to do with the effect of a particular kind of building. The pagan in his pagan temple may have marvellous feelings, but is it true worship?

It is, in other words, to mistake the appearance for the reality, and that suggests an attitude of reverence, rather than true reverence. A true worshipper is not the one who goes devotedly to early morning celebration and then claims a right to the rest of the day, but the one who worships with the heart and with the spirit. There is always the danger of assuming that we are clear about what worship means, while in truth we are being misled. But apart from those obvious dangers, I would ask a much more personal and direct question – what about our own individual and private worship? We do not have liturgies for that, we do not have ceremonies and forms, but God forbid that we should therefore assume that our worship is right and true. I ask the direct question: Do you really worship God? The first characteristic of the Christian, says Paul, is that he worships by the Spirit of God – that is real worship. What does he mean? Let me suggest some questions that I should ask myself in order to determine whether I am really worshipping in the way that the Apostle here states.

Here is my first question: Do I worship as a matter of duty or am I aware of a desire to worship? Do I find worship a chore, or does it rise spontaneously from within? You see, the Apostle defines Christians as those who worship as the result of the operation of the Holy Spirit upon them, so that worshipping God is no longer a matter of duty, it is a desire. Secondly, to put it in a slightly different form, to worship God by the Spirit means that we do not have to force ourselves to worship him, but are conscious of being moved, and being led, to worship. Is that not the acid test? Most of us know what it is to be forced to go to a place of worship. That happened to us when we were children. And perhaps when we were older, we were made to go to church, either by our parents, or because we were told it was the thing to do. We did not want to go, there was a sense of compulsion, and we gave in to it. Is there not all the difference in the world between that and being conscious of being moved, of being led, of something within which urges and directs us. There is all the difference between getting down mechanically on our knees at our bedside because it is the thing to do, and that experience which comes perhaps when we are reading our Bible, or walking along a road or meditating. We are moved, we are disturbed, we feel there is a leading of the Spirit. This consciousness of being moved inwardly and being gripped and led is the characteristic of worship by the Spirit.

To worship by the Spirit of God is not something cold and formal, it is always warm and loving and free. You remember how Paul puts it when writing to the church at Rome; he says, 'The love of God is shed abroad in our hearts by the Holy Ghost' (Rom. 5:5). If the Holy Spirit is in us there must be something of the love of God in us, and we must have this love for God so that our prayers are not cold and formal or even just beautiful. No, that is not the characteristic of worship by the Spirit; there should be warmth; there should be feeling and some kindling of the heart; there should be freedom; we should know something about being lost in praise as we worship. It is the warmth of the Spirit, not a cold formality.

But let me put it still more specifically. As men worship God more and more by the Spirit, they become less and less dependent upon means. By 'means' I mean buildings, liturgies, priests, or even other people. I suggest that if you read the biographies of the saints, indeed, if you read the lives of some people who have never left the Roman Catholic Church, but who seem to me to have been thoroughly evangelical in spite of that, without exception you will find that as men really come to know God and worship him in an evangelical sense, they begin to drop their written prayers and their liturgy and their forms, and begin to pray from the heart; their prayers become extempore. You find this in the account of the Methodist Revival of the eighteenth century. I think we all probably find that it is easier to worship God in a prayer meeting than in a formal church setting, but as we become more and more spiritual we shall be less dependent even upon our friends, and we shall know that same liberty and freedom when alone with God.

Let me go still further. True worship of God in the spirit can be tested in this way: the man who worships God in the spirit does not think of God as some distant abstraction, almost a philosophical concept, away in the distance. The man who worships in the spirit realises the presence of God; he knows that God is there at his side. If he is led by the Spirit he is aware of being in the presence of the Almighty. What a test that is of spiritual worship!

But let me suggest a last thing, and I think that this is perhaps the best of all. We can be quite sure that we worship God in the spirit when we have that perfect admixture of, on the one hand, a sense of reverence and godly fear, and on the other the spirit of adoption whereby we cry, 'Abba Father'. I want to emphasise that because there are those who may agree with everything I have said so far. They may say, 'You are perfectly right in what you say about liturgy and form and appearance, I believe in the freedom of worship about which you are speaking.' They regard free worship as something that means a lot of shouting, and perhaps the banging of a timbrel; they feel that that is real worship.

But the opposite of liturgy, and form and ceremony is not the flesh; and true spiritual worship is not in fleshly, carnal customs. Surely anyone who worships by the Spirit of God, or who worships God in the spirit, must be aware of what our Lord said to the woman of Samaria: 'God is a Spirit: and they that worship him must worship him in spirit and in truth' (John 4:24). Anyone who realises the presence of God realises something of his holiness and feels unworthy. I cannot rush into his presence. I cannot be easily familiar, I cannot shout, I cannot yield to the flesh – no, as the writer of the epistle to the Hebrews puts it, there must be 'reverence and godly fear' (Heb. 12:28). Yes, but at the same time we 'have not received the spirit of bondage again to fear; but ye have received the Spirit of adoption, whereby we cry, Abba, Father' (Rom. 8:15). That is the ultimate and true spiritual worship. I realise the holiness of God, so that I approach him with reverence and awe, and yet at the same time I know that he is my Father and I say to him, 'Abba Father.' I know that he is not just an abstraction. I know that he has loved me with a Father's love, he has even sent his Son to the cross to save me. He is concerned about me to the extent that the very hairs of my head are numbered, and nothing can happen to me apart from him.

Oh, let us test ourselves by these things! Is our worship like that? Are we worshipping God in the Spirit, or is it merely a matter of form and appearance? Do I pray and read my Bible occasionally, or do I know that the Holy Spirit is dealing with me? Am I aware of being led? They are the sons of God that are led by the Spirit of God (Rom. 8:14). He leads, he gives freedom, he kindles the love. Do we know God, do we love God, can we say 'Abba Father' to him? God forbid that we should be relying upon some wrong notion and conception of worship; God grant rather that we may be able to see that we are the circumcision because we worship him by the Spirit.

3

All in Christ

We are the circumcision, which worship God in the spirit,
and rejoice in Christ Jesus, and have no confidence in the
flesh (Phil. 3:3).

As we continue with our consideration of this verse, let me
remind you that Paul gave this particular definition of the
Christian in order to counteract the false teaching which was
being offered to the Philippians by the so-called Judaisers.
It is important that we should bear that in mind because this
definition can, in a sense, only be fully understood when we
study it in its setting. It is definitely polemical. It is not only
a positive statement, it is at the same time a contradiction of
something else about which he is writing. It is an affirmation, but it is also a denial, and it is against that background
that we see the dual element in Paul's definition.

Now it is a remarkable thing that the Apostle, in such a
brief compass, is able to give us a perfect and complete
definition of the Christian. There is nothing lacking, and if
we honestly examine ourselves in the light of this statement
we should be clear and certain in our minds and hearts as to
whether we are Christians or not. The big things, the essential things, are each one of them mentioned in this one
verse. Let us look at them again.

The first, of course, is our attitude towards God. That
must always come first. In our attempt to discover whether
we are Christians or not, we must not start with our lives, or
with our sensations or experiences. We must not merely ask,
'Am I happy? Am I successful in life? Am I committing

certain sins?' Our answers may tell us something about the Christian, but if we start and stop at that, we are obviously in a very dangerous condition. All sorts of delusions could give people such experiences – false teachings can do that – so the definition must never begin there. It must start, obviously, with our relationship to God. This is what we were looking at in chapter 2 – we worship God 'by the Spirit'. The contrast between the letter and the spirit is frequently brought out in the New Testament. And in this verse we are at once held face to face with the doctrine of God the Father and the doctrine of the Holy Spirit. We are not Christians, says Paul, unless we worship God in this way. Such worship is the result of the operation of the Holy Spirit.

So, then, having considered that, let us come to the second statement which the Apostle makes. He has opened with the words: 'We are the circumcision which worship God the Spirit . . .' and now he follows with his second statement: '. . . and rejoice in Christ Jesus.' In other words, the second great test of our Christianity is our attitude towards the Lord Jesus Christ, that is, the place which the Lord Jesus Christ occupies in our lives. Here again we come to something that the Apostle is constantly repeating. We have already seen how the Apostle concentrates attention upon this;* indeed, as has so often been pointed out, Paul was a 'Christ-intoxicated man'. Paul cannot leave Christ out, he is always talking about him. This point is obvious. The very name, 'Christian', should itself be sufficient to make us see that Christ is absolutely central. We worship God in the spirit; yes, that is right, and the big characteristic of that worship is the place that the Lord Jesus Christ occupies in it.

Now the Apostle puts it in rather a striking manner, and here, I regret to say, we must slightly correct the translation of the Authorised Version, not because it is not true, and not because it is not right, but because it does not give the

---

*See Volume 1, *The Life of Joy.*

particular shade of meaning which the Apostle is anxious to convey. In the first verse of this chapter, Paul writes, 'Finally, my brethren, rejoice in the Lord.' And here again in the third verse we read '. . . which worship God in the spirit, and rejoice in Christ Jesus.' In the Authorised Version the same English word 'rejoice' is used in both verses, but it is not the same word in the original. The word Paul uses in verse 3 does mean rejoicing, but it is a particular form of rejoicing. I am concerned to stress this because of the polemical background of this statement. Paul is dealing with these other people, these Judaisers, who are guilty of teaching error, and that is why he uses a different word at this point.

So what, then, does he mean by 'rejoice in Christ Jesus'? Well, a better translation at this point would be the word 'boast': 'We are the circumcision which worship God by the Spirit and boast in Christ Jesus', or, if you prefer it, 'glory in Christ Jesus', or 'are proud of', or, perhaps still better, 'talk loudly about Christ Jesus'. Now that is actually the meaning of the word which the Apostle employed in this third verse. You may say, of course, that anyone who boasts in Christ Jesus is rejoicing in him, but you see the difference in the shade of meaning. The other people, the Judaisers, were boasting about something else. They were boasting about the fact that they were Jews and that they had been circumcised, and had kept the law. We who are Christians, said Paul, do not boast in these things but in Christ Jesus. They were boasting, it was their great characteristic, so the Apostle deliberately uses this particular word.

It is the same word that we see in 1 Corinthians 1. There Paul is pointing out that not many mighty, and not many noble are called, and the reason, he says, is 'that no flesh should glory [boast] in his presence' (v. 29). It is the word that is here translated 'rejoice'. And we find it again in the last verse of 1 Corinthians 1 where Paul says – 'According as it is written, he that glorieth, let him glory in the Lord.' Again the same word twice over, not translated 'rejoice', but 'glorieth', and rightly so, though I suggest that an even better translation would have been this word 'boast' – 'According as it is written, he that boasteth let him boast, let him glory, let him be proud of the Lord, let him speak loudly of the Lord.'

And that is what the Apostle means here by rejoicing in Christ Jesus. It is a very profound statement and we must try to realise something of its depth. It does not merely mean believing; it does mean that, but how much more than that! You can believe in a person, or in a dynasty, or in a country and yet not be proud of it. What a world of difference there is between that and boasting in it and rejoicing in it! Many people believe in one cause or another, and are prepared to give their general support, but others are on fire on behalf of their cause, they are zealous and keen and active, and are prepared to shed the last drop of blood in their veins for it. They are proud of it, they glory in it – that is the word.

That is the attitude of those who are Christians, that is one of the hallmarks of true believers, says Paul; they boast in Christ Jesus, they exult, they not only believe on him but their whole being is moved as they contemplate him. In other words, he is all and in all to them, and because of that, they desire to ascribe all honour and glory to him. Or perhaps we can put it like this: the characteristic, always, of the man who boasts is that, as the word suggests in the Greek, he talks loudly about himself – which is what I have suggested as an alternative translation. When you describe a man as a 'boaster' you mean that he wants everybody to know what a fine fellow he is and so he speaks loudly about himself. According to this translation, Christians are people who are always talking about Christ, they are always praising him and want everybody else to hear about him. They want other people to know how wonderful he is, so they are ever paying tribute to him, and ascribing glory and honour to him. All their talking is about him, they cannot stop doing it: it is always Christ.

Think of it also in contrast with the Judaisers who were for ever talking about their nationality and about all those things that Paul mentions later. Paul, of course, knew it all so well; I have no doubt but that in writing his epistle he was not only thinking of the Judaisers, he was thinking of himself before his conversion – what a proud man he had been. It is very interesting to go through all Paul's epistles with your eye on this Greek word that should be translated boasting – I commend this to those of you who are Bible scholars – you will find that it is one of Paul's great words. He goes on to say in the next verse, 'I might also have confidence in the flesh. If any other man thinketh that he hath whereof he might trust in the flesh, I more' (v. 4) – and how often he repeats that! It was his great characteristic. But now, he says, it is not like that any longer. He now boasts in the Lord Jesus Christ. He glories in him. Christ is the one Paul talks about. 'I determined,' he says to the Corinthians, 'not to know any thing among you, save Jesus Christ, and him crucified' (1 Cor. 2:2) – rejoice, glory, boast, exult in Christ Jesus.

Now if that is what is meant by glorying or rejoicing, let us ask this question in order to elucidate the matter still further. Why does the Christian thus boast in Christ? Why should he? Why is it the hallmark and the acid test of the Christian? I do not hesitate to use such expressions. To me, the great test that differentiates between those who are Christians and those who are not is the place of Christ in their lives. Is he central, is he essential, is he absolute? If that is not our position, then, according to the New Testament, we are not Christians. What would happen to us if we suddenly heard Christ had never existed? Would our lives be unaffected? If they would, we cannot be Christians according to this definition. But why is it, then, that the Christian thus boasts and glories in the Lord Jesus Christ. Well, of course, the answer to that is the whole gospel. I will simply mention here certain central things with which you may be perfectly familiar, but I make no apology for standing with the great Apostle when he says, 'To write the same things to you, to me indeed is not grievous . . .' Not only that, if you have ever found yourself becoming tired of hearing about the Lord Jesus Christ, then you had better examine the foundations again. The saints, God's people, are never tired of praising his virtues and telling forth his glory and wonder.

What is it, therefore, that should make us boast in him alone? In the first place, it is the very fact of his person; he stands out from all others. I should boast in him and glory in him, because he is indeed the only begotten Son of God. It is the miracle of the incarnation. It is everything that Paul was describing in those first verses of the second chapter, the whole amazing process that brought the Son of God from heaven to earth, and made him live here in the likeness of sinful flesh, and assume the form of a servant and do all that he did. As you look at him, and see it all, and realise its meaning, there is only one thing to do, and that is to boast in him, and to glory and exult in him.

So our first reason is his person, and that alone is enough. We have all got a good deal of the hero worshipper in us, and how often have we boasted in man, how often have we praised great men in the world, leaders and those in high places and positions? If we have been distantly related to them, how proud we have been, how we have always liked people to know of it! Well, multiply that by infinity, and there you have the Lord Jesus Christ, the very Son of God incarnate – in the flesh – here in this world, living life as a man. If you want to boast, boast of that, and boast of the fact that you know that by the operation of the Holy Spirit upon you, you belong to him and are related to him. Boast of the greatness and the wonder and the glory of the person of Christ.

But let me move on to something else, for it does not stop at that. The Christian glories in Christ because he realises that the whole point of the incarnation was that Christ might save us from our sins and reconcile us to God. The incarnation in itself, merely as a spectacle, is something big enough and great enough to absorb all our praise and all our boasting. But when we realise the meaning and the purpose of it, when we realise that he did all that for us, for our sakes, for our sins, and for our deliverance and emancipation in every sense, does not this desire to boast become infinitely great-er? According to the New Testament, he came specifically to save us, and as we realise that, with this great Apostle, we shall feel that nothing matters but Christ alone.

Or let us put it still more personally, and this, of course, is essential because I really do want us to know what it is to boast in him. Certainly I must look at the truth objectively, but if my view is only objective, this element of boasting will not arise. The boasting comes in at the point when we realise that our personal salvation is entirely dependent upon him. That is why Paul put it like this in Galatians 2:20: '. . . the Son of God,' he says, 'who loved me, and gave himself for me.' It is an amazing thing to see the Son of God bearing the sins of mankind there in his own body on the tree. That, in itself, is enough to make me drop upon my knees and worship and praise him. But when I realise that he was doing that for me, even me, that I myself am involved, then at that point I am lost in wonder. Because he has done it all for me I boast and make my boast in him. When I realise that that is the way in which God saves me, and that there is no salvation for me apart from that, then I glory in him.

And what does all that mean for us? Well, the New Tes-tament puts this in an almost endless variety of ways. First, it is only in Christ that I really come to see my trouble and my need. Before he really saw the Lord Jesus Christ, the Apostle Paul lived a life which satisfied him. However, fun-damentally there was something wrong, and that is why, later, when he had come to the right view, he went on to say that all those things of which he had boasted had become refuse to him. Before he knew Christ he was in a kind of fool's paradise, feeling that he could justify himself, and that all was well with him. In effect, he says, 'I would have gone on living like that, had it not been for Christ; it was he who made me see myself and the wrong, and the danger of my whole position.' That is the first thing that Christ does; it is he who makes us see our sin and our need, and makes us know our desperate plight.

But thank God it does not stop at that, because the moment we see that, we then instinctively try to do something to put ourselves right, and to get rid of this sin and guilt. I know of nothing that is more depressing and discouraging, nothing that is so truly killing to the soul and spirit, than that continual fight to fit ourselves to stand in the presence of God; it cannot be done. Paul knew something about that, and it was after some such struggle, that he saw that Christ was, once more, the answer. He saw the whole meaning of the death upon the cross; he saw that Christ was there setting him right with God. He could not do it for himself, neither could anyone else do it. He saw that the whole meaning of the cross was that 'God was in Christ, reconciling the world unto himself,' that, 'God hath made him to be sin for us, who knew no sin' (2 Cor. 5:19–21). These are Paul's words. Again he writes, 'whom God hath set forth to be a propitiation' (Rom. 3:25), which means that there on Calvary God was doing something which enabled him to forgive. He had laid the sins of Paul upon Christ, and had punished them in Christ, so that Paul was forgiven and free – that is what it means. And Paul had come to see that, and he had found peace and rest and knew that he was reconciled to God.

And then the new life begins, the new strength, the new power, the new outlook, the new understanding, the new everything and – but I am attempting the impossible! You see, Paul himself seems to realise, at the end of 1 Corinthians 1, that this is something which he can never express, so he puts it like this: 'But of him are ye in Christ Jesus, who of God is made unto us wisdom, and righteousness, and sanctification, and redemption' (1 Cor. 1:30). Is there anything greater than that? He is everything. The Alpha and the Omega, the beginning and the end, the start and the finish, the All in all, and in him we are complete. Is there anything that you can conceive of or imagine that you need or want for your soul? It is all in him: 'in him dwelleth all the fulness of the Godhead bodily' (Col. 2:9). There is nothing that the soul of man can need in time or eternity but that it is all in Christ. You need pardon? There it is. You need reconciliation to God? The man Christ Jesus is the one and only mediator between God and man. You need new life and a new nature? You receive it from him. You need strength and power? He sent the Holy Spirit that you might have it. You need an Advocate with the Father? There he is, seated at the right hand of God. You tremble at the thought of death and of going to face God in the judgment? You are assured that you will be clothed with his righteousness and he will present you spotless. What else do you need? He is everything: Prophet, Priest and King, the All in all.

> He's the lily of the valley
> The Bright and Morning Star,
> He's the fairest of ten thousand to my soul.

The man who believes that, must make his boast in Christ. Christ is everything: wisdom, knowledge, understanding, a view of life, a view of God, a view of the world. Paul found all that in Christ. He had a very different view before; he used to regard the Gentiles as dogs, but now he sees them coming into the Church. He sees a whole plan unveiled and continuing.

At this point let us ask ourselves a simple question. Is Christ that to us? Do we make our boast in him? Do we glory in him? Do we say honestly that Christ is everything to us, that without him we are nothing? Do we say that we cannot even begin the Christian life, we cannot approach it, without him? He is the life, 'I am the way, the truth and the life,' he says, 'no man cometh unto the Father, but by me' (John 14:6). Is he vital to our whole outlook and all our conceiving? Do we realise that our utter and entire dependence is upon him? Do we realise that, in a sense, there is no such thing as prayer except through him? Is he at the centre of our life, on the throne of our heart?

So the second great characteristic of the Christian, says the Apostle, is that he boasts in Christ Jesus. He says with the Apostle, 'God forbid that I should glory' – this, again, is the same word 'boast' – 'God forbid that I should boast, save in the cross of our Lord Jesus Christ, by whom the world is crucified unto me, and I unto the world' (Gal. 6:14). God forbid that I should ever, for a second, boast in anything or anyone else but in him.

> In the Cross of Christ I glory
> Towering o'er the wrecks of time
> All the light of sacred story
> Gathers round his head sublime.
>
> J. Bowring

Does that strike a chord in you? If it does, you are a Christian, you are within the definition. You boast in Christ Jesus.

Let me just comment briefly on the last characteristic of the Christian – 'And have no confidence in the flesh.' I wonder why Paul went on to that, after his earlier glorious statement? I think he recognised the danger that was threatening these people at Philippi, and so he put before them what should be their attitude to God, and then at the end gave their attitude to themselves – 'no confidence in the flesh'. Let me give you some headings on this because I think that will be sufficient. Paul means, first, that he does not boast in his nationality. He used to – he was proud of being 'a Hebrew of the Hebrews' – but, now, he says in effect, 'I have no confidence in nationality any longer. My confidence is entirely in Christ.' To repose our confidence in nationality is a denial of the Christian gospel and we are emancipated from that. It is our birth in Christ which reconciles us to God, and we boast in that; not in family, not in the tribe of Benjamin, not in being Jewish, or British: birth does not count.

Other things make no difference either, as Paul shows in 1 Corinthians 1; not upbringing, nor training, for example. You may have had excellent training, it may have been one better than anybody else's, but that does not save you. You may have had the finest upbringing in the world, and yet not know him. Nor are you saved by a love and zeal for politics and economics. Paul was better than most other people: 'touching the righteousness which is in the law, blameless' (Phil. 3:6); but he had no confidence in that kind of thing. Nor did he trust in philosophy and the understanding and wisdom of this world – what a subtle enemy! One of the last things we let go of, because of our pride, is intellect – the boasting of philosophy and understanding and thought. I have no confidence in it any longer, says Paul, no confidence in the flesh. If I have any confidence in these things and not in Christ alone, I am in a dangerous position. Christ is the end as he was the beginning, and I must have my confidence in him from beginning to end. It is in him I am saved, in him I have been sanctified, it is all in him: wisdom, righteousness, sanctification and redemption. I must be entirely dependent upon him, with no confidence in the flesh in any shape or form.

That, then, is the definition of the Christian. Let me finally put it like this. The Apostle says here that we – the people who worship God by the Spirit, and who rejoice in Christ Jesus and have no confidence in the flesh – we are the circumcision. This means that all those great promises of God to the Children of Israel in the old dispensation, in the Old Testament, the promises made to Abraham, the promises repeated through Isaac and Jacob and right down the running centuries, all the extraordinary promises of God that were given to that nation now apply to us. We, the Christians in every nation, are the circumcision; we are God's Israel who worship God in the spirit and have no confidence in the flesh. All the gracious promises of God originally made to the nation of Israel are now made to the Church, to Christian people.

You and I, in other words, if we are Christians, are the inheritors of all those promises, and no one else. The nation of Israel has been put aside, as our Lord himself said, because of their rejection of him and their unworthiness; and the promises belong to the nation bringing forth the fruit thereof: the Church. And Paul is saying the same thing:

'we are the circumcision'. Oh, the tragedy that the Jews should still be claiming it for themselves! We, Christian people, are the inheritors of those gracious and glorious promises; we are the citizens of the Kingdom and we are going to reign with him and enjoy the blessings of the ever-lasting Kingdom, world without end. What a privilege! We are the circumcision, the people of God, and we prove it by worshipping him by the Spirit, by glorying in Christ Jesus, and by having no confidence in the flesh in any form.

4

The Christian Life

Though I might also have confidence in the flesh. If any
other man thinketh that he hath whereof he might trust in
the flesh, I more: Circumcised the eighth day, of the stock of
Israel, of the tribe of Benjamin, an Hebrew of the Hebrews;
as touching the law, a Pharisee; concerning zeal, persecuting the church; touching the righteousness which is in the
law, blameless. But what things were gain to me, those I
counted loss for Christ. Yea doubtless, and I count all things
but loss for the excellency of the knowledge of Christ Jesus
my Lord: for whom I have suffered the loss of all things, and
do count them but dung, that I may win Christ, and be found
in him, not having mine own righteousness, which is of the
law, but that which is through the faith of Christ, the righteousness which is of God by faith: That I may know him,
and the power of his resurrection, and the fellowship of his
sufferings, being made conformable unto his death; if by
any means I might attain unto the resurrection of the dead.
Not as though I had already attained, either were already
perfect: but I follow after, if that I may apprehend that for
which also I am apprehended of Christ Jesus. Brethren, I
count not myself to have apprehended: but this one thing I
do, forgetting those things which are behind, and reaching
forth unto those things which are before, I press toward the
mark for the prize of the high calling of God in Christ Jesus
(Phil. 3:4–14).

It seems to me that it is essential that we should consider this
passage as a whole before we come to consider its various
parts. It is an elaboration of what the Apostle has been

saying in the first three verses of the chapter, especially the third verse, in which he has claimed, you remember, that 'we are the circumcision which worship God in the spirit [by the Spirit], and rejoice in Christ Jesus, and have no confidence in the flesh'. Now verses 4 to 14 are, in a way, an exposition of the theme as stated in verse 3, and it is worked out in a magnificent and truly glorious manner in these following verses. In other words, the Apostle is here finally demolishing the false teachings and arguments of the Judaisers, who would have these Gentile Christians believe that in addition to faith in Christ it is essential for them to become Jews, that is, to be circumcised and to follow certain Jewish practices, before they can truly claim to be Christian.

The argument is something like this. These men are making claims about the importance of the fact that they are Hebrews, Jews, and they are boasting about their good works and so on. Now, says Paul, if any man has a right to boast at all, surely I am the man; and then he gives a list of what he used to be and what he used to do; but he does that only in order once and for ever to contrast his old self with this new nature which he has obtained in the Lord Jesus Christ. So we have here, in effect, one of the guarantees, and certainly one of the most eloquent statements, of what it really means to be a Christian. The Apostle, in showing the contrast between the Christian life and that other life, has given us a wonderful, positive picture of the Christian life itself, and that is what we must look at together now.

But, before we do so, there is one caution which it is perhaps necessary to make, and I say this on the basis of experience. The caution is that we must bear in mind that the Apostle here is not only describing what was true for him, he is also stating what should be true for every Christian. I have often met men who, confronted by a passage like this, have said, 'Ah yes, that is all right, that was Paul, but we are not Paul.' They mistakenly think that the unique experience which Paul had on the road to Damascus is something which puts the whole of his Christian experience in a category apart.

It is vitally important, therefore, that we should be clear about this point. Of course, the experience which Paul had on the road to Damascus was unique. Paul, you remember, going down to Damascus to persecute and massacre the Christians in that city, was given a view of the risen Lord himself. It was not a vision, it was an ocular manifestation. He really did see the risen Lord, he says so. It is quite clear that that sight of the risen Lord was given to Paul in order that he might be counted as an Apostle, because one of the distinctive marks of an Apostle was that he must have seen the risen Lord with his naked eye. So that is the sight that was given to him in a very special and remarkable manner, as he tells us in 1 Corinthians 15:8, where he calls himself 'one born out of due time'. We as Christian people do not see, and must not expect to see the risen Lord in the way that Paul saw him on the road to Damascus. But after all, that is not vital to the Christian experience, that is not what makes someone a Christian; that was only essential to the calling of an Apostle.

But in this passage here, Paul is saying what is true of him as a Christian believer, and in this, therefore, the Apostle, of all men, would have been concerned to argue that he was not in a category apart. Does he not tell us, in 1 Timothy 1:15, that he is the greatest of all sinners the world has ever known? And he makes it patently plain that he is nothing but a sinner saved by the grace of God in Christ in exactly the same way as every other Christian. So we must not challenge this magnificent statement by trying to emphasise the difference between his experience on the road to Damascus and what is known to be true of us. No, what the Apostle says here about the normal Christian experience is to be true of each and every one of us. God forbid that we should perpetuate that false Roman Catholic division between Christians and call some spiritual and some ordinary, some exceptional and some mundane. There is no distinction in the New Testament: we are all in the same position, we are all to have the same experience of God's salvation, whatever form it may take, and we are all to strive after the same things.

So with that word of caution, which I give simply because I so often have to argue with people on that point, people who are avoiding the whole challenge because they put Paul into a separate compartment, let us consider something of what the Apostle says here. As I said, at this juncture we shall only deal with this magnificent description in a general manner. We shall have to go into the details again, but I think it is important that, sometimes at any rate, we should take a composite view of the Christian life, so that some of these big principles may stand out in our minds.

What, then, does Paul tell us here, in general, about the Christian life and experience? First, he tells us that it is something that takes hold of us and masters us and holds us. That is, of course, the statement of the twelfth verse. 'Not as though,' says Paul, 'I had already attained, either were already perfect: but I follow after, if that I may apprehend that for which also I am apprehended of Christ Jesus.' I start with that verse because I suggest that, to be logical, it really must come first. Now you may say, and I would agree with you, that at this point the Apostle is undoubtedly thinking of what happened to him on the road to Damascus. It is more or less inevitable that he should do so because that was how he became a Christian. He says, in effect, 'There was I, this proud, self-righteous, boastful Pharisee, going down to Damascus truly believing I was serving God, when suddenly this great light began to shine such as I have never seen before. I saw him, and what really happened to me was that he took hold of me, he grasped me, he held me and he has held me ever since.' And, says Paul, 'my position now is that I am trying to grasp that which grasped me.'

And we find a great principle there that is true not only of Paul but of every other Christian. We all tend to want that kind of climactic experience, like the one that Paul had on the way to Damascus, but it is not a part of the preaching of the gospel to say that one must be converted suddenly. What does matter is that we should know something of what the Apostle means when he says that he has been taken hold of by something or Somebody. Whether it happened suddenly or not, does not matter – that is irrelevant – it can come in a thousand ways and forms, but what is all important is this awareness of being taken hold of by something, of being held in the grip of something: that is what is so vital to the Christian position.

The Christian, in other words, is not a man who has taken up something as an interest, he is a man who has been taken up by the interest and he cannot escape it. The Christian, therefore, can never be half-hearted, because he is conscious of this vice-like grip which holds him. I am not going too far when I venture to put it like this, because I sometimes think it is perhaps one of the most delicate tests we can ever give ourselves: Do we know what it is to feel sometimes that we would like to get away from it, but it has got us in a grip, it has mastered us? This is expressed in that well-known hymn: 'O love that wilt not let me go' – that is it. There may be times in our folly and blindness and sin when we would like to be released, but he will not let us go, we are taken hold of, and grasped firmly.

That is the first thing that is true of this new life in which Paul finds himself. 'It is not,' he says in effect, 'that I have given up Judaism and taken up Christianity; it is not that having heard something about it, I find it rather interesting, and I like reading about it and discussing it in a casual, external, objective manner. Not at all! That is not the Christian position. The thing that is characteristic of the Christian in the first place is that he is suddenly aware that this thing has taken hold of him and he cannot get away from it; he is taken up, apprehended by it, and then he tries to apprehend.'

Now this is basic, it is something one finds very difficult to put into words, and yet, I repeat, I know of nothing that is a more thorough-going test of our whole position. Is your Christian faith something that you take up and, as it were, carry in your hand like a bag? Or are you rather in the position of the slave, mastered and grasped, possessed and taken up; sometimes aware of that foolish, sinful desire to get away, and yet knowing that you cannot? That is always the New Testament picture of Christian people. They know that God has been dealing with them, God has done something to them, God is moving in their direction, God has interfered in their lives. They do not quite understand it, but they know that it is the action of God. We are apprehended – that is the first thing.

The second thing, surely, about this new life – we are only dealing with the over-all principles now, we must go into this again in detail – is that it is something that leads to a complete change of outlook and values, and that, of course, is the great theme of verses 7 and 8. It was something Paul was never tired of saying. Having given this list of his perfections as a Jew, and a proud Pharisee, he then goes on to say, 'But what things were gain to me, those I counted loss for Christ. Yea doubtless, and I count all things but loss for the excellency of the knowledge of Christ Jesus my Lord: for whom I have suffered the loss of all things, and do count them but dung, that I may win Christ.'

Now here he is describing a complete transformation, a turning point. There he was climbing upwards when suddenly he found himself looking at an entirely different landscape. I would put it like this: Christianity is never an addition to our lives, it is never something that is added on to that which we have previously had: it is central or it is nowhere. If it is not controlling the whole of your life, then you are just not a Christian. Christians are not people of whom it can be said that their lives are identical with everybody else's, they have an extra something in addition, and in the end they are seen to be Christians. No, to be a Christian, says Paul, means that at the very centre, at the very core of your being and existence, this new something has come in and controls everything. A radical change takes place when you become a Christian, you are suddenly aware of it; it is a change of outlook upon all things. I do not hesitate to use the term which the Apostle uses in verse 8 – all things have become 'loss'.

This is something which Paul elaborates in his various epistles, and I think it follows of necessity. If to be a Christian means that I have been affected profoundly at the very centre of my being, in what the New Testament calls the heart (the heart does not mean the emotion or the seat of emotions – it means the centre of the personality), if the centre of my personality has been affected, well, then, everything else must be changed. My thinking must be changed, my feeling, my willing, must be changed; and that is exactly what the Apostle claims for the Christian.

Paul says it again more explicitly in 2 Corinthians 5: 'if any man be in Christ, he is a new creature: old things are passed away; behold, all things are become new' (v. 17); and that is literally true, nothing remains the same in the heart. In verses 7–8, Paul puts it all in terms of profit and loss – 'But what things were gain to me, those I counted loss for Christ.' If you study these verses carefully for your-selves, you will notice how Paul repeats these words. He is saying that far from being gain, those things have actually become loss. He could not have expressed the entire trans-action in stronger language than he does by using that par-ticular analogy.

In what respects, then, is it right to say that life is entirely changed? Well, Paul answers that question here in these verses. He had a completely new view of himself – he who had been so proud is now ashamed of himself; before, he thought he was better than everybody else, now he sees himself as the chief of sinners. What a transformation! And that, again, is something that should be true of every Chris-tian. The more we grow as Christians, the more we should be aware of the corruption of our own hearts; and not to be aware of that is a very serious symptom. Here is a man who in terms of morality could stand face to face with any chal-lenger, and yet once he has been enlightened, he is aware of his corruption and sin, and can cry out in agony, 'O wretched man that I am! who shall deliver me from the body of this death?' (Rom. 7:24).

He also has a new view of God – he sees that his view of God has been seriously and tragically defective. He has a new view of religion. He was formerly content with an external religion, but now he becomes aware of a spiritual nature. His whole idea of how God should be approached is different. Before, he approached him in terms of his own righteousness and merit, but now he humbles himself before the throne of mercy and whispers the words, 'Jesus Christ, my Lord.'

What else? Life itself, and his whole view of it, has become different. He has been a Pharisee, a great teacher, proud of his position and with great prospects of promotion. What is his view of life now? Well, he has already told us: 'to me to live is Christ' (1:21); he has lost those false motives, and his one desire is to know Christ better and to be able to serve him more truly. He now has an entirely different view of the purpose and meaning of life, and, as he has told us in the first chapter, he has an entirely new view of death. Death is now of no account to Paul because it means to be with Christ, which is far better. And he has a new view of the Gentiles. He once regarded them as dogs, outside the commonwealth of Israel, but now he rejoices in them as beloved brothers, inheritors of the everlasting Kingdom.

That is how Paul shows us his complete transformation. But we are not only dealing with Paul, we are dealing with ourselves. Christians by definition must have an entirely different view of everything from those who are not Christians: a new vision of themselves, a different view of God and of how God is to be approached, a different view of life. Now I think this is very important at this present time. Because we are governed by new principles, we should be viewing events in a different way – our whole attitude towards everything is essentially different from the non-Christian attitude. Our view of death should be different, and our view of all other people should be different as well.

As we have seen, Paul goes so far as to say that the things that were gain to him have actually become loss. Is he thereby condemning the law of God which was given to the Children of Israel? Is he condemning the Jewish religion which was given by God? No, Paul does not say that these things are wrong in and of themselves, but he does say: 'I was relying upon them, I had a false view of them, I thought they were gain; I see now they were loss, they were the things that stood between me and Christ, therefore I regard them as refuse.'

And the Christian knows exactly what Paul means when he says that. There are many good, innocent and harmless things in this world, but because of the new view which we now have we can see that these very things are robbing us of something which is still greater, and the things which we had thought were gain are actually loss.

The next principle is that this truth, which has mastered and grasped the Christian, is something for which he is clearly prepared to lose and to sacrifice everything else. Paul expresses this in his magnificent words: 'But what things were gain to me, those I counted loss for Christ. Yea doubtless, and I count all things but loss for the excellency of the knowledge of Christ Jesus my Lord: for whom I have suffered the loss of all things, and do count them but dung, that I may win Christ.' That is not hyperbolical. Paul is stating literal facts. Those things have no meaning at all for Paul because he is now a Christian. All his wonderful pride as a Pharisee has gone. He was a highly intellectual man, he had done better in the schools than anybody else, he had sat at the feet of Gamaliel, he was at the top of the list, he was one of the outstanding teachers of the law; and to become a Christian meant for Paul that he was regarded as a fool. He was denounced by his own people, all his prospects of position and greatness were gone, he lost it all, but he does not object, he is perfectly satisfied. If I may use his own language, he is pleased with the bargain. There he was in the old life keeping a list in the ledger, but now, he says, he has something on the other side which is infinitely greater.

And, of course, he suffered persecution. In 2 Corinthians 2 he describes all that he had suffered for Christ's sake and he suffered it all perfectly happily. I sometimes think that the greatest thing he had to lose was this: here was this highly intelligent man, this man who could meet with Jews at their best, as an equal, and even surpass them, and yet he had to spend most of his subsequent life amongst Gentiles and not only that, but ignorant Gentiles, many of them slaves and serfs who did not understand and did not appreciate his greatness, even as a natural man, so that he had to work with his own hands as a tent maker. It seems to me that the greatest test of all was to have to come down to such a level and spend his life with such people. But he gloried in it, he rejoiced in it, he suffered the loss of all things, and he tells us he did it gladly.

And why was that true of him? This is the last principle. All that we have been talking about is due to one thing, and that one thing is what Paul describes here as 'the excellency of the knowledge of Christ Jesus my Lord'. That is what explains everything else, that is the thing that has mastered him, that is the thing that has changed his outlook, and for which he is prepared to give up everything. What is it about this knowledge which is so wonderful, what is 'the excellency of the knowledge'? It is almost foolish to ask such a question – but let me just give you some brief suggestions.

The nature of the knowledge itself entitles it to that description. It is knowledge that brought Paul into an immediate, direct, personal contact with the most glorious person that this world has ever seen. Paul had met Gamaliel and had sat at his feet, he had met the great theologians, he was conversant with Greek philosophy, but now he had seen someone who is in a category apart. We, too, probably meet great people in this life, but here is knowledge that can enable us to meet God, that can enable us to meet the Lord Jesus Christ and to have fellowship and communion with him. The excellency of the knowledge is because of the greatness of the Person.

And then, it was knowledge that gave him understanding of God's marvellous way of salvation. You see, there is no need to detract from human knowledge. Philosophy is very good and wonderful, you can read your literature and enjoy your music and all these other interests, but when you take them at their best and highest, and contrast them with the scheme outlined in the Bible, they pale into insignificance. The excellency of the knowledge is because of God's plan of salvation.

What else? Undoubtedly Paul thought of it in terms of what it had done for him. It had saved him and delivered him from hell. He had been going there, and he saw that this knowledge had saved him from eternal damnation. What an excellent knowledge that could put a man right for eternity and save him from perdition, that could give him a knowledge of sins forgiven and reconciliation to God! Is there any knowledge comparable to knowing that your conscience is clear, that the book is put right, that your sins are erased, and that God in mercy has forgiven you? What excellent knowledge! This knowledge, then, brings peace and joy, a tranquil, quiet mind, a joy that is greater than the world can ever know or give or take away. New life, and power to live in a manner worthy of the name of man – that is what it had given him.

And then it told him about what was going to happen to him, it gave him promises with respect to his future. It told him that he had become a child of God and because of that, was an heir, and therefore a joint heir with Christ. It gave him an insight into glory and life beyond this world and death and the grave: it showed him the perfect life that he as a Christian would share with God to all eternity. When Paul saw that, everything else had become very small and insignificant, and he says, 'I count it as dung, refuse.' The excellency of the knowledge: it is excellent in itself, excellent in what it has already done for us, excellent in what it is going to do.

So, briefly and inadequately, we have taken a general view of this amazing Christian life. Let me end with a question. Have you been possessed by that kind of life? Do you know that God has dealt with you? Have you felt the hand of God upon you? Have you been taken hold of, do you feel that he is dealing with you, do you know something of the feeling that you cannot get away from it? Are you aware of being taken up rather than of taking up? Is your outlook on life entirely different from that of the non-Christians around you? Have you seen something which makes you feel you would sooner give up everything else, rather than lose this? As you think of the New Testament gospel, do you agree with Paul that there is only one way of describing it – the excellency of the knowledge of Christ Jesus, my Lord. Is he your Lord? That is the Christian position. He makes himself your Lord and mine, he has bought us, he has purchased us, he has taken hold of us and he holds us in his mighty grasp.

5

The Righteousness of God

And be found in him, not having mine own righteousness,
which is of the law, but that which is through the faith of
Christ, the righteousness which is of God by faith (Phil.
3:9).

In verses 4 to 14 of chapter 3, Paul has been telling the
Philippians how he counts all the things of which he used to
boast before he became a Christian, but loss, 'for the excellency of the knowledge' of Christ Jesus his Lord. And here,
now, in this ninth verse, he proceeds to tell us of one more
aspect of the excellency of that knowledge. It is something
that thrills the Apostle, something that makes him feel that
anything else which comes into competition with it must not
be considered for a second – therefore we must now concentrate our attention on this. The knowledge of which Paul is
now speaking concerns the whole question of righteousness
– a word that all who are familiar with their Bibles know
very well, for it is a word that you constantly find in the
Scriptures.

What, then, does it mean? Now there is a sense in which
the question of righteousness was always a problem to the
Apostle. It is the whole question of how we can stand in the
presence of God. It was the old question propounded by Job
right back at the beginning of history: 'How should man be
just with God?' (Job 9:2). That is the problem. How is any
one of us, in this life and in this world, ultimately going to
stand face to face with God in the judgment? That is the
problem, and it is because he has discovered the gospel's

answer to it that the Apostle tells us that nothing else is of any value at all. All that he had gloried in and boasted of, he now regards as refuse, it was loss because it had stood between him and this great answer.

Now this is, of course, the outstanding theme of the New Testament, and particularly of the New Testament epistles. It is perhaps more particularly the great theme of the Apostle Paul. It is his central doctrine, which you will find him illustrating almost everywhere in all his epistles.

Take, for example, Paul's statement at the end of 1 Corinthians 1: 'But of him are ye in Christ Jesus, who of God is made unto us wisdom, and righteousness, and sanctification, and redemption.' Again, you will find it in 2 Corinthians 5:21: 'For he hath made him to be sin for us, who knew no sin; that we might be made the righteousness of God in him' – it is the same thing again. Then take Galatians 3, which is nothing but another exposition of this self-same doctrine. But perhaps the classic passage on this theme is Romans 3. It is, indeed, the theme of the whole epistle to the Romans, until you come to the practical portions, but it is especially the theme of chapter 3, and the verses from verse 20 onwards stand out prominently in this respect.

There is nothing, therefore, that is so characteristic of Paul's whole outlook as his understanding of the question of righteousness. No subject so roused him as this; and there is nothing that made him so often burst forth in hymns of praise as his understanding of it. It is, indeed, the key of the whole doctrine of the Apostle, and if we are not clear about Paul's teaching on righteousness, we shall not understand any of his teaching; it is the first, it is the centre, it is the doctrine out of which, and from which, he derives every other doctrine in his teaching; it is indeed pivotal.

But we can go further and say that throughout the long history of the Christian Church no doctrine has produced such momentous results as this doctrine of man's righteousness in the presence of God through our Lord and Saviour Jesus Christ. It was, of course, the great doctrine which was propounded by St Augustine; it was when Augustine came to see this that his whole life ·was changed and entirely reversed. It was the doctrine that changed the course of Martin Luther's life. Martin Luther had been reared in that old religion, the Roman Catholic religion, which was nothing, in a sense, but a return of the Judaisers – an attempt to earn merit, an attempt to arrive at righteousness before God by one's own efforts. When Luther saw the doctrine that Paul announces in this ninth verse, his life was immediately changed and the Protestant Reformation came into being. It was this truth that made Luther defy, not only the powerful Catholic Church of his day, but all the tradition accumulated in the centuries which had gone before. This one man alone pitted himself against all that tradition, and it was all because of the certainty of the excellency of this knowledge; his constant challenges to that Church were in terms of this particular truth. Having seen it, he was prepared to risk everything, his life included, rather than give it up. It revolutionised everything, and that has been the effect it has always had when men and women have truly understood it. This doctrine is the whole explanation of most subsequent history, not only in the Church but even in secular history – it is a pivotal doctrine.

If you want another illustration of the same thing, you will find it in the life of John Wesley. It was when Wesley suddenly came to see this truth that his life, too, was reversed spiritually; his preaching became quite new and it was attended by the results with which we are so familiar.

Now I have given those illustrations in order that we may realise something of the background against which we should always consider this doctrine. Let me put it still more emphatically and bluntly: I wonder if we can say with the Apostle Paul that the doctrine of the righteousness of God in Christ Jesus is to us the most amazing and astounding and thrilling thing we have ever heard? That is what Paul says. This is wonderful! he declares. This excellent knowledge which I have received in Christ Jesus makes me say without hesitation that I count everything else but refuse, loss, and useless.

Perhaps the best way to approach this great doctrine is to try to define the word 'righteousness'. The best definition that I have encountered is this: 'Righteousness signifieth both justice and righteousness', that is to say, righteousness means conformity to law. Now, conformity to law can express itself in two ways. Firstly, justice means conformity to the law in carrying out the judgment, or sentence, imposed by the law; secondly, it means conformity to the law in obeying the precepts of the law. Paul uses the word 'righteousness' in both senses in that third chapter of Romans to which I have already referred.

Righteousness in the sense of enforcing the law comes in verses 25–26: 'Whom God hath set forth to be a propitiation through faith in his blood, to declare his righteousness for the remission of sins that are past, through the forbearance of God; to declare, I say, at this time his righteousness: that he might be just, and the justifier of him which believeth in Jesus.'

This use of the word righteousness really means 'justice'; the words, 'to declare, I say, at this time his righteousness', refers to his justice. Christ, by his death on the cross, says Paul, justifies God's forgiveness of sins.

Righteousness in the second sense of conformity to the law, of obeying its precepts, comes in verses 20–22: 'Therefore by the deeds of the law there shall no flesh be justified in his sight: for by the law is the knowledge of sin. But now the righteousness of God without the law is manifested, being witnessed by the law and the prophets; even the righteousness of God which is by faith of Jesus Christ unto all and upon all them that believe: for there is no difference.'

Our righteousness is conformity to the law in the matter of obedience; *God's* righteousness is conformity to the law in carrying out its sentence. God is the law-giver. When he forgives us he manifests his righteousness, or his justice. It has been necessary to work this out in detail because if we do not hold these two meanings clearly in our minds, we shall find that third chapter of Romans somewhat confusing. If we bear in mind that it refers to God's part and our part, in these two senses, then I think that it will become clear.

So, then, the question that arises for us is this: how can we conform to God's holy law? What can we do in order that we may conform to the demands of the law of God in all its fulness; for that is our position and the position of every person who is born in this world. Whether we like it or not, we are under God, and we are under God's law; whether we like it or not it is a fact. Everyone who is born in a particular country is born under the laws of that country; they may say they do not care for them, but they are under the law and can be challenged by that law. In the same way we are all born into this life under God's law. God has stated and revealed his law, and we are all under it. So the question confronting us is: What can we do in order to meet the demands of God's justice? What can we do about our life in this world so that when the law ultimately faces us and challenges us with the demands that it has made, we can answer it in such a way as to be free to enjoy happiness throughout the countless ages of eternity? That is the question.

And here Paul tells us that, in the last analysis, there are only two ways of doing that. There is, first of all, the old way that he had followed as a Jew. Now that old way is one with which we are all perfectly familiar. Our system is not that of the Jews, but it is the same in principle, so that what Paul says about the whole method of seeking righteousness under the Jewish law is true of everyone who has not seen the absolute necessity of believing on the Lord Jesus Christ. And I think we will all agree that this most common and fatal obstacle still stands between men and women and belief in the gospel. Ask the average person today what it means to be a Christian and, if I am not greatly mistaken, I think you will find that almost invariably you will be told what he or she does, or tries to do – the answer will be given in terms of personal human efforts. And that is the modern statement of this old Jewish position which Paul tells us he had forsaken.

Bearing that in mind, let us examine its characteristics and these are two-fold. The first is what Paul tells us here: in that old life, he had depended upon himself, upon his own efforts, on 'having my own righteousness, which is of the law' – that is it. It was an effort to produce his own righteousness; it was a righteousness dependent upon himself and his own excellencies; it was his own diligence with regard to the keeping of the law, especially the ceremonial law; it was his personal effort.

The second thing about it was that it consisted of an outlook which conformed to the ceremonial commands of the law. Paul tells us in verse 6 that, judged by the righteousness which is in the law, he was blameless. That was part of his boasting; he was 'circumcised the eighth day, of the stock of Israel, of the tribe of Benjamin, an Hebrew of the Hebrews; as touching the law, a Pharisee; concerning zeal, persecuting the church; touching the righteousness which is in the law blameless' (vv. 5–6). In what sense was he right to say that he was blameless? Well, this is what he came to see. He had thought that under the law he was absolutely blameless and that he could stand in the presence of God and claim that, but, he now tells us, he came to see that his blamelessness was merely in the matter of outward conformity to the ceremonial commands of the law.

In other words, the Jewish law commanded that the people were to bring burnt offerings and sacrifices, they were to do certain things, and Paul had equated the law of God with that outward, external, mechanical, ceremonial of the law. In that respect he was blameless. But it was only in that respect, for Paul had come to see that the righteousness of which he had boasted so much was, in deed and in truth, nothing but his own righteousness. He saw that instead of taking the law of God as it really was, he had substituted his own understanding and interpretation of it, and was thus conforming to his own little interpretation. Paul is very fond of saying that. In Romans 10 you will find he puts it very clearly: 'Brethren, my heart's desire and prayer to God for Israel is, that they might be saved. For I bear them record that they have a zeal of God, but not according to knowledge. For they being ignorant of God's righteousness, and

going about to establish their own righteousness, have not
submitted themselves unto the righteousness of God' (vv. 1–
3). The tragedy of my countrymen, the Jews, says Paul, is
that they think that they are pleasing God; they think that
the righteousness they are working out is the righteousness
God demands, but the trouble is that they are ignorant of
God's righteousness, and are going about trying to establish
their own.

And that was, of course, the whole trouble with the
Pharisees. Our Lord constantly made the same point. Ah,
he said, you authorities, you claim you are teachers on the
subject of rejoicing in the law, and yet the whole time you
are doing nothing but worshipping your own tradition, you
have substituted the tradition and opinions of men for the
law of God. Paul had done the same thing. He had fondly
imagined that he was blameless. There he was, boasting that
he was better than others. But suddenly he came to see that
it was not God's law at all, he had simply been keeping his
own little idea of God's law – it was his own righteousness.

Now this is a tragic attitude, but it is very common, as we
have already seen. Men and women tell us that they do not
see any need to believe in the death of Christ upon the
cross, it seems to them almost immoral. 'Surely,' they say,
'if people live a good life and do all the good they can, that
is what God demands.' The answer is, that it is not – and
that is the only reply to make to such a statement. They are
constructing a law, and then having made it, and having
equated it with God's law, they say that they are keeping
God's law. But the truth is that it is nothing but their own
righteousness – they are going about to establish their own
righteousness, and have not submitted themselves to the
righteousness of God.

Now Paul came to see that the law was not just mechanical, external conformity to certain dictates; the law was this:
'Thou shalt love the Lord thy God with all thine heart, and
with all thy soul, and with all thy might' (Deut. 6:5). He
describes it all in Romans 7:7–9, and says that when he came
to see the spiritual nature of the law and its demands, when

he came to see that God demands man's total allegiance – his heart and the whole of his being – then Paul was utterly condemned and, he writes, 'I died.'

But not only that, he saw also that the law is something that pronounces judgment upon sin. The Lord said, 'The soul that sinneth, it shall die' (Ezek. 18:4); that is God's law and the punishment for sin is spiritual death and separation from God. The law first of all gives positive commandments and asks us to keep them, and then, on the other hand, it pronounces judgment. There are, therefore, these two sides to the law and Paul came to see clearly that he had failed in both respects.

So, in the light of that, what does he mean by the 'excellent knowledge'? This is the real message of the gospel, this is the wonderful thing that Christ came to proclaim, and its characteristics are these. The first is that it is God's righteousness. 'Not having mine own righteousness, which is of the law, but that which is through the faith of Christ, the righteousness which is of God by faith.' Let us be sure that we understand exactly what Paul means here. It is God's righteousness in the sense that it is God's way of dealing with the problem of righteousness; it is not the righteousness that God demands or requires, it is that which he provides. That is what makes Paul go into such ecstasies. Here are men and women who have sinned against God, trying to establish a righteousness that will please God, but they cannot, and the wonderful thing is that God, in his word, has shown us the righteousness that he himself has freely provided for fallen, helpless, sinful mankind.

Now we must be clear about that, because it is the essence of the doctrine of justification by faith. The gospel shows us how, at one and the same time, we can fulfil the demands of the law, and God can accept us without violating his own justice. The law, I would remind you again, demands that we live a life of obedience to it and honour it; it also denounces our failure to do so, and when we define 'law' we must include those two things. Something must happen that delivers me from the penalty, and something must come into my possession which enables me to give that positive assent to the law so that I may honour it by keeping it. That is my problem, and the answer is that the gospel tells us of the provision that God has made for us in that two-fold respect. The righteousness which God provides is God's righteousness and not my own. That is the first thing.

The second characteristic is that this has become possible in Jesus Christ – 'And be found in him, not having my own righteousness . . . but that which is through the faith of Christ . . .' This righteousness comes to me by my believing that which has happened in Christ. It is all made possible for me in Christ. Again, this is something of which Paul loves to speak. For example, there is his great statement in 1 Corinthians 1:30. '[Christ] is made unto us wisdom, and righteousness, and sanctification, and redemption' – it is all in Christ. This is God's way of salvation, this is his way of providing us with righteousness. Here we are in this life; we have all sinned against God and his holy law, and there will be that two-fold demand. Under the law, the condemnation of sin is death and I have to meet that. I have also to face the questions: Have I kept the law and have I honoured it? But I have not.

So how does Christ help me with that problem? Here is the answer. He came into this world, he was made of woman, made under the law. Though he was the Son of God, he was born into this world as a human being. He put himself under the law, and in his life here on earth he rendered a perfect, absolute obedience to that law of God. He never forgot it in any respect or in any detail. He gave it the maximum obedience, the maximum allegiance; he worked out a perfect, full, positive righteousness. Then on that first Palm Sunday he went deliberately to Jerusalem, and afterwards he went deliberately to the cross.

Why did he do that? He went there because the law's demands had to be fulfilled. He was innocent, pure and absolutely righteous, the law could not point a finger against him, it could not find a single blemish in him, but he deliberately took our sins upon himself, and God punished our sins there in his body on the tree. God made him responsible for our penalty; God was there inflicting his penalty upon the Son, so that in Christ we see the demand and the penalty of the law satisfied, and we see the positive demand of the law in the matter of righteousness satisfied. Thus Christ is righteous in the full sense in that he has yielded obedience to the law both in its penalty and in its requirements, and the amazing, astounding message of the gospel is that God now takes that righteousness and gives it to us – 'Not having mine own righteousness, which is of the law, but that which is through the faith of Christ, the righteousness which is of God by faith.' We can put it like this. God turns to the sinner and says, 'There is perfect righteousness and I will give you that righteousness exactly as you are.' That is the offer of the gospel; that is what Paul came to see, and without doing anything at all, exactly as he was, he received and accepted it. He saw that it was his only hope, he submitted to it, and he was saved; God pardoned him and regarded him as justified – it is the righteousness of God by faith.

Let us be clear about this point. 'Through faith' does not mean that our faith is part of the righteousness. Righteousness is entirely in Christ, nothing that we can do can satisfy that law, we can never pay its penalty, we can never conform perfectly to its demands – righteousness is in Christ. He is our righteousness, it is all in him. My faith does not make me righteous; faith is simply the generator by which I receive that righteousness. Righteousness is of God, it is God who gives it to me and the way in which that happens, says Paul, is that I, by faith, am joined to Christ – 'that I may be found in him'. My faith in him makes me part of him. I enter into a mystical union with him, I belong to him, I am in him by faith, so that everything that is true of him becomes true of me – his righteousness is my righteousness.

And the results are that as believers we are being given all the great benefits of Christ. Is it surprising that Paul spoke in such a lyrical manner? Do you realise what it means? It means that you and I are delivered from the penalty of the law. It means more than that – it means we receive the reward of obedience. Archbishop Leighton once put it like this: 'The sinner stands guiltless of any breach, yea, as having fulfilled the whole law' – that is exactly what this doctrine means. If I am in Christ, God regards me as guiltless; not only that, God regards me as one who has kept the law fully. Christ has kept it and I am in Christ. I receive all the benefits of his perfect life and atoning death exactly as I am. That is the doctrine: 'Just as I am without one plea' – with nothing, nothing at all, indeed to start to do anything is a denial of the doctrine. You can do nothing, Christ has done everything. God offers his righteousness, he offers it as a gift. It is not our righteousness he requires, it is the righteousness he gives, so that we must no longer rely upon our own efforts and endeavours and activities. We must realise that if we lived to be a thousand years old we would be no more righteous in the sight of God then than we are now. You may grow in grace, but on your death bed your only hope will be the righteousness of Christ. It is all in Christ and all you do is believe on him and, to use the New Testament image, you are covered, you are clothed by that.

In Revelation 3:18 the Lord tells the Laodiceans that they must have white raiment that they may be clothed. And you remember how we are told in Revelation 19:7–8 that the bride is clothed with a robe of perfect whiteness. This symbolises the righteousness of Christ himself. That is the gospel message, so do you not see how it came to Paul as the most thrilling thing he had heard? There is that self-righteous Pharisee trying to build up his righteousness, and suddenly he sees that it has been given him. Look at Luther praying in his cell, trying to bring about his own righteousness, and then in a flash he sees that God gives it all in Christ. Whatever I can do, I can never do that, it is a gift. Christ is absolutely righteous and God gives me his righteousness. By faith I am incorporated in him and all that is true of him becomes true of me. God will reward me for keeping the law though it was Christ who did it. The righteousness which is of God by faith – that is 'the excellency of the knowledge of Christ Jesus my Lord'.

6

Paul's Great Ambition

That I may know him, and the power of his resurrection, and the fellowship of his sufferings, being made conformable unto his death; if by any means I might attain unto the resurrection of the dead (Phil. 3:10–11).

The Apostle Paul's object in this whole passage is, as we have seen, to denounce all types of religion which would add anything to the Christian faith beyond what has been accomplished by the Lord Jesus Christ himself. In our last study, we looked at verse 9 and saw that there the first and fundamental thing in 'the excellency of the knowledge' is the truth concerning the righteousness of God which is given to us in Christ. As Paul contemplates this, he scarcely knows how to restrain himself and he piles up epithet upon epithet as he thinks of the glory of this knowledge. But that, according to the Apostle, is only the first part of it. It is the first part, and it is a very vital one, but, thank God, it does not stop at that. Paul's position is that he has come to see that everything, all this 'excellent knowledge', is there in the person of the Lord Jesus Christ – his perfect life of obedience and his atoning death.

But as Paul contemplates these things he also sees something else, and he goes on to tell us in verses 10 and 11 of this further knowledge which he has found in Christ and which he desires to know still better. In verses 10–11 he states his ambition for which he counts everything else as loss. He is straining, as he tells us, like a dog at the leash. He wants to know it, he wants to apprehend it and he wants to be held by it.

And the first thing he tells us about this further knowledge is that he is anxious to know Christ himself better. 'That I may know him'. Now it is very important that we should be clear about this statement. Paul does not say that he is anxious to have a greater knowledge about Christ. Nor does he say that he is anxious to be still more aware of certain truths concerning Christ. There was a sense in which the Apostle desired this, but what he says is something that goes well beyond all that. He tells us that he longs for a greater and more intimate personal knowledge of the Lord himself.

Now the steps in his statement are perfectly clear. He has been looking at our Lord's earthly life, and at his death, and he sees that without them he would have nothing at all: he would have no hope, nothing on which to stand. 'Already,' says Paul, in effect, 'I see that in his life and death he has done all that for me, but, thank God, he did not remain in the grave. He rose again, he triumphed over death, he appeared to his disciples and he ascended into heaven.' This was something that Paul never forgot, for he himself had literally seen Christ that midday on his journey to Damascus; he had actually seen the face of the risen and glorified Lord and he had heard his voice. In a sense, he is asking here for a more intense and deepened experience of his initial experience on the road to Damascus.

If we consider some of Paul's experiences, which are recorded in Acts and in his epistles, we shall see perhaps still more clearly what he has in his mind. There, on the Damascus road, he had that amazing sight of the risen Lord, he had communion and fellowship with him, he heard a voice and the Lord spoke to him, he had contact with the person of Jesus. But we are also told that Paul subsequently had certain visions of the Lord. The Lord appeared to him in the temple and spoke to him; there was no question about it, Paul knew he was receiving a direct message from the risen, glorified Lord. Then, in Acts we are told that when he was in Corinth he was having a difficult time trying to preach the gospel because everything seemed to be against him. So he was rather dejected – Paul knew what it was to be dejected – and when he was feeling utterly hopeless, and the task seemed to be impossible, the Lord appeared to him in the night and said, 'Be not afraid, but speak . . . for I am with thee, and no man shall set on thee to hurt thee: for I have much people in this city' (Acts 18:9–10).

Again, he tells us in 2 Corinthians 12, that he once knew a man, some fourteen years before, who had been caught up into the third heaven and heard unspeakable words – and that man was Paul himself. He had been taken hold of and had actually been in that sensitive, ethereal atmosphere above the flesh, above the world, in a sense, having immediate communion with the Lord. That is not some general mysticism; it is Christian mysticism. It is not a man feeling that he is in tune with the Infinite; it is communion with the Lord of glory himself. And, says Paul, that is what I am longing for; '. . . that I may know him', that I may get to know him better.

An example from everyday life illustrates this perfectly. You are introduced to a man whom you have never met before, and immediately you are charmed, so afterwards you say to the friend who introduced you, 'I should like to meet that man again – I should like to see more of him and get to know him better.' That is what Paul is saying. He had met his Lord, and had communion with him, and now the one thing that matters to Paul in life, is to have more and more of that. He is always expecting, always anxious, to enter into more direct and personal communion and contact.

Now this is something that should not only be true of the Apostle Paul, it is something that is meant to be true of all of us. Let us be quite clear about this. We are not likely to have a view of the risen Lord such as Paul had, because, as we have seen, that was unique. Paul had been given that view on the way to Damascus because he was called to be an Apostle, and an Apostle by definition had to be a witness of the resurrection. In effect, he says in 1 Corinthians 15, 'I did not see him during the forty days as the others did, I saw him afterwards; that special view was given to me to make me an Apostle.' We are not to have that experience, because it is not meant for us, but we are meant to have a personal, living, real fellowship and communion with the risen Lord. If as a Christian all I can say is that I believe certain things about Christ, then I am but a very young and small babe in Christ. Of course, I am to believe things about him, and my faith is to rest upon him objectively, but the Christian position does not stop there. The one who is truly Christian is the one who has this fellowship and living communion with him.

Nor does it follow that you and I, of necessity, are to have visions. These are given to some Christian people, there is no question about that – you cannot read the lives of the saints without realising that from time to time visions are given to God's people. But we must not covet them; what we are to covet is this communion, this personal intercourse and fellowship with him, and, thank God, that is gloriously possible. In the absence of a direct view, without hearing a voice, without any ecstasy, quite apart from all that, it is possible for us to say with Henry Twells:

> What if Thy form we cannot see
> We know and feel that Thou art near.

Or we can say with the writer of another hymn –

> I need Thee every hour
> Stay Thou near by,
> Temptations lose their power
> When Thou art nigh.
>
> Annie Sherwood Hawkes

No, I have not seen him, I have not had a vision, I have not heard an audible voice addressing me, but thank God I can say those words. I know he is there, and I feel his presence. That is what Paul is speaking of, and that is the thing that we should covet, and long for.

'That I may know him.' Oh, not merely believing certain things about him, but really being aware of his presence. Sometimes when you are praying alone, sometimes when you are reading the Scriptures, sometimes when you are meditating upon these things, there comes the strange awareness that there is another, someone else, present, that you are not alone, and that he seems to be speaking to you. You do not hear, but you grasp the message. You understand what he is saying. He is there encouraging you about something you have done, or perhaps chastising or upbraiding you. He is showing himself in his glory and wonder, asking you to come nearer and to spend more time with him. These are the things, this is part of the fellowship about which the Apostle is speaking.

'That I may know him.' He is risen, he is alive, the Apostle actually saw him, but it is possible to have this communion by faith and Paul longed for more of it. And the question for us is, do we also long for more of it? To me it seems more and more the one thing that should be of concern to all of us who are Christians; indeed, I think it is the one thing that differentiates the true Christian from every other person in this world. Everybody desires something; everybody is anxious to have something; you and I may have ambitions of all kinds. Now the suggestion is that the Christian is someone who says, 'What I long for, above everything else, is that I may know him better, and when I think of that, everything else becomes relatively unimportant. If by selling all I have, or forsaking all I have been hitherto, if by doing that, I could have a deeper knowledge, a truer understanding, a closer communion, I would gladly do it all.' That is the test, that was Paul's experience and it should be the experience of each of us. 'The excellency of the knowledge of Christ Jesus' in this matter of knowing him still better, is something that transcends the whole world and all its wealth, its riches and possibilities.

So the first thing Paul wanted was to know Christ: 'That I may know him.' The next thing he wanted was to be more like him. Verse 10 continues: '. . . and the power of his resurrection, and the fellowship of his sufferings, being made conformable unto his death.' You see the inevitable logic? Whenever you meet someone whom you admire, you have an instinctive feeling within you that you want to be like that person. That is equally true of our relationship with the Lord. The man or woman who wants to know him better, is one who wants to be more like him, and that was Paul's constant experience.

And here he tells us three things that are necessary before we can become more like Christ. The first is that we must know 'the power of his resurrection'. The Apostle was very fond of this picture. As you read his epistles, notice the frequency with which he repeats the idea that he is presenting in these two verses. His favourite phrase is 'to be in Christ'; the Christian is 'in Christ' and Paul explains what he means by that. He makes the bold and, as he says himself, the incredible statement, that those of us who are Christ's and who are, therefore, 'in Christ', have died with Christ. When Christ died, I died with him; but, says Paul, not only did I die with him, when Christ rose again, I rose again with him. If I am in him, that must be true; if I am attached to him by faith, if I belong to him, if I am a member of his body, then whatever has happened to him has happened to me also – buried with him in baptism, rising also with him in newness of life.

Now if you want the best exposition of that which even Paul can give, turn to Romans 6. In the first five chapters of Romans Paul has been emphasising the great doctrine of justification by faith. We must not look to ourselves and our own merits at all; we are saved in Christ, by what he has done. Then Paul imagines some clever man in Rome saying, 'I see the doctrine, if we are justified by faith, it does not matter what we do, so shall we continue in sin that grace may abound? Surely,' says this person, 'the logic of your argument is this: if it is all in Christ, then I can do whatever I like, I am covered by the blood of Christ and I am forgiven and all is well.'

'Ah,' says Paul, in effect, 'the man who speaks like that has never understood the doctrine of righteousness; he has never understood the meaning of the death of Christ upon the cross, and he is being utterly ridiculous.' Then Paul goes on to explain it in the sixth chapter. 'Romans,' he says, 'understand this, that if you are in Christ and have died with him, you have received newness of life. Well, then, walk with him in this risen life that you share with him.' And that is exactly what he is saying here in this tenth verse of Philippians 3.

No, for those who understand this doctrine there is no real danger of what is called 'antinomianism'; the people who want to know Christ better are those who want to be more like him. But what about the man or woman who comes to me and says, 'Here am I in my weakness, conscious of sin within me, temptation always around and about me, the whole world organised on the side of sin and Satan and evil. It is difficult enough to keep straight and moral at all in a world like this, and you are asking me to live the kind of life that Jesus of Nazareth lived on this earth – it is impossible.' The answer to such a person is, 'the power of his resurrection'. He is risen, he has given a manifestation of his power, and that power is being offered to us. That is the power that can become ours, however weak we are; it can lift us and raise us up in newness of life, and enable us to walk with him.

Paul puts this most dramatically in Romans 7, in fact these verses in Philippians are but a very brief synopsis of the sixth, seventh and eighth chapters of that epistle. What can I do? Paul says. I want to be better, I want to live the Christian life, but I cannot do it. I do love the law of God, I know it is right and I want to live according to it, but, 'I see another law in my members, warring against the law of my mind, and bringing me into captivity to the law of sin which is in my members. O wretched man that I am! who shall deliver me from the body of this death?' And there is only one answer, 'I thank God through Jesus Christ my Lord' (vv. 23, 25). The one who conquered sin and Satan and death, and who rose triumphant will enable me. His power can become mine, I may experience the power of his resurrected life. And as I realise more and more that I am in him and get to know him better, I shall feel his mighty power flowing into me and raising me up above myself and out of sin – 'the power of his resurrection'.

What else? The second thing that is essential to becoming more like Christ is 'the fellowship of his sufferings'. What does this mean? Why does Paul go back to Christ's sufferings after talking about the resurrection? Well I think that, experimentally, it is perfect logic. I want, says Paul, to be in him before I can become more like him, and I realise that nothing but the power of his resurrection can make me more like him. And I want to be like him in this sense, that, because I am so much like him, I shall repeat some of his experiences in my own life in this world. It is a world of sin, so that when even the Son of God came into it, he suffered because he was holy and the world was sinful. Jesus Christ could not have suffered as he did if he had not been perfect. The sufferings of the Son of Man on earth were entirely the result of sin, and, Paul says, the more I become like him, the more I shall suffer as he suffered.

It is a tremendous and a terrifying thought. Paul, in writing to Timothy who was suffering and actually grumbling, says, Timothy, my friend, you have it the wrong way round. You ought to be glad about this, 'Yea, and all that will live godly in Christ Jesus shall suffer persecution' (2 Tim. 3:12). 'The disciple is not above his master, nor the servant above his lord,' said Christ himself, '. . . if they have called the master of the house Beelzebub, how much more shall they call them of his household?' (Matt. 10:24–25). 'My brethren, count it all joy,' says James, 'when ye fall into divers temptations' (Jas. 1:2).

> It is the way the Master went,
> Should not the servant tread it still?
>
> Horatius Bonar

That is what Paul means. He says, 'I can see clearly that the more holy I become – the more I become like Christ – the more his experiences will be re-enacted in my life.'

Our Lord was 'a man of sorrows and acquainted with grief' partly because his holy soul was troubled when he saw what sin had done to his Father's creation. When he saw the foulness and the ugliness of sin, it hurt and it grieved him. So the more we approximate to our Lord and his life, the more will the sin of this world grieve and hurt us. Does it wound us? I am not asking whether we are irritated by it; a person who is merely moral can be, and often is, irritated by sin, but that is not what our Lord felt. He was not irritated, he was hurt, it grieved him, it became a burden on him. And Paul says that he longs to enter into the fellowship of those sufferings. In addition, the more we are like him, the more we are likely to be persecuted by those who do not understand him, by those who cry out: 'Away with him, crucify him.' That is what Paul means by living the life our Lord lived, and I know I am living it as I experience, in a measure, what the world did to him.

Then Paul says next, '. . . being made conformable unto his death,' which means that I become so obedient to God that, like my Lord before me, I am ready, if necessary, even to lay down my life. If it is a question of loyalty to him and his holy commandments, I do not hesitate. My Lord was confronted by that very possibility and he gave his life willingly and readily so that God's holy will might be done. And I, too, says Paul, shall be so dead to sin, so dead to the world, so dead to everything that is not of him or is opposed to him, that, like my Lord before me, I will be able to give my very life, even, if necessary, unto death itself.

There, briefly, are the three steps in becoming more like Christ – knowing the power of his resurrection, sharing the experiences of his sufferings, even being made conformable unto his death. But, lastly, Paul's ultimate ambition was to be with Christ in glory. 'That I may know him, and the power of his resurrection and the fellowship of his sufferings, being made conformable unto his death; if by any means I might attain unto the resurrection of the dead.' You see the steps: more frequent communion with him, more like him, then ultimately with him for ever. Paul could never get away from those steps; let us make sure we understand them:

verse 9, justification – his righteousness;
verse 10, sanctification;
verse 11, glorification.

These are the inevitable, indelible steps. Note, too, that you cannot be justified without being sanctified, and without being glorified. You remember how Paul put it in Romans 8: 'For whom he did foreknow, he also did predestinate to be conformed to the image of his Son, that he might be the firstborn among many brethren. Moreover whom he did predestinate, them he also called: and whom he called, them he also justified: and whom he justified, them he also glorified' (vv. 29–30). Those are the steps and it is all in Christ.

Now let us be quite clear as to what Paul means here when he says, 'If by any means I might attain unto the resurrection of the dead.' 'But I thought,' says someone, 'that every person who has lived on the face of this earth is ultimately going to rise at the last day?'

True, there will be a general resurrection of the dead. Every one of us is going to be raised one day, that is inevitable, that is the decree of God for all mankind, but that is not what Paul means here. He means this other truth to which we have just referred; he is looking forward, not to the resurrection that is going to lead to the second death, to damnation and to hell, but to the resurrection of the just, the resurrection of the righteous, the resurrection that leads to glory, to be for ever with the Lord.

Paul is looking forward to that state into which all Christian people shall finally enter, in which they will be entirely free from sin. It is incredible, but it is going to happen. You and I, if we are in Christ, shall rise, and no trace of sin will be left in us. There will be no such thing as an evil thought or imagination; we shall be blameless and faultless, without spot or blemish; the eye of God will detect nothing amiss in us and we shall be glorified, perfect, even as he is. Paul works that out in the last verse of this third chapter: we look at him 'who shall change our vile body, that it may be fashioned like unto his glorious body, according to the working whereby he is able even to subdue all things unto himself'. The day is coming when sin shall not only be taken out of my soul and spirit, but even out of my body. There will be nothing imperfect in it, I shall have a new glorified body, I shall be like him. This is how John puts it: '. . . it doth not yet appear what we shall be: but we know that, when he shall appear, we shall be like him; for we shall see him as he is' (1 John 3:2).

> Changed from glory into glory,
> Till in heaven we take our place,
> Till we cast our crowns before Thee,
> Lost in wonder, love, and praise.
>
> Charles Wesley

That is what Paul longed for above everything else – the day that was to come, the glorious day of the resurrection. Again he refers to it in that eighth chapter of Romans. He says the whole creation is looking forward to it, even the animals, the birds, the flowers, everything groaning as they wait for it. The whole world is to be renovated, there is to be a new heaven and a new earth, and everything is waiting for the manifestation of the signs of his glory – the final glorification.

Christ lived the perfect life, he died the atoning death, he was buried in a grave, he has risen and has entered into the glory, he is living the life of glory and all who are in Christ are certain of the same glory. The extent to which we realise something of this is the extent to which we shall know, with the Apostle Paul, what it is to long for it, and to say that in the light of this everything else is unimportant, it is rubbish. The world and its kingdoms and all its glories, what are they as I think of that other glory? And, therefore, my ambition is: 'If by any means I might attain unto the resurrection of the dead' – and an entry into that glory.

7

The Ultimate Goal

Not as though I had already attained, either were already
perfect: but I follow after, if that I may apprehend that for
which also I am apprehended of Christ Jesus. Brethren, I
count not myself to have apprehended: but this one thing
I do, forgetting those things which are behind, and reaching forth unto those things which are before, I press
toward the mark for the prize of the high calling of God
in Christ Jesus (Phil. 3:12–14).

On any showing, this is a most remarkable and important
passage. I suppose that in many ways it is one of the Apostle's most familiar statements, but it has also led to much
controversy and misunderstanding.

These three verses are part of the statement which the
Apostle is making with respect to his own faith and his own
position. You remember the background: he has set out to
contrast the position of the Judaisers with that of Christianity, and he puts it in terms of his own experience – as well
he might, for he himself had experienced the position of the
Jews, and he had given years of his life in an attempt to
make himself acceptable in the sight of God before being
given this understanding of the truth as it is in Christ Jesus.

And in what a glowing, moving and dramatic way he
finally contrasts these two positions! Once he had obtained
this excellent knowledge that is in Christ, all else seemed to
him not only trivial, but indeed a hindrance. And he goes on
to say that he would gladly sacrifice everything else that
remains to him – though he has sacrificed so much already –

313

if that were necessary in order to win Christ and be found in him, not having his own righteousness which is of the law, but that which is through the faith of Christ, the righteousness which is of God by faith. Paul's ambition is to 'know him, and the power of his resurrection, and the fellowship of his sufferings, being made conformable unto his death; if by any means I might attain unto the resurrection of the dead.' And then there follows the passage that we are going to consider now.

This is an important statement, if only from the standpoint of Paul himself. He is a subject well worthy of our consideration: one of the greatest men of all times, judged by any standard, one of the outstanding masterminds of history and the world. This passage is important simply because it helps us to understand him and his position more clearly and more truly. But, after all, we are not here to take merely a theoretical interest in the great Apostle, fascinating though that is from the standpoint of theology and psychology. We are concerned about this statement because it has a very definite relevance to us, because it has something to tell us about our own state and position.

While we recognise clearly that the Apostle is a man of gifts and that, as an Apostle, he stands in a category apart, we must nevertheless understand that what Paul says of himself as a Christian is to be true of every Christian. The Apostle himself makes that quite clear; he says, 'we are', and he constantly includes other Christians with himself. In this particular section he writes in the first person singular because he is dealing with his own experience, but what he says about himself should be true of all of us as Christian people and should therefore be a part of our experience, too. So it becomes urgently important for us to discover exactly what the Apostle is really saying about himself here.

Furthermore, our experience depends upon and follows from what we believe, so that if our belief as to what is possible to us and for us is wrong, then it is more than likely that our experience will be correspondingly wrong. There can be no doubt but that many, if not most, of the difficulties in the

Christian life and experience arise from a failure to understand the doctrine, from a failure to understand the possibilities that are laid open to us by this glorious gospel. So the
vital question for us to consider is what, in reality, the Apostle is saying in these verses about himself and his experience.

What is he saying? People generally answer that question
with one of two opposing answers – but I want to suggest
that both answers are wrong. The first answer is that we are
told here that Paul is saying he is uncertain of his salvation.
If ever you have been engaged in a discussion on the question of assurance of salvation, or if you do become involved
in such a discussion with people who have some knowledge
of their Scriptures, I think you will find that those who lack
assurance themselves go even further than that and say that
no one should be certain of salvation; and they are very fond
of quoting these verses. They say, 'How can a man be certain of his salvation when the great Apostle himself was not?
"Brethren I count not myself to have apprehended" – does
that not mean,' they say, 'that the Apostle was not certain?
Does it not show that his whole position was that he hoped
he would eventually be saved? Is he not there showing, and
has he not been suggesting that, in the previous verses? "If
by any means" – does that not denote uncertainty? Does not
the language he uses at that point specifically show that the
Apostle, great as he was, nevertheless was not sure that he
was saved, was not certain that his sins were forgiven and
was not confident that he was a child of God? He hoped he
was going to be eventually, but he was uncertain about it.'

That, then, is the suggestion that has often been put forward. But an argument like that, it seems to me, at once
brings us face to face with a vital principle. Whenever we
are confronted by a difficult text, there is always the danger
of basing our doctrine upon that alone instead of taking it in
the light of the whole teaching of the Scriptures. Now I
think I can show you that the language that the Apostle uses
at this point in no way supports the suggestion that he is
uncertain of his salvation. Indeed, if we say that he is, then

we are forced to the conclusion that the Apostle is contra-
dicting what he has stated so categorically and explicitly in
various other places in his writings: 'I know whom I have
believed, and am persuaded that he is able to keep that
which I have committed unto him against that day' – that is
the statement of the Apostle Paul in 2 Timothy 1:12; or
again, he says in Romans 8:38 and 39, '. . . I am persuaded,
that neither death, nor life, nor angels, nor principalities,
nor powers, nor things present, nor things to come, nor
height, nor depth, nor any other creature, shall be able to
separate us from the love of God, which is in Christ Jesus
our Lord.'

Then in this very epistle, you remember, in chapter 1:6,
he says, 'He which hath begun a good work in you will perform it until the day of Jesus Christ.'* Is that the language
of uncertainty? 'For to me to live is Christ, and to die is
gain,' he continues in verse 21, and in verse 23: 'For I am in
a strait betwixt two,' on the one hand, 'having a desire to
depart, and to be with Christ; which is far better.' I ask
again, is that the language of a man who is uncertain of his
position, the language of a man who is merely hoping that
he may eventually be saved or that somehow or other, in
spite of everything, he may find himself among the
redeemed? Surely the language of the Apostle is an utter
contradiction of that suggestion. If ever a man wrote out of
a full, abounding confidence in that which he knew concerning himself and his position in Christ, it was this man
– 'For whom he did foreknow, he also did predestinate to
be conformed to the image of his Son, that he might be the
firstborn among many brethren. Moreover whom he did
predestinate, them he also called: and whom he called,
them he also justified: and whom he justified, them he also
glorified' (Rom. 8:29–30). That is his language. 'Who shall
lay any thing to the charge of God's elect? Paul asks in
Romans 8:33. The thing is impossible. No, the Apostle is
certain of his salvation, he is assured; 'For we are the

---

* See Volume 1, *The Life of Joy.*

circumcision, which worship God in the spirit, and rejoice in Christ Jesus, and have no confidence in the flesh.' All his language everywhere, and even here in Philippians, makes it quite impossible for us to say that the interpretation of these verses is that Paul is uncertain of his salvation.

Then let me put to you the other suggestion that has been offered, which is the exact opposite of the one I have just been outlining. It is held by those who agree that Paul was certain of his salvation. These people feel that since the Apostle was absolutely certain of his salvation, the only way to explain these verses is to say that Paul means he has not yet finished his life's journey, he has not arrived at the ultimate resurrection of the dead. They solemnly put forward that as an explanation of these words. They say Paul's statement can only mean, 'If by any means I might arrive at the resurrection, but, brethren, I have not arrived yet.'

But this, surely, is yet another suggestion which is not only patently inadequate, but is, indeed, even ridiculous. It would mean in effect that the Apostle, actually writing or dictating a letter to the people at Philippi, tells them, 'I am still alive and in this world; I am still going forward in the journey.' But that is unnecessary, the fact that he is writing tells them all that there is no need for a man who writes a letter to say he is still alive!

So, then, if we cannot accept either of these two suggestions, what is our interpretation of what the Apostle says? Well, there seem to me to be three main statements in the section from verses 10 to 14. Here is the first: Paul tells us that Christ has laid hold of him, and still holds him, in order that he may arrive at a particular goal – 'Not as though I had already attained, either were already perfect: but I follow after, if that I may apprehend [lay hold of, grasp] that for which also I am apprehended of [laid hold of, held by] Christ Jesus.' That is the first great statement. In other words the Apostle is telling us here that as he went down to Damascus on that famous occasion, he was suddenly laid hold of by the Lord Jesus Christ. He was grasped – that is what 'apprehended' means. We still use the word in this sense, though not as frequently as in the days of the Authorised translation. However, we still talk about the police apprehending a man when they hold him in order that certain investigations may be made. Paul says he was apprehended by Christ; Christ had put his hand upon him, and was holding him still.

But, you notice, he says that this happened to him for a certain, specific reason: '. . . if that I may apprehend that for which also I am apprehended'. Paul was apprehended for this particular reason. Now that, it seems to me, is the key to understanding this particular statement. What was it that Paul was apprehended for? Why was he laid hold of on the road to Damascus? In a sense, he has already been telling us. He was grasped by Christ, not merely that he might know forgiveness, and not merely that he might give up the attempt to work out his own righteousness. He was laid hold of not merely that he might cease from persecuting the Christian Church, and not merely that he might be delivered and emancipated from that which was wrong.

Why, then, was he apprehended? Well, for this positive reason: he was saved, as is every other Christian, in order that he might eventually reach a particular goal, and he describes that goal in verse 10 – that he might know Christ fully and perfectly; and not only that, but that he might become like Christ, that he might know 'the power of his resurrection, and the fellowship of his sufferings, being made conformable unto his death'. The Apostle is very fond of teaching this particular truth. This is how he puts it in his letter to Titus: 'For the grace of God that bringeth salvation hath appeared to all men, teaching us that, denying ungodliness and worldly lusts, we should live soberly, righteously, and godly, in this present world; looking for that blessed hope, and the glorious appearing of the great God and our Saviour Jesus Christ; who gave himself for us, that he might redeem us from all iniquity, and purify unto himself a peculiar people, zealous of good works' (Tit. 2:11–14). That is the same idea exactly.

The goal, then, that Paul tells us has been set before him,

the thing for which he has been apprehended, is that he may come to that intimate knowledge of Christ, that perfect communion, and that he may be delivered, not only from the guilt of sin, about which he is perfectly certain, but also from the power and pollution of sin, and become like Christ in his life, in his death, in everything; that he may reproduce in his life the kind of life that was lived by the Lord Jesus Christ himself. I have been grasped for that, says Paul. So that is the first statement. Our Lord laid hold of him that afternoon on the road to Damascus in order that he might enter in along that path. And that is the Apostle's ambition – to arrive at that.

Then his second statement tells us that he has not arrived at that goal. Oh yes, he knows he is saved; he realises that his ultimate salvation is as certain as anything can be; he is in Christ and knows he is going to be with Christ – there is no question about that; he has left all these other things behind him and has given up any belief in any other righteousness. He now has that righteousness which is by faith in Christ Jesus and he knows his ultimate destiny. But what he is dissatisfied about is his failure to arrive at that goal for which he has been arrested – the experimental knowledge of Christ and his conformity to Christ in his whole life and living. 'Not as though I had already attained' – Paul is not referring to the resurrection nor, as I have shown, is it necessary for him to say that he is alive – no, it is, '. . . that I may know him, and the power of his resurrection.' I have not attained to that, says Paul, and that is what I am pressing after. He has not reached the goal for which he has been apprehended and so his third statement is that he longs to arrive at it and he strains every nerve in order that he may do so: '. . . reaching forth unto those things which are before, I press toward the mark . . .'

These are the three things which the Apostle says in these verses: he defines the goal, the ambition of the Christian; he confesses that he has not attained unto it; and he tells us that his whole concern in life is to arrive at it and that he is doing those things which are necessary to arrive there. So, having explained the Apostle's words, let us proceed to deduce the doctrine; in other words, let us apply what the Apostle says about himself to ourselves.

Now this is a matter about which there is a great deal of confusion and there is much loose talk on the one side and on the other. There are those who claim more than the Apostle claimed and there are those who do not claim as much. Those two dangers are always present. Some people say that you must not claim that you are sure of your salvation; you must just say that you are doing your best and are hoping to reach that goal at the end. Others maintain that Christians in this world are already perfect and should certainly claim that they have attained to such a state of perfection. We shall see, however, that the Apostle avoids both these statements and is saying something quite different here. The doctrine can be put like this.

First, there is no such thing as perfection in this life and world, it is impossible. The case of the great Apostle alone is, in and of itself, quite sufficient to satisfy us upon this matter once and for ever. 'Not as though I had already attained,' says this mighty man of God, 'either were already perfect.' Paul himself was not perfect.

'But,' says someone, 'does he not go on to say in verse 15, "Let us therefore, as many as be perfect"?'

But surely the Apostle would not contradict himself within a few verses! The word 'perfect' in verse 15 is one of those limiting terms that we find used by the Apostle in many places. For example, in 1 Corinthians 2, he says, 'Howbeit we speak wisdom among them that are perfect' (v. 6). He is contrasting those who are babes with those who are in a more advanced position; he says he cannot give the higher doctrine to the people at Corinth because they are still babes in Christ, they are 'yet carnal' (1 Cor. 3:3). 'Howbeit,' he says in effect, 'we speak wisdom to those who are more advanced and mature.' And in Philippians 3:15 he says the same thing: 'Let . . . as many as be perfect . . .' It is not absolute perfection, it is relative. But in verse 12 it does mean absolute perfection: I have not already been made perfect, he says, I have not arrived at that.

Thus, it is obvious that the great Apostle is not satisfied with the life that he is living; there are elements in his life which cause him a good deal of dissatisfaction. On the basis of this one instance, without going any further or quoting other Scriptures, which I could easily do, we can lay down the principle that perfection is not possible in this life. What right have we to claim that it has happened to us? The Apostle does not claim that it has happened to him.

'Then,' someone asks, 'why is it that God does not make perfection possible to us here?' To which the only ultimate answer is that we do not know. All we do know is that if it were God's will for us to be made perfect by the operation of the Holy Spirit upon us it would happen. 'But why does God not do that?' someone insists. However, there are certain questions that you and I should not ask; all we know is that he has chosen not to do so.

Certain answers can be put forward. It may well be that because of sin and its effect upon us, God leaves us just as we are in this life to keep us humble, lest we boast, lest we fail to realise our utter dependence upon him. It is our failures that drive us back to him, it is our consciousness of imperfection that keeps us in communion with him. God has chosen to do this even as he did in the lives of the Children of Israel; it seems that God works in that way. I do not understand it, but I simply recognise the fact that the great Apostle says he is not perfect, and from that I deduce that we are not meant to be perfect in this world.

Let me put it negatively: claims to perfection are based upon two errors, and the first is an incomplete self-examination. People who claim to have arrived at a state of perfection – and there have been such, you read of them in history – have generally done so because they have been guilty of not examining themselves completely. They have said that because they are not guilty of certain sins, they are perfect; they have not examined the heart or the imagination; they have not realised that in the matter of perfection our state is as important as our actions.

The second error is the error of setting up too low a standard. People see that they are better than they were before because they no longer commit certain sins. They also find themselves better than other people around them – and they think therefore that they have reached perfection. But their standard is too low. Let me remind you that the standard the Apostle sets for himself and all Christians is nothing less than this: to know Christ in a perfect state of communion and fellowship; to know the power of his resurrection delivering us not only from acts of sin, but from thoughts of sin, from the machinations of sin, and from this toying with sin, delivering us from the guilt and power and pollution of everything connected with sin; that is the standard and nothing less. It is the fellowship of his sufferings, being made conformable unto his death. And no one can honestly claim that he or she has attained unto such a standard.

Then my next proposition is that perfection and complete sanctification are not to be attained suddenly. I think that obviously follows as the next step. Those who teach a kind of perfectionism would have us believe that this is a state that one can achieve suddenly. They often tell us that it has happened in a Convention or in a meeting, that suddenly they have received this other blessing and have been made perfect. They say there was a sudden transition from one condition to another.

Now, surely, the language of the Apostle here denies any such doctrine. He speaks of 'following after': '. . . this one thing I do, forgetting those things which are behind, and reaching forth unto those things which are before, I press towards the mark.' There is nothing sudden about it; his whole picture is one of development and progress. He is like a man running along the road, going step by step and yet ever going forward. There is no sudden transition from a state of improvement to a state of perfection. Indeed, a good illustration, used by Paul and the other New Testament writers on the same subject, is that of the 'babe in Christ', where the whole idea suggests growth and development, with steps and stages. Or take again Paul's other example of the plants and the flowers. He talks about the husbandman planting seeds (for example, 2 Cor. 3:6–7), and in that illustration there is the same idea. Perfection and complete sanctification must never be conceived of as something that happens suddenly. In a meeting or a convention you may have a new view of the love of God, but that is very different from perfection and complete sanctification. The Apostle's method is 'pressing forward', striving and going forward, step by step and stage by stage.

That leads me to the next important principle. This progressive work means activity for us and not passivity. The teaching on perfection is almost always a teaching that is connected with passivity. We are told that people will persist in striving after holiness, in trying to sanctify themselves, but that the thing to do is to 'let go and let God'. The Apostle's language, on the other hand, is this: 'I follow after'; 'This one thing I do, forgetting those things which are behind . . . I press forward.' He talks in 1 Timothy 6:12 about fighting 'the good fight of faith.' All these expressions are indicative of great activity on the part of the Christian in the matter of salvation. In the matter of our righteousness and justification we can never say too often that we do nothing, we can do nothing, it is entirely the work of Christ. But once we are saved and given this new life, then the progressive work of sanctification does not call for passivity, and we are exhorted to activity.

The last principle in this doctrine is that our consciousness of imperfection, far from robbing us of assurance of salvation, is, in a sense, almost the ground of assurance of salvation. And that is so in this way: I suggest to you that the only people who speak like Paul are those who are saved, those who have life in them. The vast majority of men and women in the world do not say that their greatest ambition is to 'know him, and the power of his resurrection, and the fellowship of his sufferings, being made conformable unto his death'; they are not interested, that is not their ambition at all; they are interested in things that are almost the exact opposite. But, surely, the people who say, 'I am dissatisfied,

I am conscious of my imperfection, I am aware of sin, I am not what I ought to be, "O wretched man that I am! who shall deliver me from the body of this death?"' – they are the people who have spiritual life in them.

Do you, as you look at yourself in the light of the truth, feel, like Paul, that you have not attained, that you have not arrived, that you have not grasped, that you are much too far back along the road and wish you were further forward? If you do, then it is a proof that you have spiritual life. If this is your ambition, far from suggesting uncertainty about whether or not you are Christian, it is proof that you are.

Finally, let me apply what I have been trying to say by asking a few questions. Are we satisfied with our lives? The Apostle Paul was not. Look at him, look at the life he lived. Here was a man who had seen Christ, who had had visions, who had heard an audible voice. Here was a man who had been lifted up into the third heaven, a man who had preached the gospel day and night. But he was not satisfied. Are we complacent? Do we feel we are all right simply because we are better than the vast majority of people who do not darken the doors of a place of worship? Are we content with our lives? If we are, we are very different from this Apostle. Do we long to go forward? Paul, this mighty servant of God, longed to go still further forward along the road, he was straining to arrive at the goal. Can we say that we are advancing in that way? Are we striving with all our might to do so?

Well, there is this great and vital doctrine which is taught by the Apostle at this point. It is a picture of the Christian. Christians are assured of their salvation; they see clearly what they are meant to be and they know that they are not; but they long to be and they give all their energy in order to arrive. May God deliver us from a false doctrine of perfection, and implant within us and encourage the growth within us of this principle that was so plainly evidenced in Paul, this realisation of the ultimate standard, this longing for it and this determination to spare no effort in order to arrive at it.

8

The One Thing

Not as though I had already attained, either were already perfect: but I follow after, if that I may apprehend that for which also I am apprehended of Christ Jesus. Brethren, I count not myself to have apprehended: but this one thing I do, forgetting those things which are behind, and reaching forth unto those things which are before, I press toward the mark for the prize of the high calling of God in Christ Jesus (Phil. 3:12–14).

In our last study we considered these words mainly from the standpoint of what I may describe as their theological import. We have here, as you remember, a personal statement made by the Apostle – which was something he did but rarely. Paul only makes use of his own personal experience when it is essential for him to do so, for example, if he is to define his title as an Apostle or if his authority as a teacher is being queried. He calls upon his own experience here because it is clearly the best way of confuting the argument being put forward by the Judaisers who wrought such havoc in many of the early Christian churches.

So we have seen that Paul's description of the Christian's position in general terms is this – assurance with regard to the ultimate, dissatisfaction with present attainments. But having said that, we come now to a more practical consideration of the Christian position, for in these three verses the Apostle not only describes his state in theological terms, he also describes in detail what we may call the method of the Christian life. The Apostle gives us here a more intimate

picture of his own spiritual life and the discipline of his
Christian living than he does anywhere else in all his writings, and that is why these three verses are of supreme
value. He gives us this one insight and glimpse into his own
normal daily procedure; he tells us how he is dealing with
this sense of dissatisfaction which he feels with his present
attainments, and how he is pressing onwards and forwards
to that ultimate goal towards which his face was set.

These verses, then, are of great practical importance to
us, and we should thank God for them because I think
that most of us must tend to think of this great Apostle in
a way which is not altogether true. It is very easy to think
of him as some person altogether apart whose life, therefore, is of no value and significance to us. There are so
many things about Paul that mark him out as an exceptional man; he was exceptional by birth, exceptional in his
ability, and exceptional in his training; and then his conversion took place in such an exceptional and unusual manner.
He was given visions, and had such unique experiences
that, unless we are careful, it is very easy, as we read the
various references to him in the New Testament, just to
think of him as some kind of miraculous person standing in
a category quite on his own, and to think of his life as
purely miraculous.

It is very difficult to think of Paul having the struggles and
conflicts which we experience as Christian people. I suppose
that most of us – some of us especially – tend to idealise the
Apostle's life to such an extent that it almost becomes of no
value to us as an example and illustration of Christian living.
But here, in these few words, Paul disabuses our minds of
any such ideas. Here, I think, he shows us very plainly that
he finds it absolutely essential to work according to a given
plan; that his life is not just a succession of miraculous
events, but that he is the man he is because of his conformity
to certain fundamental principles, and it is there that his
case becomes of such value to us.

To put it in a directly practical form, we can ask ourselves
a question: Are we anxious to have Paul's experience? Are

we able to speak of life as this man spoke of it? Can we say that there is a sense in which what may happen to us in the future is a matter of supreme indifference to us? Can we say with Paul that whether it is going to be a life of imprisonment or whether it is going to be death, it is really immaterial, for, 'to me to live is Christ, and to die is gain'? Are we, as he was, in the position of being able to say, '. . . I have learned, in whatsoever state I am, therewith to be content' (4:11)? Can we say, 'I can do all things through Christ which strengtheneth me' (4:13)? That is Paul's experience; the question is: Have we longed to know that? How is that to be attained? How can we arrive at it?

Here, I suggest to you, the Apostle answers those questions. If we would have the experience of the Apostle, we must live the life of the Apostle. If we would share these amazing things that are recorded in the life of the saints of God, then we must conform to the pattern of their life. And it is of great interest to me to observe that all these people seem to conform to the same pattern. It does not matter whether you take the biographies of the saints who lived in the first century, or those of the twentieth, you will find that some essential things are always there they always live in a certain manner, and that manner is described perfectly in these three verses.

So then, as we come to consider the passage in detail, let me emphasise what I would call the two controlling principles in Paul's life. The first, which stands out very clearly, is that Paul did not live off his experiences. We read the story of his conversion, we read his account of the visions he was given, and of how, on one occasion, he was caught up into the third heaven and saw and heard things unspeakable, and yet nothing is so clear about the life of this man as that he did not live on those experiences. Indeed, in 2 Corinthians 12 he tells us quite explicitly that though he might boast about these things, he did not do so. He rather gloried in his infirmities and weakness and in the apparent perplexities of life, for he tells us that though he had these extraordinary experiences, he also knew what it was to have a thorn in the flesh and though he prayed

that it should be removed the Lord did not take it away.
Paul prayed that prayer three times, but the thorn did not
go, and for a time he was bewildered by this. However, he
came to understand the reason when the Lord said unto
him, 'My grace is sufficient for thee' (2 Cor. 12:9) and then,
Paul tells us, he arrived at his ultimate philosophy, '. . .
when I am weak, then am I strong.'

That is the first great principle which we must always bear
in mind. Many Christians are in trouble because they try to
live off their past experiences. They remember their experiences and try to draw something from them; they are, as it
were, drawing on some capital which was given to them in
the past, and they are receiving nothing in the present. Paul
denounces that; it is not his method at all. He does not grasp
at the past, or live off his experiences; his method is active,
pressing forward into the future.

This leads to the second principle underlying the Apostle's conception of holiness and spirituality: that the Christian life is not passive. I need not stay with that because I
dealt with it in our last study, but I do think it is right that
we should hold it in our minds as we come to consider Paul's
spiritual method. We must not think of Paul as a man who
spent most of his time in contemplation, either upon his
knees or sitting waiting. There is nothing of the so-called
'spiritual method' of the Roman Catholic view of sanctity
and holiness, with its 'dark night of the soul' and its passivity
and abnegation. You cannot find it in the verses we are considering, or anywhere in the life of this Apostle – his life is,
indeed, the very antithesis of that kind of passivity.

And so, bearing these two principles in mind, we come to
Paul's method of living. In a sense, Paul here tells us that his
life was nothing but an exemplification of what he has told
the Philippians to do. In their case, you remember, his rule
for them was given in verses 12 and 13 of the second chapter. 'Wherefore, my beloved, as ye have always obeyed, not
as in my presence only, but now much more in my absence,
work out your own salvation with fear and trembling. For it
is God which worketh in you both to will and to do of his

good pleasure.' That is the method. It is this apparent paradox in the Christian life. It is a working on our part and yet a realisation that we could not work unless we were being worked upon. It is a realisation that it is of God and yet that God has allowed to us, who have been given new life, our part and our portion – 'work out . . . for it is God that worketh in you.' That is what we see perfectly illustrated here in this practical method of the Apostle.

It is, of course, something he tells us everywhere. Take, for instance, the first chapter which we have already considered.* There he tells the Philippians that he is 'confident of this very thing, that he which hath begun a good work in you will perform it until the day of Jesus Christ' (v. 6). And yet, in spite of that confidence, he says in 1:9, 'And this I pray, that your love may abound yet more and more in knowledge and in all judgment' – and so on. The Apostle assures them of the ultimate, and of what God is doing, and then immediately follows that by an exhortation to activity and to work.

Those, therefore, are the principles behind the detailed method which we can now consider. So let us look at it like this. What is the character of the Christian life? According to the Apostle it is a striving, a struggle, an effort, an endeavour ever onwards and upwards in the direction of that goal in the distance, of which he has been given a view. Now let me introduce you to the terms – and all I am doing at this point is making one or two comments upon the words which Paul uses in these three verses. 'I follow after,' he says. It is not as though he had already grasped, or were already perfect, but, 'I follow after'. That is one of his terms, and then he has another in verse 14: 'I press toward . . .', and what is interesting is that in the original these two expressions are exactly the same word. And what is still more interesting is that it is precisely the same word which he has already used in the sixth verse. You remember how he gave an account of his life before his conversion –

---

* See Volume 1, *The Life of Joy*.

'Concerning zeal, persecuting the church . . .'? Now the word translated there as 'persecuting' is the word translated 'follow after' and 'pressing toward' in this passage.

And that gives us a perfect picture of the character or the nature of the Apostle's life. When we read the account of the Apostle's conversion in Acts 9 we see clearly his zeal and enthusiasm in persecuting the Church. He went to the rulers at Jerusalem and asked them for authority, for papers, to go down to Damascus to persecute the Christians. There never was a man keener on his job, there never was a man more zealous! He hated these Christians and spared no effort to wreak havoc amongst them. There he went down the road, breathing out threatenings and slaughter, persecuting the Church. And that is the way in which he is living the Christian life. Just as he once followed after the Christians and hounded them and sought them out in every nook and corner, so he is now following after this thing for which he has been apprehended: 'I follow after', 'I press toward', 'I persecute'. That is the description which he gives of his life as a Christian.

But Paul is not content even with that. In order to show us this zest, this keenness, this enthusiasm, he adds still another word: 'Brethren . . . forgetting those things which are behind, and reaching forth . . .' Now 'reaching forth' is even stronger than 'following after' or 'pressing toward'. Paul is using an illustration familiar from the Greek games. He is picturing a man running in a race and it is a wonderful pen-picture. You can almost see the man reaching forth, stretching forward with his hand. You know the anxiety of the man who is running a race – he stretches out his hand; it doesn't help him, but it does show his desire to win, to touch the finish before he gets there. His hand is stretched out, he is striving, pressing on, trying to grasp it – reaching forth.

That is the kind of Christian the Apostle Paul was. You see his keenness. He is a man who has seen something – a glorious possibility, the prize, and wants to get there. Paul is pressing on, he is running, he is stretching forth with all his power. In his unregenerate days Paul used that power to persecute, but now it has been harnessed and turned in the other direction. He is all out for this glorious, tremendous thing that lies there ahead of him in the future. That is the character, that is the nature of the Christian life. That, according to the Apostle, is the sort of person which the Christian is meant to be.

Now I should fail in my task as a preacher at this point if I merely painted the picture and then moved on, because there is surely a question which we all must ask ourselves: Is that a picture of us? We know what it is to be enthusiastic about something but is this keenness, which is in every one of us by nature, channelled in the direction of the ultimate goal of the Christian? That is the question. It is because it was true of him, that Paul could say with such confidence, 'To me to live is Christ, and to die is gain.' Christ is everything, and Paul is confident and assured.

Very well, if that is the nature or character of the Christian life in general, let me ask the next question, which is a still more practical one. How can we arrive at that goal? If we have seen it, and know about it, if our eye is fixed upon it; if we are in this race and if we are aiming at that goal, then how are we to get there? What are the Apostle's rules? How did he run in this race? What are the principles on which he operated? Let me just mention the terms – they are all here. The first is *self-examination*. 'Brethren,' says Paul, 'I count not myself to have apprehended,' or, 'I reckon not myself to have apprehended.' Now that denotes self-examination. Here is a man who examines himself. This is a great subject; every one of these four points I am going to note is worthy of not only one study to itself, but a whole series of studies. But as we are living in this twentieth century and not in the great days of the Puritans of the sixteenth century, we must just hurry on and note them in passing instead of spending two or three studies on each one of them!

Self-examination is a subject which can very easily be misunderstood. It does not mean that Paul was morbid, or

introspective; it does not mean that he was always feeling
his own spiritual pulse and taking his own spiritual temperature. No, but it does mean that he did not live on assumptions concerning himself. He was always looking at the standard and was constantly being measured by it. Perhaps one
of the greatest dangers confronting us as Christian people is
the danger of being content to go on assumptions, the
danger of thinking that because we are in a certain position
we are all right. I trust that I am not unjust in saying this,
but is not complacency perhaps one of our greatest dangers?
I feel that because I am not guilty of certain sins I am all
right, and I cease to examine myself. How easy it is to be
content with conversion and never to go any further. Paul
was always looking at himself and examining himself, in
order to make sure that he was still pressing forward
towards that goal. He was not satisfied with himself, and he
was not satisfied because of this self-examination, and he
exhorts others to do the same. Examine yourself, he says,
make sure that you are in the faith.

And this is something we constantly need to do. It is, of
course, one of the functions of preaching to encourage that.
Increasingly, I consider it the business of the preacher to ask
questions, and that is one of the first questions we must ask.
How often do we stop to examine ourselves? Do we dislike
self-examination? Do we face ourselves, or do we try to get
round it by doing good, by giving attention to this or that,
and in this way attempt to salve our own conscience? Now
this is the first essential. We should ask the Holy Spirit to
search us; we should meditate upon these things; we should
make notes, if necessary, of obvious weaknesses. We must
be honest and true with ourselves and face ourselves in the
mirror of the perfect law of liberty. Self-examination – 'I
count not myself,' says Paul.

Then let us hurry to the second word, which is *concentration*. 'One thing I do.' That is Paul's way of describing his
concentration. Let us look again at the man running in a
race. The man who runs in a race must not be interested in
the landscape. If he begins to look at the mountains and the

charm of the flowers in the hedgerows, he will not win the race; he must be intent on one thing only. There was a story I once read in a newspaper which struck me as a charming and perfect illustration of what I am saying. An agriculturist was describing how he was driving his car along a narrow road on his way to visit a farm, when suddenly he came upon a flock of sheep and a sheep dog. His problem was how to get past these sheep. Then he described the amazing way in which the sheep dog dealt with the situation, how he kept and had his eyes upon the flock and made his calculations, running backwards and forwards. But the interesting thing was that a little terrier belonging to a nearby house came out and tried to pick a quarrel with the sheep dog, coming at him and barking at him. The writer of the article pointed out the magnificence of that sheep dog who completely ignored the yapping terrier. He knew he had a great job to do – he had to get his sheep past the car – so he did not pay any attention to the terrier: 'One thing I do,' said the sheep dog.

That is the way in which Christians are to work. They do not look at these distractions – the world is full of distracting interests, some of them legitimate, some not. But those who want to be like the Apostle Paul do not look at them – only at one thing – concentration! They do not look around, they do not allow themselves to be interested in things that are going to distract them from their purpose; they keep their attention upon it. Furthermore, they are not fitful and spasmodic in their Christian life. God knows how we find ourselves searched by a word like this. Is it not the case with most of us that we constantly make resolutions about what we are going to do, but we are always going to do something; we make a start and then we stop. We start running, but those who know us know that before midday we will probably be lying down. This spasmodic, fitful Christian living! The Apostle says, 'One thing I do'; it is regular and it is constant. The Christian life is impossible without discipline. We must control ourselves, we must divide up our time, we must realise, in a world that is so set against us, that if we do not discipline our spiritual life we shall certainly find ourselves in trouble.

And then the third great principle is 'forgetting those things which are behind'. And here again the most important point, of course, is that we must be quite clear what Paul means. He does not mean that the Christian should deliberately forget the past experiences, nor does he say that he himself forgot about his conversion, he never forgot it. He does not say that he had forgotten all the things that had happened to him. No, he does not mean that. What, then, does he mean? He means that we must not rest upon our past experiences, we must not be for ever looking back upon them in a self-satisfied way in order to pride and preen ourselves upon them. It is like the man in the race. His business is not so much to consider how far he has arrived along the track as to discover how near he is to the goal that is ahead of him. What a temptation it is always to be looking back!

Of course, there is a sense in which that is perfectly legitimate. If you have ever climbed a mountain, you are probably acquainted with this very thing. If you look at the summit as you are climbing you feel discouraged, but when you look back, you feel better. That is all right as long as you do not stop to admire your achievement. That is what the Apostle is warning us against. Those who are always looking back are those who are not likely to be going forward very rapidly or securely. That is why I have felt that when people are repeatedly called upon in meetings to tell the experience of their conversion, though it may be good for those who are listening, it is probably very bad for those who give the experience. Anything which tends to cultivate this tendency to look back and to talk about past experiences or past achievements comes into conflict with the Apostle's great principle here. No, 'forgetting those things which are behind'. I would even put it as bluntly as this: do not look back in a spirit of self-satisfaction even upon your orthodoxy. You may have made great sacrifices for Christ's sake – forget it, and think of the things still awaiting you! That is what Paul means. Anything which makes us look back with a desire for self-admiration threatens our spiritual progress.

But lastly, of course, and, indeed, supremely, there is the importance of keeping our eye on the goal and on the prize, for is it not obvious that if we do that, the other things follow of necessity? And that was Paul's greatest secret: 'That I may apprehend that for which also I am apprehended.' The Apostle always looked at that; he saw that goal, and, of course, seeing the goal he did not want to look back on his past achievements. They were good and wonderful, yes, but now, looking at the goal, how poor they were, how small! And that, it seems to me, is the secret of the Christian life. Those who have their eye on the goal do not want to compare themselves favourably with other people; no, they see their own imperfections. That does away, too, with jealousy and envy. They do not want to look back, what they do want is to get to the goal. The Apostle kept his eye, his gaze, fixed upon that.

What, then, is that goal? We have already described it – 'That I may know him, and the power of his resurrection, and the fellowship of his sufferings, being made conformable unto his death . . .' That I might attain unto that final resurrection of the just and enter into glory – that is it, that is the one thing that counts with Paul. I rather like the one word which puts together all that we are considering in these verses: 'I press toward the mark for the prize of the high calling . . .' In the margin of some Bibles you will find another phrase – 'the upward calling'. It does not matter which you use, the idea is just this: it is a call that comes to us from on high, or, if you prefer it, it is a call to us to go upwards. The call raises us and summons us to ultimate glory in the presence of God himself.

That is the final secret. We must not compare ourselves with the sinful world around and about us; we must not compare ourselves with Christians who are obviously further back than we are in the race. No, we have been called, grasped, apprehended by Christ, to know him, to be like him, to be for ever with him. Christians are people who see that, and never lose sight of it. Nothing matters with them but attaining unto that, so they press onwards, they stretch forward, they are always reaching up, and they do so by watching themselves and their achievements, by this utter concentration upon the goal and by being forgetful of everything that has happened hitherto.

That, it seems to me, is the Apostle's method, the discipline of Christian living. So the effect of it should be something like this. Not a day should pass in our lives but that we should deliberately and solemnly remind ourselves of these things. I am destined for that glory. I am in Christ, I am going to be perfected in Christ – that is the goal. Do I know him? Am I like him? Am I being made conformable unto his death? I have been apprehended by Christ for that and that should be the centre of my life, the object of my every ambition.

God grant that we all may so see the goal, that we may be so charmed and attracted by it, that we shall have an eye for nothing but that – the prize, the mark of the high calling of God in Christ Jesus.

9

Belief and Conduct

Let us therefore, as many as be perfect, be thus minded:
and if in anything ye be otherwise minded, God shall
reveal even this unto you. Nevertheless, whereto we have
already attained, let us walk by the same rule, let us mind
the same thing. Brethren, be followers together of me,
and mark them which walk so as ye have us for an ensample. (For many walk, of whom I have told you often, and
now tell you even weeping, that they are the enemies of
the cross of Christ: whose end is destruction, whose God
is their belly, and whose glory is in their shame, who mind
earthly things) (Phil. 3:15–19).

Here in these verses, and, indeed, in the two following verses also, the Apostle Paul is applying what he has just been
saying about himself to the situation of the members of the
church at Philippi. In verses 4 to 14 we have seen, how, in
order to deal with the difficult subject of the Judaisers, he
gave an account of himself and of his experiences. He
described how he had been brought out of Judaism into the
Christian position, and he elaborated that statement in the
way that we have been considering together for a number of
studies.

But it is not Paul's intention simply to write about himself; his concern is to help the members of the church at
Philippi. It is possible that he might be put to death at any
moment and he is naturally anxious to safeguard their whole
future position. He has introduced himself merely by way of

337

an illustration; his purpose is to apply all he has said, in order that his readers might put into practice in their lives the governing principles of his own life and conduct. Here, then, he sums up the whole of the experience he has just been relating, and he sums it up to enforce it and apply it to the Philippians.

If we would know, therefore, how to live a full, successful and happy Christian life, the kind of life which the Apostle lived, if we would enjoy the experiences in the Christian life that he so singularly enjoyed, then Paul tells us here exactly what we have to do. Perhaps the best way to consider this is first of all just to indicate the various points and principles which Paul enunciates in these verses, and then, having commented upon them one by one, to look at the philosophy at the back of it all. The great theme is the inter-relationship of faith and practice, belief and conduct, but before we come to work out the teaching in terms of a principle like that, it might be good for us to note the separate items as the Apostle enumerates them.

The first thing Paul tells us is that we must have the right belief. 'Let us therefore, as many as be perfect, be thus minded . . .' Now the Apostle Paul is very fond of this word 'mind'. You notice how in this very section he keeps on repeating it. In the sixteenth verse he says, 'Nevertheless, whereto we have already attained, let us walk by the same rule, let us mind the same thing'; and in verse 19 he ends the description of those unworthy believers by adding 'who mind earthly things'. Again, back in the second chapter, he uses exactly the same word. In exhorting these Philippians to consider one another and to help one another, he says, 'Let this mind be in you.' In Romans 8, also, he points out that the difference between the natural and the spiritual person is that those who are of the flesh 'do mind the things of the flesh', whereas those who are spiritual 'do mind the things of the spirit' (Rom. 8:5). It is an expressive term and it generally means that these are the things which not only interest, but greatly concern people; they are the things with which people spend a lot of time, the things about which they form strong conclusions. That is why I put it in the form of a principle.

So we must make certain, first of all, that we have the right belief: 'Let us therefore, as many as be perfect . . .,' says Paul. I need not point out again the meaning of the word 'perfect', because I referred to it when we were dealing with it in verse 12 where Paul says, 'Not as though I had already attained, either were already perfect.' In that verse it is an absolute term, here in this fifteenth verse it is relative. It means those who are matured and have reached the adult state, those who have advanced so far in the Christian life. But what is it that we have to be clear about? Well, surely, this third chapter, which is pre-eminently the theological chapter of the four, itself answers that question.

Paul is warning the Philippians that there are two main errors which they must avoid at all costs. The first is the one dealt with at such length, the error of the Judaiser. 'If,' says the Apostle in effect, 'you are still prepared to listen to these people who teach and believe that unless you are circumcised you are not truly Christian, if you are going to put that into practice, then your whole Christian position is undone. It is no use exhorting you to live the Christian life so long as you have the wrong mind about the Christian faith.' In other words, Paul is, as it were, coming back to verse 3 where he says, 'For we are the circumcision, which worship God in the spirit, and rejoice in Christ Jesus, and have no confidence in the flesh.' We have to be absolutely certain about that, we must not be in any state of hesitation in our minds as to what it is that makes a person a Christian. Beware of the error of Judaism!

But there is also a second danger to which he has been referring in outlining his own experience. The Philippians must be equally clear about the error of perfectionism. Both these things must be avoided: Judaism and perfectionism. Judaism generally presents itself as a belief in the power of man to save himself by his own works, or in man's reliance upon his birth, upbringing or nationality, these purely carnal and natural things which the Apostle tells us he has left behind once and for ever. We must avoid all that and realise that as Christians we are in a spiritual realm and we must not 'mind' – or set our minds upon – earthly things, but heavenly things.

That is one danger, and the other is this equally dangerous error of perfectionism which, almost invariably, has been accompanied by what is commonly known as antinomianism. In other words, it is quite clear from this passage that there were people in the church at Philippi who were threatening the life and the peace and the welfare of that church. There were people in the early Church (and they have appeared in the Church from time to time ever since) who believed that they had arrived at a state of perfection and who then, on being shown that they were guilty of certain things, did not hesitate either to try to explain those sins or defects away, or to say they did not matter. It was, they said, the flesh, but they themselves were all right. And that is the essence of antinomianism: it says that as long as I am in Christ, it does not matter what I do; as long as I am truly Christian, my practices are quite irrelevant.

Now the Apostle says that we must be perfectly clear about these two things – 'Let us therefore, as many as be perfect, be thus minded', and by being 'thus minded' he means that we must be perfectly clear about the whole basis of our position. You must, says Paul, agree with what I have just been saying – that we must press on, that we do not rest upon our oars, that we do not say we have arrived, or that we have done all we have to do to maintain this state of perfection to which we have attained. It is not that, Paul says, but rather, our lives in this world must be ever pressing forward towards the mark and the prize and the goal. We must not congratulate ourselves on our achievements but be ever 'stretching forth'. We must be 'thus minded' – we must get rid, once and for ever, of the dangers presented by the Judaisers and by the perfectionists.

Now this is as true today as it was when the Apostle wrote this letter to the church at Philippi. We must always start with doctrine and with belief. There is no hope at all in the

Christian life if we are wrong at the very basis and foundation of our whole position. Therefore we agree with the Apostle and realise that the first thing is to have a right mind about these matters, so that if we are asked what it means to be a Christian we know exactly; we realise that we have a foundation which is solid because it is based upon the teaching of Scripture itself. That is the first principle.

But then Paul hurries on to the second point, which is equally important, and it is this: that we must practise that belief and walk in a manner that is consistent with it. 'Nevertheless, whereto we have already attained, let us walk by the same rule, let us mind the same thing.' Now, 'walking by the same rule' just means that we should put into practice that which we have already agreed about as being the right and correct belief. The Apostle is particularly insistent about this. Everywhere in his epistles you find him saying that there is no purpose in having the right belief unless we put that belief into operation. 'Let us therefore, as many as be perfect, be thus minded: and if in any thing ye be otherwise minded, God shall reveal even this unto you.' There are certain things, says Paul, which are absolutely central and vital. There must be no argument and no discussion about them, we must all be clear about them. But, he says, there may be other things about which you are not quite clear – 'if in anything ye be otherwise minded'. If there are certain aspects of the Christian life or of the Christian faith about which you are not clear in your minds, do not lose hold of your Christian faith and practice because of them.

This is surely a very healthy principle. The Apostle's way of dealing with those difficulties and with some intellectual perplexities is this: practice! Put into operation the central things about which you are certain and if you do that, God will then reveal unto you the truth concerning those other things. Do not spend the rest of your life arguing about the things which are not clear to you. There are certain matters in connection with the Christian faith about which Christian people have never been unanimous. I need not mention them now in detail, but Christians differ about Church gov-

ernment, for example. We are familiar with that in this
country. No man can say that one view is the truth and no
other. No, but about justification by faith you can and must
say that, and that is the distinction which the Apostle is trying to bring out. About justification by faith, about the
uselessness of works in the matter of saving one's own soul,
there is to be no question at all, we must all be thus minded,
it is dogmatic and definite.

But there are other matters about which we may not be
clear: a particular form of baptism, for instance, or a particular interpretation of prophetic teaching – pre-millennial,
post-millennial and a- or non-millennial. Now those are in
the realm where no one can say, 'This is the truth and there
is no other.' There is room for legitimate difference of opinion, and the saints of God have differed about these matters
throughout the ages. Very well, says Paul, get hold of the
essential things, put them into practice, and if you do that
honestly, then you can be perfectly sure in your mind that
God will reveal to you those other matters about which you
are not clear and certain at the moment. He does not say
when this is going to happen, but he does say that eventually
we shall be given clear teaching.

That, then, is the distinction. We must always maintain in
our minds that there are some things that are absolutely
essential to salvation, and there are other matters which are
not, though they may be important. So the essence of wisdom in the Christian life is to draw a sharp distinction
between these two things; never to regard the essential
matters with indifference and never to regard matters which
belong to the realm of indifference as if they were essential.
We must never mix matters about which there can be no
certainty in this life with matters which are central and all-
important in Christian living.

Anyone who is familiar with Church history, will realise
what an important principle this is. Have we not all known
Christian people who have made their Christian life
unhappy simply because they would take things which we
cannot arrive at with any certainty and make them tests of

orthodoxy, and insisted that we should agree with them absolutely before we could have fellowship with them? How much harm has been done in the Church because of that, because men and women would not implement the teaching of the Apostle at that point. 'Let us therefore . . . be thus minded: and if in anything ye be otherwise minded, God shall reveal even this unto you' – that is it. Out with Judaism! Out with perfectionism! 'Let us walk by the same rule, let us mind the same thing'; practise what you are certain of, put into operation that which is beyond a doubt, be careful and diligent always to implement these central matters about which there can be no discussion. I hope that all who are following me in this argument will join me in admiration of the balance and the sanity of Christian teaching, and I trust that we can see that most of the heresies of the Church, and also most of the unhappy divisions in the Church – for I would differentiate between happy and legitimate differences and unhappy divisions – have been due to the fact that men and women have failed to grasp this teaching and to draw these vital distinctions between central and peripheral, between absolute and doubtful.

The next piece of advice which Paul gives us is an exhortation to follow good examples – 'Brethren,' he says, 'be followers together of me.' Here again we cannot but be amazed at the magnificence of the Apostle's teaching and especially at his condescension. He is concerned about doctrine, and in order to help the members of the church at Philippi he says, in effect, 'I have given you the teaching in that bald, unvarnished, theoretical manner, but if you really want to know what I mean, let me put it like this: follow my example, and not only my example, but follow the example of those who are your teachers.' Now there is very little doubt but that he is referring partly to the two men of whom we read in the second chapter, Epaphroditus and Timothy. These men had helped in the teaching and the building up of the church at Philippi, he has already made reference to them, and Paul is exhorting the Philippians to look at them – people they have known.

Notice, too, the way in which the Apostle turns from himself and includes the others: 'Be followers together of me, and mark them which walk so as ye have us for an ensample.' I am not quite sure that I agree with those people who think this is said by the Apostle merely out of modesty. What he means is that he does not hesitate to ask them to follow him – that is not egotism on the part of the Apostle, it is simply stating a literal truth. This man who had been saved by the Lord Jesus Christ, and had given his whole life to pleasing his Lord, was the man who had a right to ask others to imitate and follow him. He does so frequently in his letters, and yet no man who has a spiritual mind at all would feel like charging the Apostle with pride. There was never a more humble man than Paul; his life was such that he could turn to these people and say, I am presenting you with an example and illustration, and this is the illustration: 'Not that I have already attained or were already perfect, but I follow after.' That is what he tells them to follow. 'I am exhorting you,' he says in effect, 'to do the very thing that I am doing myself. I am not satisfied with my life and achievements, so I am pressing on towards the mark and the goal. Be followers of me, do the same thing I am doing. But it is not only true of me, it is true also of Epaphroditus, and of Timothy.' And he thus exhorts these members of the church at Philippi to follow their great and glorious example.

Once again, is there anything that can be of greater practical value to the Christian who is anxious to live a truly Christian life than to follow such good examples? Is there anything that so helps us in our endeavour to attain unto that ultimate goal than to read the lives of God's saints, the biographies of good, godly men and women? Speaking for myself, I can certainly testify that I have found nothing of greater value and encouragement. You see the truth in practice; you see it translated from the realm of pure teaching and put into operation. To me it is one of the saddest features of the life of the Church today that so often people are ignorant of the great saints of the past. Our fathers were familiar with them and spent a lot of time reading about them and these great biographies are still available. Surely nothing can do us greater good than to read and study them, that we may follow their example even as the Apostle exhorts us at this point.

The last piece of advice which Paul gives is that we should take warning from bad examples: 'Many walk, of whom I have told you often, and now tell you even weeping, that they are the enemies of the cross of Christ . . . who mind earthly things.' It is not only right to follow good examples, it is equally important that we should observe these illustrations of bad Christian living. We are provided with many of them in the Bible itself, and there is no doubt that this is why the cases of these men and women are recorded there; they are set up as great warnings to God's people. We find the story of Cain, of the people of Sodom and Gomorrah, and we have the example of the Children of Israel; these various illustrations have surely been recorded for our benefit – we are told of people who have not lived the godly life and we behold what has happened to them.

And can we not find the same thing in subsequent Church history? Nothing is more valuable and useful than familiarising ourselves with the great history of the Church in the past, keeping our eye on the positive and the negative, as the Apostle exhorts us at this point. Here is the Apostle's prescription for a happy, successful and full Christian life; be absolutely certain in your mind about the things that are vital, and the moment you are certain of them, put them into practice.

But Paul is inculcating here a doctrine on the whole question of the relationship between faith and practice. Let me note what I regard as his essential teaching in this matter. The first thing, surely, is that our belief will always determine our conduct. The Apostle and his friends lived the life they lived because they were 'thus minded'. Paul lived the life he lived because he had seen the error of Judaism and has been delivered out of it; he had seen the positive truth concerning Christ and he had also seen the error of perfectionism. Thus the Apostle's conduct as he ran the Christian race was determined by the belief that he held.

In exactly the same way, he tells us, the conduct of people who are living unworthy lives and 'whose end is destruction' is also the outcome of their belief. The trouble with them is that they 'mind earthly things'; their real interest is in the world and in life as it is lived in this world. Their mind, their concern, their interest, their thoughts are earthbound, and Paul says that they are the people of whom we can say, 'their god is their belly', and 'their glory is in their shame'. Why? because 'they mind earthly things'. A man's conduct is finally determined by his belief and by his faith.

Is that not being painfully proved and manifested in this modern world of ours at this present time? Look at the conduct of the vast majority of people. What explains it? Well, surely, the simple answer is that they hold a wrong belief. That is why education, culture and all these things cannot save the situation. The trouble with the world for the last fifty years or so has been this: it has said, 'Yes, Christianity is all right, but we need not be bothered about Christian dogma and doctrine.' The world would like to hold on to Christian ethics, that is why it is so fond of praising the Sermon on the Mount, but it does not want all this talk about Jesus of Nazareth being the Son of God, and about his incarnation, and his death upon the cross. So the world has brushed aside Christian doctrine and has fondly believed that it can hold on to that which it thinks is good in Christian ethics. But that is impossible in the light of what the Bible says about belief and Christian teaching. It is useless for a man to say he believes in God, but does not see any need to keep the Ten Commandments; and it is equally idle to expect people to believe in the Ten Commandments without believing in God – which is the first commandment. Faith determines conduct and the modern world is nothing but an eloquent exhibition of the soundness of this fact. We must start with the belief and faith principle, for a man's conduct always expresses what he ultimately believes.

Let me put that in a slightly different form in a second

principle. Conduct is the best index to the nature and the value of our belief. In other words, show me a man's conduct and I can tell you his belief. That is the reason why the Apostle here so constantly exhorts these Christians to make certain that their conduct is in accordance with their belief. In Titus 2:3, Paul uses the expression 'as becometh holiness' – that is his argument for holy living. 'Can you not see,' he says in effect, 'that it is truly inconsistent to say you believe one thing, if you are doing the exact opposite?' That is the New Testament argument for sanctity and holiness. If we believe that Christ died for our sins in order to deliver us out of that realm, how can we continue in sin? It is utterly inconsistent and the Apostle does not hesitate to say that there is no value at all in the supposed faith and belief of a man who constantly lives the other life – 'Be not deceived; God is not mocked' (Gal. 6:7). It is possible for a man to make a whole series of intellectual assertions, but if he lives his life altogether in the other direction, it is proof positive that his faith is not of the slightest value and is indeed not real faith at all. There is no difference in this between James and Paul; they are saying exactly the same thing in different ways. A man's conduct is the final proof and testimony of the reality or the value of his profession and belief.

And then, lastly, the ultimate test of a man's belief and conduct is the cross. 'Many walk, of whom I have told you often . . . that they are the enemies of the cross of Christ . . .' Notice here that Paul says these people are the enemies of the cross of Christ. What really proves the ultimate error of the Judaisers is that they are doing away with the cross. Those who tell me that they can put themselves right with God by living a good life, are enemies of the cross of Christ because, in effect, they are saying that the cross of Christ will not save them. The friend of the cross says, 'Nothing but that cross can save me.' Any one who in any way adds to or detracts from it is an enemy of that cross – that is the final condemnation of the Judaiser and of the moraliser. All people who say that by their own efforts they can fit themselves to stand in the presence of God, are the enemies of the cross, they are detracting from its glory.

But you can do exactly the same thing in your conduct, says the Apostle. He is talking about people who are living the wrong kind of life, whose gods are their lusts, their passions, their carnal nature, who live for these things, who 'mind earthly things'. Paul says equally of them that they are enemies of the cross of Christ. Is there any class of person who brings the cross into greater disrepute than that? Have you seen people who talk about the cross and say that Christ died for them, and yet they are living an immoral life? I have seen a man in a drunken condition proclaiming that he believed that Christ died for him – preaching the cross as it were – and yet his very conduct not only denied it, but proved that he was an enemy of that cross. He brought it to shame and into disrepute.

If we believe what we claim about this cross, how careful we must be. By our behaviour, by our conduct, we can show we are the enemies of the cross, we can cause men to ridicule, blaspheme and laugh at it. Not only that, we are really denying its purpose and its function. Let me remind you of how Paul put it to Titus. He says Christ died, in order that he might 'purify unto himself a peculiar people, zealous of good works' (Tit. 2:14). Why did our Lord die that death on the cross? Why did he go to Calvary? There is the answer: that he might separate these people from sin, from iniquity, from shame, and make of them 'a people zealous of good works'. So if I am not zealous of good works, if I am living a sinful, worldly, carnal life, I am obviously the enemy of the cross of Christ.

The cross, therefore, is the ultimate test both of my faith and belief, and of my conduct and practice. What a tremendous responsibility there rests upon those of us who are Christians! How careful we must always be to see that these two things are intimately related, for as long as we keep the cross in front of us as the touchstone of our lives, we can never go far astray. Is the cross vital and everything to me? Does my life proclaim that I believe that he died there for me, not only that my sins might be forgiven, but that I might be delivered from the whole realm of sin and might become a child of God, being prepared by God for the glory that yet awaits me with him?

My faith determines my conduct; my conduct is a proclamation and statement with regard to my faith; and both of them together are always tested ultimately by what they say about the cross. God grant that we may all be people whose whole life, faith and conduct are centred there.

10

Citizens of Heaven

For our conversation is in heaven; from whence also we look for the Saviour, the Lord Jesus Christ: who shall change our vile body, that it may be fashioned like unto his glorious body, according to the working whereby he is able even to subdue all things unto himself (Phil. 3:20–21).

An alternative translation of these verses – which is more or less that of the Revised Version – would be this: 'For our citizenship is in heaven; from whence also we look for the Saviour, the Lord Jesus Christ: who shall change this body of our humiliation, that it may be fashioned [or made conformable] unto the body of his glorification, according to the energy of his power whereby he is able to subdue all things unto himself.'

We must all agree, I am sure, that these verses are a grand climax to a great chapter. We have worked through this third chapter of Paul's epistle to the Philippians in several studies and we have seen that, from time to time, individual statements in it stand out prominently and are some of the most magnificent statements ever made by this great Apostle. It is a chapter full of great and noble and wonderful things. It is a unique description of the Apostle's own experience; his clear and unmistakable definition, several times over, of the Christian; and we have seen the seriousness with which he rejects the false teaching of the Judaisers and the Antinomians and various other people. But above all, running through it all, there is an exalted and magnificent conception of the Christian life and the individual Christian position. And here in these two verses Paul winds it all up and brings it to a glorious and magnificent climax.

That is the way in which we approach these two verses. They must be regarded as the summary of everything that Paul has been saying in the great argument in this chapter. It is, therefore, perfectly true to describe these two verses as another reminder of just what it means to be a Christian. They express the essence of the position of the New Testament gospel as the Apostle puts it here. As we have seen, he has exhorted the members of the church at Philippi to follow his example: Be followers of me, he says, and of all who walk in the way I walk. And he has reinforced it by a negative; there are those, he says, 'of whom I have told you often, and now tell you even weeping, that they are the enemies of the cross of Christ: whose end is' not this glory to which we are moving but – destruction. Their God is not the Lord Jesus Christ, but their carnal lusts and passions; their glory is not the glorification that awaits us, but their shame, and they mind earthly things. That is their ultimate trouble. But, Paul concludes, 'our conversation [our citizenship] is in heaven.' In other words, he gives this particularly glorious definition here of the whole Christian position because he is anxious to make a final appeal to them for holy living and for running along this road of sanctification.

But before we come to look at these two verses in detail, it is, I think, important that we should bear in mind that one great principle: our citizenship is in heaven. This is typical of the New Testament appeal for holiness, which is always expressed in terms of what we are. That is where New Testament holiness is – I do not hesitate to say it – essentially different from morality. Morality is always interested in actions per se, that is why it has to produce particular arguments, whether in the matter of drink or of anything else. The whole business of morality is to show defects; but while the gospel does not deny all that, it is never the basis of its appeal. The New Testament never tells a man to avoid drunkenness because of the effect upon his body; the Christian teaching is that a man is not to be guilty of drunkenness because he is a citizen of heaven, a child of God. The argument is on a higher plane and, as I said, this is something we must always bear in mind.

I emphasise this because I believe much harm has been done to the Christian cause and the Christian Church because of that sad confusion between morality and New Testament holiness; because of a concern about details at the expense of principle; because of the failure to see that there is a different setting altogether to the New Testament concern about life and living and about holiness and conduct. It is the difference between Judaism and Christianity; between that concern about detail and the law, and this other grand and glorious conception of a state and position.

So, having reminded ourselves that we must never lose sight of this great principle, let us consider how Paul describes the Christian at this point. We can best divide our subject into two headings which suggest themselves at once. The Christian is to live this type of life, he is to follow Paul and all others who are partakers of the Christian life, and he is to do that first and foremost because he is what he is, and secondly, he is to do it because of what he hopes to be. Now let us take the first reason. What is a Christian? The Apostle's answer is that in the first place the Christian is a citizen of heaven; the Authorised Version has, 'Our conversation is in heaven', others have said that it should be translated: 'we are a colony of heaven' – they all mean the same. To me, the important thing to emphasise is the word *is* – our citizenship *is* in heaven. I put that emphasis in order to show that the Apostle is not saying, 'our citizenship will be in heaven', but it is so now!

In other words the authorities have agreed that the word 'is', that is used here by Paul, is the word which means 'being already in existence and manifesting itself'; or, as Dr Lightfoot puts it, 'our citizenship is even now in heaven'. It is even now already a fact – not that we are going to be, but that we are. And here again we are confronted by one of the primary, fundamental, New Testament doctrines. This is just another way of stating the doctrine of regeneration and of the rebirth. As we look at a great description like this of the Christian, does it not make us feel that the little definitions of the Christian that are so often current at the present time, are not only inadequate but almost insulting? Think of describing the Christian simply as one who lives a morally decent life! Perhaps I should not speak like this of morality, I do not do it in any controversial spirit, but because I am jealous of this glorious life we have in Christ and with the Apostle, and it makes me weep to think of the Christian life as just a good life, a life which is just a little better than that of the average person. Christians are people who are already citizens of heaven, people who have been translated and elevated.

Let me give you some of Paul's other statements which put this whole matter so perfectly. For example, in writing to the Ephesians, he says, 'But God, who is rich in mercy, for his great love wherewith he loved us, even when we were dead in sins, hath quickened us together with Christ, (by grace ye are saved;) and hath raised us up together, and made us sit together in heavenly places in Christ Jesus' (Eph. 2:4–6). The Christian is already sitting together with Christ Jesus in the heavenly places – we are there in a spiritual sense, we are citizens of heaven. Or take the way in which Paul puts it in his letter to the Colossians, where he says exactly the same things again: our Lord, 'hath delivered us from the power of darkness, and hath translated us into the kingdom of his dear Son' (Col. 1:13).

Now this is a conception which is so magnificent that it tends to elude us. It was difficult for the members of the church at Philippi, suffering as they were, to realise that they were already seated in the heavenly places in Christ. It is equally difficult for us today, and yet this is the first thing we must lay hold of. We are not citizens of that heavenly kingdom because we have taken up naturalisation papers; you can be a citizen of any other country by going through a legal procedure, but you remain the same person that you

were before. That is not the New Testament conception. We
are citizens of heaven because we have been born again, we
are citizens by birth. We have not paid any price in order to
obtain our citizenship; it is not a question of a legal transaction; we have been made, we are new beings, we are partakers of the divine nature, we are sons of God. We are in the
kingdom and have our citizenship by birth and blood, and
by nothing less. So the claim that Paul makes for the Christian is that the Christian is essentially different from all
those who are not Christians.

The Apostle has, of course, got in his mind the contrast
he has drawn of those people who are living an unworthy
life, those people he has been calling the enemies of Christ
– 'You should not for a moment even contemplate living
like that,' he says in effect, 'you do not belong to the same
realm. They belong to the kingdom of this world, you are
citizens of heaven' – that is the New Testament position. As
Christian people, if we are at all worthy of the name, we are
at this moment essentially different from those who are not
Christians, not just a little bit better, not merely different on
the surface, but different in our being as the result of the
rebirth. We have a new citizenship, we are in Christ, and
because we are in Christ, we are seated in the heavenly
places with him. Certain things will happen to us before we
finally arrive in heaven, but our citizenship is as definite now
as it will be then. There will be a physical translation when
we die, but spiritually we are there already, we belong
there. This point will become clearer as we move on to a
further elaboration of the Christian.

What, then, does this citizenship mean? Why does the
Apostle put it in this way? Perhaps the best way of explaining it, is to elaborate that contrast at which I have already
hinted. Every living person, according to New Testament
teaching, is in one of two kingdoms – there are only two, the
kingdom of heaven and the kingdom of this world; the kingdom of God and the kingdom of Satan. The Apostle and the
other New Testament writers talk about the kingdom of
Satan, the dominion of Satan and the god of this world.

They talk about the prince of the power of the air who controls the lives of those who do not believe, and about the kingdom of darkness – these are the terms they use. And over and against all these is this other kingdom, the kingdom of God, the kingdom of heaven, the kingdom of his dear Son, the kingdom of light, and so on. There is no mean between these two opposites, there is no neutral ground; if we are not in the kingdom of God, we are in the kingdom of Satan, it is one or the other. So here, as he emphasises the fact that our citizenship is in heaven, Paul is saying that we are in a different kingdom and we claim a different allegiance.

The first characteristic of a kingdom is the king, the head of the state, the one to whom you give allegiance. Paul is drawing a contrast here. Of those other people, he says their 'god is their belly' and by that he means that they live to their instincts, their lusts, their passions; these are the things that govern and control them, and that is where their allegiance is. You can test where a man's allegiance is by the way he spends his time and money and energy. A man's treasure is where his heart is, and his heart is where his treasure is, as our Lord puts it in the Sermon on the Mount. A man very soon shows what and who his god is. But the position of Christian men and women is that their King is the Lord Jesus Christ, their King is God, he is supreme in their life, and they give their allegiance to him, and to nothing and to no one else. Christians are entirely different in that respect from non-Christians. The thing that must always be true of them is that they are conscious that their lives are dominated by God, that their first concern is the will of God, and his good pleasure.

You see, again, how different that is from morality. You can be perfectly moral without thinking of God, you can be doing a lot of good and living a decent life but God never enters into your thoughts. No, says Paul, that is not the way of the Christian. If you are a Christian you are in a relationship with God, God is your King and your thoughts, therefore, are about him.

The second characteristic is that the Christian lives under a different law, he lives a different type of life, under a different system. Take, for instance, the great argument worked out by Paul in Romans 6. He says, Before you became a Christian you were under the dominion of sin and of Satan but now you are under that dominion no longer. There is nothing, in other words, that is quite so ridiculous as to talk about men and women having a free will: that is not true, we are born in sin, and are under the dominion of sin and of Satan. And that is why people go further and further into sin; they are slaves of the things they do. In Luke 11:21 our Lord talks about the strong man armed who 'keepeth his palace, his goods are in peace' – that is Satan controlling the lives of men and women, while, of course, persuading them that they are at liberty.

This is something that can be easily understood in the international and in the political world at the present time. There is a form of tyranny which persuades you that you are free. And that is what Satan does – he persuades men that they are free, though they are bound in his dominion. But Christians are not in that position. They have been taken out, they are in the kingdom of God, they have a different law, they are subject to different rules and regulations. The whole ordering of their life is different, they have literally been taken right out of one kingdom and translated into another. As citizens of this new kingdom, they are aware of a new code altogether. As there are different customs and rules in the different countries, so there is an essential difference between the kingdom of God and the kingdom of Satan, and the people who are now citizens in the kingdom of God, are aware of altogether new ideas about life. They see things in a different way because they are aware of a new law: this perfect law of liberty.

And the third important thing that is true about citizenship is that it entitles us to different rights and privileges. As citizens of a country, we are entitled to do certain things which people who are not citizens are not entitled to do. In the Christian life this is something of vital importance. As citizens of heaven we have a right of audience with the King, a right of access to the throne, a right of taking our petitions to him and of making our requests to him. The Bible is full of these things. It tells us that God is particularly interested in his people. Speaking to the people through Amos, he says, 'You only have I known . . .' (Amos 3:2). He knew all the other nations, in a sense, but here it means to know in an intimate way. God is particularly concerned and interested in his people, he is in a unique relationship to them. And that is something that you find elaborated in the New Testament. Our Lord himself said to Christian people 'The very hairs of your head are all numbered' (Matt. 10:30). Nothing can happen to you without your Father knowing it. God our Father is interested in us in this intimate sense.

Is this not something upon which we should ponder and meditate at a time like this? Wherever you may find yourself, and in whatever position you may be; you may be at the end of the earth and surrounded by enemies, you may be in the most impossible position – you always have this right of access to your King. As the Psalmist puts it, 'From the end of the earth will I cry unto thee' (Ps. 61:2). These are privileges and rights which belong, inherently, to the citizens of the kingdom.

But let us move on now to something which is, in a sense, of more practical importance and something which we need to emphasise in these days. What are the implications of this citizenship? Now, of course, when Paul tells us that our citizenship is in heaven, he is not teaching that the Christian should not take any interest in this world and the affairs of this life. It is a spiritual relationship, and he is anxious to emphasise that. If I do take an interest, as I should, in this life and world, I must do it in a different way from the man or woman of the world who is not a citizen of the kingdom of heaven. In other words, the Christian, though he is in the world, is not of it. How trite and yet how profound this is; we are in this world like everybody else, but as Christians we are not of it. Many hymns have this kind of teaching, and they often express it by saying that this world is not our home; if we are Christians we are away from home.

> I am a stranger here,
> Heaven is my home

says the old writer, and every Christian should say that.

During the last hundred years people have rather scoffed at that kind of teaching, but as Christians we must come to see that we are but a colony here; our citizenship, our home, is there in heaven. We must be unworldly in that sense and our interest in this world should arise solely from the fact that we believe that it is God's world and we bemoan the havoc that men and women are making of it. It is not that we think that it is the only world and the only life, and that we may as well settle down in it and enjoy ourselves. Not at all! But we believe in restraining the evil, because this world belongs to God. At the same time, if I say I am not of this world, then I must realise the dangers of life in the world, the iniquity, the sin, the arrogance, the foulness that is in it. I am increasingly coming to the conclusion that there is no sounder test of whether people are truly Christians or not, than their view of life in this world. The criterion is not only whether we say we believe certain articles of the faith. Christians who are new men and women and who have a new nature must of necessity take a different view of life in this world from those who are not Christians – it is a thorough and absolute test. The Christian sees the danger of life in this world, and is constantly aware of it; or, to use the Apostle Paul's language, Christians 'mind' other things; their interest is in something else.

Now whether we like it or not, and strange as it may sound to ears which have become so accustomed to a worldly emphasis, New Testament Christians, as is true of Christians in every great period of revival and reawakening, had their minds and their affections set on things above, not on things of the earth. As I said, that does not mean that Christians retire out of life and take no interest in the affairs of this world – but heaven is the place on which their minds are set. They are looking at the things that are not seen, or, to go still further, their pride is in that heavenly citizenship. We all know how citizenship always leads to pride. Some of the deepest thinkers today are telling us that the main cause of our trouble is the pride that people take in national sovereignty, and there is undoubtedly a great truth in that, it can be very dangerous. But pride in citizenship is inevitable, and a true citizen is proud of the fact that he is a citizen. That comes first, that is the thing he boasts of, that is the thing for which he is prepared to sacrifice his life and everything.

Christian people, are we as ready to die for the citizenship which we have in heaven, as we are for our earthly kingdom? I am not setting these two up as opposites; it is just my way of reminding us all that our pride in our heavenly citizenship should be infinitely greater than the pride we have in any earthly position. We should desire the pride of the kingdom of heaven, and, above everything else, it should be our greatest ambition to be worthy of it. 'England expects every man this day will do his duty' – yes, and God and the kingdom of heaven expect it! Though you are away from home, remember that the honour and the dignity of the great kingdom to which you belong is in your hands. There are those other people around and about you who do not belong to your kingdom; they are watching you and they will judge your country by you. Therefore, says the Apostle, remember what you are and live a life that is worthy of this high calling of the heavenly citizen.

But finally, let us briefly consider the Christian's hope. Christians are people who live this kind of life because of the hope that is set before them. This is, perhaps, the greatest and most glorious consolation and encouragement that a Christian can ever have. Our position in the world is exactly as Paul described the position of the Philippians. We are in a world that is utterly hostile to us. It is controlled by Satan and sin, and all these evil forces are arrayed against us. Not only that, we ourselves are not perfect – 'Not as though I had already attained . . . brethren, I count not myself to have apprehended' – there are weaknesses and defects in us, the very body itself gives us trouble, it is weak and subject to disease and finally to death. That is our position in this world, surrounded by enemies and weaknesses, troubles within and without. How can we go on? What is the use of telling us that we are citizens of heaven? It seems almost a mockery.

No, says Paul, 'For our conversation is in heaven; from whence also we look for the Saviour, the Lord Jesus Christ: who shall change this body of our humiliation, that it may be fashioned according to the body of his glorification, according to the working of his mighty power whereby he is able to subdue all things unto himself.' You see what he means? This is the ultimate consolation. We are looking forward to something, and that something is the return of the Lord Jesus Christ. He is going to return and when he returns he will conquer hell; he will vanquish every foe – Satan, sin, evil and iniquity. Everything that belongs to the kingdom of darkness he will finally rout and utterly consume. We look for the Saviour, the Lord Jesus Christ. Life can be hard, and it may be worse; we may have to suffer persecution, we may have to face some of the things that other Christians are facing at the present time. All this may come to us. This is our answer: Let hell rage, let the kingdoms of this world arise in their fury, whatever they may do we know that the day is coming when the Saviour will return, our Lord Jesus Christ. He will come from his throne in heaven back to this world as King. He will have the ultimate victory over all and will reign supreme.

But it does not stop at that. When he comes he is going to do something else that, in a sense, is even more wonderful for us. I read in the New Testament of that glory, of my standing in the presence of God and seeing the holy angels and seeing my Saviour as he is. I think of this renovated earth and heaven where everything has been made anew and I ask: How can I dwell in such a realm or live under such conditions knowing myself to be what I am? Here is the answer: Paul says that the Lord is even going to change my vile body – that is, the body of my humiliation – the word 'vile' in the Authorised Version is an unfortunate translation. What he is saying is that the difference between the body of infirmity (Paul was subject to such infirmities and we know, too, that with some people sin is associated with the body) and the glorious future that awaits me is this; he is going to deliver me from everything that is humiliating, it is all going to be taken away and I shall be given a new body. On the road to Damascus Paul saw the risen Lord in all his glory. The brightness was such that it struck him to the ground, and, Paul says, I am to have a body like that. It will be like the glory which came to our Lord on the Mount of Transfiguration, a glorification which will fit us and enable us to spend our eternity in the presence of God. That is what we have to look forward to. You may be weak, you may be tired, you may be conscious of imperfection, but, says the Apostle, go on pressing on down the road, you are not doing it on your own, the Saviour is coming.

That, then, is the final appeal which he makes to all of us – press on, but as you are pressing on, keep your eye on the distance, look forward to the glory, wait for him: 'Whence also we look for the Saviour.' What a word the word 'look' is! It means that we do not look at other things. It is a very powerful word and it means patient waiting, eagerly expecting and anticipating.

That, then, is how the Apostle appeals to men and women for holy living and for the sanctified life. We as Christian people are citizens of heaven. We belong to that realm and the day is coming when the King will return. Then we shall enter into our inheritance and we shall be completely changed. Sin will be entirely removed with all its effects and influences, and, perfect and glorified, we shall dwell with God in the glory for ever and ever. That is our birthright, that is our position. Is it necessary even to appeal to all of us to be worthy of our high calling and to glory in Christ and in his cross, and live for him?

11

The Life and Work of the Church

Therefore, my brethren dearly beloved and longed for, my joy and crown, so stand fast in the Lord, my dearly beloved. I beseech Euodias, and beseech Syntyche, that they be of the same mind in the Lord. And I intreat thee also, true yoke-fellow, help those women which laboured with me in the gospel, with Clement also, and with other my fellow-labourers, whose names are in the book of life
(Phil. 4:1–3).

We come now to these first three verses of the fourth chapter, and the very word 'therefore' at the beginning of the first verse reminds us that there is a close connection between what the Apostle is now beginning to say and what he has just been saying at the end of the third chapter. There we looked at that glorious doctrine of the coming again of our Lord, conquering his enemies, ridding the world of evil and indeed even changing this, the body of our humiliation, and fashioning it, that it might be made conformable to the body of his glorification according to the energy of that great power of his, whereby he is able even to subdue all things unto himself. It is a mighty doctrine, no greater is to be found anywhere. 'Therefore . . .' says the Apostle; and once more he does something that is characteristic of him. He never states a doctrine for the sake of stating it, he always applies it, and here he begins to apply what he has just been saying.

I always find these transitions in the thought of the Apostle Paul particularly fascinating. I can never quite decide for

myself whether he is greatest when he declares his doctrine
or when he applies it; I try to discuss this question with
myself, and frankly, I cannot arrive at any conclusion. I find
him equally fascinating, equally moving, whichever he does.
For the truth about the Apostle is that whether he is stating
doctrine, or whether he is applying it, he is always doctrinal.
He is incapable of handling a problem except in terms of
doctrine, so it really makes very little difference whether he
is asking us to look at the great declarations objectively, or
whether he is putting them in a practical, and immediate
and subjective, manner.

So, here, we are dealing with the application, but, as I
hope to show you, we shall find that it is full of doctrine, full
of teaching, and we shall see that once more Paul proves
himself incapable of even handling the problem of quarrelling within the church without putting it in the great context
of the whole truth. This 'therefore' is the connecting link
and all Paul is going to say about this problem must be considered in the light of what he has been saying about the
coming again of our Lord, 'from whence' – from heaven –
'we look for the Saviour'. In addition, we must remember
the emphasis he has laid upon the fact that as Christian
people we are already citizens of heaven; not 'going to be',
we are. And if all that is true of us – 'therefore' that brings
us to this particular question.

The Apostle here is still dealing with what we may call the
doctrine of the Christian Church. He is doing this because of
the particular problem that has arisen in the church at
Philippi, but he cannot deal even with that minor problem
without the whole character of the Church coming in. So we
have here what we can describe as Paul's amazing picture of
the nature of the Christian Church, and of the character of
her life; and in doing that the Apostle does something else.
I suggest it is quite unconscious, but he also gives us a wonderful picture of himself. I confess that it was a real temptation to me, in thinking about these three verses, and
meditating upon them, to divide this matter into two,
because we have here two pictures, one of Paul the pastor,

and the other of the church in which he ministered. I have
decided, however, that we cannot go into detail here with
the picture of Paul himself, except perhaps, as it appears
when we deal with the other doctrine; but I cannot refrain
from pointing out the way in which Paul addresses this
church: 'My brethren, dearly beloved and longed for, my
joy and crown, so stand fast,' again it comes – 'my dearly
beloved.' That is to be the relationship between a minister
and the members of his church, and any minister who reads
words like these must feel humbled and almost humiliated.
That is the relationship between pastor and people, this
burning, blazing love. Most of the Philippian church had
entered into the kingdom as the result of Paul's preaching,
so he calls them his joy and crown. They constitute a kind
of garland which he will wear on the great day, a crown of
victory. He loves them dearly, and here he gives us an
extraordinary picture of this intimate, loving relationship.

Consider also the remarkable humility displayed by the
Apostle. Notice how he addresses Euodias and Syntyche –
he does not command, he beseeches them. This supreme
evangelist and teacher, this great Apostle, asks these two
women to come together. Please, says the Apostle, will you
. . .? He might have commanded them, but he does not, he
comes right down to their level and he begs them. It is a
wonderful insight, in passing, into the character of this noble
man of God.

But we must give our attention now to what these three
verses tell us about the doctrine of the nature and character
of the Christian Church. The problem with which the Apostle has to deal is the trouble in the church at Philippi
between these two women, Euodias and Syntyche. These
two, for some reason or other, are quarrelling and causing
trouble in the church, and Paul, loving the church as he
does, and anxious as he is for her perfection, has to deal
with that trouble. And his way of doing so is to put the dispute in the setting of the whole doctrine of the Church. Oh,
if the Christian Church had always remembered that, how
many troubles would have been avoided! Every problem, it

does not matter how small and insignificant, must always be put into its larger context. In a church there is no such thing as an isolated problem. You cannot consider such a problem without considering it in the light of the nature of the Church, and this is how Paul does it here.

He has three main things to say about the Church. The first concerns the task of the Church, which, according to the Apostle, is to 'labour in the gospel'. He speaks of Euodias and Syntyche as 'those women which laboured with me in the gospel'. Paul has already introduced us to this same thought at the beginning of the epistle; in chapter 1:5 he thanks the Philippians for their 'fellowship in the gospel from the first day until now'; they had been working or labouring with him – it was their fellowship, their partnership in the gospel. Then in the eighth verse he says, 'For God is my record, how greatly I long after you all in the bowels of Jesus Christ'; and also in the seventh verse, 'Even as it is meet for me to think this of you all, because I have you in my heart; inasmuch as both in my bonds, and in the defence and confirmation of the gospel, ye all are partakers of my grace'; and again in 1:27; it is the same thing in all these verses.

Clearly, therefore, that is the primary task of the Christian Church. It is a missionary task; that is always Paul's conception of the Church, and that is the New Testament picture of it. The Church is a body of people set in a world that is under the control of sin and Satan, a world opposed to God, a world that is rushing unconsciously to perdition. So what, in view of that, is the business of the Church? It is to hold forth the gospel, it is to speak to that world and to tell it about its sin and its desperate condition, to tell it about the Saviour and the only way of salvation – that is the business of the Church. Paul himself travelled over that ancient world doing just that, and wherever he got a body of people together he formed them into a church and told them to go out and do the same thing. He thanks God for the members of the church at Philippi because they are doing that work with him; they have helped him; they are all partakers in this ministry.

The Book of Acts is full of this. We read not only of the Apostles themselves but of the most ordinary Christians, who were all scattered abroad as the result of persecution, and wherever they went they preached the word. The record of the early Church in the first century bears abundant and eloquent testimony to the fact that the gospel was spread, in the first place, by the ordinary Christians. By telling people about it and living it in their daily lives, they spread it abroad.

But apart from that, this very section which we are considering together here impresses this upon our minds. This 'true yoke-fellow' was doing the same work, together with these women who had laboured with Paul in the gospel, and Clement also and those other fellow labourers. The missionary task of the Church is a task for every single individual Christian. We are all meant to be involved in it. The Church was in danger of losing sight of this particular truth many years ago, when the churches and chapels were full and when it was the fashionable and popular thing to be a Christian, and, surely, there is a very real danger of our forgetting it at this present time. For never was there a time, perhaps, when the individual Christian should realise his or her importance in this matter so much as today; in our daily life and living, we are to spread abroad this Good News.

It is to be done in many ways; we are not all to do it by preaching from pulpits. In a sense, we can all preach it, we are all to be engaged in prayer, prayer for the preaching and the propagation of the gospel and prayer for the souls of men and women. Then we can all do it by witnessing in our lives, and by the way in which we conduct our business, or practise our profession. People will see that there is something different about us, and then we can give the explanation. We can also bring others to listen to the word of God and we ourselves can attend meetings where the word of God is preached. Now every one of these people in Philippi, Paul tells us, was a helper; they were all taking part in the work and it is quite clear that they were taking part in some of those ways.

Do you know that you take part in the preaching of the gospel by being present? It is an encouragement to the preacher. I frankly confess that I never quite understand those who feel that it is sufficient for them, in desperate times like this, to attend the house of God but infrequently. When people who may not have been to church for years come into the house of God, they are impressed by the fact that large numbers of people still believe in listening to the gospel. So, my Christian friend, if you feel you have no gift, let me assure you here and now that you are one of those people whose name is written in the Book of Life, and your presence in a service of worship is a great help.

In addition, the Apostle makes it very plain in all his epistles that there were those who helped in the propagation of the gospel by just ministering to his own personal need. Take, for instance, the man called Onesiphorus. In 2 Timothy 1:16 Paul thanks God for that man because when he was a prisoner in Rome, Onesiphorus went and visited him. Now Paul was an outstanding mighty man, and you would have thought he would have been quite above any need like that, but he thanks God for this man who visited him in his bonds, and cheered up the great Apostle who was feeling a certain amount of depression. There is an endless number of ways in which we can all preach the gospel, and become labourers together in it, and spread it abroad.

But, above all, we do it by making the gospel attractive to others and awakening an interest in it as we live the Christian life. We can be such people that those who come into contact with us will know that there is something different about us and want to know the explanation.

But let me go on to something still more important. If labouring in the gospel is the great task of the Church, let us consider certain essentials to the performance of that task, and this is the burden of these three verses. Certain things are essential, and the first is that we should realise the lordship of Christ. Notice what the Apostle longs for:

'I beseech Euodias, and beseech Syntyche, that they be of the same mind in the Lord.' Now we have always got to start there – the lordship of Christ. All the Apostle's appeals were made in these terms. When dealing here with this little trouble that has arisen in the church at Philippi, Paul does not appeal to these women to put it right for his sake. He does not say, 'You are spoiling my church.' He does not beg them to put this thing right for the sake of his reputation. Not at all! He says, 'in the Lord', for the Lord's sake. Neither does he appeal to them to put this right for their own sake, or for the reputation of the church at Philippi. The New Testament never does that, it always makes its appeal in the name of the Lord. Perhaps the New Testament Christians were not as interested in the local church as we are. We are so fond of talking about our church or our denomination and it is always in this personal sense. But the Apostle says, 'in the Lord', and for this good reason: it is the Lord's work.

You remember that mighty statement in chapter 1:6? It is the Lord's work. He began it, and it is he, says the Apostle in the second chapter, who is keeping it going: God is working in you 'both to will and to do of his good pleasure'. And it is he who is going to bring it to its final consummation. Once more it must strike us, that if only the Church had been careful to observe this, how different its history would have been. It is the Lord's work; we would never have been in the Church but for the grace of the Lord. It is not our Church, it is the Church of God. The glory, therefore, must be his, the honour must be his, he must be in control and our every decision must be taken in his presence, for he is supreme. The Lord himself bought the Church with his own blood; it belongs to him and everything in the Church must always be put in that relationship. If only we were careful to start at that point, most of our difficulties would immediately and automatically disappear.

The second thing we are exhorted to do, the second essential principle for the Christian Church, is to 'stand fast in the Lord'. This, again, is one of Paul's great phrases. He says the same thing to the church at Corinth: 'Watch ye, stand fast in the faith, quit you like men, be strong' (1 Cor. 16:13). He has already told the Philippians to do this: 'Only let your conversation be as it becometh the gospel of Christ: that whether I come and see you, or else be absent, I may hear of your affairs, that ye stand fast in one spirit . . .' (Phil. 1:27) – stand firm, if you like, it means the same thing. Stand fast in the Lord. What does Paul mean when he uses this expression? We can put it like this: we must stand fast in the faith. You see the sequence? The task of the Church is a missionary task, she is to preach the gospel, she is to tell forth this good news, to bring salvation to men and women, but she cannot do that unless she is sure of her faith. Paul does not say stand fast together, but stand fast in the Lord, stand fast in the faith.

I am not anxious to be controversial at this point, but these days we hear a good deal of talk about ecumenicity, and with the general spirit of such talk we are all in agreement. But I am here to assert that, even before that, comes this truth: stand fast in the Lord. How can I stand fast and firm with the man who denies the deity of my Lord? How can I stand shoulder to shoulder, and in rank, with a man who does not believe in miracles and in the supernatural? How can I keep in line with a man who denies the substitutionary aspects of the atonement? No, we are not merely exhorted by the Apostle to stand together and present a common front against the enemy, not at all! That is not my standard, that is not what brings us together. It is the truth, the truth concerning the Lord himself. Stand fast, says Paul, do not compromise. Stand fast in the truth and hold on to what you know to be right. Put the Lord first, because if you are true to him, and stand fast in him, you can do mightier things than a great army that is uncertain about its truth and doctrine.

Furthermore, if you do not stand fast in the Lord, then you do not have a gospel to preach. If the Church is uncertain of her own message, how can she evangelise? The strength of the Church lies in her message and the power of the Holy Spirit. Alas, how often has she forgotten this! What a temptation it is to concentrate on being highly organised and to think that if we can present a great crowd it will have an impact upon the people. History denies that. Churches were filled a hundred or so years ago, but in spite of that we are faced with the present position. Numbers never convince. It is the truth that convinces, and the great thing for us is to put this first. We must stand firm in the truth, in the message, for without it we have no power. We may be very nice and kind to one another, but that will not convince the world of sin, and bring them to Jesus. The truth alone can do that. That is the second thing.

Then the next principle is that we must also be 'of the same mind'. 'I beseech Euodias, and beseech Syntyche, that they be of the same mind in the Lord.' Once more you see what a perfect picture this is of the Church. Here is the Church, her task is to be a missionary Church, she must be careful that she is doing everything for the Lord, and that she has the right message. She must not play with it or compromise with it in any sense. That is the danger of the heresy with which Paul has been dealing in the third chapter; it is one of the dangers that arises from within. And another danger was arising within the church at Philippi. These two women are clearly quarrelling with each other, they are trying to form rival factions and the Apostle beseeches them to stop, because such a thing will spoil the record, it will upset the whole testimony of the church and will overthrow everything he is trying to do.

We must be careful, therefore, not only to guard against heresies that come from without, but against our own spirits too, against the subtle temptations that arise from within ourselves which can spoil the work. That is the way in which the Apostle puts it negatively. We must not be like Euodias and Syntyche who were forming factions. They were not speaking to each other, they were trying to corrupt the people around them; there was a whispering, and they were refusing to work with each other. If only you realised, says the Apostle, that you are all under the Lord and that none of you would be in the Church but for his grace, you would not do this thing – stop doing it!

But let me show you how he puts it positively; I will just note the interesting words which Paul uses. 'I intreat thee also, true yokefellow, help those women which laboured with me in the gospel.' Now there has been much dispute about who is meant by 'yokefellow', but what the Apostle is saying is, 'You dear helper, help these women to come together.' And I am particularly entranced by the description which the Apostle gives here of this helper of his. He calls him 'true yokefellow'. You see the picture, do you not? Think of that long pole with the cross bar and a bit of leather at each end and an ox on each side of it. The oxen are yoked together and the secret of successful ploughing is that the two go forward together. And here was a man whom the Apostle describes as a true yokefellow. He was always doing the right thing, he was pulling together with Paul; that is the spirit which is needed in the Church.

Then Paul tells us that these women had once been doing the right thing: 'I intreat thee also, true yokefellow, help those women which laboured with me in the gospel.' That was the tragedy of Euodias and Syntyche; there was a time when they had been glad to help, when they had laboured with the Apostle in the gospel. Now it is a pity that the Authorised Version here uses this word 'laboured' because in this verse Paul refers to other people as 'fellow-labourers', and in the Greek it is not the same word. What Paul is actually saying is this: Help these women who were fellow athletes with me in the past. It is a picture of a group of athletes in a team – the Olympic games or something like that – and the whole secret was that you put loyalty to your team first. You did not run in the race to gain honour for yourself, you were working in a team; you were fellow athletes. Paul is saying that in the past Euodias and Syntyche had sacrificed everything in the interests of the Church and of the Lord. Help them to come back to that, says Paul.

That should be the spirit of a team: we should be working

together; or, as Paul puts it later on: we must be fellow workers, fellow labourers. Or perhaps, to put it at its very highest, our ambition should always be to become like the Apostle Paul himself. You notice the spirit of love that encompassed him and the way he loved the members of this church. You notice the humility. As we have seen, instead of commanding these women, he beseeches them, he is almost in tears as he comes down to their level. 'I beg you,' says Paul. 'Please put this right.'

Notice, too, Paul's wisdom and his discrimination. He does not command the two women, he *pleads* with them, he beseeches them; but when he has a man like this, whom he describes as his true yokefellow, he intreats him.* That is the thing needed in the Christian Church – discrimination in the way in which we deal with people. Why is this spirit so important? It is because, if the Church is not right in this respect, she grieves the Holy Spirit, and if she grieves the Holy Spirit, she loses her power and she cannot be a missionary Church. Moreover, if the Church fails in her spirit, it is a denial of the message she preaches, and above and beyond it all, it is dishonouring to the Lord himself and, after all, the Church is his.

So, then, those are the things that are essential – the lordship of Christ, standing fast and firm in the truth and guarding our spirits against every kind of subtle temptation. But let us finish with Paul's last great point – the encouragements to the performance of this task. How glorious they are! Paul says, 'I intreat thee also . . . help those women . . . with Clement also, and with other my fellow-labourers whose names are in the book of life.' Am I going too far when I suggest that what the Apostle was really saying was this: 'Not only these women and Clement, and all those other people – I have forgotten their names, it does not matter, these names are written in the book of life.' I know of

---

* In the Greek two different words are used and the second word is not as emphatic. The New International Version here uses the words 'plead' and 'ask', which perhaps makes Dr Martyn Lloyd-Jones' point even more clear. (Ed.)

no greater encouragement than that. Do you remember what our Lord said to his disciples who went out to preach? They were full of pride and elation; they said, 'Lord, even the devils are subject unto us through thy name,' but our Lord said to them, 'Rejoice not, that the spirits are subject unto you; but rather rejoice, because your names are written in heaven' (Luke 10:17, 20).

Beloved Christian people, that is the greatest ambition and the highest privilege we can ever have – that our names are written in the book of life. Here is your encouragement. All is known to God. The world may never know, the Church herself may never know what you have been doing. It may have been some quiet work behind the scenes and the devil may tempt you and say, 'Why go on with it? Why bother with it? Everybody talks about the man in the pulpit and certain obvious officials, but is your work worth going on with? Stay at home and do nothing!' But let me remind you of this, your name is written in the book of life. The minister may know nothing of what you are doing and neither may anyone else, but God knows it. Nothing you do goes unrecorded and your Father who sees in secret shall himself reward you openly. Remember also that he is the Judge; the books will be open to him and he is absolutely just. Do not feel that somebody else is having greater credit than you. That may be true on earth, but when you come before him it will not be true. You will have justice, all your humblest actions are recorded and known. He is absolutely fair, you need never fear. Do not worry what man may do unto you, the Lord is our judge and he is our keeper.

Furthermore, let me remind you that your reward is certain and glorious. If your name is written in that book, you are going to the glory and ultimately it does not matter very much what man may do to you. As Paul puts it once and for ever at the end of that mighty fifteenth chapter of the first epistle to the Corinthians, 'Forasmuch as ye know that your labour is not in vain in the Lord.' And so:

Go labour on, spend and be spent
Thy joy to do the Father's will.

H. Bonar

Your names are written in the book of life. Seeing that privilege, and holding on to it, go on with your work to the glory of the Lord.

12

Rejoice Always

Rejoice in the Lord alway: and again I say, Rejoice (Phil. 4:4).

As we come now to consider this well-known exhortation of the Apostle Paul, it is important for us to remember that the whole history of the early Church, and indeed all the New Testament epistles, can only be understood in the light of the pouring forth of the Holy Spirit upon that infant Church in Jerusalem. It is one of those historical events that is in series with the great crucial events recorded in Scripture, with the story of the Children of Israel in the Old Testament, the call of Abraham, the calling out of Egypt, the crossing of the Red Sea and the crossing of Jordan. It is in a series with events like the incarnation, the birth of Christ, his death, his resurrection, and ascension.

Pentecost is an event which we must always hold firmly in our minds, because apart from that we cannot hope to understand either the Book of Acts itself, or any one of the New Testament epistles. Someone has said that the Acts of the Apostles might well be named the 'Acts of the Holy Ghost', and whether that is so or not, it is clear that the Holy Spirit did dominate the life of the early Church. You notice the constant repetition in Acts of phrases like, 'the Spirit hath not said', or 'the Spirit said' or 'the Spirit indicated' – the life of the Church was dominated by the power

This sermon was preached on Whit Sunday, 1948.

375

of the Holy Spirit.

And the same thing is to be seen in the New Testament epistles. The kind of life that is depicted in them and in Acts is the kind of life that is produced by the working and operation of the Holy Spirit. The Christian life is the fruit, to use Paul's term in Galatians 5, of the Spirit and of his working and operation. In the New Testament itself that is sometimes stated explicitly – we have an instance of it in Galatians 5, where Paul specifically says, 'The fruit of the Spirit is love, joy, peace, longsuffering, gentleness, goodness, faith, meekness, temperance' (vv. 22–23). That is the kind of personality, or the kind of life which the Holy Spirit produces. But even where it is not stated explicitly, that doctrine is implied everywhere in the epistles. The life that they depict, and the appeals that they make for the Christian life, are almost all made in terms of the doctrine of the Holy Spirit – if you like, they take the doctrine of the Holy Spirit for granted.

Let me give you a perfect illustration of what I am saying. Take this fourth chapter of Philippians which we are now studying. Here in this section the Holy Spirit is not mentioned by name at all, so that if you read it superficially you might say that here is a passage which has nothing to do with the doctrine of the Holy Spirit. But wait a minute! What is Paul talking about in this section? In the first three verses he mentions love – 'Therefore, my brethren, dearly beloved'; and you remember that verses 2 and 3 are nothing but a great appeal to Euodias and Syntyche to love one another and to co-operate together. Furthermore, Paul appeals to all the other members of the Church to help them. The first three verses are a great exposition of love.

Then here we come to verse 4, 'Rejoice in the Lord' – joy. Then the next verse says, 'Let your moderation be known unto all men' – longsuffering. Then you go on – 'be careful for nothing'; and 'the peace of God' – love, joy, peace, longsuffering. That is a perfect illustration of the point I am making. Sometimes Paul states this doctrine of the life of the Holy Spirit explicitly, but implicitly it is everywhere.

This is something which is fundamental to our understanding of the whole New Testament doctrine of the Christian life. This chapter is nothing but another exposition by Paul of the fruit of the Spirit – love, joy, peace and so on. That is the essential background, therefore, to understanding these particular words in the fourth verse. Here Paul puts his emphasis upon one of these fruits of the Spirit – joy. 'Rejoice in the Lord alway: and again I say, Rejoice.'

Now there is nothing, perhaps, that is more typical of New Testament doctrine than just that injunction. It is something you find running right through the New Testament from the beginning to the end. Nothing was more characteristic of the life of the first Christians than this element of joy. Our Lord himself, you remember, had promised his followers that he would give them joy which the world could not take away. He said, 'You are going to be disappointed when you see me arrested and crucified, but your joy will be restored to you' (John 15:11; 16:22).

You cannot read the Book of Acts without being impressed by the amazing way in which these people were actually able to rejoice in the most untoward and difficult circumstances. In Acts we read how some of them were arrested, put into prison, and beaten, and when they came out they praised God that they had been accounted worthy to suffer for his name – they rejoiced in tribulation. When you go through the whole story you will find that in spite of the malignity of their enemies, in spite of the contradiction of the world around them, they continued to rejoice.

Then as you read the epistles you will find this great, dominating quality of joy everywhere in the life of the people. Read how Paul puts it in Romans 14:17: 'For the kingdom of God is not meat and drink; but righteousness, and peace, and joy in the Holy Ghost.' Peter, writing to similar people about the Lord Jesus Christ, says, 'Whom having not seen, ye love; in whom, though now ye see him not, yet believing, ye rejoice with joy unspeakable and full of glory' (1 Pet. 1:8). And even in the Book of Revelation, if we look at its general message instead of losing ourselves in the details, we see that it is a book which is intended to do one thing: to teach people at such a time, and in subsequent periods of the history of the Church, to rejoice in spite of adversity and difficulties, trials and troubles.

So it is everywhere, but as I have already pointed out, it is particularly the theme of this epistle to the Philippians. Paul's real reason for writing the letter was to teach these people how to rejoice in every kind of circumstance; and we have seen, therefore, how he has taken up various things that tend to rob Christian people of their joy, and how he has dealt with them one after another. To begin with, the Philippians were worrying about him; that is in the first chapter. Then various troubles within the Church tended to create discord, so he has to put that right, and he does so by giving us a great illustration of Christ in his humiliation and incarnation – 'Let this mind be in you, which was also in Christ Jesus.' Then they were troubled about the illness of Epaphroditus; Paul tells us that in the second chapter. Next, we have seen in the third chapter that he moves on to the great question of heresy and of wrong living and of how wrong belief can always rob people of their joy. And then comes this dispute between Euodias and Syntyche.

So this is Paul's great theme, and back he goes to it again. You can compare this letter to a kind of symphony. The theme is the question of joy; Paul plays his variations on it, and then he goes back to it. He has already told us at the beginning of the third chapter that this is his theme: 'Finally my brethren, rejoice in the Lord . . .' But he has not finished yet: 'Rejoice in the Lord alway: and again I say, Rejoice,' he says in 4:4. So he goes on repeating it. But why? Is it not clear that it was the thing that Paul desired for these people above everything else? It was their heritage as Christian people, and to Paul it was a tragedy that any Christian should be unhappy. Unhappiness was a denial of their profession of faith. They were missing something, they were being robbed of what is the most glorious thing about the faith, and so the Apostle could not leave it alone. He did not know whether he was to live much longer – he said that

it was very doubtful, and he did not know whether he pre-
ferred to go or to stay. But, he said in effect, 'Whichever I
do, the thing that I am concerned about is that you should
be right, and that no one should rob you of this joy in the
Holy Spirit that is possible for you and all who are true
believers in the Lord Jesus Christ.'

So now as we approach it, let me ask a question. Do we
know this joy? Do we have it in our lives? Is it a living fact
in our experience? Are we rejoicing in the Lord? Let us,
then, look at this together, bearing in mind the whole doctrine of the Holy Spirit and of his coming upon the Church
on that day of Pentecost. Let me suggest the first principle:
the nature of the joy. What is the character of this joy? Here
let us note two points. The first is that it is something positive. That needs emphasis because we must always differentiate between this Christian quality of joy and mere negative
resignation. Like the Apostle, I go on repeating this point
because I think that, in a day and time like this, one of our
grievous dangers is to mistake the stoical spirit of negative
resignation for Christian courage, fortitude and joy. But
Paul is not advocating that they should adopt a negative
attitude to the things that are happening to them. No, it is
essentially positive: 'Rejoice . . . and again I say, Rejoice.'
You can hear him tapping it out like a bugle call. Christian
joy is stimulating and stirring; never must we think of it as
just something negative and passive.

Or, to put it another way, it is not merely a state of indifference. This, again, must constantly be repeated because
the whole subject is so subtle. I suppose the more scientific
mankind becomes, the more he becomes prone to the subtle
temptation to mistake psychological solutions to problems
for spiritual solutions. Let me explain. The child shows his
feelings, whether pleasure or displeasure, satisfaction or dissatisfaction, and the more primitive people do exactly the
same thing. But as we get older, and as the whole world gets
older, there is a tendency to hide our feelings. Up to a point,
that is perfectly right, but it can be a very real danger and it
becomes a danger when it would have us feel and think that

the Christian attitude towards problems is an attitude of indifference, as though people should say to themselves, 'Well, the only way to go through this life without being hurt is to put on a protective mechanism of indifference which says, "I don't care what anybody says, or what may happen to me."' The idea is that if you put up a screen of indifference around yourself, you will not react violently to the things that are happening to you.

But that is not what the Apostle has in mind here. People who hide themselves behind a screen of indifference do not have any joy; nor do stoics with their negative resignation. Paul is talking about a joy that is positive; it is active and there is an emotional element in it. It does not curb us, there is power and life in it – it is a spirit of exultation. 'Rejoice' – that is surely active and positive!

The second characteristic which I must note is that it is a specific joy. It is a joy in the Lord – 'Rejoice in the Lord alway; and again I say, Rejoice.' The New Testament never just exhorts people to be happy or tells them to cheer up while it gives out psychological sympathy. That is something it never does, and that is why I again suggest that there is perhaps no greater travesty of the gospel of Jesus Christ than psychological teaching which presents itself in Christian terms. A presentation of the gospel which will have us cheer up, or do something to make ourselves feel happier for the time being, is a denial of the gospel of Christ. We are to rejoice in the Lord. There is no need for a stoical mechanism here, it is something direct and immediate, and it is in terms of the Lord.

In other words, the joy that the Christian is to experience is a joy that is based solidly upon Christian truth and doctrine. You notice that it is only after Paul has told them to, 'Stand fast in the Lord,' that he tells them to, 'Rejoice in the Lord,' and anything which is not based on the doctrine concerning the Lord Jesus Christ is not joy. Many agencies can make us happy. Indeed, you can take alcohol and you may feel happy and full of joy – but it has nothing to do with the joy of the Lord. Paul is not talking about joy in a general sense, but about specific joy. He is not merely concerned with whether or not we are happy; his concern is that, because we are Christians, we should rejoice.

And so, having thus outlined the nature of Christian joy, let me say something about the hindrances to this joy. There are many, and I obviously cannot deal with them all in one study, so I shall simply try to pick out the more obvious ones mentioned in this context.

First of all, there is a hindrance to some people over the whole question of the mechanism of this joy, over the way in which it comes to us, of how it becomes available. Some people have an initial intellectual difficulty about this because here in this verse the Apostle confronts us, and tells us to, 'Rejoice in the Lord.' 'And yet,' says someone, 'in Galatians 5 Paul says that the "fruit of the Spirit is love, joy, peace . . .".'. How can this be something that I do and yet be the fruit and operation of the Spirit?' We are all familiar with the argument, it has gone on in the Church from the very beginning, the apparent conflict between the two types of Christian life, the life of activity and the life of passivity, of meditation; the contrast between those who believe that the thing to do in the Christian life is to be always engaged in activity, and those who believe in contemplation and in the mystical, monastic conception of the Christian life.

But when you examine the Scriptures more closely you will see that there is no contradiction. Take Galatians 5: before Paul tells us that 'the fruit of the Spirit is love, joy . . .', he has already said, 'Walk in the Spirit, and ye shall not fulfil the lust of the flesh' (5:16). The two things are there together in the same chapter. Thus we reconcile the apparent contradiction in this way – it is as we practise these things that the fruit of the Spirit will be manifested in our life. It is perfectly true that I cannot create or produce joy myself, but if I listen to and obey the dictates and leading of the Holy Spirit within me, if I practise the Christian life, if I work out the doctrine of the Holy Spirit, then the Holy Spirit will plant this fruit of joy within my life. We cannot find joy merely by rushing into activity or merely by sitting

in contemplation. To try one or other of these two possibilities alone, is certain to lead to disaster. We must do
both: we must meditate upon the truth and we must practise
it, and as we do so the Holy Spirit will flood our lives with
joy. That is not a theory only, and it is not only the teaching
of the New Testament. If you read the lives of the saints,
you will find it confirmed in abundance. We can also confirm
it ourselves, thank God; it is literal, actual, present-day
experience in the Christian life.

The second cause of failure to have this joy which is in
Christ is the failure to be in the right relationship to him;
that is why I emphasise 'in the Lord'. Many people do not
know the joy of the Lord today for the one and only reason
that they have never truly realised their own poverty, empti-
ness and deadness. Most people who have never experienced the joy of salvation are people who have never seen
their full need of salvation. This may sound paradoxical, but
how true it is! Our Lord put it perfectly in the Sermon on
the Mount: 'Blessed are the poor in spirit: for theirs is the
kingdom of heaven . . . Blessed are they which do hunger
and thirst after righteousness: for they shall be filled.' You
see, the only people who are going to be filled are those who
hunger and thirst; the people who are going to have endless
spiritual wealth and riches are the paupers in the realm of
the spirit. There are many people who never know the joy
of the Lord because they have failed to see themselves as
miserable sinners. The only way to be happy in Christ is to
be desperately unhappy without him.

In other words, there are people who have never known
the joy of salvation because they are relying upon themselves and their own works. They still feel they can live the
Christian life in their own power, and that they can put
themselves right with God. But if you want to be filled with
the joy of the Lord, you have to be absolutely empty, you
have to see yourselves as wretched, hopeless sinners, you
have to know that nothing you can do will avail you anything, but in utter poverty and helplessness you have to
come to him. Then you are likely to know the joy of the

Lord, and not until then. Or to put it another way: such people have never cast themselves utterly upon him. Those are the two essentials to receiving this joy – experiencing the utter misery of conviction of sin, as the New Testament reveals us to ourselves in all our hopelessness and woe; and then, empty handed, coming to Christ and casting ourselves upon his mercy and his bounty, his love and compassion, and saying to him –

> Nothing in my hand I bring
> Simply to Thy Cross I cling.
>
> Augustus Toplady

If you have anything in your hand, you will never get it filled from him; you have to come with nothing at all and then you will receive his joy.

And that is confirmed abundantly by the subsequent history of the Christian Church. It is the people who have said the most terrible things about themselves, as they are by nature, who have rejoiced most in Christ Jesus. It is those who have said, 'Vile and full of sin I am,' who have been able to say, 'Plenteous grace in Thee is found.' And the people who have never quite admitted that they are vile sinners are the people who have never rejoiced in Christ Jesus and have never known the abundance of Christian living. We must be right about this, we must be in the right relationship to Christ or we will never know the joy and happiness, the peace and love, that he can give.

And that leads me to the next hindrance. There are many who lack the joy of the Lord because they fail to maintain that right relationship with him. You must not only enter into it, you must maintain it, and you do this in your spirit and in your attitude towards one another. These two women who were quarrelling in the church had certainly lost their joy; you cannot have the joy of the Lord if your spirit is not wholesome and clean. It grieves the Spirit and he goes away. Therefore, if we want to have the joy of the Lord we must maintain the right spirit.

Furthermore, we must also maintain the right practice –
we must live and walk in the right way. This is obvious from
what Paul said to the Galatians. If we are guilty of certain
practices and sins, we cannot know the joy of the Lord; as
our Lord said, 'Ye cannot serve God and mammon' (Matt.
6:24). If you want the joy of the Lord, you must forsake
other things. Walk in the Spirit, be led by the Spirit, and you
will experience the joy of the Spirit.

And the next thing which Paul mentions here – 'Let your
moderation be known unto all men' – he has already dealt
with earlier so he goes on to the following injunction: we
must maintain contact with Christ by prayer and communion. 'In everything by prayer and supplication with
thanksgiving let your requests be made known unto God.'
So I have not only to watch my spirit, I must spend a certain
amount of time in talking to him. That is the source of joy; he
alone can make me truly happy. What fools we are in this
Christian life! We depend on so many other things, but the
secret of the saints has always been the time they spend in conversation and communion with the Lord and in meditation
upon him. We must maintain that contact; we must go to the
source and fount of joy and go there readily and frequently.

And then, too, we must maintain this contact with him by
never allowing ourselves to be tyrannised by circumstances.
That is the most common cause of a loss of joy – the tyranny
of events and circumstances. So many things come between
us and him, and rob us of his presence and joy. Oh, these
things that tend to worry us and cause us to be pulled down by
anxiety! We think about them, they always seem to be coming
up, and we go on worrying about them, and as we do so we
become miserable, breakdowns occur and all such troubles.

Those, then, are some of the things that rob us of the joy.
Now let us come to the positive side. If these are the things
that rob us of joy, how can we maintain it? And the answer
is quite simple: we must avoid all those things that prevent
us concentrating upon him – 'Rejoice in the Lord alway . . .'
Look on him, consider him, meditate upon him, his person,
his work, all he has done, his death, his resurrection, his send-

ing forth of the Holy Spirit. Consider, too, the things he is going to do, the whole of the New Testament scheme and plan for life, and the ultimate, that glorious hope that nothing can ever rob us of. These are the things; meditate upon him, on his person, and upon all the glory of his work.

And lastly, let me ask a question. Is this state of joy something that can continue? Is it always possible to know it? And Paul's answer is, Yes, always! 'Rejoice in the Lord alway: and again I say Rejoice.' You can say that of nothing else; every other source of joy and happiness must, of necessity, sooner or later fail us. Some people are foolish enough to find their joy in their work. As far as it goes that is all right, and apart from the gospel, it is not a bad thing. But, my friend, a day is coming when you will lose your work – you will become old or ill. What a tragic thing it is to see such people. They were so happy when they were working, but when they are laid aside they do not know what to do with themselves. They have been dependent for joy and happiness upon their own efforts and exertions.

Then think of the men and women who are only happy when they are successful. Our reply to them is, 'Uneasy lies the head that wears crown' – there are always others seeking that crown. You may be successful but look at that other person who is coming up fast, and who will soon beat and excel you. You will become tired, your powers will fail and somebody else will take your place. It is a tragedy that one sees in the lives of professional men and women. They have been happy in the days of their success and achievement, they are joyful as they reach the summit of their profession, but then they begin to come down the other side, and it is much more difficult to come down, than to go up. The pathos of such people! How foolish it is to let our joy depend upon our circumstances, because we live in a world where it is true to say, 'Change and decay in all around I see.' Circumstances are bound to let you down sooner or later. Do not depend upon them.

No, there is only one thing that never fails: it is to rejoice in the Lord. And this does not fail, because it is always con-

cerned about the soul and its destiny; it is concerned about
something which is safe and sure, something which the
world can never affect because it is in Christ. This joy is
beyond the reach of all those other powers, and you work it
out like this: you say, 'Circumstances may certainly vary and
may fail me, but nothing can affect my relationship to
Christ. It does not matter what the world may do to me, my
relationship to him cannot be affected by it.' You remember
Paul's argument? 'For I am persuaded, that neither death,
nor life, nor angels, nor principalities, nor powers, nor
things present, nor things to come, nor height, nor depth,
nor any other creature, shall be able to separate us from the
love of God, which is in Christ Jesus our Lord' (Rom. 8:38–
39).

In other words, you may be in prison, but there you may
still find Christ. You may be stripped and rid of everything,
but not of your soul or your eternal destiny, nor of the glory
that awaits you in Christ – these things are beyond circumstances. To go even further, let me show you how you can
rejoice in the Lord even in failure, even in sin. Is that a dar-
ing statement? No, 'Rejoice in the Lord alway' – even when
I have failed or sinned? Yes, in this way – if as a Christian
I fall into sin, the Holy Spirit will convict me, and that will
make me miserable. But if I am truly led of the Spirit I will
not stop at that. I will go back to Christ, I will go back to
Calvary's hill, to the blood that was shed, the blood that still
cleanses me, and as I go back I know I am washed and
cleansed, and so I rejoice. If I am truly a Christian, if the
Holy Spirit dwells within me, he must minister to my joy,
and as I go back in contrition and shame, penitent and conscious of my unworthiness, his love is great enough to cover
my sin and my failure. So I go back and I find it is greater
than I thought it was. I have made a fresh discovery of his
love and his mercy and compassion, and in my sin and failure I am made to rejoice all the same. Rejoice in the Lord
always, in life, in death, in sins or failure, whatever may be
happening to you, whatever your circumstances, 'Rejoice in
the Lord alway: and again I say, Rejoice.'

13

Moderation

Let your moderation be known unto all men. The Lord is
at hand (Phil. 4:5).

As one reads the various letters of the Apostle Paul, nothing
is more instructive and interesting than to observe the way
in which statements and remarks, which are apparently
casual, are nevertheless parts of a very definite logical system, and have a logical sequence of ideas which clearly gripped the Apostle's mind as he was writing them. As you read
the first few verses of this fourth chapter, you might at first
sight come to the conclusion that what you have here is a
series of outstanding injunctions, given one after another
without any definite order, which the Apostle worked out as
they came into his mind. But on closer examination, we find
that each one of these specific and particular injunctions is
related to the others, and that they all go together to form a
composite and complete whole.

In other words, the injunction we are considering
together now follows, I think you will see, directly from the
one we were considering in our last study on the fourth
verse, where Paul says, 'Rejoice in the Lord alway: and
again I say, Rejoice.' Now this injunction here follows
directly from that one because, as I think we all must agree,
nothing is so likely to rob us of our joy as trouble in our own
spirits or trouble in our relationships with other people. Let
me emphasise again that Paul's mastering idea in this epistle
is the whole question of joy, that is what he is really

concerned about, and so he talks about the various things that tend to rob us of the joy, and this happens to be one of them. We must pay attention, negatively, to our own spirit and condition and do so especially in relationship to other people.

But we must also look at this from another standpoint. The Apostle was not only concerned about the happiness and joy of the members of the church at Philippi, he was equally concerned that they should be displaying and portraying the Christian character in all its fulness. We have seen something of his love for these people; he speaks of them as his brethren, 'dearly beloved and longed for, my joy and crown'. Yes, but however great his love was for them, his love for his Lord was still greater, and it always urged and compelled him to write these various letters and exhortations to the early Christians in order that they might lead the Christian life in all its fulness, and all its glory. He wanted them to show, if one might use such an expression, the handiwork of God in salvation. In the last study we made the point in passing that miserable or unhappy Christians are not only a very poor advertisement for the gospel of Jesus Christ but they also detract from the glory of the Lord, if they are not showing the possibility of the Christian life in its fulness. And if that was true about the injunction to rejoice in the Lord, it is equally true with respect to this injunction that we are now considering, because it is an essential part of the Christian character, that we should let our moderation be known unto all men. It is as vital to the Christian character that we should exercise and display moderation, as it is that we should rejoice always and glory and exult in the Lord under all conditions.

So, then, these injunctions are very closely connected and interrelated. You cannot have true joy in the Lord if you are wrong on this point, and your Christian character is not complete unless this further aspect is also present.

Now it seems to me that a very interesting question for discussion, in a church fellowship meeting, or in any gathering of Christian people who are concerned about the Christian life, would be this: Which is the more difficult, the injunction in verse 4, or this one in verse 5? Which is harder, to rejoice in the Lord always, or to let our moderation be known unto all men? I commend to you a meditation upon that theme. May I suggest certain ideas to you as you embark upon that process. As far as I am concerned, this injunction in the fifth verse is altogether the more difficult of the two. I find it easier to rejoice in the Lord always, than to let my moderation be always known unto all men. Why is that? I would suggest these reasons. In verse 4 the Apostle is exhorting us to a certain state, and condition. He is concerned there about what we ought to be, but here he is concerned with the application of that state, and I think you will agree that to apply a truth is generally much more difficult than holding or possessing the truth itself.

Let me explain what I mean. I am sure we all know something of this – I am alone in my room, reading my Bible, and I come across this injunction to rejoice in the Lord. So I think of all the arguments that the Apostle provides me with to rejoice in the Lord, and there, all alone, I can rejoice. But it is very much more difficult to continue doing that when I meet my fellow men and women, and when I come face to face with trouble and difficulty. To accept theory is generally easier than to practise it, and in this verse we are in the realm of application. Or let me put it like this. I feel that to rejoice in the Lord is easier than to let my 'moderation be known unto all men,' because when I am exhorted to rejoice in the Lord always, I am exhorted to express something, whereas in this exhortation I am exhorted to practise restraint; and I would not hesitate to say that to restrain oneself is always more difficult than to express oneself. There is something essentially positive about rejoicing in the Lord; you want to sing and to praise God; the whole of your being is involved. Yes, but when you are told, 'let your moderation be known unto all men,' the element of restraint comes in. It is not that it is negative (I shall show that it is positive) but there is a negative element in it.

Or let me put it like this. The injunction in verse 4 is

easier than that in verse 5 because in verse 4 I am being exhorted to look at my Lord, whereas in verse 5 I am exhorted to be like my Lord. It is easy to rejoice in the Lord while you look and meditate upon him, while you think of his work, and as you are looking at him objectively in his work. Yes, but here I am asked to do something more difficult, I am asked to reproduce him. I am asked to conduct and comport myself exactly as he did when he was here on earth, and facing the trials and contradictions in life that I myself have to face. So, then, here in many ways we are face to face with one of the highest demands of the Christian gospel. I think we can safely say that the gospel, in a sense, never calls us to a greater height than it does here with regard to our life, our conduct and practice. Indeed, I would say that it is much easier to rejoice, even in tribulations, than it is to let my moderation be known unto all men.

That is why I thank God that the Apostle, true to his method, as he is always and without exception, not only gives me the injunction but also couples it with doctrine. There is no Christian for whom I feel more sorry than the one who has not yet realised the all-importance of doctrine. We have already noticed that the Apostle never gives an injunction without giving doctrine at the same time. In verse 4 he was not simply saying 'rejoice', but 'rejoice in the Lord', that is the doctrine: it is 'in the Lord'. And here again, the Apostle does not just say, 'Let your moderation be known unto all men,' he adds, 'the Lord is at hand'. That is mighty doctrine, and I thank God for it, because only a full understanding and realisation of what Paul means by that doctrine can ever truly enable me to carry out the injunction. This is something so characteristic of this Apostle. He never asks us to do something without at the same time showing us how it can be done. He never shows us the height we have to climb without pointing us to the source of power that will enable us to climb; never one without the other. The New Testament is not interested in the fact that we should just live a certain type of life for the sake of doing so, the doctrine is fundamental and absolute.

Bearing all this in mind, then, let us look at the injunction directly. What does Paul mean by moderation? Let us first deal with two negatives before we come to the positive. By moderation, Paul does not mean just good nature, something which is animal. He is not talking about psychology or temperament. Nor, secondly, is he referring to what we may call a looseness, a flabbiness and lack of definition. That cannot be what the Apostle means by moderation, because he has already been saying to us, 'Stand fast in the Lord.' Never forget that these commands must all be taken together; this is one in a series of injunctions. The people who are to be moderate in all things are the people who are to stand fast in the Lord at all costs. They are not compromisers; they are not men and women who, because they believe nothing in particular themselves, can be indulgent with respect to everybody else. Nor are they people who, because they lack purpose, believe in a kind of coalition with every other person. No, they are to stand fast in the Lord. So we must get rid, once and for ever, of the idea that moderation means a kind of indifference, a vagueness, a nebulous attitude towards truth and life and everything else; the kind of person who is 'all things to all men' in a wrong and unworthy sense; a man who is always ready to compromise at all costs, 'peace at any price'. Not at all! Nothing is further removed from the grand and magnificent character of the Apostle. No, it is much more difficult than that. There are people, let us grant, who seem to be born like that, but you see that the Apostle is obviously not concerned about that, because he is writing to many different kinds of people. There were all sorts of people in the church at Philippi, as there are all types in the Church today, so Paul's injunction is not just to be worked out like that.

So we can put it positively like this: this word 'moderation' means control of oneself and one's spirit, and is shown by self-control, self-mastery, possession of one's spirit and of one's activity. It means not urging one's own right to the uttermost – that is the first idea inherent in these words. I must be free from that spirit that insists upon the last ounce

in every single situation. It means the capacity to differentiate between what is really of vital importance and what is
not, to stand like a rock by the things that are vital, but to
be reasonable about the things that are not. It means not
pressing my bargain to the very last drop of blood, it means
being prepared, at times, and if necessary, to have less than
is due to me for the sake of the Church and for the sake of
others, but above all, for the Lord's sake. 'Let your moderation be known unto all men': not grasping, not so carried
away that your whole spirit is involved. In other words, it is
not so much what you are doing as the way in which you do
it.

Let me put it another way. This word 'moderation'
undoubtedly conveys the idea of forbearance, that is, a condition in which one is not easily offended. Here you are,
says the Apostle, you are members together of the Church
of Christ, and I am exhorting you to be so in control of your
spirits, your mind and your whole selves that you cannot be
easily put off and offended. We have already looked at that,
you remember, in the case of Euodias and Syntyche –
touchy, sensitive people, always ready to be offended. We
all know something about this, the Lord have mercy upon
us! It is a great and wonderful and noble quality of the
Christian character, this quality of not being easily
offended. Some people have a control and mastery over
themselves, so that though darts are thrown, they do not
find a sensitive place. Let me make it clear again that I am
not advocating a kind of stoic indifference, or a negative,
passive condition. No, this quality is essentially active. If
you have it, it means that you have Christian grace in your
personality, so that when these darts come, you can somehow receive them, and not worry about them – longsuffering, able to bear and forbear, not easily offended.

But it goes even further than that. It means that you have
an active consideration for others. You see the steps in the
definition of this word? First, in and of yourself you are prepared to have less than is your due. Second, when you come
into contact with people who are irritating and difficult, you

have some kind of shock absorber as far as they are concerned. Ah, yes, but you must go further if you want your moderation to be known unto all men: you must actively and positively consider them; you must try to find excuses for them and seek an explanation for their way of behaviour. You might say, 'Well, after all, they are having a difficult time,' or, 'I believe that person was born with a difficult temperament.' You are all the time trying to explain them to yourself, trying to take the edge off harsh and difficult behaviour. You go out of your way to meet people and to make up for any deficiency there may be in them – consideration for others, trying to understand them, and indeed to help them, and to make things easier for them. That is an essential part of this word 'moderation'.

Let me go still further. Notice the kind of person the Apostle is, notice the quality of his personality – a personality that never reacts violently to anything. Let your moderation be known unto all men, in all times and circumstances and under all conditions. Let me work it out like this. The Christian is never to react violently in any realm, not even with respect to joy. Your moderation is to be known unto all men, even in times of happiness. I need not stay with this. Is there anything more obvious and sad in the modern world than the lack of moderation in men and women who are enjoying themselves? They are carried away, right out of control, intoxicated by joy. But the Christian is never to be like that, there is to be an element of control even in his joy, and still more, perhaps, in his sorrow. At times of grief and sorrow the Christian is never to react too violently. Do not misunderstand me, I am not saying he is not to be natural. The Christian was never meant to be unnatural and God forbid we should ever think that. Christians are not only people who know joy, they know grief and sorrow – perhaps more than anybody else – yes, but it does not master them. This is the trouble: so often we are either overjoyed, on the mountain top, or we are down in the depths of despair. But Christians should not be like that, they must never react violently – there is always to be this control, in joy and in sorrow. They are never to be over-animated or over-depressed, but must always maintain a kind of balance and pose; they are to be controlled.

Yet I must make this important addition: they do all this in a spirit of cheerfulness; they are never to be morose, or sullen. Once more we must differentiate between the self-control of the Christian and the control of the Stoic. The Stoic accepts things, but the Christian's moderation is cheerful. There is a great deal of stoicism in the modern world; the world shows amazing self-control, but what a cold thing it is! There is no cheerfulness in it. That sort of control is not what Paul is talking about. You are to be controlled and happy at the same time, and you are also to have even this joy in moderation. Let me give you a perfect illustration of it. Paul, in writing to the church at Corinth, said, 'Now I Paul myself beseech you by the meekness and gentleness of Christ . . .' (2 Cor. 10:1) – the meekness and gentleness of Christ! And that is the Apostle's exhortation here to these Philippian Christians.

Again, I want to emphasise the fact that we are all called upon to show this moderation; Paul is not merely writing to certain people who may be balanced by temperament. No, even though you may be naturally impulsive, it does not matter, you are exhorted to let your moderation be known unto all men. Someone may ask whether this is possible for every type of personality; is it not asking for the impossible? I reply that it is possible to all. Let me give you a proof of that. I was reminded of it forcibly when attention was being called to the fact that it was the anniversary of the death of that great Christian statesman, William Gladstone. I remember once reading of something that Mrs Gladstone said to John Morgan about her husband. She said, 'You must remember that he had two sides, the one impetuous, impatient and unrestrainable, the other all self-control, able to dismiss everything but the great central subject, able to put aside what was weakening or disturbing. He achieved this self-mastery and sanity in the struggle from the age of twenty-three or twenty-four, first by the natural power of his character, and secondly by much wrestling in prayer to reach this injunction, "Let your moderation be known unto all men."' And Gladstone achieved it, this wonderful grace of the Christian character.

But of course, the supreme example of all is the example of our Lord himself. The Apostle Peter puts this very clearly when he says, 'Christ also suffered for us, leaving us an example, that ye should follow his steps: who did no sin, neither was guile found in his mouth: who, when he was reviled, reviled not again; when he suffered, he threatened not; but committed himself to him that judgeth righteously' (1 Pet. 2:21–23). Peter has already said: 'Servants, be subject to your masters . . . not only to the good and gentle, but also to the froward . . . For what glory is it, if, when ye be buffeted for your faults, ye shall take it patiently? but if, when ye do well, and suffer for it, ye take it patiently, this is acceptable with God' (1 Pet. 2:18–20). That is it – our Lord himself was like that; follow in his steps, be like him; 'Let your moderation be known unto all men.'

So, then, let me ask a second question. How is this to be manifested and to whom? And the answer is that we manifest it in practice, we reveal it in our lives and dealings with others. Yes, let me emphasise once more that we are to show this moderation to all men – to everyone, whether they are nice or not, whether they are loving and gentle, or cruel and harsh; whether they are tyrants or whether they are our greatest friends.

Not only that, we are to show moderation in every sphere and in every department of life. We are to show it when we are contending for the faith and standing fast in the Lord. In other words, we are to stand for the truth, yes, and we are to do it in this way. We must watch our spirits, there must be no harshness and no kind of petty-fogging legalism. We must learn to differentiate between what is vital and what is comparatively unimportant. We are to express and show this moderation in our business or in our profession. We are to let people see, by the way we transact our business, that we are Christians. This does not mean that we are to suffer wrong in a legal sense. No, the Apostle Paul himself appealed to Caesar and objected when he was thrown into prison without a trial. It does not mean that, but it does mean that we are always certain that we are not fighting only for ourselves, we are fighting for the truth – and how difficult it is at times to do that! How difficult it is to differentiate between holy zeal or righteous indignation, and the mere expression of a harsh, critical, judgmental spirit. We are told to behave with moderation to all men and at all times, and I would say that there is no greater testimony for the power and the grace of the gospel, than men and women who are showing their moderation in this way.

Let me finish with a word of encouragement which the Apostle provides to enable us to do this. How can we ever reach such a state? What is there that can help us? Here is the answer: 'The Lord is at hand.' This is the Apostle's way of telling us that we must learn increasingly to be indifferent to this world and its ways. As Christian people we have an entirely new view of life, we see things always in the light of the Lord, we see everything in the light of the salvation that he brought, by his life, by his birth, his death, his resurrection and ascension. We see it all in the light of the fact that he is going to return again to the earth, to conquer all his enemies and to bring in an entirely new order. The Lord is at hand.

There are those who try to argue that by these words Paul meant that the Lord is always near, but the whole context is surely against that. It is true, he is always near, but in many ways this is a greater truth. In all we do we must always remember that the Lord may return at any time. His coming is always at hand, yes, but we do not know when, and so we must always live in the realisation that he is coming. And that works out like this. If we always remember that the Lord is coming, we shall always remember that this world and life are nothing but a kind of preparatory school; we are but pilgrims and strangers here, we are here today and gone tomorrow. Very well then, if we always bear that in mind, we have already gone more than half way to displaying this moderation. It is because people think that this is the only life and world that they fight for the last ounce; but what are sixty, seventy or eighty years compared with eternity? 'The Lord is at hand' – remember that.

These words also remind us that he is the Judge, and not we ourselves. How ready we are to judge, but he is the Judge. The Lord is at hand. I am not the judge, and when I am reminded of that it solves many of my problems for me. Not only that, I am reminded of the truth that we ourselves shall be judged, and we shall have to render up an account for our lives and our deeds; therefore be careful in your judgments. You remember how Christ put it, 'Judge not, that ye be not judged. For with what judgment ye judge, ye shall be judged: and with what measure ye mete, it shall be measured to you again' (Matt. 7:1, 2). Do not forget, then, when you feel like condemning, that you yourself are going to be judged. The Lord is at hand, and when you realise that, you are prepared to overlook a great many things in this life and world.

But further, we must not be anxious to obtain the retribution or justice to which we feel we are entitled. The Lord himself will judge evildoers, or anybody who may have wronged us here, because everyone will have to stand before Christ. Do not worry, do not feel you must have immediate revenge. Paul says, 'Dearly beloved, avenge not yourselves, but rather give place unto wrath: for it is written, Vengeance is mine; I will repay, saith the Lord' (Rom. 12:19). If you believe that, you will be sorry for the people who have wronged you, you will tremble as you think of them having to stand before God, and your moderation will already be in active operation.

Or, finally, let me put it like this. You may be having a hard and difficult time – Paul does not minimise it – people may be very cruel and unkind, your position may be really grievous. You may be having to bear something terrible, people may be constantly nagging at you, day after day, night after night. But whatever you may have to suffer or endure in this life, the Lord is at hand and he is preparing an amazing reward for you. When he comes, and when the reign of glory begins, you will be with him, you will be reigning with him, and you will be sharing in his joy and all his glory. My friend, if your name is written in heaven, if you belong to him, your reward is absolutely certain. There is joy in glory awaiting you that you cannot imagine or conceive. So, then, remember that he is coming, the Lord is at hand – keep looking at that.

In other words, once more, you are just exhorted to do what our Lord did. This is what the epistle to the Hebrews says about him: 'who for the joy that was set before him endured the cross, despising the shame' (Heb. 12:2). Or consider how James puts it, 'Be patient therefore, brethren, unto the coming of the Lord. Behold the husbandman waiteth for the precious fruit of the earth, and hath long patience for it, until he receive the early and latter rain. Be ye also patient; stablish your hearts: for the coming of the Lord draweth nigh. Grudge not one against another, brethren, lest ye be condemned: behold, the judge standeth before the door' (Jas. 5:7–9).

Need I say any more? That is not a bit of psychology. Be moderate in all things. 'The Lord is at hand.' Your whole life is in that setting. As you realise that he is the judge and not yourself, as you realise the vengeance that he will manifest on sin and evil, and on all who have been wrong, and have harmed him and his people, pray for those who are going to suffer. But above all, contemplate being with him, spending eternity in his glorious presence, and sharing in that joy that is set before him. 'Let your moderation be known unto all men.'

14

The Peace of God

Be careful for nothing; but in every thing by prayer and
supplication with thanksgiving let your requests be made
known unto God. And the peace of God, which passeth
all understanding, shall keep your hearts and minds
through Christ Jesus (Phil. 4:6, 7).

This is undoubtedly one of the noblest, greatest and most
comforting statements which is to be found anywhere in any
extant literature. One is tempted to say that about many
passages in the Scriptures, and yet from the standpoint of
our personal lives in this world, and from the standpoint of
practical experience, nothing has greater comfort for God's
people than these two verses. We saw in our last study how
an unquiet spirit, a grasping desire to have our own way, so
frequently robs us of our joy; and here in these verses Paul
goes on to consider another factor that is perhaps more
problematical than any of the others which tend to rob us of
the joy of the Lord, and that is what we may well describe
as the tyranny of circumstances, or the things that happen to
us. How many they are, and how often they come! Here the
Apostle deals with this question in a final manner. It is
remarkable, as you read through the Bible, to notice how
often this particular subject is dealt with. A very good case
can be made out for saying that all the New Testament epistles
face this particular problem, and were designed to help the
first Christians deal with it. They lived in a very difficult world
and had to suffer and endure a great deal; and these men,
called of God, wrote their letters in order to show them

399

how to overcome these things. It is the great theme of the New Testament; but you find it also in the Old Testament. Take the third and fourth Psalms, for instance. How perfectly they put it all. The great problem in life is, in a sense, how to lay oneself down to rest and sleep. 'I laid me down and slept,' said the Psalmist (Ps. 3:5). Anybody can lie down, but the question is, can you sleep? The Psalmist describes himself surrounded by enemies and by difficulties and trials, and his mighty testimony is that in spite of that, because of his trust in the Lord he lay down, and slept, and he woke safe and sound in the morning. Why? Because the Lord was with him and was looking after him.

That is the theme of so much of the Bible in the Old Testament and in the New that it is obviously a subject of supreme importance. I sometimes feel that perhaps nothing provides such a thorough test of our faith and of our whole Christian position as just this matter. It is one thing to say that you subscribe to the Christian faith; it is one thing, having read your Bible and abstracted its doctrine, to say, 'Yes, I believe all that, it is the faith by which I live.' But it is not always exactly the same thing to find that faith triumphant and victorious and maintaining you in a state of joy when everything seems to have gone against you and has well nigh driven you to despair. It is a subtle and delicate test of our position because it is such an essentially practical test. It is far removed from the realm of mere theory. You are *in* the position, you are *in* the situation, these things *are* happening to you, and the question is, what is your faith worth at that point? Does it differentiate you from people who have no faith? That is obviously something of very great importance not only for our peace and comfort but also, and especially at a time like this, from the whole standpoint of our Christian witness. People today tell us that they are realists and practical. They say that they are not interested in doctrine, and are not very interested in listening to what we say, but if they see a body of people who seem to have something that enables them to triumph over life, they become interested at once. This is because they are unhappy, and frustrated and uncertain, and fearful. If, when in that condition themselves, they see people who seem to have peace and calm and quiet, then they are ready to look at them and to listen to them. So that both from the standpoint of our own personal happiness and our maintenance of the joy of the Lord, and also from the standpoint of our witness and our testimony in these difficult days, it behoves us to consider very carefully what the Apostle has to say in these masterly statements about the way to deal with the tyranny of circumstances and conditions.

The matter seems to divide itself up quite simply. First of all he tells us what we have to avoid. There are certain things we must avoid, says the Apostle – 'Be careful for nothing.' That is a negative injunction – something to avoid. Now let us be clear about the term 'careful'. 'Be careful for nothing,' says the Authorised translation, but you will find another translation even better: 'Be anxious for nothing,' or 'Be anxious about nothing.' 'Careful' means 'full of care', that means anxiety, harassing care, nervous solicitude, tending to brood or to ponder over things. It is the word our Lord used in the Sermon on the Mount – you remember that section in the sixth chapter of Matthew: 'Take no thought . . .' It means do not be over-anxious, do not brood and ponder, do not meditate overmuch upon, do not have this nervous solicitude about the thing. That is the meaning of the term.

It is important, in passing, that we should understand that the Bible nowhere teaches us not to make ordinary provision for life, or not to use commonsense. It does not encourage laziness. You will remember that Paul in writing to the church at Thessalonica, said: 'If any would not work, neither should he eat' (2 Thess. 3:10). 'Careful' here, therefore, does not refer to wise forethought, but must be interpreted as anxiety, this harassing, wearying, wearing care. That is the thing the Apostle tells us we must avoid at all costs.

But you notice that he does not stop merely at that negative injunction. There is a very profound piece of biblical psychology here. The Apostle shows us how we tend to get into this state of nervous, morbid, brooding anxiety. You notice that he tells us it is all due to the activity of the heart and mind – 'The peace of God, which passeth all understanding, shall keep your hearts and minds through Christ Jesus.' It is the heart and the mind that tend to produce this state of anxiety, this morbid care and solicitude.

This is a profound piece of psychology, and I am emphasising it because later on we shall see how vital it is, in applying the Apostle's remedy to ourselves, that we should grasp and understand his psychological explanation of the condition. What Paul is saying, in other words, is that we can control many things in our lives and outside our lives, but we cannot control our hearts and minds. 'This condition of anxiety,' says Paul, 'is something which, in a sense, is outside your own control, it happens apart from you and in spite of you.' And how true that is to experience. Recall any occasion when you were in this condition of anxiety. Remember how it could not be controlled. You were lying awake and you would have given the whole world if you could only sleep, if you could but stop the heart and the mind from going on working, from revolving and thinking and so keeping you awake. But your mind would not let you sleep, your heart would not let you sleep. The heart and the mind are outside our control. Here is profound psychology indeed, and the Apostle does not hesitate to use it. Here, once more, we come across the wonderful realism of the Scriptures, their absolute honesty, their recognition of man as he is. So the Apostle tells us that in this way the heart and the mind, or, if you prefer it, the depth of one's being, tends to produce this state of anxiety. Here the 'heart' does not only mean the seat of emotions, it means the very central part of one's personality. The 'mind' can be translated by the term 'thought'. We have all, alas, experienced this condition and we know exactly what the Apostle means. The heart has feelings. If a dear one is taken ill, how the heart begins to work! Your concern, your very love for the person, is the cause of the anxiety. If you thought nothing of the person you would not be anxious. There you see where the heart and the affections come in. Not only that – the imagination! What a prolific cause of anxiety is the imagination. You are confronted with a situation, but if it were merely that, you would probably be able to lie down and go to sleep. But the imagination comes in and you begin to think, 'What if this or that should happen? Everything is fairly under control tonight, but what if by tomorrow morning the temperature should be up, or what if this condition should arise and lead to that?' You go on thinking for hours, agitated by these imaginations. Thus your heart keeps you awake.

Or, then, not so much in the realm of imagination but more in the realm of the mind and of pure thought, you find yourself beginning to consider possibilities and you put up positions and deal with them and analyse them and you say, 'If that should take place we shall have to make this arrangement, or we shall have to do that.' You see how it works? The heart and the mind are in control. We are the victims of thoughts; in this condition of anxiety we are the victims. The heart and the mind, these powers that are within us and which are outside our control, are mastering us and tyrannising over us. The Apostle tells us that this is something which at all costs we must avoid. I need not dwell upon the reason for that. I think we must all know it from experience. In this state of anxiety we spend the whole of our time reasoning and arguing and chasing imaginations. And in that state we are useless. We do not want to speak to other people. We may appear to be listening to them as they speak in conversation, but our mind is chasing these possibilities. And so, alas, our testimony is useless. We are of no value to others and above all we lose the joy of the Lord.

But let us hurry to the second principle. What have we to do in order to avoid that inner turmoil? What does the Apostle teach us here? This is where we come to that which is peculiarly and specifically Christian. If I do nothing else I trust that I shall be enabled to show you the eternal difference between the Christian way of dealing with anxiety and the psychological way or the commonsense way. Some may think that I am rather hard on psychology but let me indulge in a little apologia. Psychology, I believe, is one of the most subtle dangers in connection with the Christian faith. People sometimes think that they are being sustained by the Christian faith when what they have is merely a psychological mechanism; and it breaks down in a real crisis. We do not preach psychology, we preach the Christian faith.

Let me show you, then, the difference between the Christian way of dealing with anxiety and this other method. What does the Apostle tell us to do when we are threatened by anxiety? He does not just say, 'Stop worrying.' That is what commonsense and psychology say: 'Stop worrying and pull yourself together.' The Apostle does not say that for the good reason that to tell a person in that condition to stop worrying is useless. Incidentally, it is also bad psychology. If you happen to be a strong-willed person you can hold these things from the conscious mind with the result that they then go on working in the unconscious mind. That is what is called repression – a condition which is even worse than anxiety. But not only that, it is so idle to tell the average person to stop worrying – that is why I say Paul's 'psychology' is so important. It is the very thing he or she cannot do. They would like to, but they cannot. It is like telling a hopeless drunkard to stop drinking. He cannot, because he is helplessly in the grip of this lust and passion. In the same way the Bible does not say, 'Do not worry, it may never happen.' This is a popular psychological slogan and people think it is very wonderful – 'Why worry, it may never happen?' But if anyone says that to me when I am in this state, my reaction is: 'Yes, but it *may* happen.' That is my problem. What if it does happen? That is the essence of my problem, so it does not help me to say it may never happen.

Another negative is this. People tend to say to those wretched people who are anxious and worried, 'You must not worry, it is wrong to worry, and all the worry in the world will not make any difference.' Now that is perfectly true, it is sound commonsense. The psychologists in their turn say, 'Do not waste your energy. The fact that you are worrying is not going to affect the position at all.' 'Ah, yes,' I say, 'that is all right, that is perfectly true; but, you know, it does not get at the source of my trouble for this good reason. I am concerned with what *may* happen. I agree when you put it to me that worrying is not going to affect the position, but the position remains and it is the position that is causing me this anxiety. What you say is perfectly true, but it does not deal with my particular situation.' In other words, all these methods fail to deal with the situation because they never realise the power of what Paul calls 'the heart' and 'the mind' – these things that grip us. That is why none of the psychology and commonsense methods are finally of any use.

What, then, does the Apostle say? He puts his remedy in the form of a positive injunction: 'Let your requests be made known unto God.' That is the answer. But now, here, it is of vital importance that we should know precisely and in detail how to deal with this. The Apostle says, 'Let your requests be made known unto God.' 'Alas!' says many a sufferer. 'I have tried, I have prayed; but I have not found the peace you speak of. I have not had an answer. It is no use telling me to pray.' Fortunately for us, the Apostle realised that also, and he has given us particular instructions for the carrying out of his injunction. 'Be careful for nothing; but in every thing by prayer and supplication with thanksgiving let your requests be made known unto God.' Is the Apostle just tumbling out one word after another, or is he speaking advisedly? I can show you that he is indeed speaking advisedly as he shows us how to let our requests be made known unto God.

How are we to do that? First he tells us to pray. He differentiates between prayer and supplication and thanksgiving. What does he mean by prayer? This is the most general term and it means worship and adoration. If you have problems that seem insoluble, if you are liable to become anxious and overburdened, and somebody tells you to pray, do not rush to God with your petition. That is not the way.

Before you make your requests known unto God, pray, worship, adore. Come into the presence of God and for the time being forget your problems. Do not start with them. Just realise that you are face to face with God. The idea of being face to face is inherent in the very word 'prayer'. You come into the presence of God and you realise the presence and you recollect that presence – that is the first step always. Even before you make your requests known unto God you realise that you are face to face with God, that you are in his presence and you pour out your heart in adoration. That is the beginning.

But following prayer comes supplication. Now we are moving on. Having worshipped God because God is God, having offered this general worship and adoration, we come now to the particular, and the Apostle here encourages us to make our supplications. He tells us that we can take particular things to God, that petition is a legitimate part of prayer. So we bring our petitions, the particular things that are now concerning us.

We are now coming nearer to letting our requests be made known. But wait, there is still one other thing – 'by prayer and supplication with thanksgiving'. That is one of the most vital of all these terms. And it is just here that so many of us go astray when we are in this condition with which the Apostle is dealing. I trust it is unnecessary that I should digress to point out that in connection with these steps the Apostle was not merely interested in liturgical forms. What a tragedy that people should take an interest in the form of worship in a mere liturgical sense. That is not what the Apostle is concerned about. He is not interested in formality, he is interested in worship.

Thanksgiving is absolutely essential for this reason: if, while we pray to God, we have a grudge against him in our hearts, we have no right to expect that the peace of God will keep our heart and our mind. If we go on our knees feeling that God is against us, we may as well get up and go out. No, we must approach him 'with thanksgiving'. There must be no doubt in our heart as to the goodness of God. There must be no question or query; we must have positive reasons for thanking God. We have our problems and troubles but there on our knees we must ask ourselves: 'What can I thank God for?' We have to do that deliberately and it is something that we can do. We must remind ourselves of it. We must say, 'I may be in trouble at the moment, but I can thank God for my salvation and that he has sent his Son to die on the cross for me and for my sins. There is a terrible problem facing me, I know, but he has done that for me. I thank God that he sent his Son, our Lord Jesus Christ, into the world. I will thank him for bearing my sins in his own body on the tree, I will thank him for rising again for my justification. I will pour out my heart in thanksgiving for that. I will thank him for the many blessings I have received in the past.' We must just work out with our mind and with all our energy the reasons for thanking and praising God. We must remind ourselves that he is our Father, that he loves us so much that the very hairs of our head are all numbered. And when we have reminded ourselves of these things we must pour out our heart in thanksgiving. We must be in the right relationship to God. We must realise the truth concerning him. Therefore we must come into his presence with a loving, praising, worshipping, adoration and confident faith and then make our requests known unto him. The prayer that Paul advocates, in other words, is not a desperate cry in the dark, not some frantic appeal to God without any real thought. No, we first realise and recollect that we are worshipping a blessed, glorious God. We worship first and then we make our requests known.

Then the next principle is the gracious promise of God to all who do this. We have seen what we have to do, we have been instructed how we are to deal with it, and now comes the gracious promise to those who do what the Apostle has just been telling us. This is, of course, the best of all, but we must learn how to look at it. Have you noticed the promise, have you noticed its character, have you noticed that it does not even mention the things that are worrying you? That is the peculiar thing about the Christian method of dealing with anxiety. Does the Apostle say, 'In all things – these things that are worrying – make your requests known and God will banish and remove them all?' No, Paul does not say that. He does not mention them, he just says nothing about them. To me that is one of the most thrilling things about the Christian life. The glory of the gospel is that it is concerned about us and not about our circumstances. The final triumph of the gospel is seen in this, that whatever our circumstances, we ourselves can be put right and maintained. It does not mention our condition, it does not talk about these things that are harassing and perplexing, it does not say a single word about them. They may or they may not happen, I do not know. Paul does not say that the thing feared is not going to take place, he says that we shall be kept whether it happens or whether it does not happen. Thank God, that is the victory. I am taken above circumstances, I am triumphant in spite of them.

That is the great principle. We all tend to be tyrannised by circumstances because we depend upon them, and we would like them to be governed and controlled, but that is not the way in which the Scripture deals with the situation. What the Apostle says is this: 'Make your requests known unto God, and the peace of God which passeth all understanding, shall keep your hearts and minds.' He will keep you absolutely safe from these things which are keeping you awake and preventing your sleep. They will be kept outside, and you will be kept in peace in spite of them.

Again, I would point out that never does the Apostle say that if we pray, our prayer in and of itself will make us feel better. It is a disgraceful thing that people should pray for that reason. That is the psychologists' use of prayer. They tell us that if we are in trouble it will do us good to pray – very good psychology, thoroughly bad Christianity. Prayer is not auto-suggestion.

Neither does he say, 'Pray, because while you are praying you will not be thinking about that problem, and therefore you will have temporary relief.' Again, good psychology but bad Christianity.

Neither does he say, 'If you fill your mind with thoughts of God and Christ these thoughts will push out the other things.' Once more, good psychology but nothing to do with Christianity.

Neither does he say, and I say this advisedly, 'Pray, because prayer changes things.' No, it does not. Prayer does not 'change things'. That is not what the Apostle says, that is again psychology and has nothing at all to do with the gospel. What the Apostle says is this: 'You pray and make your requests known unto God, and God will do something.' It is not your prayer that is going to do it, it is not you who are going to do it, but God. 'The peace of God, which passeth all understanding' – he, through it all, 'shall keep your hearts and minds through Christ Jesus.'

I must say a word about that expression 'keeping' your hearts and minds. It means garrisoning, guarding – a number of words can be used. It conjures up a picture. What will happen is that this peace of God will walk round the ramparts and towers of our life. We are inside, and the activities of the heart and mind are producing those stresses and anxieties and strains from the outside. But the peace of God will keep them all out and we ourselves inside will be at perfect peace. It is God who does it. It is not we ourselves, it is not prayer, it is not some psychological mechanism. We make our requests known unto God, and God does that for us and keeps us in perfect peace.

What shall we say of this phrase: 'The peace of God, which passeth all understanding'? You cannot understand this peace; you cannot imagine it; in a sense, you cannot even believe it; yet it is happening and you are experiencing it and enjoying it. It is God's peace that is in Christ Jesus. What does he mean by that? He is telling us that this peace of God works by presenting the Lord Jesus Christ to us and reminding us about him. To put it in terms of the argument of the epistle to the Romans: 'If, when we were enemies, we were reconciled to God by the death of his Son, much more, being reconciled, we shall be saved by his life' (Rom. 5:10).

'All things work together for good to them that love God, to them who are the called according to his purpose.' 'He that spared not his own Son, but delivered him up for us all, how shall he not with him also freely give us all things?' (Rom. 8:28, 32). 'I am persuaded, that neither death, nor life, nor angels, nor principalities, nor powers, nor things present, nor things to come, nor height, nor depth, nor any other creature, shall be able to separate us from the love of God, which is in Christ Jesus our Lord' (Rom. 8:38, 39). The argument is that if God has done that supreme thing for us in the death of his Son upon the cross, he cannot forsake us now, he cannot leave us half-way, as it were. So the peace of God that passeth all understanding keeps our hearts and minds through, or in, Christ Jesus. In that way God guarantees our peace and our freedom from anxiety.

I end with a word on the last principle, which is the all-inclusiveness of the promise. 'In nothing be careful' – 'Be careful for nothing, but in all things . . .' It does not matter what they are, there is no limit in it. Beloved Christian, whatever it is that is tending to get you down, tending to make you a victim of this anxiety, this morbid care, harassing and spoiling your Christian life and witness, whatever it is, let it be known unto God in that way, and if you do so it is absolutely guaranteed that the peace of God which passeth all understanding shall guard, keep, garrison your heart and mind. That mighty turmoil of heart and mind within you will not affect you. Like the Psalmist, you will lay yourself down and you will sleep, you will know this perfect peace. Do you know this, have you got this peace? Is this another bit of theory or does it actually happen? I assert that nearly two thousand years of Christian history – the story of the Christian Church – proclaim that this is a fact. Read the stories of the saints and the martyrs and the Confessors. And, you get the same evidence in contemporary stories. Recently I read of an experience told by John George Carpenter, until a few years ago the General of the Salvation Army. He tells how he and his wife had to part with their daughter, a lovely girl, of whom they were so fond and proud and who had dedicated her young life to foreign mission work in the East. Suddenly she was taken ill with typhoid fever. Of course, they began to pray, but John Carpenter and Mrs Carpenter somehow felt, although they could not explain it, that they could not pray for that child's recovery. They went on praying but their prayer was – 'Thou canst heal her if thou wilt' – they could not positively ask God to heal her, only – 'Thou canst if thou wilt.' They could get no further. They went on like that for six weeks and then this beautiful girl died. The very morning she died John Carpenter said to Mrs Carpenter, 'You know, I am aware of a strange and curious calm within.' And Mrs Carpenter replied, 'I feel exactly the same.' And she said to him, 'This must be the peace of God.' And it was the peace of God. It was the peace of God keeping the heart and mind quiet in the sense that they could not upset the person. There they were, they had made their request known in the right way, and to their amazement and astonishment – they were almost chiding themselves because of it – this amazing calm and peace had come to them. They could not understand it, and that was the only explanation – 'It must be the peace of God.' It was. Thank God for it. You and I cannot explain these things, they overpower us; but he is almighty. With prayer and supplication and thanksgiving, therefore, let your requests be made known unto him, and he, through his peace in Christ, will keep your heart and mind at rest and in peace.

15

The Hebrew and the Greek Mind

Finally, brethren, whatsoever things are true, whatsoever
things are honest, whatsoever things are just, whatsoever
things are pure, whatsoever things are lovely, whatsoever
things are of good report; if there be any virtue, and if
there be any praise, think on these things (Phil. 4:8).

We come, in these words, to the last of the series of exhortations which the Apostle Paul addresses to the members of
the church at Philippi. The word 'finally' indicates quite
clearly that the Apostle is finding it very difficult to end this
letter. He so loves the members of the church at Philippi, his
attachment to them is so great because of the special
relationship that exists between them, and the whole character of the church is such that the Apostle feels drawn to
them in an exceptional manner, and he has thoroughly
enjoyed writing this letter to them. He finds it difficult,
therefore, to finish it, and yet he must, and so, apart from
certain further remarks of a more personal character, he
brings the letter to an end with this general exhortation.
Now these words are probably very familiar to all of us. In
the days when people used to put framed texts upon their
walls, you would often find this verse facing you. It is one
which is often quoted, and yet I suggest that perhaps no
words which were written by the Apostle Paul are so open
to misunderstanding. They have frequently been misunderstood; and have been the attacking ground of a great discussion which has gone on in the Christian Church almost
from the beginning. Therefore I feel that as we look at this

412

verse nothing is so important as the question of our approach to it.

There are certain verses in the Bible of which it can always be said quite truthfully that our approach to them is vital and determines our exposition. For those who are interested in this matter of exegesis and exposition, that is a very important principle. It is always dangerous to take a verse in isolation; no verse should be taken out of its context, but that is especially so with regard to some verses. For instance, it would be possible to approach this verse by taking the different words and terms that the Apostle uses and giving their exact meaning, and then to regard that as an adequate interpretation. But I want to try to show you that that is quite inadequate with a verse like this, and that here, especially, our whole approach to the statement is of supreme significance. In other words, the question that arises at once is this: What exactly is the Apostle Paul talking about here? And that immediately introduces us, as I have already reminded you, to the great discussion that has obtained from the very earliest days of Christianity, and has divided Christian people into two groups.

The problem which is posed for us by this particular text is the whole problem of the relationship between Christianity and culture. Now I am sure that many, if not most, Christian people, are interested in that question, because it is of very real significance and importance. Indeed, it behoves us to arrive at some decision with regard to this whole matter because it really is one of the most urgent and relevant problems confronting the Christian Church at this very moment.

We can put this in its setting by approaching the subject historically. If you go far back into history, you will find that the problem raised here is the difference between the Hebrew mind and the Greek mind – it is as old as that! In the ancient world two ways of thinking confronted men and women – the Hebrew outlook upon life, and the Greek outlook, and they were very different. In a sense, the fight that you find in the Bible – and you certainly find it in the subsequent history of the Christian Church – is this conflict between the Hebrew and the Greek, these two attitudes with regard to life. Let me note briefly some of the characteristic differences between the two outlooks.

Now the Hebrew always tends to be active; the Greek, on the other hand, tends to be abstract. The Hebrew believes in salvation by deeds and by actions, while the Greek believes in salvation by ideas. The Old Testament, which is the quintessence of the Hebrew outlook, is the story of God doing things – that is the Hebrew concept of salvation. Not ideas about salvation, not thoughts, not concepts, but God acting, God intervening, that is the Hebrew emphasis, whereas to the Greek everything tends to be a matter of ideas. Salvation is an idea, something that you work out in terms of thought, by passivity and contemplation – it is salvation by thoughts and ideas.

Then another important distinction is that the Hebrew is characterised by emotion and passion, whereas the Greek, I would say, is characterised by sentimentality and control. I think you will see the importance of these distinctions.

If you look at the great Hebrew prophets, whose writings we have in the Old Testament, you will find that they are full of emotion, full of movement, full of rugged strength, tearing asunder, blasting with force and with power. The Greek, on the other hand, does not like passion or emotion; at least, he likes controlled emotion which becomes sentimental; everything must be very orderly. The Greek does not stress power and might so much as beauty and order, arrangement and control. To put it, perhaps, in a word, the essential difference between the Hebrew and the Greek is the difference between the prophetic and the educative.

Now you see the importance of this at the present time. There are people in the Church who say that what we need is a great teaching ministry; but there are others who say that what we need, above everything else, is a prophetic ministry. They say it is not enough to present ideas by teaching – no, you need something more profound and fundamental and the prophetic note is the note that is needed. You can see that the decision of the Church with respect to these two things will affect her ministry. In this you also see the difference between those modern men and women who just need to have ideas presented to them and those who need the prophetic power that will blast and rend and convict and lead to conversion – the mighty activity of God. That is the essential background to this verse that we are looking at now.

So there you have, right away back in history, the difference between the Hebrew and the Greek. But the moment the Christian Church came into being, the problem became very acute, the moment this gospel was preached in Europe and in the Greek areas of the world, the great fight began. The tendency was for the Greek outlook, the philosophical outlook, to impose itself upon the essentially Hebrew idea of salvation, and to control and modify it. That is why you find a man like the Apostle Paul going out of his way, in writing to the church at Corinth, to say that he does not preach Christ 'with the wisdom of words, lest the cross of Christ should be made of none effect' (1 Cor. 1:17). He is warning the people against philosophy, against this science of learning, this Greek conception.

Now the authorities are all agreed in saying that for the first three or four centuries the Christian gospel had to fight for its very life against Greek philosophy: the idea of turning the gospel with its activity, with its prophetic emphasis, into just another, though perhaps the best and the greatest and the most perfect, of the philosophies. But let us come down the ages and see how this fight was continued. You see it showing itself clearly in the sixteenth and seventeenth centuries, especially, first of all, in the sixteenth. I am referring to the conflict between the Reformation and the Renaissance, for the two things came together at that time – the revival of learning and the revival of religion – and there was a great fight between them. In a sense, it was represented by two people: Martin Luther and Erasmus. On the one hand, Luther the prophetic preacher of the gospel, believing the Hebrew idea; on the other hand, Erasmus with his ideas on teaching and with his knowledge and culture. It is very interesting to read the correspondence between these men, because there you will see a great elaboration of this question.

Then move on to the seventeenth century where you find the same thing once more, and here it is the conflict between Puritanism and Anglicanism – I mean Anglicanism in a general term. It was a fight between the Puritan idea of worship, which was simple, direct and immediate and which emphasised emotion, trembling in the presence of the Holy God, and being subject to the activity of God; there was a conflict between that, and the idea of worship that lays emphasis on forms, ceremonies, ritual, beauty of diction and language, ornate buildings and the Greek concept of beauty and goodness, as well as truth. And this great fight beween the Hebrew and the Greek in terms of Puritanism and Anglicanism has persisted throughout the centuries. You find it in the last century in a striking manner. In the eighteenth century, as a result of the evangelical awakening, the Hebrew idea came into the ascendancy with revival, conversions and God doing things. Ah, yes, but in the last century, as the result of the so-called 'Enlightenment' and a new interest in the Classics and in learning and in knowledge, the Greek idea began to percolate back, and its influence upon the interpretation of Scripture has been most profound. Indeed, the vast majority of theological ideas today show the decided influence of the Greek outlook upon salvation. Think of the men during the last century, men such as Emerson, Ruskin, Matthew Arnold and people like that, they are typical Greeks, and over against them you have the evangelicals with their Hebrew emphasis, and these two viewpoints are ever fighting against each other.

I call your attention to this because it is my profound conviction that the state of the Church today, in this and in most other lands, is entirely to be attributed to the fact that the Greeks have gained the ascendancy, that the old idea of the prophetic message is being pushed into the background, and the idea of worshipping God in terms of ideas and thoughts is gaining ground. You must not talk about conversion – that was all right in prophetic times, but there is no longer any need to be converted. No, you just absorb the idea, and, in this way, the whole world is going to be saved. That is the Greek conception in contra-distinction to the Hebrew.

And, of course, we are face to face with this self-same thing at the present time. But today it is a fight between Christianity and what is called Western, or European culture. Now it behoves us to examine this matter seriously and carefully. Is it the business of the Church to contend for that culture? I am not expressing any opinion on modern-day culture other than that it is very good, but I must ask whether it is the business of the Church merely to preach that type of culture, or whether it is the job of the Church to preach the prophetic Hebrew gospel, the activity of God, the need of conversion?

Are we simply standing for the propagating of certain values which have been useful in life and conduct, or are we to preach doom and judgment? Are we to call upon God, to repent and humble ourselves, and thus have personal dealings with God? That is the question, and you see it is of vital moment to the whole future of the Christian Church.

Now all this arises because of the eighth verse of Philippians 4. When we look at this verse, the question that we ask at once is this: What is Paul saying? Is he, just for once in his life, and for the only time in his writings, suddenly taking the Greek view? Is Paul just telling these Philippian people, 'Now, then, familiarise yourselves with Greek culture and spend your time in thinking about these things'? That is the question. You can see that our approach to this verse matters supremely, because this is the favourite verse of those who advocate the Greek outlook. If you ever have a discussion with them on the relationship between Christianity and culture, I can assure you that they will produce this verse – it is the only one they can produce – and they say that here the Apostle Paul is putting before us this Greek idea.

They are, however, in one difficulty, and it is interesting to notice how they all have to grant it – Paul uses the word *virtue*: 'Finally, brethren . . . if there be any virtue . . .' and immediately they begin to write their notes: 'Now,' they say, 'this is striking. That word virtue was a pagan word, and isn't it remarkable that this is the only time that the Apostle ever used it?' They have to acknowledge that Paul knew all about Greek culture, he was a man well-versed in these things, he was a cultured man, and yet they have to admit that in all his writings this is the only place where the Apostle uses this word. It was something the Greeks believed in and it was the basis of their philosophy. Greek philosophy was nothing but a constant appeal to men to exercise virtue, it was a moral appeal. But Paul uses the word just once, here, and that is why they are in difficulties.

But the question that arises for us is what exactly does the Apostle mean in this verse? There are a number of ways in which people traditionally have approached and interpreted this verse. The first is what I would call the sentimental approach and interpretation. Certain people who read these words, or see them upon the wall, say, 'How beautiful!' And they never get any further; it is the aesthetic approach. They say as they read verse 8 aloud to themselves, 'How wonderful!' I need not stay with this. If there is one thing with which the Apostle must never be charged it is with sentimentality. Sentiment, passion, yes; emotion, yes; but sentimentality, never – it is utterly foreign to the essential Christian character.

The second approach is what I would describe as an interpretation in terms of what is called 'the science of thought'. This is important, because it does seem to me that far too often, as Christian people, we confuse this so-called 'science of thought' language with the message of the Christian gospel. What it says is that you must fill your mind with beautiful thoughts, with poetry, good literature or music. That is the appeal of the gospel. If we fill our minds with these beautiful, lovely, uplifting thoughts and ideas, we shall be saved and emancipated from everything that tends to be unworthy and to drag us down.

You are familiar with this; you see it in the books and journals. We are told that last thing at night we must make sure that we have beautiful thoughts in our minds; it will not only help us to sleep, it will help our whole life and outlook, and we will wake up feeling fresher and brighter. 'Surround yourself,' people say, 'with beauty in poetry, literature and music, and in various other ways, and as you go on doing this, you will gradually become a better and better person.' Now there are Christian people who use this verse in that way, fondly imagining that that is what the Apostle is advocating: we must fill our minds with these wonderful things, and as we do so we will gradually be achieving salvation. That is the science of thought or mind culture, and it is a typical Greek outlook – it is excellent psychology, but an abuse of the Christian gospel.

And then there is what I might call the semi-Christian interpretation of this verse. It appeals to those who do believe that salvation is only possible in terms of the death and resurrection of our Lord, but who also believe that this type of thing has come as an addition and supplement to the gospel, and that it will help us perfect our salvation. This view says that the way to avoid sin and to live a good life, the way to be happy and to maintain our joy, is just to take these good and beautiful and true ideas and think about them, meditate upon them and surrender ourselves to them. Then, as we do so, we will become better people.

But the answer to all that is an eternal 'No!', and that for two main reasons. First of all there is a general reason, and then a specific reason indicated by Paul in verse 8 itself. First, these views are a misinterpretation of the whole of the New Testament teaching. The New Testament never asks us to contemplate ideas, it always calls upon us to look at the Person. That is the essential difference between the gospel and philosophy, between the Hebrew and the Greek. I would remind you once more that there was nothing that Paul was so afraid of as that the doctrine of the cross should be turned into a philosophy – and how easy it is to do it! To maintain, for example, that 'death is essential to life', or that there is 'a principle of sacrifice in life', is to turn the doctrine of the cross into a philosophical idea, and it is exactly the same with the resurrection. Have you not noticed, as you come to Eastertime, how people start sentimentalising about 'life', saying how the seed that was sown has died and that now the life germ has come out of death, and that there you see resurrection as a principle of life because you see it everywhere? And the glorious fact of the resurrection of Christ is philosophised in that way into a general principle of 'resurrection'.

Now that is something which the New Testament never does. The New Testament is concerned about facts, it is concerned about a Person, Paul said of him, '. . . that I may know him, and the power of his resurrection . . .', not a general principle of rising in life. No, the eternal Son of God was literally born as a babe in Bethlehem; it is not an idea, it does not belong to Greek mythology, it happened. He suffered and endured, he literally staggered up to Golgotha, he was nailed to the tree – these are not ideas. They happened! See him, look at him. He died and was buried, a stone was rolled to the mouth of that grave, but it was removed and he emerged. He came out literally in the body, he showed himself again. All along we are exhorted to consider him, and to consider these facts, while we are told that what he has done is all sufficient.

'But,' says someone, 'surely if that is all true, doesn't this other idea help? Isn't it still a good idea, and won't it help with my salvation if I fill my mind with beautiful words and thoughts and music?' No, that is the cloven hoof of the devil, that is where the devil comes in. The gospel of Jesus Christ needs no assistance, it needs no supplement, nothing can save a man but what God has done in Christ. If the whole of Greek culture and the Greek outlook failed to save the world, if it failed in the greater thing, do we need to call in its assistance in the lesser thing? Out upon the suggestion! 'But of him are ye in Christ Jesus, who of God is made unto us wisdom, and righteousness, and sanctification, and redemption' (1 Cor. 1:30). He is the life, I do not need your plus. He is the beginning and the end, he is all and in all, and in him dwelleth all the fulness of the godhead bodily. I do not need Greek culture, I do not need science of thought, I have all in him. I will admit no assistance, no supplement.

And, of course, it is not a mere theory. I think I can show you clearly that the history of the last hundred years proves my contention. We have heard a great deal about this other idea during that time. We have not preached the prophetic gospel; we have not stressed the need for repentance and conversion and an utter humiliation before God; we do not like the term 'vile sinner', we are too polite! We work on the Greek idea, but what has it led to? You see what happens when we call in the assistance of culture to help us? Look at the modern world, look at the life lived by men and women, look at the moral muddle throughout the whole world. No, the very idea must be dismissed; people like to be told to fill their minds with beautiful thoughts, so to use this verse in the Greek sense is a danger to men and women because it panders to their pride.

Then, as I have tried to show you, it detracts from the glory and perfection of the work of Christ upon the cross. I can put that in terms of one particular illustration in order to show you the difference between these two things which we have been discussing together. Take the problem of dealing with fear, or the problem of dealing with unworthy thoughts, perhaps the problem of jealousy. Now the person who is troubled about one of these things is afraid of being alone, he is afraid of what will happen. The Greek idea believes in what is called subjugation. Here you are, alone, and you begin to be fearful, so at once you start thinking about things that are beautiful, lovely and pure, and as you are filling your mind with these thoughts you forget your fear, you have got it under control. So in that way you are harnessing that fear, you are attaching it to something higher, and as you do this, you get rid of your fear or these unworthy thoughts, and instead you have these beautiful and lovely ones.

Now that is not the New Testament method of dealing with the problem and for this good reason: it means that you are not facing yourself or the temptation honestly. While the Greek method tells you not to think about it, the Christian method tells you to look it straight in the face. The Christian, the gospel method, never tells you to avoid thinking about sin, it tells you to face it, and to think about it. And here is the essence of the whole matter and that is why, by nature, people prefer the Greek to the Hebrew. The Christian way of dealing with fear is like this. It comes to you and it says, 'Do you say that you, as a Christian, are afraid like this? Do you say that you, who believe that God loved you and sent his only begotten Son to die on the cross for you and rose again to justify you, do you say you cannot trust him with your little life? Do you say the God who has done the greater thing is not going to look after you?' The gospel does not say, 'Now think beautiful thoughts and forget the others.' The gospel comes to you and says, 'Are you as a Christian harbouring thoughts like that? Did Christ die in order that you should go on thinking in that way and living in that way? Face yourself,' says the gospel, 'look at your own imperfections, and then look into the face of Christ upon that cross and ask God to have mercy and compassion upon you.' That is the Christian method, not science of thought, but looking at yourself in the light of Christ and what he has done for you, bringing that sin, that foul, ugly sin immediately to him, facing it and yourself in his holy presence, and believing truly and absolutely and implicitly in his power.

In view of all this, I would suggest to you that what Paul was saying to the Philippians was this: Your whole thinking and all your actions must be controlled by the gospel. He was still concerned about their joy and peace, and this is his last word about it. In effect, he says, 'If you want to know that peace of God that passeth understanding, if you want to experience the joy of the Lord, then, in addition to what I have told you negatively, remember this positively: your whole life and thought and your actions must be controlled by the gospel. You must not think things that are incompatible with it.' And then he puts it in a positive form. The things we are to think about must be compatible with the gospel. They must be true, true in that ultimate sense, they must be serious, they must be reverent. Christians are essentially serious people because they have seen themselves as lost sinners saved only by the death of Christ on the cross, and those who have seen that must be profoundly, fundamentally serious. I do not say that they are solemn but I do say that they are serious and reverent; there is a seriousness in their whole outlook upon life. They must be just, and their thoughts must be pure, clean and unadulterated; lovely, in the sense that they will lead people to look at and love them; of good report, well spoken of; of virtue, moral excellence; of praise, moral approbation from the practice of the truth.

That is what the Apostle says. As Christian people we must see to it that the whole of our life, our very thoughts and ideas, everything, are under the mighty control of the risen Lord. Every thought must be brought into subjection to him. As we read in 2 Corinthians 10:5, we must bring everything into captivity to Christ; Christ must control our minds and the whole of our thinking. So let us beware of the subtle danger of confusing the general culture, which is good in and of itself, with the glorious gospel of God in Jesus Christ. Let our whole life be a tribute and a testimony to our Redeemer's praise.

16

How to Know God's Peace

Those things, which ye have both learned, and received,
and heard, and seen in me, do: and the God of peace shall
be with you (Phil. 4:9).

Let me remind you again that these two verses, the eighth
and ninth, constitute the Apostle's final exhortation to the
members of the church at Philippi, and we have seen that
they are particularly comprehensive. The eighth verse,
which we considered in our last study, stresses mainly the
thought of the Christian, the realm in which thinking should
be exercised, the way in which the gospel limits intellectual
life, and it defines the things about which the Christian life
should meditate. Then here in this ninth verse we come to
the other great section of the exhortation, and this is the
more practical part. Here Paul is concerned to emphasise
what the gospel has to say to us in the realm of conduct and
of action.

Here, then, in this final exhortation, we are reminded of
some fundamental principles with regard to the gospel
which we can never and, indeed, must never forget. The
Apostle is here, in a sense, giving a summary of everything
he has been trying to say. It is as if he were saying, 'I have
now gone into the details, I have dealt with these particular
problems, I have tried to visualise the temptations that you
may meet and all I have been saying to you can be put like
this: let your whole life be dominated in this way by the gospel, and then all will be well with you.' And that, I would
say, reminds us of two fundamental principles with regard to

the gospel. The first is that the gospel is not something which we add to our lives, it is rather, something which should entirely dominate them.

We must constantly repeat this, because I believe that a most subtle danger, which tends to assail us all, is the danger of making our Christianity some kind of addition to our lives, instead of seeing that the New Testament teaches everywhere that the gospel controls the whole of life. There is to be nothing in the life of the Christian that does not come under the control and domination of the gospel. In other words, in this exhortation the Apostle is reminding us that all our thinking, all our intellectual activity, must, to use his words in 2 Corinthians 10:5, be subjected to, or made captive to, the Lord Jesus Christ.

Now the life of man on earth can be divided into these two categories. Our whole existence here is a matter of thinking and of doing; and the Apostle teaches us that in both respects we are to be controlled by the gospel. He has given us the characteristics of the gospel in the realm of thought; the gospel is concerned only with things that are honest, things that are just, things that are pure and lovely and of good report, everything that belongs to the moral excellence and everything deserving of praise. And here, in conduct, it is exactly the same – 'These things which ye have both learned, and received, and heard, and seen in me, do': – your thinking and your acting are to be dominated entirely by the gospel of Jesus Christ.

The Christian life, therefore, is not merely a modification of the natural life, it is a new life, and Christians do not merely add something to their lives, they are people who have been changed at the centre, they are entirely different. Now we need not stay with this, but this, surely, is something which is basic in the New Testament teaching. 'If any man be in Christ, he is a new creature' (2 Cor. 5:17), not an improved creature, nor a renovated creature, but a new creature, a new creation; he is altogether different, his entire life is something that should present a striking contrast to those who are not Christian. Christians do not think in the same way, they do not live in the same way; there is this new power and purpose on the very throne of their being, dominating their activity and thinking, that covers the whole of their lives. All that is suggested by this great exhortation.

Then the second great principle is what the Apostle here shows us very plainly with regard to the New Testament doctrine of holiness. The New Testament teaching of holiness, or sanctification, is never presented as a law. This is something that tends to lead us astray. There is always the danger of turning New Testament holiness into moralities, but the two things are entirely different. The New Testament never gives a list of rules and regulations, it never tells us to do, or not to do, various things, that is the law. But the New Testament does not do that; holiness, it tells us, is rather something which is not only essential, but is inevitable if we truly desire to enjoy the blessings of the Christian gospel. I am never tired of putting it like this. The New Testament doctrine of holiness is an appeal to our Christian commonsense; it is an appeal to our reason. It does not come, as it were, in the form of a dictator saying, 'Do these things!' No, it rather comes and says, 'If you really want to enjoy the fulness and the blessings of the gospel of Christ, then there are certain things that you must do.'

That is why we must realise that there is no need to denounce people who are not living the holy life. The New Testament seems to me to be sorry for them. There is no need to denounce Christians who are not doing their utmost to live the Christian life, because, poor things, they are suffering enough as it is. They are missing the greatest things the gospel has to give. The New Testament regards as pathetic these people who claim that they desire the blessings of the gospel and yet are not doing the one thing that is essential to receiving them. They are deceiving themselves, they are foolish; is that not the term which our Lord himself used – the foolish man who built his house upon the sand? That is the New Testament way of proclaiming this doctrine of holiness and of sanctification. It comes to us with this great appeal, and tells us, 'Here are the blessings that are possible, but if you desire to receive them, you must pay attention to what always accompanies them.'

In other words, the New Testament blessings are always conditional. This is just another way of saying that one of the most important words in verse 9 is the last 'and': 'These things which ye have . . . seen in me do; *and* the God of peace shall be with you', that is, 'If you do this, then that will follow.' That is the New Testament way of offering these blessings. Indeed, search your Bible from beginning to end and you will find that all the promises of blessing are conditional. In the Old Testament, was that not true of the Children of Israel? That was the blunder which they made; they forgot that all that God had promised to Abraham, and their receiving the land and dwelling in it, was conditional. This was expressed in one of the commandments – 'Honour thy father and thy mother: that thy days may be long upon the land which the Lord thy God giveth thee' (Ex. 20:12). God promised the Children of Israel that they should possess that land only so long as they obeyed his commandments and lived life in accordance with his holy will. Read again about the two Mounts, the Mount of blessing and the Mount of cursing (Deut. 11:29). So long as the people obeyed the Lord they were blessed, but when they disobeyed they were cursed. And you remember how those foolish people thought that as they were the people of God, nothing could disturb them, but they forgot that the promises are always conditional. Or read also the preamble to the Ten Commandments in Exodus 19. It is all there, always this 'if', so if the condition is not observed, we have no right to expect God's blessing.

Then when you come to the New Testament, you find exactly the same thing. Take the Beatitudes from the Sermon on the Mount: 'Blessed are the meek . . . Blessed are the poor in spirit' and so on. These are the people who are blessed; yes, there is always the condition: you must be meek and poor in spirit; you must hunger and thirst after righteousness if you want to be filled. We are not told that we shall be filled because we are Christians, no, we have to hunger and thirst, and then we shall be filled, and blessed. And now we find this great exposition of that principle here in the ninth verse of this last chapter of Philippians.

So let us look at this statement, and analyse it into its component parts. The subject divides itself quite simply. The first principle taught here is the vital importance of practice, or of action and conduct. It is this little word *do*. You have heard these things, says Paul, you have learned them, and you have seen them in me; yes, but you must do them. Here you are, beloved Philippians, facing your uncertain future and here am I, a prisoner in Rome. I may never see you again, I may be put to death tomorrow, I do not know. But I do know that if you live this life, if you practise these things, then you have nothing to fear at all, the God of peace shall be with you, and nothing can ever harm you. You see the perfection of the Apostle's method? In verse 8 he has dealt with the realm of thought. Ah, but the Apostle knows the subtle danger that is always confronting us, the danger of being content with theoretical knowledge, the danger of being satisfied with doctrine only, the danger of failing to put into practice that which we know.

Let me underline again the emphasis which is placed upon this doctrine from the beginning to the end of the Bible. Was that not the whole trouble with the Pharisees? They were resting upon their knowledge of the law, and they felt that they knew it all so well; but the trouble with them was that they did not practise it. They were teachers, yes, but it is not enough to know these things, you must put them into operation. Or, take Paul's great demonstration of this principle in Romans 2. 'The trouble with the Jews,' Paul says, 'is that they think that because they are the people to whom the law was given, all must be well. But,' says Paul, 'the knowledge of the law does not save, it is the practising of the law that puts a man right with God, and they are relying upon their knowledge without the practice. You foolish men,' he continues, 'you are relying upon the fact that you are aware of God's commandments, but you must practise them.' That is his way of showing how the Jews are guilty, before God, of not receiving the salvation of Jesus Christ.

James says the same thing: The man who knows these things, but does not practise them is like a man who looks at his face in a mirror, and when he has turned away immediately forgets what he has seen. James shows that it is the man who looks into the perfect law of liberty, and 'continueth therein' who is going to be blessed (Jas. 1:22–27). Nothing is more dangerous for us than to be content with a mere superficial acquaintance with God's law. Our Lord says, 'If ye know these things, happy are ye if ye do them' (John 13:17). Ah, yes; you are not going to be happy merely because you know them; rather, happy are you if you put them into practice, and live them out in your daily life.

Or take that great warning in Matthew 7, the picture of the two houses, the house on the rock and the house on the sand. What do they represent? 'Whosoever heareth these sayings of mine, and doeth them . . .' says our Lord, 'I will liken him unto a wise man, which built his house upon a rock' (Matt. 7:24). But the man who builds his house upon the sand is the man who hears these sayings of Christ but does not do them. He has heard what the gospel has to offer him and he is aware of it, but he does nothing about it, and the foolish man imagines that all is well. But when trial comes, that house is utterly demolished. He has not done these things, he has been content with a theoretical knowledge, an academic acquaintance. So the Apostle in this last exhortation is warning the Philippians against that dread and terrible error. 'I have been with you,' says Paul in effect, 'and you have known and received certain things from me. Not only have you heard me speak, you have seen them enacted in my life, and I beseech you to put them into practice. Do not be content with a mere acquaintance with these things, live them out in your daily life, then the God of peace shall be with you and only then.'

Now it seems to me that two main difficulties arise at this point. I feel that many of us are missing so much in the Christian life because we just have not put this apparently obvious principle to the proof, and I think that this is so for two reasons. One is, of course, the very delight that some of us, by nature, tend to take in theoretical knowledge and truth. There are still some people who enjoy reading philosophy, theology and things of that kind. In my opinion, the consideration of reality and truth is the highest intellectual process of which man is ever capable. Look at the great doctrine expounded in this truth! Yes, but the greatest danger with such people is that they are content with that theoretical interest. You can be a great student even of the Bible and live a life that is utterly contrary to it. There are many such people, alas! There have been many whose chief hobby in life has been the dissection and analysis of the Bible. They were interested in its numerics and various other things, but they were rather hard and harsh, and often failed in some of the elementary principles of the Christian life. I mention this because we are so often told that this is the main cause of the modern turning away from the gospel. People say, 'I don't want to be like that Victorian whose head was so full of theology and an understanding of the Scriptures but who failed so tragically in his daily life,' and this criticism is often justified. This danger does face that type of individual. It is the masterpiece of Satan to make us put theory and practice into separate watertight compartments, to make men so interested in the Book that they forget to apply its teaching. What you have seen, says Paul, practise!

The second difficulty is this. There are some people who seem to miss the blessing of the gospel of salvation because they always think of it in terms of some experience, something which has to happen to them. They spend their lives waiting for an experience. Many wait for certain meetings, because they have heard of people who have been to such meetings and who have received great blessings, and they say, 'That is what I want. I will go and get this great blessing which the gospel has to give. The thing to do is to go to that meeting and then it will happen to me.' But such waiting for experiences is a denial of this teaching; you need wait for nothing. Begin to practise the plain teaching of the Scriptures; it is not an experience to be received. You may, of course, suddenly see this truth in a meeting; that is quite all right – the message may come home to you there. You may have specific experiences, you may have some emotional feeling, there are many such things, but the teaching of the New Testament is that without the practising of the precepts, we are not entitled to expect any of the promises. The Holy Spirit, said the Apostle Peter to the first people who listened to him, is given to them that obey God. Without that obedience we have no right to expect the blessings of the Holy Spirit.

But now let us come to something still more practical and immediate. If I say that without practice we cannot expect the God of peace to be always with us, what is it that we have to practise? Paul puts it quite simply: 'Those things, which ye have both learned, and received, and heard, and seen in me, do.' That is not egotism; the Apostle Paul was entitled to speak like that. 'Thank God,' says Paul, in effect, 'I have known these blessings of the gospel, and if you want to know them, then practise the things which you have learned and seen in me.' He does not hesitate to tell them to live the kind of life that he had lived in their presence. And that is a very valuable principle for us. We are to discover what we should do both by reading the Scriptures themselves and also by looking at the example of the saints.

Now here is something that to me is not only of great importance but also of great interest. I have often observed, when I have read the biographies of saintly, godly men and women, that they always conform to a pattern. The saints are remarkably alike. If you read the life of any one of them, you will always find that their life was based on certain very simple principles. The saintly life is always a very simple life, it is the ungodly whose lives are complicated. Sin always brings complications. It did at the very beginning, when man sinned and lied to cover his sin; and the moment men and women come back to God and live godly lives, their lives conform to a very simple pattern.

Thus, if you look at Paul, if you look at any one of the

saints who have ever adorned the Church, you will find that
there are certain simple things which they never fail to practise and to which they pay the most rigorous attention. Let
me just note them. You may think, as I mention them, that
they are almost puerile, and yet, as we examine ourselves, I
think we must admit that it is because we fail in these simple
things that we miss so much in the Christian life. Here, then,
are some of the principles by which the saints lived. First
and foremost, came their attitude to God. The first characteristic always of the saints was that they desired to live to
his glory. That, of course, expresses itself in a desire to
know God better. You have seen me, said Paul to the
Philippians, and what was the big characteristic in my life?
It was my great ambition to 'know him, and the power of his
resurrection, and the fellowship of his sufferings.' Do you
not see standing out in my life this great desire to glorify
God and to know him better?

Can we say that that is the chief thing in our lives? We
have many interests, many of them quite necessary and perfectly legitimate, but as we examine ourselves can we say
that this stands out above everything else, that our highest
ambition is to know God better, that our greatest endeavour
in life is to live to the glory of God? Take any of the saints –
Paul, Augustine, Luther, Calvin, Wesley – look at them,
and you will see that this is the dominating feature of their
lives. Yes, but let us be quite practical, how can we test
whether this is true of us? Well, it always expresses itself in
various practical ways, and the most obvious is that the
saints read as much as they could of God's revelation of
himself. 'These things, which ye have seen in me, do.' What
are they? First and foremost, reading the text book. If you
would know God, then go to God's revelation. If you want
to know him you cannot avoid it. Spend your time with the
Scriptures, long to understand them; say, as Peter puts it,
that as a newborn babe you thirst for the pure milk of the
word that you may grow thereby (1 Pet. 2:2).

Then, next, obviously, is prayer. If you like a person you
want to spend as much time as you can with that person. If

we want to know God better, surely we need to spend time talking to him. How much time do we spend in prayer, in secret, in public, in praying about these things, in talking to God about our own unworthiness, asking him to reveal himself more and more? 'These things do' – if you want the God of peace to be with you, it is a matter of doing, not waiting for experiences. You just start reading your Bible, and then you go on and begin to pray. You may say, 'But I can't pray.' Then talk to God about it. Tell him it is your desire to know him better and to spend time with him. Is it not obvious? Do these things, says Paul.

Furthermore, the attitude of the saints towards themselves inevitably follows. They realise their sinfulness, and therefore they humble and humiliate themselves and do their utmost to mortify their imperfections – you will find this in the biography of any saint. So how do they do this? By spending time in self-examination, which is one of the most difficult things to do in this busy world. But if a man would humble and humiliate himself before God, he must make time to examine himself and his life. He must examine it in the light of Scripture, and in the light of the lives of the saints. He must see where he fails; he must constantly survey his own heart, bringing out the hidden things and dealing with them. Self-examination – how the saints have concentrated upon that!

What else? The next thing is their attitude towards the world in which they find themselves. This again is inevitable. The saints have always regarded this world as a sinful place, opposed to God and opposed to the highest interests of the soul. They have, therefore, done their utmost to avoid its influence, its selfishness and worldly lusts, and they have broken with such things. I am not enunciating this as a law, I am just telling you what you can see in the lives of Paul and all God's saints. They have always seen that the world is opposed to our highest and best interests – that it is always dragging us down, and having seen that, they have renounced it, cost what it may.

What is their attitude towards those who are not Christians? It is to see them as victims of sin and Satan, and the saints have therefore felt sorry for them, and have spoken to them about these things. They have tried to enlighten them, to warn them of the danger to their souls; they have not hesitated, at the risk of being persecuted and laughed at, to remonstrate with them and to try to appeal to them to see the truth of God as it is in Christ Jesus.

So, to sum it all up, the saints have always regarded life as but a journey, a pilgrimage. They have regarded themselves as people travelling through this wilderness to God and to glory, and their eye has ever been upon that. Everything that stands between them and that, everything that has been opposed to that, has been avoided; they have concentrated on this one thing – godliness.

Now I have merely summarised the teaching of the Bible, you will find it in many places. Paul, for instance, in writing to Titus, sums it all up by saying that we are taught this: '. . . denying ungodliness and worldly lusts, we should live soberly, righteously, and godly, in this present world; looking for that blessed hope, and the glorious appearing of the great God and our Saviour Jesus Christ . . .' (Tit. 2:12–13). That is it – that is what we are to practise.

So we have seen the importance of practice and of what we have to practise and now, finally, let us look at the reward of such practice. Here it is – do these things: 'and the God of peace shall be with you'. Does anyone feel that I have been too narrow, that this is a very narrow kind of life and that it is hardly worth living? 'Avoid this, read the Bible, pray – isn't that an apology for life?' But this is what the gospel says, 'Those things . . . do: and the God of peace shall be with you.' So is the price too great? My dear friend, no one can decide that for you, you decide that for yourself. All that I would say is that if you want the God of peace to be with you, then do these things. That is what Paul had been doing, that is what the saints have always done. 'Is there any difference,' asks someone, 'between the peace of God spoken of in the seventh verse and God's peace here in this ninth verse? Verses 6 and 7 say ". . . let your requests be made known unto God. And the peace of God . . . shall keep your hearts and minds . . ."; but here Paul says, "the God of peace shall be with you".'

There is no essential difference. In verse 7 you have the particular application, but in verse 9 you have a general statement: 'Live this life,' says Paul in effect, 'and God himself will always be with you and he is the God of peace'. Peace is his great characteristic. There is peace in the love of God because he is holy; he is a God of peace and he wants to be at peace with you. That is the whole meaning of the gospel, that is why Christ came. Men and women had become miserable because they had rebelled against God and God sent Christ to make peace. The meaning of the cross is that God is making peace with his enemies, who have rebelled against him, making it possible for them to be at peace with him. Christ has blotted out our sin and therefore we can be at peace with God. And, too, he makes me at peace with myself, because as he removes sin out of my life, the stress and the strain and the struggle go and I find a strange peace. He makes me live at peace with others and he enables me to be in a state of peace whatever my circumstances and conditions and surroundings may be.

That is the promise and oh, what a gracious and glorious promise! Walk in the light in that way, says Paul, and God will be walking with you. That is the picture. It is exactly like Enoch of old: 'Enoch walked with God' (Gen. 5:24), and God walked with him. So here is Paul's promise to the Christians to whom he was writing: You walk in that way and the God of peace will be with you. Difficulties may arise, but he will quench them. Whatever happens he will ever be with you. 'Those things, which ye have both learned, and received, and heard, and seen in me, do: and the God of peace shall be with you.' In life, in death, always, his promise is: 'I will never leave thee, nor forsake thee' (Heb. 13:5).

Is he that to you? Do you know him? Have you found him by your side in the days of trouble? During illness and disease, trouble and unhappiness, is he with you? What a wondrous possibility! But that is the condition: Do these things and then, if you do, he will indeed be with you always.

17

Learning to Be Content

> But I rejoiced in the Lord greatly, that now at the last
> your care of me hath flourished again; wherein ye were
> also careful, but ye lacked opportunity. Not that I speak
> in respect of want: for I have learned, in whatsoever state
> I am, therewith to be content. I know both how to be
> abased, and I know how to abound: every where and in
> all things I am instructed both to be full and to be hungry,
> both to abound and to suffer need (Phil. 4:10–12).

We have, in the words of Philippians 4:10–12, one of those
portions of Scripture which always makes me feel that there
is a sense in which the only right and proper thing to do after
reading them in a church service is to pronounce the
benediction! One trembles at the very approach to such
exalted, noble words, recalling as they do one of the high-
water marks in the Christian experience of this mighty
Apostle to the Gentiles. Yet it is our business, though we
approach them thus with fear and trembling, to try to
analyse and expound them. With the end of the ninth verse
in this chapter the Apostle has reached the end of the particular exhortations which he was anxious to address to the
members of the church at Philippi. He has really finished
with his doctrine, but he still cannot close the letter. There
is one other thing he must do, and that is he must express
his profound gratitude to the members of the church at
Philippi for the personal gift which they had sent to him,
while he was held in prison in Rome, by the hand of their
friend and brother, Epaphroditus.

That is one of the reasons why Paul was writing the letter at all. The Philippian church had sent him some gift. We are not told what it was, whether it was in money or in kind, but they had sent him some gift by their emissary Epaphroditus. Epaphroditus is now going back to them, and Paul sends the letter with him. Having finished with his doctrine, he wants to thank them for this expression of their love and solicitude for him in his suffering and his imprisonment. That is what Paul proceeds to do in these ten verses running from verse 10 to verse 20. There is nothing, I always feel, about this great epistle, which is more interesting than to observe in detail the way in which the Apostle does everything; and the way in which he offers his thanks to the members of the church at Philippi is full of instruction and of interest. It is quite clear that this question of thanking the members of the church at Philippi for their gift and for their kindness presented the Apostle with a problem. You would have thought that there could surely be no problem in thanking people who have been kind and generous, and yet to Paul it is obviously a problem. It takes him ten verses to do this thing. You often find him dealing with a mighty doctrine in a verse or two, but when it comes to just thanking the members of the church at Philippi for their goodness and kindness, it takes him ten verses. You notice also how he goes on repeating himself. 'Not that I speak in respect of want,' and later on, 'Not because I desire a gift.' There is a kind of argument and he seems to find it difficult to find the right words.

Paul's trouble was something like this. He was very anxious to thank the church at Philippi for their kindness. But at the same time he was equally anxious, if not more anxious, to show them that he had not been waiting impatiently for, or expecting, this expression of their kindness, and still more that he was in no sense dependent upon their goodness and generosity. In that way he finds himself confronted with a problem. He has to do these two things at one and the same time – he has to express his thanks to the members of the church at Philippi, and yet he has to do it in a way which will not in any sense detract or derogate from the reality of his experience as a Christian man, dependent upon God. That is why it takes him ten verses. It was the problem of a Christian gentleman, sensitive to the feelings of others. And what a great gentleman this Apostle was, how concerned about the feelings of others. As a gentleman he is anxious to express his profound gratitude and to let them know that their kindness really did move him very deeply, and yet he is concerned, on the other hand, to make it abundantly clear to them that he had not been spending his time wondering why they had not thought of his needs, and suffering because they had not sent him something there in prison. He wanted to make it perfectly clear that that had never been his condition at all, and what we have in these ten verses is the Apostle's method of resolving that particular problem.

Now the thing we have to grasp about Christian truth is that it is something that governs the whole of our life. The Christian gospel dominates the entire life of the Christian. It controls his thinking, as we see in verse 8, it controls his actions, as we see in verse 9. And now, in these ten verses, we see how a Christian, even in such a matter as returning thanks for a kindness, does so in a way which is different from the way of a person who is not a Christian. The Christian cannot do anything, not even in a matter like this, except in a truly Christian manner. So here the Apostle, at one and the same time, shows his indebtedness to his friends, but his still greater indebtedness to the Lord. Paul was always jealous for the reputation of the Lord, and he was afraid that in thanking the Philippians for their gift he might somehow give the impression that the Lord was not sufficient for him. He must keep that first. He loves these Philippians very dearly and he is profoundly grateful to them. But he loves his Lord still more, and he is afraid lest in thanking them he might somehow give even a suspicion of a suggestion that the Lord was not sufficient for him, or that he had been depending upon the Philippians in an ultimate sense.

So he sets out in this mighty passage, with its staggering and astounding affirmations, to show the primacy of the Lord and the all-sufficiency of the Lord, while at the same time showing his gratitude and his indebtedness and his love towards the Philippians for this manifestation of their personal care and solicitude for him. The essence of the matter is found in verses 11 and 12. Here we have the doctrine – 'Not that I speak in respect of want: for I have learned, in whatsoever state I am, therewith to be content. I know both how to be abased, and I know how to abound: every where and in all things I am instructed both to be full and to be hungry, both to abound and to suffer need.'

We must now look at this great doctrine which Paul announces in this way. There are two big principles here. The first, of course, is the condition at which the Apostle has arrived. The second is the way in which he has arrived at that condition. They constitute the subject matter of this tremendous statement.

Let us first look at the condition to which the Apostle has attained. He describes it by the word that is translated here as 'content' – 'I have learned in whatsoever state I am, therewith to be *content.*' It is important that we should get at the precise meaning of this word. Our English word 'content' does not fully explain the Greek. The word Paul uses really means that he is 'self-sufficient', independent of circumstances or conditions or surroundings, 'having sufficiency in one's self'. That is the real meaning of this word which is translated 'content'. The affirmation made by the Apostle is that he has arrived at a state in which he can say quite truthfully that he is independent of his position, his circumstances, his surroundings and of everything that is happening to him. Now that that was no mere rhetorical statement on the part of the Apostle is made very clear in the records that we have of this man and of his life in different parts of the New Testament. There is, for instance, an interesting example of it in Acts 16 which describes Paul's first visit to Philippi where the recipients of this letter lived. You remember how he and Silas were arrested and beaten and thrown into prison with their feet made fast in the stocks. Their physical conditions could not very well have been worse, yet so little effect did that have upon Paul and

Silas that 'at midnight Paul and Silas prayed, and sang praises unto God' (Acts 16:25). Independent of circumstances, 'content in whatsoever state I am'. That is what you find also in the famous passage in 2 Corinthians 12, where Paul tells us how he learned to be independent of 'the thorn in the flesh'; he was self-sufficient in spite of it. You remember also how he exhorts Timothy to take hold of this principle by saying: 'Godliness with contentment is great gain' (1 Tim. 6:6). 'There is nothing like it,' he says in effect. 'If you have that you have everything.' Paul was an old man by then and he writes to the young man Timothy and says: The first thing you have to learn is to be independent of circumstances and conditions – 'Godliness with contentment'. These are but a few of many similar illustrations to which we might call attention.

The teaching of the New Testament, however, not only affirms that this was true of Paul, it makes it very clear that it is a condition into which we should all, as Christian people, enter. You remember how our Lord makes this point in Matthew 6:34 – 'Take therefore no thought for the morrow.' Be not over-anxious and worried about food, and clothing and things of that kind. That is the glorious, mighty independence of what is happening to us, that we should all know and experience. It is self-sufficiency in the good sense.

But it is most important that we should have a clear understanding in our minds as to what this means. The word 'content' tends to provoke certain misunderstandings about what the Apostle is teaching. You can so interpret this statement by Paul as more or less to justify the charge that the Christian gospel is nothing but 'the opium of the people'. There is a tendency on the part of large numbers of people today to feel that the Christian gospel has been a hindrance to the forward march of mankind, that it has been a drag on progress, that it has been nothing but 'the dope of the people'. They say that it is a doctrine which has taught people to put up with all kinds of conditions whatever they may be, and however disgraceful and unjust. There has been a violent political reaction against the gospel of Jesus Christ because people have so misinterpreted this kind of text as to put it this way:

> The rich man in his castle,
> The poor man at his gate,
> God made them, high or lowly,
> And order'd their estate.

C.F. Alexander

Now that is just rubbish and a blank denial of what the Apostle teaches here. Yet how often has it been interpreted like that. It is a matter of great regret that one who could have written the hymn, 'There is a green hill far away' should have been guilty of such a violation of the teaching of the Bible – 'The rich man in his castle, the poor man at his gate'. Were men meant to be like that and to stay like that for ever? The Bible never teaches that; it does not say that men and women should be content to remain in poverty, that they should never endeavour to 'better' themselves. There is nothing in the Bible that disputes the proposition that all people are equal in the sight of God and that all are entitled to equality of opportunity. Grievous harm has been done to the Church of Christ because a statement such as this in our text has been misinterpreted in that way.

Neither does it mean mere indifference to circumstances. That is but the negative resignation of a pagan stoicism, and is far removed from the Christian position. What, then, does it mean? The Apostle says here that he is not mastered or controlled by circumstances. If you can improve your circumstances in fair and legitimate ways, by all means do so; but if you cannot, and if you have to remain in a trying and difficult position, do not be mastered by it, do not let it get you down, do not let it control you, do not let it determine your misery or your joy. 'You,' says the Apostle, 'must come into the state in which, whatever your conditions, you are not controlled by them.' That is what he affirms of himself. 'Whatever my condition or circumstance,' he says in effect, 'I am in control. I am master of the situation, I am not mastered by the situation. I am free. I am at liberty. I do not depend for my happiness upon what is happening to me. My life, my happiness, my joy and my experience are independent of the things that are going on round about me, and even of the things that may be happening to me.' I would remind you again that Paul was actually in prison, probably chained to a soldier on his right and another on his left, when he uttered these words, yet even in that condition he can say that he is independent of circumstances. 'My life,' says Paul, 'is not controlled and determined by what is happening to me; I am in a state and condition in which I rise right above them. These things are not the determining factors in my life and experience.'

Now that is his claim, and he was most anxious to emphasise the fact that it is an all-inclusive claim. Observe his words again. Having made the general statement, he now amplifies it: 'I know both how to be abased, and I know how to abound: every where and in all things I am instructed' – again he goes back to it – 'both to be full and to be hungry, both to abound and to suffer need.' He was anxious to make the all-inclusiveness of his claim perfectly clear. Let me put the opposites in series. He knows how to be abased, he knows how to be hungry and to suffer need; on the other hand, he knows how to abound, how to be full and to have plenty. It would be interesting to discuss the relative difficulty of these two things. Is it more difficult to have a contented mind when abased, or when abounding? I do not know whether we can ever answer the question. They are both extremely difficult and one is as difficult as the other. Can I be abased without feeling a sense of grudge, or without being worried? Can I suffer the need of food and clothing, can I be abased in my profession or office or work, can I somehow or other be put down and still remain in spirit exactly as I was before? How difficult it is, to take second place, to be hurt, to be insulted, to see others suffering in the same way, to suffer physical need or pain – to know how to be abased, how to be hungry, how to suffer need in some respect. One of the greatest tasks in life is to discover how to suffer any or all of those things without feeling a sense of grudge, without complaint or annoyance or bitterness of spirit, to discover how not to be worried or anxious. Paul tells us that he has learned how to do that. He has experienced every kind of trial and tribulation and yet he is unaffected by them.

Then take the other side. 'I know how to abound,' says Paul. 'I know how "to be full", I know how to enjoy plenty.' What a difficult thing this is. How difficult it is for the wealthy person not to feel complete independence of God. When we are rich and can arrange and manipulate everything, we tend to forget God. Most of us remember him when we are down. When we are in need we begin to pray, but, when we have everything we need, how easy it is to forget God. I leave it to you to decide which is the more difficult. What Paul says is that in either of these positions he is perfectly free. Poverty does not get him down, riches do not carry him away and make him lose his hold. He says that he is not dependent upon either, that he is self-sufficient in this sense, that his life is not controlled by these things, that he is what he is apart from them. Whether he is 'to abound' or to 'suffer need', it does not matter.

But he is not content with that, he goes still further and says, 'In all things, everywhere', which means in everything and in all things, every single thing in detail, all things together. Now Paul divides it up like this quite deliberately. He wants to say that there is no limit to what he can do in this respect – 'In every single, particular thing I am like that.' Then he adds: 'Now I will put them together – in all things, whatever may happen to me, I am self-sufficient, I am not dependent upon them, my life and happiness and joy are not determined or controlled by them.'

That, according to the Apostle, is the way to live, that is Christian living. It is good for us to face this mighty statement. We are living in days and times of uncertainty, and it may well be that the first and the greatest lesson we have to learn is how to live without allowing circumstances to affect our inner peace and joy. And yet perhaps there was never a time in the history of the world when it was so difficult to learn this lesson as it is today. The whole of life is so organised at the present time as to make it almost impossible to live this self-sufficient

Christian life. Even in a natural sense, we are all so dependent on the things that are being done for us and to us and around and about us, that it has become most difficult to live our own lives. We switch on the wireless or the television and gradually become dependent upon them, and it is the same with our newspapers, our cinemas, our entertainments. The world is organising life for us in every respect and we are becoming dependent upon it. There was a good illustration of that in the early days of the last war when the blackout regulations were first imposed upon us. We used to hear of something which was described as the 'boredom of the blackout'. People found it almost impossible to spend a succession of nights in their own homes doing nothing. They had become dependent on the cinema, the theatre and various other forms of entertainment, and when these things were suddenly cut off they did not know what to do with themselves. That is the very antithesis of what Paul is describing here. But increasingly it is becoming the tendency in life today; increasingly we are becoming dependent upon what others are doing for us.

This, alas, is not only true of the world in general, it is becoming true also of Christian people in particular. I would suggest that one of the greatest dangers confronting us in a spiritual sense is that of becoming dependent upon meetings. A kind of 'meetings mania' is developing, and there are Christian people who seem to be always at meetings. Now meetings are undoubtedly of great value. Let nobody misunderstand me and imagine that I am saying that you should only go to a place of worship on a Sunday. Meetings are excellent, but let us beware lest we become so dependent upon meetings that one day, when we find ourselves ill and laid upon our bed we do not know what to do with ourselves. We can become too dependent even on Christian meetings – even on a Christian atmosphere. A man was discussing with me the other day what is referred to as the 'leakage' that takes place among the members of certain Christian organisations mainly concerned with young people. There is a very real problem here. While they are in the atmosphere of the Christian organisation these young people are keen and interested, but in a few years' time they have become lost to the Church. What is the cause of the leakage? Very frequently it is that they have become too dependent upon a particular fellowship, so that when they go out into the world, or move to another district where they are no longer surrounded by all this Christian fellowship, they suddenly flag and fall. That is the kind of thing against which the Apostle is warning us. We must beware of the danger of resting on props, even in Christian service and witness. The Apostle therefore exhorts us to get into that state in which we shall be independent of what is happening around and about us even in these things. We must cultivate this glorious self-sufficiency.

Professor Whitehead uttered a great truth when he said in his definition of religion, 'Religion is what a man does with his own solitude.' You and I, in the last analysis, are what we are when we are alone. I confess that in a sense it is easier for me to preach from a pulpit than it is to sit alone in my study; it is probably easier for most people to enjoy the presence of our Lord in the company of other Christians than when alone. Paul would have us enjoy what he himself was enjoying. He had a love for the Lord that rendered him independent of all that was happening, or that might happen – in everything, in all things, wherever he might be, whatever was happening, he was content. Abased or abounding, in need or plenty, it did not matter, he had this life, this hidden life with Christ.

Let us consider briefly the second matter which we find here, namely, how the Apostle reached this condition. Here again he makes a very interesting statement. You notice that he says: 'I have learned,' or better, 'I have come to learn.' I thank God that Paul said that. Paul was not always like this any more than any one of us. He had 'come to learn'. He has another interesting word also. He says: 'Everywhere and in all things I am *instructed* both to be full and to be hungry.' The authorities are all agreed here in saying that what he really says is, 'I have been initiated', 'let into the secret', 'let into the mystery'.

Paul says that he has come to learn how to be in this condition. Now there are many intimations in the New Testament that this was particularly difficult for him. Paul was sensitive, proud by nature, and, in addition, he was an intensely active being. Nothing could have been more galling for such a man than to lie in prison. He had been brought up a Roman citizen, but here he is enduring bondage, not spending his life among great intellectual people, but among slaves. How does he manage it? Ah, he says, I have come to learn, I have been let into the secret, I have been let into the mystery.

How did he come to learn? Let me try to answer that question. In the first place, it was by sheer experience. I need only direct your attention to 2 Corinthians 12, especially verses 9 and 10 about 'the thorn in the flesh'. Paul did not like it. He struggled against it; three times he prayed that it might be removed. But it was not removed. He could not reconcile himself to it. He was impatient, he was anxious to go on preaching, and this thorn in the flesh was keeping him down. But then he was taught the lesson: 'My grace is sufficient for thee.' He came to a place of understanding as the result of sheer experience of the dealing of God with him. He had to learn, and experience teaches us all. Some of us are very slow to learn, but God in his kindness may send us an illness, sometimes he even strikes us down – anything to teach us this great lesson and to bring us to this great position.

But it was not by experience alone. Paul had come to learn this truth by working out a great argument. Let me give you some of the steps of the argument which you can work out for yourself. I think that the Apostle's logic goes something like this. He said to himself:

1. Conditions are always changing, therefore I must obviously not be dependent upon conditions.

2. What matters supremely and vitally is my soul and my relationship to God – this is the first thing.

3. God is concerned about me as my Father, and nothing

happens to me apart from God. Even the very hairs of my head are all numbered. I must never forget that.

4. God's will and God's ways are a great mystery, but I know that whatever he wills or permits is, of necessity, for my good.

5. Every situation in life is the unfolding of some manifestation of God's love and goodness. Therefore my business is to look for each special manifestation of God's goodness and kindness and to be prepared for surprises and blessings because, 'Neither are your ways my ways, saith the Lord' (Isa. 55:8). What, for example, is the great lesson that Paul learned in the matter of the thorn in the flesh? It is that 'When I am weak then am I strong.' Through physical weakness Paul was taught this manifestation of God's grace.

6. Therefore I must not regard circumstances and conditions in and of themselves, but as a part of God's dealings with me in the work of perfecting my soul and bringing me to final perfection.

7. Whatever my conditions may be at this present moment they are only temporary, they are only passing, and they can never rob me of the joy and the glory that ultimately await me with Christ.

I suggest that Paul had reasoned and argued it out like that. He had faced conditions and circumstances in the light of the Christian truth and the Christian gospel, and had worked out these steps and stages. And having done so he says: Let anything you can think of happen to me, I remain exactly where I was. Whatever may happen to me, I am left unmoved.

The big principle that emerges clearly is that Paul had learned to find his pleasure and his satisfaction in Christ and always in Christ. That is the positive aspect of this matter. We must learn to depend upon him and in order to do that we must learn to know him, we must learn to have communion with him, we must learn to find our pleasure in him. Let me put it plainly – the danger with some of us is of spending far too much of our time even in reading about him. The day may come, indeed will come, when we shall not be able to read. Then comes the test. Will you still be happy? Do you know him so well that though you become deaf or blind this fount will still be

448 THE LIFE OF JOY AND PEACE

open? Do you know him so well that you can talk to him and listen to him and enjoy him always? Will all be well because you have always been so dependent upon your relationship to him that nothing else really matters? That was the Apostle's condition. His intimacy with Christ was so deep and so great that he had become independent of everything else.

Finally, I believe that what most helped him to learn this lesson was his looking at the great and perfect example of Christ himself. 'Looking unto Jesus . . . who for the joy that was set before him endured the cross, despising the shame' (Heb. 12:2). Paul 'looked unto him' and saw him and his perfect example. And he applied it to his own life. 'While we look not at the things which are seen, but at the things which are not seen: for the things which are seen are temporal; but the things which are not seen are eternal' (2 Cor. 4:18).

'I have come to learn in whatsoever state I am therein to be self-sufficient and independent of circumstances.'

Christian people, can you say that, do you know that state? Let this become first with us, let this become our ambition, let us strain every nerve and do everything we can to get into this blessed state. Life may force it upon us, but even if circumstances do not, the time is bound to come, soon or late, when earth and every earthly scene will pass away, and in that final isolation of the soul we shall be alone, facing death and eternity. The greatest thing in life is to be able to say with Christ himself at that hour: 'And yet I am not alone, because the Father is with me' (John 16:32).

May God in his infinite grace enable us all to learn this great and vital lesson, and to this end let us offer frequently that prayer of Augustus Toplady:

> While I draw this fleeting breath,
> When mine eyelids close in death,
> When I soar through tracts unknown,
> See thee on thy judgment throne,
> > Rock of ages cleft for me
> > Let me hide myself in thee.

18

The Final Cure

I can do all things through Christ which strengtheneth me
(Phil. 4:13).

Here again we are confronted by one of those staggering statements which are to be found in such profusion in the epistles of this great Apostle to the Gentiles.

Nothing is more misleading, as one reads the letters of the Apostle Paul, than to assume that when he has finished the business which he set out to do, he has at the same time finished saying great and mighty things. We should always keep an eye on his postscripts. You never know when he is going to throw in a gem. Anywhere, everywhere, in the introduction to his letters, in the postscripts to his letters, there is generally some amazing insight into the truth or some profound revelation of doctrine.

We are here, in a sense, looking at the postscript of this letter. The Apostle finished the business at the end of verse 9 and he is now just offering his personal thanks to the members of the church at Philippi for their goodness to him personally, for the gift which they had sent. But, as we have already seen, the Apostle could not do that without being involved at once in doctrine. Anxious as he is to thank them, he is still more anxious to show them, and to show to others, that his sufficiency is in Christ, and that whether he is remembered or forgotten by men, he is always complete in the Lord. And it is in that connection that we come to this thirteenth verse.

I say that this is a staggering statement – 'I can do all things through Christ which strengtheneth me.' It is a statement that is characterised at one and the same time by a sense of triumph and by humility. Paul sounds at first as if he is boasting, and yet when you look at his statement again, you find that it is one of the most glorious and striking tributes that he has ever paid anywhere to his Lord and Master. It is one of those paradoxical statements in which the Apostle seems to have delighted; indeed, it is the simple truth to say that Christian truth is always essentially paradoxical. It exhorts us at one and the same time to rejoice, to make our boast, and yet to be humble and to be lowly. And there is no contradiction, because the boast of the Christian is not in himself but in the Lord.

Paul was very fond of saying that. Take, for instance, the statement: 'God forbid that I should glory, save in the cross of our Lord Jesus Christ' (Gal. 6:14), or again: 'He that glorieth, let him glory in the Lord' (2 Cor. 10:17). There is the exhortation on the one hand for us to be boasting; yes, but always boasting in him.

Now this statement belongs to that particular category and perhaps the best way for us to approach it is to give an alternative translation. The Authorised Version is, in a sense, quite correct, but it does not really bring out the particular shade of meaning the Apostle was anxious to convey. It says: 'I can do all things through Christ which strengtheneth me.' But I suggest that a better translation would be: 'I am strong or made strong, for all things in the One who constantly infuses strength into me.' The authorities agree that the word 'Christ' should not appear in this text, and we need not boggle at that. Paul actually put it like that. What the Apostle is really saying is not so much that he can do certain things himself, as that he is enabled to do certain things, indeed all things, by this One who infuses strength into him. In other words, we have in this verse the ultimate and the final explanation of what Paul has been saying in the preceding verses. There, you remember, he says – 'I have learned, in whatsoever state I am, therewith [therein] to be content. I know both how to be abased, and I know how to abound: every where and in all things I am instructed both to be full and to be hungry, both to abound and to suffer need.' We have seen that there the Apostle is saying that he has come to learn. He was not always able to do this. Paul had had to learn how to be content in every state, how to be self-sufficient, how to be independent of circumstances and surroundings. He had had to learn, indeed he goes on to say that he had been 'initiated' into the secret of how to do this. That is the meaning of 'I have been instructed', and we have seen some of the ways in which the Apostle had been led. We have seen that he had come to this knowledge by experience, by logical reasoning out of his Christian faith and by cultivating a personal, intimate knowledge of the Lord, looking to him and his glorious example.

But it is here, in this thirteenth verse, that we have the ultimate explanation. The real secret, says Paul, which I have discovered, is that I am made strong for all things in the One who is constantly infusing strength into me. That is his final explanation. Now I need scarcely remind you that that is the point to which the Apostle always returns. Paul never works out an argument without coming back to it. That is the point to which he always brings every argument and discussion; everything always ends in Christ and with Christ. He is the final point, he is the explanation of Paul's living and his whole outlook upon life. And that is the doctrine which he commends to us here. In other words, he is telling us that Christ is all-sufficient for every circumstance, for every eventuality and for every possibility. And, of course, in saying that, he is introducing us to what in many ways we may describe as the cardinal New Testament doctrine. The Christian life, after all, is a life, it is a power, it is an activity. That is the thing we so constantly tend to forget. It is not just a philosophy, it is not just a point of view, it is not just a teaching that we take up and try to put into practice. It is all that, but it is something infinitely more. The very essence of the Christian life, according to the New Testament teaching everywhere, is that it is a mighty power that enters into us; it is a life, if you like, that is pulsating in us. It is an activity, and an activity on the part of God.

The Apostle has already emphasised that in several places in this very epistle. Let me remind you of some of them. In the first chapter he says that he is 'confident of this very thing, that he which hath begun a good work in you will perform it until the day of Jesus Christ' (verse 6). 'I want you,' says Paul in effect, 'to think of yourselves as Christians in that way. You are the people in whom God has started to work; God has entered into you, God is working in you.' That is what Christians really are. They are not just men who have taken up a certain theory and are trying to practise it; it is God doing something in them and through them. Or listen again in the second chapter, verses 12 and 13: 'Work out your own salvation with fear and trembling. For it is God which worketh in you both to will and to do of his good pleasure.' It is of his own good pleasure that God is working in us both to will and to do – our highest thoughts, our noblest aspirations, our every righteous inclination is from and of God, is something that is brought into being in us by God himself. It is God's activity and not merely our activity, and that is why Paul tells us in chapter 3:10 that his supreme ambition in life is: 'That I may know him, and the power of his resurrection . . .' All along he is interested in this question of the power and of the life.

You find Paul saying exactly the same thing in other epistles. What is Paul's great prayer for the Ephesians? He prays that they might know 'the exceeding greatness of his power to us-ward who believe, according to the working of his mighty power, which he wrought in Christ, when he raised him from the dead' (1:19–20). He goes on in Ephesians 2:10 to say that we are 'his workmanship, created in Christ Jesus.' You remember also the great statement at the end of the third chapter: 'Unto him that is able to do exceeding abundantly above all that we ask or think, according to the power that worketh in us.' Now, that is characteristic New Testament doctrine, and if we have not grasped it we are surely missing one of the most glorious things about the Christian life and position. The Christian, essentially, is a man who has received new life. We come back again to what I am never tired of quoting, namely, John Wesley's favourite definition of a

Christian. He found it in that book by Henry Scougal, a Scotsman who lived in the seventeenth century, and in the very title – *The life of God in the souls of men*. That is what makes a Christian. The Christian is not just a good, decent, moral man; the life of God has entered into him, there is an energy, a power, a life in him and it is that that makes him peculiarly and specifically Christian, and that is exactly what Paul is telling us here.

Let me begin by putting this negatively. The Apostle is not telling us in this great verse that he has become a Stoic. He is not saying that as the result of much self-culture, he has developed an indifference to the world and its surroundings, and that as a result of discipline he has at last been able to see that he can do all things or bear all things because of this culture. It is not that. Let me remind you that the Stoic could do that. Stoicism was not only a theory, it was a way of life for many people. Read the lives of some of the Stoics and you will find that as a result of this outlook they had developed a kind of passive indifference to what might happen in the world. You may have heard or read of the Indian fakirs, men who have so developed the power of the mind that they control their physical bodies, and by concentration on mind culture can develop an immunity or indifference to what may be happening to them and round and about them. It is also the great principle which characterises many Eastern religions, such as Hinduism and Buddhism. All those religions are basically religions which are designed to help people to die to circumstances and surroundings, and to develop an indifference to the world that is round and about them, to go through this life and world unaffected by circumstances. Now the point I want to make is that the Apostle is not teaching some such doctrine. Paul is not telling us that he has become like the Eastern mystics, he is not saying that he has developed this stoical philosophy to such a point that nothing can affect him.

Why am I so concerned about this negative emphasis? The reason which compels me is that all such teaching is really hopeless, all those religions are finally pessimistic. Stoicism, in the last analysis, was profound pessimism. It really came to this, that this world is hopeless, that nothing can do any good, that the thing you have to do therefore is to get through life as best you can and just refuse to let yourself be hurt by it. The Eastern religions are, of course, entirely pessimistic. They regard matter in itself as evil, they regard the flesh as essentially evil; everything, they say, is evil, and the only thing to do is to get through life with a minimum of pain and to hope that in some subsequent reincarnation you will be rid of it altogether and at last be absorbed and lost for ever in the absolute and the eternal, ceasing to exist as a separate personality.

Now that is the very antithesis of the Christian gospel, which is not negative but positive. It does not regard matter as essentially evil nor the world as essentially evil in and of itself in a material sense. But we reject the negative view *in toto*, supremely because it fails to give the glory and the honour to the Lord Jesus Christ. That is the thing about which Paul is most concerned. Paul wants us to see that his victory is based upon his association with Christ. In other words, we come back to our original definition once more – to be a Christian is not only to believe the teaching of Christ and to practise it, it is to be so vitally related to Christ that his life and his power are working in us. It is to be 'in Christ', it is for Christ to be in us. Now these are New Testament terms – 'in Christ', 'Christ in you the hope of glory'. They are found everywhere in these New Testament epistles.

We can put our doctrine in this form. Paul is saying that Christ infuses so much strength and power into him that he is strong and able for all things. He is not left to himself, he is not struggling alone and vainly against these mighty odds. It is a great power from Christ himself which is entering, and has entered, into his life, and it is there as a dynamo, as an energy and strength. 'In this,' says Paul, 'I am able for anything.'

Now this is surely one of the most glorious statements Paul ever made. Here is a man in prison, a man who has already suffered a great deal in his life, a man who knows what it is to be disappointed in so many ways – persecuted, treated with derision and scorn, even disappointed sometimes, as he tells us in the first chapter, in his fellow-workers. There he is in prison, in conditions calculated to produce dejection in the stoutest heart, facing perhaps a cruel martyrdom – yet he is able to send out this mighty challenge: 'I am able to stand, to bear all things in the One who is constantly infusing strength into me.'

I am anxious to put this doctrine like this at the present time. There are those who feel that at a time like this, it is the business of the Christian preacher and the Christian Church constantly to be making comments on the general situation. There are many people who say: 'Are you dealing only with matters of personal experience while the world is as it is? Is it not remote from life? Have you not read your newspaper or even heard the report on the wireless? Don't you see the whole state of the world? Why don't you make some pronouncement on the world situation or on the state of the nations!' My simple answer to such talk is this. What I, or a number of preachers, or the entire Christian Church, may say about the whole situation will probably not affect it at all. The Church has been talking about politics and the economic situation for many years but with no noticeable effect. That is not the business of Christian preaching. The business of Christian preaching is to say to the people: In this uncertain world, where we have already experienced two world wars within a quarter of a century, and where we may have to face yet another and things that are even worse, you must ask yourself, 'How am I going to face it all? How can I meet it all?' For me to give my views on international politics will not help anybody; but thank God there is something I can do. I can tell you of something, I can tell you of a way which, if you but practise and follow it, will enable you, with the Apostle Paul, to say, 'I am strong, I am able for anything that may happen to me, whether it be peace or war, whether it be freedom or slavery, whether it be the kind of life we have known for so long or whether it be entirely different, I am ready for it.' It does not mean, I must repeat, a passive, negative acquiescence in that which is wrong. Not at all – but it does mean that whatever may come, you are ready for it.

Are we able to speak the language of St Paul? We have already known certain tests and trials, and more may well be coming. Can we say with this man that we have such strength and power that whatever may come we are ready for it? The Apostle had power that enabled him to bear anything that might happen. How are we to obtain this power?

There is a great deal of confusion concerning this, and all I want to do is to try to lessen that confusion.

Many people spend the whole of their lives in trying to obtain this power, and yet they never seem to have it. They say: 'I meet other Christians who have this, but I never seem to get it.' Or, 'I would give the whole world if I could only get this power into my life. How can I get this power?' They spend their life trying to obtain it and yet they never do. Why is this? I think the main trouble is due to a failure on their part to recognise and to realise the right respective positions of the 'I' and the 'him', or the 'One', who is mentioned by the Apostles. 'I can do all things,' or 'I am able for all things through the One who is constantly infusing strength into me,' or, to put it in the words of the Authorised Version, 'I can do all things through Christ which strengtheneth me.' Now there is the crux of the whole matter – the right relationship and the correct balance between 'I' and 'Christ'.

There is a great deal of confusion at this point. The first cause of confusion is an emphasis on that 'I' only. In a sense, I have already dealt with that. It is what the Stoic does, it is what the Hindu or the Buddhist does, it is what all these people who go in for 'mind culture' are constantly doing. And we have seen that this is inadequate. But perhaps the final reason for its inadequacy is that it is a type of teaching that is possible only for people who have a strong will power and who have time to cultivate this will power. Indeed, I agree entirely with what Mr G. K. Chesterton said was his main objection to the simple life, namely, that you have to be a millionaire in order to live it. You need the time, and if you are a working man you have neither the leisure nor the opportunity – you have to be a millionaire before you can live the simple life. Is it not exactly the same, or indeed more so, with this other teaching? If you happen to be born a highly intellectual person and have the time and the leisure you can give your days and your weeks to concentration and to the culture of the mind and spirit. That is no gospel for the person who has neither the leisure nor the energy, and especially not for those who have not the intelligence. We must not over-emphasise the 'I'.

That is one error, but there is another, which is at the other extreme. As there are some who over-emphasise the 'I', there are those who tend to obliterate the 'I'. Let me put it in terms of something which I read in a religious journal. This is their definition of a Christian. The Christian, said that article, is:

> A mind through which Christ thinks,
> A voice through which Christ speaks,
> A heart through which Christ loves,
> A hand through which Christ helps.

My reply to that in terms of my text is – nonsense. And it is not only nonsense but a travesty of Christian teaching. If the Christian is a mind through which Christ thinks, a voice through which Christ speaks, a heart through which Christ loves and a hand through which Christ helps, where is the 'I'? The 'I' has vanished, and 'I' has been obliterated, the 'I' is no longer present. The teaching represented by that quotation is that the Christian is a man or woman whose personality has gone out of existence, while Christ is using his various powers and faculties. Not using him but using his voice, using his mind, using his heart, using his hand. But that is not what Paul says. Paul says: 'I can do all things through Christ which strengtheneth me.' Or listen to him elsewhere. You remember what he says in Galatians 2:20: 'I live; yet not I, but Christ liveth in me.' Is there in these verses an obliteration of the 'I'? 'I live, yet not I, but Christ liveth in me: and the life I live in the flesh, I live by the faith of the Son of God, who loved me, and gave himself for me.' The 'I' is still there.

We must, therefore, if we are to be just to this doctrine, safeguard the true position. The Christian life is not a life that I live myself and by my own power; neither is it a life in which I am obliterated and Christ does all. No, 'I can do all things through Christ.' I wonder if I can best put this by telling you of how an old preacher, famous in the last century, once put it when preaching on this very text. Those old preachers used sometimes to preach in a very dramatic way. They would have a kind of dialogue with the Apostle in the pulpit. So this old preacher began to preach on this text in this way: 'I can do all things through Christ which strengtheneth me.'

'Wait a minute, Paul, what did I hear you say?'

'I can do all things.'

'Paul, surely that is boasting, surely you are just claiming that you are a superman?'

'No, no, I can do all things.'

Well, the old preacher kept up the dialogue. He questioned Paul and quoted every statement made by Paul in which he says that he is the least of all saints, etc. 'You are generally so humble, Paul, but now you say, "I can do all things," haven't you started boasting?'

And then at last Paul says: 'I can do all things through Christ.'

'Oh, I am sorry,' said the old preacher, 'I beg your pardon, Paul. I did not realise there were two of you.'

Now I think that puts it perfectly. 'I can do all things through Christ.' 'There are two of you.' Not I only, not Christ only, but Christ and I, two of us.

Very well, then, let us put the doctrine like this. What is the right way to approach this question of power? How can I get this power which Paul tells us was being infused into him and which made him strong and able to stand and bear all things? May I suggest an analogy? I do so with hesitancy and trepidation because no analogy is perfect, and yet to use one can help us to arrive at the truth. What is vital, in this connection, is the matter of the approach, or, if you prefer a military term, the strategy. Never is the strategy of 'the indirect approach' more important than it is here. You know that in military strategy you do not always go straight at the objective. Sometimes you may appear to be going in the opposite direction but you come back. That is the strategy of the indirect approach and that is the strategy that is needed here.

Let me put it, then, in terms of an illustration. This question of power in the Christian life is like the question of physical health. There are many people in this world who spend most of their lives in seeking health. They spend their time and money going round from Spa to Spa, from treatment to treatment, from physician to physician. They are seeking health. Whenever you meet them they begin at once to talk about their health. The big thing in their lives is this question of health, and yet they are never well. What is the matter? Sometimes the trouble is due to the fact that they forget first principles, and the whole explanation of the state they are in is that they eat too much, or take too little exercise. They are living an unnatural life, and because they eat too much they produce certain acids and these acids produce conditions that call for treatment. They have to be told to eat less or to exercise more, or whatever it may chance to be. Their problem would never have arisen were it not that they had forgotten the first principles, the fundamental rules of life and living. Because of this, they develop an unnatural situation and a condition that needs treatment. Now I suggest that that is analogous to this whole subject of power in one's life as a Christian. Health is something that results from right living. Health cannot be obtained directly or immediately or in and of itself. There is a sense in which a man should not think of his health at all. Health is the result of right living, and I say exactly the same thing about this question of power in our Christian lives.

Or let me use another illustration. Take the question of preaching. No subject is discussed more often than power in preaching. 'Oh, that I might have power in preaching,' says the preacher and he goes on his knees and prays for power. I think that that may be quite wrong. It certainly is if it is the only thing that the preacher does. The way to have power is to prepare your message carefully. Study the word of God, think it out, analyse it, put it in order, do your utmost. That is the message God is most likely to bless – the indirect approach rather than the direct. It is exactly the same in this matter of power and ability to live the Christian life. In addition to our prayer for power and ability, we must obey certain primary rules and laws.

I can therefore summarise the teaching like this. The secret of power is to discover and to learn from the New Testament what is possible for us in Christ. What I have to do is go to Christ. I must spend my time with him, I must meditate upon him, I must get to know him. That was Paul's ambition – 'that I might know him'. I must maintain my contact and communion with Christ and I must concentrate on knowing him.

What else? I must do exactly what he tells me. I must avoid things that would hamper. To use my illustration, if I want to be well, I must not eat too much, I must not get into an atmosphere that is bad for me, I must not expose myself to chills. In the same way, if we do not keep the spiritual rules we may pray endlessly for power but we shall never get it. There are no short cuts in the Christian life. If in the midst of persecution we want to feel as Paul felt, we must live as Paul lived. I must do what he tells me, both to do and not to do. I must read the Bible, I must exercise, I must practise the Christian life, I must live the Christian life in all its fulness. In other words, I must implement what Paul has been teaching in verses eight and nine. This, as I understand it, is the New Testament doctrine of abiding in Christ. Now the word 'abiding' makes people become sentimental. They think of abiding as something passive and clinging, but to abide in Christ is to do what he tells you, positively, and to pray without ceasing. Abiding is a tremendously active thing.

'Well,' says the Apostle, 'if you do all that he will infuse his strength into you.' What a wonderful idea. This is a kind of spiritual blood transfusion – that is what Paul is teaching here. Here is a patient who has lost much blood for some reason or another. He is faint and gasping for breath. It is no use giving him drugs because he has not enough blood to absorb them and use them. The man is anaemic. The only thing you can do for him is give him a blood transfusion, infuse blood into him. That is what Paul tells us the Lord Jesus Christ was doing for him. 'I find I am very feeble,' says Paul, 'my energy seems to flag and sometimes I feel I have no life blood in me at all. But, you know, because of this relationship, I find he infuses it into me. He knows my every state and condition, he knows exactly what I need. Oh, how much he gives me! He says, "My grace is sufficient for thee," and so I can say, "When I am weak then am I strong." Sometimes I am conscious of great power; there are other times when I expect nothing, but he gives everything.'

That is the romance of the Christian life. Nowhere does one experience it more than in the Christian pulpit. There is certainly romance in preaching. I often say that the most romantic place on earth is the pulpit. I ascend the pulpit stairs Sunday after Sunday – and I never know what is going to happen. I confess that sometimes, for various reasons, I come expecting nothing; but suddenly the power is given. At other times I think I have a great deal because of my preparation; but, alas, I find there is no power in it. Thank God it is like that. I do my utmost, but he controls the supply and the power, he infuses it. He is the heavenly physician and he knows every variation in my condition. He sees my complexion, he feels my pulse. He knows my inadequate preaching, he knows everything. 'That is it,' says Paul, 'and therefore I am able for all things through the One who is constantly infusing strength into me.'

That, then, is the prescription. Do not agonise in prayer, beseeching him for power. Do what he has told you to do. Live the Christian life. Pray, and meditate upon him. Spend time with him and ask him to manifest himself to you. And as long as you do that, you can leave the rest to him. He will give you strength – 'as thy days, so shall thy strength be' (Deut. 33:25). He knows us better than we know ourselves, and according to our need so will be our supply. Do that and you will be able to say with the Apostle: 'I am able [made strong] for all things through the One who is constantly infusing strength into me.'

19

All Our Need Supplied

> Not because I desire a gift: but I desire fruit that may abound to your account. But I have all, and abound: I am full, having received of Epaphroditus the things which were sent from you, an odour of a sweet smell, a sacrifice acceptable, wellpleasing to God. But my God shall supply all your need according to his riches in glory by Christ Jesus (Phil. 4:17–19).

In these verses we have the final statement that the Apostle has to make with regard to this question of the gift that has been sent to him by the members of the church at Philippi while he is a prisoner in Rome. They have sent him the gift, obviously a large and generous one, through Epaphroditus, and now that Epaphroditus is going back to Philippi, the Apostle is anxious to convey his thankfulness. We have already considered what he has to say about this matter, and we have seen the profound theological implications that are involved. We have emphasised his great concern that the Philippians, much as he loves them, should not imagine that he is finally dependent upon them. That is his difficulty, how to thank them profusely without giving the impression that he is dependent upon them, and how to thank them without detracting from the glory of God, and we have seen how he contrives to do that. But here we come to the end of his statement and once more we see clearly how anxious he still is that the Philippians should hold this matter in the right perspective; that is why he goes on repeating himself. He is jealous for the honour, the glory and the reputation of the

Lord, and he is anxious that they should know that he finds his complete fulness in Christ – there must be no mistake about that.

Yet he is also anxious that they should realise that he deeply appreciates their thoughtfulness for him. As he tells them this, he pays them a very great compliment. He says they are the only people who have sent him a gift. We cannot stay with this – it is a great subject in and of itself – but we must remember how careful the Apostle was that no one should ever think that he preached the gospel in order to make money. You will find him dealing with that subject in 2 Corinthians 11, as indeed he has already dealt with it in 1 Corinthians 9. Suggestions were being made that he went around to make money, that he was commercially minded. In fact, Paul was so concerned about the gospel, and above all about the Lord himself, that he refused any payment from them, but went on working with his own hands as a tent-maker, in order to support himself so that no one could ever say that he was making money out of the cross of Christ.

Now this is a great subject, and we should realise how many of the troubles of the Christian Church have arisen because the Church has not always remembered the apostolic pattern. The Church became very wealthy and powerful in a worldly sense, but she lost her spiritual power. Someone wisely pointed out that as long as the Church could say, 'Silver and gold have I none,' she could repeat the miracles of the Apostle Peter, but when the day came that she had much silver and gold, then she became a worldly power, a secular institution using Christian terminology, and she ceased to function as the power of God among men. I only touch upon that in passing. The point I am emphasising is that the Apostle here reminds the Philippians that in view of the fact that that is his method and the way in which he lives, he does greatly appreciate the gift they have sent. For some reason, the other churches did not realise his sufferings, but twice over the Philippians had sent him a gift and he appreciated it profoundly. But then he is a little bit unhappy about it – 'notwithstanding ye have well done' – this reminder that they had done it once again; then: 'not because I desire a gift' – back he comes to it once more. It was a wonderful thing for them to do, but God forbid that they should think or imagine that he had been unhappy until their gift came, or that he could not get on without it. Even if he could, that did not lessen their generosity, but it does establish again the fulness of the supply that is to be found in God through our Lord and Saviour Jesus Christ. In other words, the great thing the Apostle is anxious about here is that the Philippians should be quite clear in their minds about this whole question of the satisfaction of our needs as Christian people while we are here on earth.

Now he has some very interesting things to say about this. Take the phrase 'giving and receiving' in verse 15. The Philippians have given, and Paul has received, and Paul goes on to enunciate three principles in connection with Christian generosity, Christian benevolence, Christian charity, or the principles of charity in the lives and conduct of Christian people. The first is that our generosity is always a very thorough test of the real value of our Christian profession. Paul loved this church at Philippi because they were such excellent Christian people, and they proved that by sending gifts to him.

Let us reconstruct the picture. These Philippians were Gentiles, the Apostle Paul was a Jew; you remember the animosity that there was between Jew and Gentile, the bitterness and hatred on both sides, the Jew regarding the Gentile as a dog and the Gentile regarding the Jew almost as a barbarian because he did not know any philosophy. Then this Jew comes to preach in Philippi and these people are converted and become a church. Later they hear of the Apostle's need, and they immediately send him a gift, and they do that twice. There is only one explanation of that, says Paul, it is their Christian love, their understanding of the gospel and what it means. They love this man because he has brought them something that is of greater value than the whole world. Here is a man who has brought them peace with God and a new love and understanding and joy, this joy which he goes on repeating. They owe everything to him, and, therefore, when they realise that he is in need and is suffering, they must do something about it, their very Christian love makes them do it.

Now that is something that we find emphasised very frequently in the New Testament. The Apostle teaches the Corinthians how to do this and we find the same teaching, in that famous parable spoken by our Lord when he went into the house of a man called Simon the Pharisee. A woman who was a sinner came and fell at his feet. She washed his feet with her tears and wiped them with the hairs of her head, and anointed them with ointments, while Simon the Pharisee had done nothing for him. Then our Lord, realising Simon's disapproval of the whole incident, told the story of the two debtors who had been forgiven their debts, and he showed how the one who had been forgiven the greater debt loved the creditor most. 'In the same way,' says our Lord in effect, 'that woman shows that she realises what I have done for her.' We express our love and understanding by what we do, and I think the principle is self-evident. If we really believe the gospel, then we must believe that nothing is more important in the world today than the propagation of that gospel; that should be our greatest concern. That is why it has always seemed to me to be a contradiction of New Testament teaching to have to appeal for funds, either for local churches or for the missionary cause. No, this matter puts us under judgment; people who really believe and love the Lord are those who know something of that constraining power which makes them say, 'I can do no other.' 'For God loveth a cheerful giver' (2 Cor. 9:7).

That, then, is Paul's first principle. The second principle – we must be careful how we put it, and yet the Apostle puts it quite distinctly – is that Christian charity and benevolence is a marvellous investment. 'Not because I desire a gift,' says the Apostle in verse 17, 'but I desire fruit that may abound to your account.' Now this is a very striking statement. Paul puts it like this: I am profoundly grateful to you for these gifts that you have given to me, but, you know, what really pleases me most is not the benefit I have derived myself, but the way in which I can see that your account, your deposit account, has been mounting up as the result of this; I am pleased because of the interest that is going to accrue to your account – 'he that hath pity upon the poor lendeth unto the Lord' (Prov. 19:17).

Again, this is a principle which is taught in several places in the New Testament. In Luke 16:9 our Lord says, 'Make to yourselves friends of the mammon of unrighteousness; that, when ye fail, they may receive you into everlasting habitations.' His teaching is: 'Make right use of your money, or the wealth that you may have received in this world. Use it in such a way, and do so much good with it, that you will be laying up for yourselves friends in heaven, so that when you fail, there will be people there to receive you.' In other words, you are doing this now, yes, but you are preparing for yourself in the future. You cannot exercise Christian charity and benevolence without unconsciously benefiting yourselves at the same time.

The Apostle Paul says the same thing in 1 Timothy 6 where he tells Timothy to exhort those who are rich in this world to use their wealth for the good of others. Why? 'Laying up in store for themselves a good foundation against the time to come, that they may lay hold on eternal life' (vv.17–19). You appear to be giving, but in this marvellous, mysterious manner you are laying up, you are getting interest which will be put to your deposit account, says Paul. We must handle this matter carefully. The Apostle is not exhorting the Philippians to be benevolent *in order* that they may build up an account, and our Lord is not teaching that in the parable in Luke 16. This is a glorious doctrine – you can do nothing as a Christian but that it has an ultimate repercussion, and the glory of this benevolence is that though you are apparently giving, you are going to receive.

The third principle on this subject is that though, in a sense, the Philippians had given their gifts to Paul, in reality they had been giving them to God. That is the message of the eighteenth verse: 'I have all, and abound: I am full, having received of Epaphroditus the things which were sent from you, an odour of a sweet smell, a sacrifice acceptable, wellpleasing to God,' Now that is the most glorious and wonderful thing of all. 'This gift of yours to me,' says Paul in effect, 'is not only something that I have received, it is like a sweet smell in the sight of God.' The Children of Israel were told to take offerings to God of a 'sweet smelling savour' and this is a wonderful picture of that – it is the pleasant odour that comes up from the offering. God descended to the level of the understanding of the Israelite people, and spoke in this anthropomorphic manner in order that he might describe the pleasure he derived as the people brought their offerings. We all know how pleasant it is to smell the aroma of a flower, and these gifts were like that to God. Paul says that these particular gifts to him personally have emitted that delightful odour, the aroma of this beautiful act has been wafted right up into heaven, and God, on his eternal and everlasting throne, has been well-pleased with it.

This is the supreme principle with regard to this whole matter of giving and receiving. Our Lord has established this once and for ever in the story of the woman with the two mites which make a farthing. She dropped them into the box and few people saw her or knew anything about it. Great gifts were being given, yes, but she gave all she had, and that little act was wafted to heaven and God saw it. It is exactly the same with all Christian giving. Anything we may do to help a Christian cause, or to help Christians individually, any act that we may perform for Christ's sake, because we have been animated and moved by our love to him, though we may think we are doing it only to that person or cause, any such act is taken right up out of that level and is something that God sees and blesses. Thus Paul is saying to these people that in reality it is not so much that they have given a gift to him, as that they have taken their sacrifice, their sweet smelling savour, to God and he has received it, and he loves his people because of it.

Have we not felt, as we have considered these statements of the Apostle, that that is the way in which the Christian Church should be operating? Is it not tragic to think that churches have to have sales of work and fêtes, and have to call in the world and its entertainments, in order to maintain the cause of Christ, and that they have to call in important people who are not spiritual, just in order to increase the funds? It is a tragedy that we do not realise that the Christian teaching with regard to giving and receiving is that we do it all in the sight and presence of God; it is to him like a sweet smelling savour.

But there is something else to add which, in a sense, is still more important. What the Apostle is concerned about finally is that these Philippians should thoroughly understand that in the whole matter of living the Christian life, they must avoid any morbid, sinful anxiety with regard to the whole question of how they are to live and what is going to happen. And here Paul lays down this amazing principle in the nineteenth verse: 'But my God shall supply all your need according to his riches in glory by Christ Jesus.' How does Paul come to say that? He is thanking them for what they have done for him, he was in need and they had superabundance, and he sends them that message. 'Philippian people,' says Paul in effect, 'at the moment I am in prison. You are out of prison and able to help me, and I am very grateful for it. But the day may come when you yourselves may not be able to give. The position may be reversed, and you may be the ones in need. But do not worry, whatever your state or position may be, "my God shall supply all your need". That is my position. I have told you that I have learned in whatsoever state I am therein to be content, and you must learn the same thing. And the secret of it all is that "my God shall supply all your need according to his riches in glory by Christ Jesus."'

Here, then, unmistakably, is the great New Testament teaching with regard to the whole vexatious subject of how, as Christian people, we are to live in this world and what our attitude should be to the very necessities of life itself. It is one of the most remarkable things the Apostle has ever said, coming in the same category as his other statements which we have already considered: 'I have learned . . .' and, 'I can do all things through Christ.' Our Lord teaches this self-same thing in Matthew 6, in the Sermon on the Mount: 'Take therefore no thought for the morrow . . .'; do not spend so much of your time in considering what you shall eat or drink . . . 'Consider the lilies of the field . . . sufficient unto the day is the evil thereof.' That teaching is repeated many times. And it is what the Apostle is repeating at this point in his letter to the Philippians.

I do not know how you feel, but I can never read words like these without feeling, and I say it deliberately, that the main trouble with us as Christian people is that we are such fools. How we rob ourselves of the riches of grace! How, with our worldly wisdom, we put our little limits upon what God offers us, and oh, how we rob ourselves of so much of the joy of salvation, and the glory of Christian living! Take a man like Paul. Was there ever a happier man than this? Take many another saint who has adorned the Christian Church. These people appear at first sight to be so reckless and yet how wonderful their lives have been! Well, this is the great doctrine and you can find it in the Old Testament as well. David at the end of his life said, This is my testimony, 'I have never seen the righteous forsaken, nor his seed begging bread'. That is the Old Testament counterpart of this statement of Paul's.

So, then, let us analyse it. Here is a promise made by God to his people that our every need shall be supplied. Let us consider first of all the greatness of the promise, or, if you like, the greatness of the supply. What is my position as a Christian? According to Paul, my position is that God is concerned about me – *my God*. What have I to draw upon? God is in charge, God is there handling the resources. But Paul has not done with that; he describes it further. He calls it 'his riches in glory', or, 'his glorious riches'. What is the wealth of God? No one can answer the question: 'The earth is the Lord's, and the fulness thereof' (Ps. 24:1). This sub-

ject is sometimes handled in Scripture with an element of
what I do not hesitate to call divine humour and irony. You
read Psalms like the forty-ninth or the fiftieth and you see
how God speaks to the people, some of whom thought that
their sacrifices to God were going to benefit him, and the
reply is, 'For every beast of the forest is mine, and the cattle
upon a thousand hills' (Ps. 50:10)! God is the owner of
everything; he brought everything into being out of nothing.
What is the wealth of God? It is equal to his glory, which is
absolute and eternal. 'His riches in glory.' I would commend
to you, as an interesting, fascinating and moving study, to
go through these epistles of Paul and make a note of the
parallel statements to this. For example, 'Unto him that is
able to do exceeding abundantly above all that we ask or
think' (Eph. 3:20) – that is it! You cannot describe it. The
riches of his grace, the riches of his glory are illimitable.

But you can see, even then, that Paul feels that that is not
enough, he must add to it: 'My God shall supply *all* your
need' – there is no limit, it does not matter what it is. And
yet I think we must be careful, as we interpret that, lest we
wrest the Scriptures to our own destruction. It is literally
true to say that with God all things are possible and that
God can and will supply all our needs. Yes, but you and I
are not always the best authorities as to the state of our
need. He does not say, 'My God shall supply all your
luxuries,' but, 'My God shall supply all your *need*,' and what
you and I need, and what we think we need, are not always
exactly the same. No, we are not promised luxury, but all
our need; whatever it may be, my God shall supply it, there
is no limit in that sense.

But the Apostle uses still another word to convey this
benevolence: the word 'supply'. Now it is very interesting to
note that in the original Greek the word translated here as
'supply', is the word which is translated in the previous verse
as 'I am full' – 'I have all things and abound.' So that what
Paul is saying is this: my God shall satisfy to the full all your
need according to his riches in glory by Christ Jesus. God
will fill you to the very brim with everything that he sees you

truly and really need.

That, then, is just a glance at the greatness of the promise. I wonder, Christian people, whether we realise as we should, and are as conscious as we might be, of the fact that this promise applies to us. This is certain, this is without any equivocation at all, this is what is promised to God's people. He, with all that wealth, is behind us, and he knows all our need.

But let me mention, in the second place, what I must call the limitation to the promise. 'My God shall supply all your need according to his riches in glory by [in] Christ Jesus.' Yes, there is a very definite limit to this promise. The statement about God supplying all our needs is not made to the world at large, it is not made to everybody; it is a particular statement, a particular promise, and it is limited by Christ Jesus. It almost sounds contradictory for me to say that it is limited in Christ Jesus. Is there any limit to Christ? No, there is not – and yet there is! Paul means that God's largesse and beneficence come through a particular channel and that channel is Christ Jesus. I know that God makes his sun to rise upon the evil and upon the good, and upon the just and the unjust; that is common grace and God's general beneficence. But this is a particular promise; it is something personal and individual that comes only through the channel of Christ Jesus – all the treasures of the riches of God's grace come only through him.

This is a fundamental of the whole of the New Testament teaching, so it means that unless and except we are in this particular relationship to God, this promise does not apply to us. This promise is only made to those who, having seen their desperate plight and condition and lost estate, have run to Christ and given themselves to him, and are being incorporated into him, and are members of his body. It is made to no one else; the promise is confined to Christians, to those who are in Christ Jesus in this relationship, who are connected to the channel, who are recipients of the grace of God in salvation. So there is a very definite limit to the promise in and of itself; it is illimitable, but it is confined to the channel of Christ, what he has done in his life and death and resurrection. He is calling his people unto himself and it is for them, and for them alone.

So we have seen the greatness of the promise, and the limitation of the promise, and that in turn brings me to the last principle, which is the certainty of the promise. 'My God shall supply . . .' There is no doubt about it, it is not contingent, it is not uncertain, it does not say, 'perhaps', 'maybe'. No! 'My God *shall*.' 'As certainly as I am writing to you,' says Paul in effect, 'this will happen to you. I know, I am certain, these are his terms.' Now Paul does not say that he knows exactly how God is going to do it, and we do not know either. 'God moves in a mysterious way, His wonders to perform.' You read the story of men like George Muller, and you see the kind of way in which God works, but sometimes he takes away in order to give, and we have all, perhaps, had experience of that in some small way or other. He seems to empty before he fills, but he does it, and he will do it. It is certain. It is absolute.

What, then, are the arguments for the certainty? Let me note them. If you and I are in Christ, we are in a very particular relationship to God; if we are in Christ, we are partakers of the divine nature, we are members of the household of God, we are of his family and we belong to him. What a staggering statement, but it is the simple truth. If we are in Christ, then we are and 'heirs of God, and joint-heirs with Christ'. We are children in this amazing personal relationship; God has become our Father, and you remember the argument that our Lord himself deduced from that? He said, 'The very hairs of your head are all numbered' (Matt. 10:30), and further, 'If ye then, being evil, know how to give good gifts unto your children, how much more shall your Father which is in heaven give good things . . .' (Matt. 7:11). All these are astounding statements of the fatherly interest and concern of God in us. The analogy is there on the very surface. Just think how parents anticipate their child's need; the child does not have to ask, they are there watching, they see the need where even the child does not see it. And God is like that to us if we are in Christ; he is going to supply our every need because he is our Father.

But there is something even greater; there is that remarkable argument used by Paul in chapters 5 and 8 of his epistle to the Romans. It is one of those great logical arguments that is based on the proposition that if the greater is true, the lesser must inevitably follow: 'For if, when we were enemies, we were reconciled to God by the death of his Son, much more, being reconciled, we shall be saved by his life' (Rom. 5:10) – it is inevitable. Or, again, he says, in chapter 8:32, 'He that spared not his own Son, but delivered him up for us all, how shall he not with him also freely give us all things?' There is no need to argue; the God who sent his only begotten, his well-beloved Son to the cruel cross on Calvary, where his blood was shed and his body was broken, in order that we rebel sinners might be saved and pardoned and redeemed, God, who has done that for us, is not going to forsake us in lesser matters like food and drink and clothing and these temporal things. No. 'He which hath begun a good work in you will perform it until the day of Jesus Christ' (Phil. 1:6). The greater that he has already done is a guarantee that he will certainly do the lesser. 'My God shall supply all your need according to his riches in glory by Christ Jesus.' The blessed security of the Christian is not only in things spiritual, it is even in things material, if we obey these conditions. The promise of God is absolute.

20

My God

But my God shall supply all your need according to his riches in glory by Christ Jesus. Now unto God and our Father be glory for ever and ever. Amen (Phil. 4:19–20).

The Apostle here, as we saw in our last study, is comforting the Philippians, and reminding them that their future is perfectly safe and secure. Whatever might happen to them, whatever experience they might be called upon to undergo, he is confident and assured that their supply will always be at hand because it will all be supplied in full by God himself. We considered the terms in which he puts that argument before them: the greatness of God and the illimitable character of his wealth and riches. We saw, too, that it all comes through Christ, and Paul is certain of it, because of the powerful argument that the God who has done the greater thing in the death of Christ, cannot leave them now, after they have been brought into the Christian life. Paul produces this argument in order to give the Philippians a sense of confidence and assurance.

In this study I am anxious to concentrate attention on the particular way in which Paul puts all this: '*My God* shall supply all your need . . .' He has already used the expression 'My God' in the third verse of the first chapter, where he says, 'I thank *my God* upon every remembrance of you;' and you will find that he uses this, or the similar expression, 'My Lord', in many other places as well.

Now this is something which was very characteristic of the Apostle. You cannot read any of his epistles, or any of his recorded speeches or sermons in Acts, without being impressed at once by the personal note which always came into every statement. This personal experience is always there, and he never writes without your being conscious of a warmth and a growing devotion. Whatever else may be said about the epistles, that, I think, must be granted by everyone. Obviously, the man is writing out of a rich personal experience – there is nothing academic and remote about these letters. They are not only pastoral, and you not only sense the love which exists between the Apostle and the people to whom he is writing, but also his every reference to God and our Lord Jesus Christ has a note of personal intimacy, devotion and love. Indeed, the juxtaposition of these two words, 'my' and 'God', remind us of what is, after all, the central feature of the Apostle's religious life, and the dominant characteristic of all the New Testament writers also. In other words, they are a perfect blend of doctrine and experience.

Now I think that a very good case could be made out for saying that most of the troubles which the Christian Church has experienced throughout her long history have been due to the fact that Christian people have not been careful enough to see that these two elements were present at the same time and the same place. Our tendency is to emphasise the one or the other, and often the one at the expense of the other. There are those who emphasise and stress doctrine: they talk about God, they are aware of the doctrine and the truth concerning God, that is their great interest. God is the subject of their constant study and research, the big theme that occupies their mind and attention, and they are aware, not only of the doctrine of God, as God is taught in the Bible, but also of how that doctrine has been elaborated by the Church in many a Council. They are learned, erudite and knowledgeable, and yet, somehow, you cannot help feeling that their interest and concern is purely academic and theoretical, that they are engaged in a kind of science. As one man takes a physical science and tries to discover truth concerning it, these men seem to have taken up, as their interest in life and the field of their scientific quest, the knowledge of God. The result is, of course, that they give the impression that they have what has been termed 'dry as dust' theology. The knowledge is there, the doctrine is there, the awareness of truth is there, but nothing more. Never do they give the impression that they are talking about 'my God'. The various truths appear almost to be abstractions and isolated concepts concerning some august and supreme being – doctrine and no more.

But, on the other hand of course, you have those who go to the other extreme. It is personal experience that receives the prominence and the emphasis. They tell you that they know no doctrine and, frankly, they are not interested. They have a lot to say about the 'dry as dust' theologians, who can argue with such cleverness and produce their casuistry, but who seem to be devoid of a personal knowledge in their hearts and minds and experience. These others talk of their experiences, what they have felt, what they have proved and known. The whole emphasis is upon themselves. They have got something; they certainly have had the experience, and they are talking out of it and about it, but their whole emphasis is on that and they say, 'It is no use talking to me about doctrine. Don't ask me to explain the doctrine of God, or the doctrine of the incarnation or the atonement. I don't understand these things, but I have felt and experienced something.'

I think you will agree with me that this is the tendency: either the one extreme or the other. But that is something which can never be said of this great Apostle, or any of the New Testament writers. The glory of their position is that the two things come together. God, yes; but also 'my God'. Doctrine *and* experience, the objective *and* the subjective. The grand statement of truth and yet the experimental, or, if you prefer it, the experiential knowledge of that truth.

So that is what the Apostle reminds us of in dealing with this question of the security of the Christian believer, and it is the ultimate ground of his assurance and confidence. You need not worry about the future, says Paul, '*my* God shall supply all your need according to his riches in glory by Christ Jesus.'

Here, then, surely, is a statement which deserves our very careful attention and analysis. Let me put it to you first and foremost by asking a question. Do we habitually speak of God as 'my God'? Do I, as a Christian, instinctively use that expression? Do I say from the depths of my being, 'My God, how wonderful Thou art'? Do I speak of *my* Lord Jesus Christ? Is this a natural expression of my religious life and of my Christian experience? Paul, as I will show you as we look at verses 19 and 20, does not confine this to himself. 'Our God' – for the Philippians and everyone else; he is 'our God and Father'.

There are, then, certain things we can deduce. Firstly, the Apostle speaks about a God whom he knows. This, perhaps, we can emphasise by putting it in opposition to a number of negatives. Paul's worship and religion were not superstition. It is possible for us to think that we are worshipping God and yet be guilty of superstition. Paul brings that charge against the citizens of Athens. 'As I walked about the streets of your city,' he said in effect, 'I observed that you are too superstitious and I have observed your altar to the Unknown God' (Acts 17). There are those who say with W.E. Henley, 'I thank whatever gods may be for my unconquerable soul.' They do not know God, but believe vaguely that there is a great Power. It is a religion of fear and dread, an awareness of something indefinable, tremendous, far away in the distance, somewhere. This numinous idea is not what characterises the worship and religion of the Apostle Paul. His is not a superstitious religion. God is a reality, a Person with whom he does business and with whom he has conversation and communion.

Secondly, let me put it like this: clearly, the God he speaks of is not merely the God of philosophy. This again is an important negative. There is, of course, the God of philosophy. There are schools of philosophy which would teach us and have us believe that the existence of God can be proved. There are those who arrive at God as a result of a number of arguments as elaborated by Thomas Aquinas. The philosophers themselves talk a great deal about God, but the God of the philosopher tends to be an abstraction, a sort of philosophic 'x' that is essential to the scheme and system. He is what they call the 'ultimate reality' or the 'absolute'. Oh, the pride of knowledge with which they tend to use the term! It is as if they think they are superior to the humble Christian who talks of 'my God'. Now that is the tendency of the philosopher. Let no one misunderstand me; I am trying to indicate the terrible danger of confusing this mere philosophical conception with the God of whom Paul speaks – 'my God', someone whom he knows.

Thirdly, the God of whom Paul speaks is not only the God of theology – and here I am trying to be scrupulously fair. Unfortunately, it is possible for us to speak of a God who is nothing but a theological conception. It is an advance and yet it is something very different from the God about whom the Apostle speaks in our text here. It is possible for us to be interested in the Bible because it is incomparably the greatest book in the world, and to a man of intelligence there can be no more fascinating study than the study of this book. Then you begin to read books about the Bible, and you come up against the greatest minds the world has ever known, incidentally, the greatest philosophers in this Christian era. But here they are, combining knowledge with a study of this book, and they elaborate this doctrine, and they talk about the God of revelation who has done this and that, but still you may only be dealing with an abstraction, with God who figures in this book much as one would deal with a character in a Shakespeare play. You have read the play so often that the character has almost assumed reality for you – and yet, of course, he has not. He is a fiction that Shakespeare conjured up in his mind and put in his play.

Now there is a terrible danger that God may be to us someone like that; essential to our theological system, but not someone we know. The theology of the Bible is a mighty intellectual concept, and the terrible danger is that God may only be a part of that scheme to us. No, that is not the God of whom the Apostle writes and so constantly speaks. Paul knows God. God is not merely some vague, indefinable

Spirit, breaking in and doing something terrifying and alarming; nor is he 'the ultimate' – someone who is essential to an understanding of the history of the Jews to whom Paul belongs. No, to Paul he is a reality, someone he knows – 'my God'. The God I know, the God of experience to whom I speak, who is more real than life itself. The Apostle Paul knew God. But we cannot stop at that.

Our second main deduction is that Paul loves God. This is not an exaggeration. Do you not detect it in the phrase 'my God'? He not only knows him, he is proud of him. He tells us something about the character of God. He does not tremble in the presence of God as he thinks of God's might and power and his illimitable sway. The reason is given in the next verse: to Paul God is also 'Father'. Here is another interesting theme – the frequency with which Paul refers to God as the 'God and Father of our Lord Jesus Christ'. This is an exposition of our Lord's statement, 'He that hath seen me hath seen the Father' (John 14:9). God is like that. He is the Father of our Lord Jesus Christ; he is our God and our Father; and the result is that Paul loves God.

Now we are used to these statements; they sound so simple, but how profound they are! The commandment is that we should love; not only that we should believe and accept a number of principles and statements, but 'Thou shalt love the Lord thy God with all thine heart, and with all thy soul, and with all thy might' (Deut. 6:5). Love God! How easy it is to slip over a phrase like this – 'my God'.

Do we love God? Or do we rather feel that he is someone who is set over against us, some great Power from whom we cannot escape, someone who seems to thwart us and prohibit us from doing the things we want to do? Is that our thought of God, or can we say that we love him? 'My God', in the sense of possessing, as the lover possesses the object of his love; one who is dear to us.

Thirdly, Paul also tells us something about the character of God. He is defining God here in contradistinction to other gods. Let us remember that the Apostle was writing to the Philippians, and until Paul went to Philippi they were pagans, apart from a few Jews and proselytes. They were, of course, polytheists. Even as in Athens, so they had pagan temples and altars in Philippi; they had been brought up in the atmosphere of polytheism and worshipped gods of silver, wood and stone. Reminding the Philippians once more of the great change in their lives, Paul says in effect, 'Let me remind you that you need not worry; I am basing my confidence on my God, not on the gods you used to worship.' God is not like the other gods that foolish people in their blindness are still worshipping, but 'my God'. Paul defines him and his characteristics. What are they? These are two things we must emphasise at this point.

In the first place, God is the only true and living God. Again, you will find Paul elaborating this in many places. In his address in Athens he tells the people that God is not someone who lives in temples of gold or silver (see Acts 17), he is not dependent upon man. God is the Eternal, the Creator, the Artificer and Sustainer of everything that is; glorious in holiness and power – 'my God'. Now that is something which we need to hold constantly in our minds. The God who is our Saviour, the Father of our Lord Jesus Christ, is also the Creator. This is where doctrine is so important. He exists from eternity to eternity. He has made everything out of nothing. He is the one to whom 'the nations are as a drop of a bucket, and are counted as the small dust of the balance' (Isa. 40:15). He is the only true and living God, the Creator. He is in that sense the 'absolute' and more of the philosophers. Paul, in other words, was anxious to remind them that this is not a superstitious belief, a figment of the imagination – 'the God of whom I am speaking is the living God'. He is a Person, and he has not only created everything and sustains everything, but everything is subject to his dominion and reign: 'The Lord reigneth.' This God of whom I am speaking will 'never leave thee, nor forsake thee' (Heb. 13:5).

Secondly, he is the covenanting God – the God of the covenants. If you read Deuteronomy 29, you will see that it is one of the places where this great idea of God covenanting himself to people is emphasised and elaborated. The God of whom I am speaking, says Paul, is not a God at whom you arrive through superstition or philosophy, but is based upon a revelation. God has been pleased to manifest himself, to tell us about himself, to reveal his great purpose with regard to men and women, to reveal his great plan of salvation. He has told us these things in such a way that I am entitled to speak of him as 'my God'. -

Let me remind you of some passages: Genesis 17:8: 'And I will give unto thee, and to thy seed after thee, the land wherein thou art a stranger, all the land of Canaan, for an everlasting possession; and I will be their God.' That word 'their' is important. God is going to be 'their God' in a particular way.

Jeremiah 31:33: 'But this shall be the covenant that I will make with the house of Israel; after those days, saith the Lord, I will put my law in their inward parts, and write it in their hearts; and will be their God, and they shall be my people.' That is the great covenant. God made it originally with Abraham and went on repeating it until you come to Christ; then you get the New Testament elaborations of the same covenant worked out by Paul, for example in 2 Corinthians 6:16: 'For ye are the temple of the living God; as God hath said, I will dwell in them, and walk in them; and I will be their God, and they shall be my people.' Then there is a great exposition in Hebrews 8 where the author again refers to the new covenant – 'I will be to them a God, and they shall be to me a people' (Heb. 8:10). The Covenant of God! Now this is something of which our fathers used to talk a great deal, but which we, alas, have allowed to fall into desuetude. This covenant of God with his own people: I am going to confine myself to you, my people; you are the people of my peculiar possession; I will be your God in a sense that I am not going to be a God to anyone else.

Therefore, beloved Philippians, says Paul, have no concern or worry about your future.

But let me emphasise the other side. If God is a God who has committed himself to Paul, Paul has committed himself to God. He is the God to whom I have given myself, says Paul, and whom I acknowledge. I have covenanted myself to him. There are two sides, two parties to a covenant. God covenants himself to us, but we must covenant ourselves to God, and, says Paul, I have done so.

But lastly, Paul says 'My God' in order to tell them that God is a God whom he has proved. Paul not only knows him and loves him and is aware of his profound characteristics, but – 'My God shall supply all your need.' I know him, says Paul, I am not writing theoretically; I have staked my whole life, my everything on him. Once I came to know him truly, I gave myself to him. I staked everything, on him and on the truth concerning him, and, here Paul says, in effect, 'I have never been disappointed.' Never!

Read again 2 Corinthians 11 and 12 and Paul will tell you something about his experiences – beaten with rods, ship-wrecked, misunderstood, maligned, starving, almost killed as a result of being stoned – and yet his statement is always that the Lord delivered him out of them all.

There is a glorious example of this in Paul's second letter to Timothy: 'At my first answer [trial] no man stood with me, but all men forsook me' (4:16). This mighty Paul, who had preached and done so much for others, who suffered so much, was on trial, and no man stood with him but all forsook him! 'I pray God,' he says, 'that it may not be laid to their charge. Notwithstanding the Lord stood with me, and strengthened me . . . and the Lord shall deliver me from every evil work, and will preserve me unto his heavenly kingdom' (vv. 16–18). 'I will never leave thee nor forsake thee'. Paul has proved that.

Philippians, says the Apostle, 'my God shall supply all your need.' That is the sort of God he is; I have tested him; I have proved him; he has never let me down, never failed. 'My God' – the God I know, the God I love, the God I can guarantee, the God I can vouch for, as it were, the God who never fails, the God who has said, 'And, lo, I am with you alway, even unto the end of the world' (Matt. 28:20).

So I ask the same question here that I put at the beginning: Can you say 'my God'? Do you know him? Is he real and living to you? Do you love him? Have you proved him and tested him?

What enables us to have this experience? I cannot deal with this in detail, so I merely mention it. All this has come true for Paul because he has gone to God through Jesus Christ. The Lord himself has said to him, 'I am the way, the truth, and the life: no man cometh unto the Father, but by me' (John 14:6). You can never know God except in Jesus Christ. You may know the philosophical abstraction, the logical concept, but the only people who really know God are those who realise that they do not know him, and that they can never arrive at that knowledge by themselves. And in utter hopelessness and helplessness they cry out to God, 'I do not know you,' and then they believe that they are simply asked to abandon themselves to God to take charge of them. In utter helplessness they ask Christ to reveal God and they go on asking until they are able to say 'my God' through Jesus Christ.

Do what Paul did. Surrender to God, and, if you do, trust him; then you will come to know him – and not without. The Holy Spirit is given to those who obey God. If you obey by coming to Christ, and giving yourself to him, he will give you the Spirit of adoption whereby we cry, 'Abba, Father' – 'My God'.

21

The Fellowship of the Saints

Salute every saint in Christ Jesus. The brethren which are
with me greet you. All the saints salute you, chiefly they
that are of Caesar's household (Phil. 4:21–22).

In these verses the Apostle, in a kind of second postscript,
is just conveying the greetings of himself and his fellow-
workers and, indeed, of all the members of the church at
Rome, to the members of the church at Philippi. You will
find that this is something which he puts in practically all his
epistles. He not only writes for himself, he writes for all the
Christians who are with him wherever he happens to be.
But, what interests us in this additional postscript is the
extraordinary and beautiful picture which the Apostle gives
of the nature and life of the early Christian Church. It is not
his intention to do that, but in conveying his greetings, he
does incidentally – and, in a sense, almost of necessity – give
us this idyllic picture.

Now there are times when I feel, and feel very strongly,
that perhaps one of the greatest needs of the Church today
is the need to recapture this New Testament picture. You
cannot read the epistles and observe the character of the
Church at the beginning without being impressed at once by
the striking and strange departure from this pattern which
has taken place. We must admit that, in general, the Christian Church has become formal, set, and more or less lifeless. You read these New Testament passages and you get
these little glimpses, in the introductions and postscripts
especially, and you are given a picture of a very wonderful

fellowship, of a body of people meeting together to worship God, to consider our Christian gospel, and to share their experiences. The thing that stands out at once is the fellowship, the love, and this peculiar quality of intimacy and understanding. The New Testament itself describes the Church as the body of Christ, and is often at pains to remind us of the nature and relationship of the different parts. The New Testament Church was clearly a Church thrilling with life, with power and with fellowship and understanding. If you try to conjure up in your mind a meeting of the early Church, and contrast it with a typical meeting in a church today, you must be strangely impressed by the remarkable and extraordinary difference. When you think of the tendency in the Church to pay increasing attention to the building, to forms and ceremony and ritual, and to the development of a kind of hierarchy, offices and things of that kind, then does it not strike you that you cannot find it in the New

Testament? In the New Testament, the Church is primarily a fellowship, and there is an atmosphere of intimacy and love. There is an absence of formality and of that word which has, alas, been emphasised so much in the last hundred years – dignity. The form was apparently irrelevant. These people were concerned about the substance, and the result was that some of the churches met in houses; they met wherever they could, but because they were met together in this way and manner, it was a church.

So we are given just a glimpse into that in this brief second postscript. The things that strike us at once are the active nature of the fellowship and the spirit of unity. It does not matter what town they lived in, or what country, they all seemed to be one in the amazing love which they had for one another and in their interest and concern for one another. The Philippian Christians were concerned about the Christians in Rome; the people in Rome sent their greetings to the Philippian Christians; and it is the same in all the epistles. It does seem to me that this is a thorough test of our whole position as Christian people. Do we feel this special interest in other Christian people? Are we concerned to read about them? Are we concerned about their condition? Are we concerned about their sufferings?

I ask these questions at a time like this when we are finding ourselves back in a state which is strangely similar to that which obtained in the New Testament era. Do we ever give a thought to so many Christian people all over the world who are suffering, and who are not free to worship as we are? In the early Church what stood out was the interest the Christians had in one another. What was happening to the others? Were they suffering persecution? There was a great desire to help one another, and to help spread the gospel in all lands and amongst all peoples. This was a special feature of the lives of these early Christians. Thus, in sending their greetings to one another, they simply underlined and emphasised the point that the Church is indeed the body of Christ and that there is a peculiar unity among the members, as there is between the members and our great and glorious Head.

The word of salutation reminds us at once of that, but I want to go beyond that now, and concentrate attention on something additional. Paul makes a very significant statement here: 'Salute every saint in Christ Jesus . . . All the saints salute you, chiefly they that are of Caesar's household.' Now that is the striking thing at this point. The two phrases together give a picture of the Christian Church and of its members, but I feel that this particular phrase tells us something very special and additional about the Christian. In order that I may help you to retain the thought in your mind, let me suggest it in terms of the following proposition:

Firstly, what it means for anyone to be a Christian. Christians are saints.

Secondly, anyone can be a Christian.

Thirdly, one can be a Christian anywhere.

The first, then, is that we must be clear in our minds what it means for anyone to be a Christian. What is a Christian? The Apostle answers that question by his repeated use of this word *saint*, or *saints*. And again, of course, we see at a glance how the Church throughout the ages has tended to depart from the New Testament pattern. When we hear the word 'saint', do we not all instinctively think of a special type of church member, an exceptionally 'Christian' person? The Church, in her use of this term 'saint', has departed radically from the use made of it in the New Testament. Despite the Protestant Reformation, we think of the saint in terms of Roman Catholic teaching; we regard a saint as an unusual Christian who is canonised by a body of men because of some peculiar merits or outstanding virtues. So we would hesitate to call ourselves saints. We are far too fond of saying that we are 'far from being a saint', as if we were afraid that someone might regard us as saints!

This is a radical departure from the New Testament, for, according to New Testament teaching, every Christian, every member of the Christian Church, is a saint. Read the introductions to the epistles – 'to the saints that are in Rome . . . in Corinth . . .', 'called to be saints', every one of them. 'Salute every saint,' or, to put it in more modern language, 'Give my greetings to every single saint in the church.' In other words, the Apostle not only speaks of every single, individual member of the church at Philippi as a saint, but regards them as such. You cannot be a Christian without, at the same time, being a saint. So that clearly means that our definition of what constitutes a saint has somehow gone astray. A saint, according to the Bible, is someone who has been set apart, a holy person. As you read the New Testament, you will find references to the 'holy mount', and this refers to a mountain which was set apart by God and consecrated. There was no change in the constitution of the mountain as such, but God set it apart. The 'holy vessels', too, were vessels of the Temple which were consecrated; blood was poured upon them and they were set apart for use in the Temple.

That, then, is the key to the understanding of what the New Testament means by 'saint'. First and foremost, a saint is a person who has been called out of the world by the almighty God. We were born in sin and shapen in iniquity but then the grace of God in Jesus Christ came to us and apprehended us, sought us out, and set us apart. We are set apart as God's special, holy people; people whom God has marked out for himself. In such people God is taking a special interest – they are the people whom he is anxious to use for a very special purpose.

So that is the New Testament conception of a member of a church: someone who has been dealt with by God in a way that differentiates him or her from all those outside. It is very important that we should hold on to this primary and initial meaning of the word 'saint', and that in the first instance we should not think of what we do or do not do, but rather of what we *are*. And we are conscious, therefore, that, in spite of all our sinfulness and unworthiness, God has been dealing with us, God has disturbed us, there is something different in us from what was once true of us, or of the average person. If God is in my thoughts and if I want to serve him more truly, then I am a saint, because that is not true of the average person. The natural man cannot understand God, nor the things of the Spirit of God. The natural man is enmity against God. The majority of people are not concerned, so why are we? Is there any explanation except that God has done something to us? Christians, church members, saints, are people who are set apart by God for his great and glorious purposes. They are his special people.

And that, of course, leads us inevitably to say that the people who realise the truth of these things set out to live holy lives. The secondary meaning of 'saint' is one who is trying to live a holy and godly life, well-pleasing in God's sight. Now that is what is meant by being a Christian. The thing to emphasise is not so much what we are trying to do, but, rather, our awareness and consciousness of being separated by God. As the vessel was set apart, as the mountain was set apart, so we have been put into a different category. Christian men and women are special, exceptional people in this world; they cannot help it, because it is the action of God upon them, and so, with the New Testament Christians, we ought to rejoice in this fact and in our distinction, in the fact that we are set apart in this separate order, we are this separate group of people, here in this world of time. This is what it means for anyone to be a Christian.

Our second proposition is that anyone can be a Christian – and let no one misunderstand what I mean. I arrive at that conclusion in this way: 'Salute every saint in Christ Jesus,' says Paul. 'The brethren which are with me greet you. All the saints salute you, chiefly they that are of Caesar's household.' So I find that I have to deduce the following points: Jews and Gentiles can be Christians. It is the Apostle Paul who is writing, and he is a Jew. Who are his fellow-workers? One of them is 'Luke, the beloved physician', another is Demas, and in addition there are certain other people to whom he makes reference. In Rome some are Jews but many of them, most of them probably, are Gentiles and, indeed, dividing it up still further, some of these Christians were actually servants in Caesar's household. Some are slaves, some free men, some of them members of the so-called nobility connected to the very person of the Emperor himself. That is the nature and constitution of the Church – neither Jew nor Greek, bond nor free, male nor female, but all one in Christ Jesus.

That is why I maintain that anyone can be a Christian. It is not a matter of nationality; it is not a question of being born in a particular country nor of belonging to a certain tradition. Neither is it a matter of a particular psychological temperament. We are aware how certain people, claiming for themselves an unusual degree of intelligence, often maintain this, saying that being a Christian is a matter of temperament. Some people have, they say, 'a religious temperament' – (if not 'complex') – and they think that this whole matter can be easily dismissed in that way. If you have some particular bent or temperament, then you will be a Christian; if you have not, then you will not be a Christian, but do not worry about it.

The simple answer to that is to read any one of the epistles. Indeed, you need not go any further than to study the twelve Apostles, and immediately you will find that men of every conceivable temperament are to be found side by side in the Christian Church, all coming from different cultures, essentially different in themselves, and yet all together in the Church, rejoicing in the same hope. This is one of the most glorious characteristics of the Christian Church, for it is a reminder to us that, after all, what makes us Christians is what God does to us. We are Christians because of the action of God, and therefore questions of temperament or intelligence are quite irrelevant. The facts support this theory. In the Church there have always been people of every conceivable type and permutation and make-up, and they are still to be found today. There are still Jews and Gentiles in the Church; men and women of scientific and artistic outlook; men and women with various trainings and differing antecedents, from every conceivable culture. All over the world you still see it.

That is what makes the Christian Church the most romantic place on earth. You never know what is going to happen; because of this truth there is hope for all; no one is 'beyond the pale'. Now I am anxious to emphasise this: 'All the saints salute you, chiefly they that are of Caesar's household.' Who would ever have expected to find members of the Church in Caesar's household – in that Imperial household, subject to the life that was so characteristic of an ancient court? This was an amazing, almost an unbelievable thing. Do you remember, too, how we are told that even the disciples, the Apostles themselves, when they were told of the conversion of Saul of Tarsus were at first a little doubtful? 'Can it happen?' they said. Was Saul really and truly a Christian? But that is the very thing that the gospel does; 'Saints in Caesar's household'.

I had the privilege once of hearing the Home Director of the China Inland Mission giving a short account of a visit he had made to China, and I heard him say that of all the things he had seen in China, the most amazing was a church that he visited in a prison. Fantastic work had been going on, and a number of men had been converted, and so a church had sprung up among prisoners in a prison. I also had the privilege of listening to a German evangelical pastor who was visiting this country. He said that the most remarkable work in Germany today is going on among ex-S.S. men, who had been guilty of the most terrible atrocities. They had awakened to the horrors of their past life, and there were a great number of conversions among them. 'The saints in Caesar's household.'

Now I want to apply that by means of an illustration. In my pastoral experience, I sometimes have the following difficult problem to deal with: parents come to me because their child has become interested in, or is proposing to marry, somebody who is not a Christian. This person is not interested in Christianity, never observes the Sabbath, and so on, and the Christian parents feel it is the end of all things and utterly hopeless. But what I have to say to such people is this. When you are in the realm of the gospel no one is hopeless. It is not impossible. Saul of Tarsus – the last man you would have thought of – was converted. There are 'saints in Caesar's household'. Christian people, never allow yourselves to regard anyone as hopeless. The gospel is the power of God. If you have a problem like that, pray for the conversion of this other person. It happens. Slaves, free men, anybody, anywhere, can, by the grace of God, become Christians. Let us, then, as we remember this phrase about the saints in Caesar's household, always bear that in mind lest we be discouraged or even fall guilty of denying the gospel itself.

Lastly, one can be a Christian anywhere. 'All the saints salute you, chiefly they that are of Caesar's household.' I must emphasise that a little and qualify it. You can live as a Christian anywhere, voluntarily or involuntarily, without any limit. In other words, there is no need for special circumstances and conditions. Some people think that you cannot be a Christian unless you come out of the world, but that is the fundamental error of monasticism. The 'saints in Caesar's household' – Christians in the most difficult circumstances imaginable! There are people who, when they are converted, think that they must of necessity change their occupation or go from one house to another. The lesson here is that you can be a Christian anywhere, and you must not have the feeling that you need to have particular circumstances and conditions before you can practise the Christian life. We must witness to it wherever we chance to be. Those people belonged to the household of Caesar. They were servants and slaves, or maybe high ranking officials in Caesar's household. The gospel had taken hold of them in Caesar's palace and there they were, witnessing to the Christian life.

Let me apply this particularly to those who, in the words of our text, are 'saints that are in Caesar's household'. As Christians, we are all the same and it is the business of all of us to bear our witness wherever we may chance to be, but there are differences. We are in different places and in different circumstances, and the whole art of the Christian, if I may so put it, is to realise the special way in which we can witness in special places. Today there are people who are 'saints in Caesar's household'. I am thinking of school teachers, doctors, and sisters and nurses in hospitals, government officials and various other people. The Bible has a good deal to say on this subject. You remember Nehemiah, the cup-bearer to the King, and the story of Esther? If there was ever a 'saint in Caesar's household' it was Esther, and the same is true of Daniel and his companions. Special conditions, calling for certain special truths. As saints in Caesar's household, these people have to realise certain special things. Let me speak directly to any 'saint in Caesar's household' who may be reading this book now. You are confronted by exceptional dangers. The greatest danger is of being ashamed of the gospel because you are intelligent, and because you are among intelligent, intellectual people who are more prone to scoff than anyone else, and more likely to try to slight it. You may therefore find you are taking part in various Christian activities at home, but are doing nothing to witness where you happen to be working.

The next danger is that of compromising your principles, perhaps out of ambition, because you are anxious for success. There is nothing wrong in a righteous ambition, but if it once makes you compromise your Christian position, it is wrong. You must exercise exceptional care, for you are being watched very carefully. Probably you are being watched more carefully than anyone else. Irritability, bad temper, scamping work – all these things are being judged by others.

You have been placed where you are and you have exceptional opportunities. You find children under your care, or patients in a sick bed who are beginning to think about death and eternity – I need not elaborate. The Christian in an exceptional position has an exceptional opportunity.

So let me just add a word about the rules you must follow. In a way, there is but one rule: keep your loyalty to Christ always in the first position; if you do that, you can never go wrong. Loyalty to Christ first, always. Do your work as well as you can, because the better you do your work, the better Christian you are. Christian students, try to obtain your First; come out on the top of the list. It is a wonderful testimony for Christ. Loyalty to Christ first, then do all your work with all your might. Then be wise: 'as wise as serpents, and harmless as doves' (Matt. 10:16). Be wise in the way in which you introduce the gospel, and bear your witness. Do not be foolish; do not do it mechanically; do not make yourself a nuisance to people. Remember the uniqueness of the position, its exceptional character, and pray to God to give you his wisdom that you may testify truly.

Remember, always, that loyalty to Christ comes first; because of your very special position you may be tempted and tried beyond all others. It happened to the 'saints in Caesar's household' right at the beginning. It was they who had this first great test. There came an Emperor who claimed that he was a god and he demanded that everyone should say, 'Caesar is Lord,' and the first people who were asked to do this were the members of his own household. Officials came to them and said, 'You must say, "Caesar is Lord." We are not objecting to your being Christians, but in addition you must say, "Caesar is Lord."' And, to their everlasting and eternal glory be it said, they refused to say it. They said: 'There is but one Lord, the Lord Jesus Christ.'

Even if it meant being cast to the lions in the arena their loyalty to him came first. They went on doing their work in Caesar's household and then at that point, as Daniel and Esther, they took the risk. They lay down their lives for their Lord and Master. That is the rule to employ; we must be loyal to him to the ultimate limit, even if it should involve death.

But, lastly, let me say a word of encouragement to all 'saints in Caesar's household'. If you are true and loyal, then it will happen to you as with the early 'saints in Caesar's household'. Having thus gone on with their work, they eventually had to take their stand and thousands of them were massacred. But you remember what happened? The day came when Caesar himself became a Christian. How did it happen? It was because of what the Roman Emperors and their advisers had observed about these Christians. Just a handful of people at the first, but they were saints; they were God's people and they held it a supreme honour to be accounted worthy to suffer for his name's sake. That ancient world observed this, and eventually even Caesar himself became a Christian. 'The blood of the martyrs is the seed of the Church,' and men and women who stand thus for Christ and for truth can be certain that their witness will be honoured, and they themselves will be given the crown of glory and have a special reward in glory.

'The saints in Caesar's household' – exceptional dangers, but exceptional opportunities. The one absolute rule of loyalty to him, and an assurance that if you are loyal, your stand and your labour will never be in vain. Thank God for the privilege of being part of such a fellowship – the fellowship of the saints, the people of God.

22

The Grace of the Lord Jesus Christ

The grace of our Lord Jesus Christ be with you all. Amen
(Phil. 4:23).

We come now to the last of our studies in this great epistle
to the Philippians. Perhaps a better translation of our text is
the Revised Version which puts it: 'The grace of our Lord
Jesus Christ be with your spirit.' These are the last words;
they express the Apostle's final prayer for these people who
were so dear to him, and whom he loved so much in the
Lord. But it is very important for us to realise that this is no
mere formal ending to a letter; it was not just a casual,
expressive phrase used by the Apostle. I have often
emphasised this particular truth. Paul never wrote anything
in a casual manner, and if we have learned nothing else in
working through Philippians, it is good for us to have learnt
that nothing must be taken lightly in an epistle by this great
Apostle. His apparent asides are often packed with doctrine, his postscripts are full of truth and instruction. Unlike
us, who often end a letter with some formal expression
which we do not stop to consider, or use a meaning we are
not careful to weigh, Paul, when he uses an expression like
this, means exactly what he says. And here in this final
word, this final prayer, he really is offering what I do not
hesitate to describe as the most comprehensive prayer that
any person can ever offer on behalf of another.

You will find that the Apostle is very fond of this particular expression; he ends his letters to the Galatians and to

Philemon in the same way, and, with a slight variation, you
will find this expression somewhere or other in most of his
epistles, either in the remarks at the beginning, or in a final
word of salutation like this. It is, then, something which the
Apostle means literally, and in this one verse he sums up
everything that he has been saying to the Philippians. You
remember how often we have been made to realise that the
Apostle's object is to encourage and strengthen these Philippians. He wants them to know the joy of their salvation; he
himself knows what it is to thrill with this glorious experience, and to have a joy in the Lord which nothing can
change and affect. Though he is in prison he still rejoices,
and he wants them to rejoice. He may be allowed to live on,
and he may visit them again, or he may be put to death, he
does not know. But whether it is life or death, the one great
thing is that the Philippians should so understand and grasp
the truth, that they will have this joy – 'Rejoice in the Lord
alway, and again I say: Rejoice.'

That is his theme, and it is for their sakes that he takes up
these various questions, these various things that tend to rob
us of joy, and he deals with them and explains them, and
then he gives his positive exhortations. That is his whole
object: he wants them to live at the full height of this wonderful salvation into which they have been brought by the
Lord Jesus Christ. And what better way is there to express
all that than in this very verse – 'The grace of the Lord Jesus
Christ be with your spirit.' If that is so, if you have that salvation, then all these other things are included. So nothing
greater can be desired or requested for any of us than that
the grace of the Lord Jesus Christ should be present with us
and controlling our spirits.

Thus, you see, we have here one of Paul's great, comprehensive statements, and all I want to do now is to look at
it with you and, by splitting it up into its component parts,
to see something of the all-inclusiveness of this petition.

'The grace of the Lord Jesus Christ': now there you have,
first of all, a statement which, as we have seen, is so often
found in Paul's letters. We often speak of Paul as the

Apostle of faith, and it is perfectly true, but I am not sure that a better term would not be 'the Apostle of grace'; it is his great theme and he can never get away from it. To follow this word right through the epistles and to observe the various things Paul has to say about it makes a most fascinating and interesting study. Of course, there is a sense in which the word baffles description and transcends understanding. Ultimately, grace is something which I feel, and it cannot be described accurately. Perhaps the nearest description we can give is that it is unmerited and spontaneous favour. That is what is really meant by grace in this instance: unmerited favour, something that arises spontaneously in the heart of God himself, something which man does not deserve at all, in any sense. Grace is not in any way a response to something that is good and noble in man; it is God looking upon man, blessing him in spite of what he is and in spite of what is so true of him. That is the essence of the biblical doctrine of grace. Though man had sinned against God, and rebelled against him and had been so utterly unworthy of God's blessing, God looked upon him, and in his infinite grace decided to bless him.

You notice how often at the beginning of these letters you find an expression like this: 'Grace, mercy and peace . . .' Now those are three very interesting words, and the old theologians used to be fond of discussing the question of the right order in which those words should come. They generally agreed in saying that though that is perhaps the best formal way in which to use them, actually, in the mind of God, the order should be: mercy, grace and peace. By that, they meant that God in heaven looked down upon earth and upon man, and saw man in his misery, his unhappiness and wretchedness as the result of sin. And the first thing that God felt was pity – that is mercy; he felt merciful towards man. And then, feeling mercy and pity, God decided that he must do something about it, and so grace came in. Man deserved nothing, nothing whatsoever, but in spite of that, God in his grace looked upon him and thus decided to shower upon him his love and favour. As near as we can ever get to it, that is the meaning of the word grace; it is unmerited, spontaneous, self-generated, not produced by anything outside God, but coming out of the being and the heart of God himself; the love of God expressing itself in this way towards man – grace.

Then in Paul's prayer we come to the words 'the Lord Jesus Christ'. Go again through this epistle to the Philippians and count up the number of times in which the Apostle uses this expression 'the Lord Jesus Christ', or 'Christ Jesus'; I find it astounding and amazing. From this alone it is clear that the very centre of Paul's religion, and his whole faith and Christian life, is the Lord Jesus Christ himself. Of course Paul worshipped God the Father, yes, but what Paul is out to teach everywhere is that were it not for the Lord Jesus Christ he would never have known the Father. Martin Luther was very fond of putting this point in this way. He used to say, 'I know no God but Jesus Christ.' Now he was not guilty of heresy there; what he meant was this: I cannot know God except in Jesus Christ. It is what our Lord himself said: 'I am the way, the truth, and the life: no man cometh unto the Father, but by me' (John 14:6). So he is the centre, he is essential, and the Apostle can never forget that fact.

Many times in the course of these studies we have emphasised this truth. Paul never forgot his experience on the road to Damascus. He had disliked the Lord, he had blasphemed him and felt that he was an impostor, and he had done his best to massacre and exterminate all the followers of Christ. And then he saw him, and from that moment the Lord Jesus Christ dominated the life of this man. Christ was at the centre of Paul's experience; Paul lived for him: 'To me to live is Christ, and to die is gain' – why? – that 'I may be with Christ; which is far better.' And his ambition was: 'that I may know him, and the power of his resurrection . . .' He looked for him and his glorious appearing. The Lord is coming out of heaven, as he has gone back into heaven, and he is going to change these bodies of ours and fashion them like unto his glorious body.

'I can do all things,' says Paul, 'through Christ which strengtheneth me' – Christ is always at the centre. And here, in his very last word, Paul gives him the pre-eminence again; he cannot speak a last word to anybody except in terms of Christ.

I just note these things in passing because they seem to me to remind us again of our whole position. Is the Lord Jesus Christ like that to us? In this prayer the Apostle is again enunciating his great doctrine – the Lord Jesus Christ – Jesus, Jesus of Nazareth. We are not concerned about philosophy or theory; our whole faith centres on a Person, someone who literally walked the face of this earth. 'We have not followed cunningly devised fables . . . but were eyewitnesses of his majesty' (2 Pet. 1:16). Our whole position depends upon someone who was born as a babe in Bethlehem, someone who lived in Nazareth and worked as a carpenter, a young man who went out preaching at the age of thirty, and did astonishing things for three years – Jesus.

And the whole teaching of Paul is that the person who appeared as a man amongst men is none other than the Lord God Jehovah, God the Son, the Lord Jesus Christ. Jesus is Lord, he is God, and he is also the Christ, the Messiah, the one whom God anointed and whom God set apart for the specific purpose of working out this great plan of salvation that mankind might be rescued and redeemed. Here, you see, in his final prayer and last word, Paul holds us face to face with the great central doctrine, the unique deity, the godhead, of Jesus of Nazareth; Jesus is Lord, Jesus is God, and he is the Messiah, the one who is set apart for the work. It meant his birth, his death, his resurrection; it meant shedding his own blood to purify man, that man might be reconciled to God. It is all here.

But now let us take it as a whole again: 'The grace of our Lord Jesus Christ.' What does Paul mean by this? Well, he uses this expression because, let me emphasise this again, the grace of the Lord Jesus Christ is the beginning and the end of our Christian salvation. There is no better way of expressing this, perhaps, than the way in which the Apostle put it in 2 Corinthians 8:9, which is one of the most glorious things the Apostle ever said: 'For ye know the grace of our Lord Jesus Christ, that, though he was rich, yet for your sakes he became poor, that ye through his poverty might be rich.' That is it, that is the perfect summary of the whole way of salvation. It is the grace of the Lord Jesus Christ that makes it all possible; if it were not for that we would have no faith or salvation. He, there in heaven and in glory, full of the glory of eternity and of the Father, came and made himself poor. We need not stay with this, we have already considered it all* in the second chapter of this great epistle – 'Let this mind be in you, which was also in Christ Jesus: who, being in the form of God, thought it not robbery to be equal with God: but made himself of no reputation, and took upon him the form of a servant, and was made in the likeness of men: and being found in fashion as a man, he humbled himself, and became obedient unto death, even the death of the cross.' That is the grace of the Lord Jesus Christ.

Now that is the beginning of our salvation, but it is also the continuation of our salvation, it is the whole basis of our perseverance in faith and it is the only thing that guarantees the ultimate end and consummation of our salvation. 'The grace of the Lord Jesus Christ' is responsible for the whole of our salvation from beginning to end. 'By grace are ye saved through faith; and that not of yourselves: it is the gift of God' (Eph. 2:8). Those are the Apostle's statements, so that this great verse, 'The grace of the Lord Jesus Christ' is a vitally important one for us to hold on to, because the Apostle means that we may experience all of God's gracious purposes with respect to us in Christ Jesus our Lord.

Having said that, let us come on to the second expression. 'The grace of the Lord Jesus Christ be with your spirit,' says the Apostle, and there, too, is something which is of real significance. Why does he say 'with your spirit'? It seems to me that the only adequate answer to that question

---

* See Volume 1, *The Life of Joy*.

must be put in this way. Our spirits are the highest part of our natures; everything that is central and most important is ultimately in the spirit. It is by our spirits that we are capable of communion with God. We are body, soul, spirit, and the spirit is the highest – body is that which is animal, soul that which links us to one another, but the spirit is a kind of link between ourselves and God, even in spite of the Fall. The spirit within us asks for that completion which God alone can give; it is the very highest part of our being and nature. The spirit of man is that in man which still, in spite of sin and the Fall, marks us out from the animal and reminds us that mankind was originally made in the image and likeness of God. Ultimately, of course, it is true to say that our spirit controls the whole of our life. So you see why the Apostle prays very deliberately that the grace of the Lord Jesus Christ might be with their spirits. If our spirit is that which ultimately controls our whole life, how important it is that the grace of the Lord Jesus Christ should be controlling it, and that is why the Apostle puts it like that.

Let me put it negatively. I say that our spirits are much more important than anything else, so the condition of our spirits is very much more important, for instance, than our actions. Proverbs 16:32 puts this point very well: 'He that is slow to anger is better than the mighty; and he that ruleth [controls] his spirit than he that taketh a city.' What a profound word of wisdom that is! We very foolishly tend to think that what one does is the most important thing, but according to that ancient wisdom, and to the Apostle Paul who was teaching the same thing here, the control of one's own spirit is very much more important than anything one may possess. There have been men in the history of the world who have had great intelligence, some have been kings, and princes, some military leaders, but because they could not control their own spirits, they have ruined everything. More important than capacity and ability to do things is this ability to be something, and especially this ability to be in control of one's spirit, and to see that one's mind and heart are in a true and correct state.

Or, to use another negative, it is more important for us to use our spirits correctly than it is for us to pay too much attention to the things that happen to us, and I have no doubt that that also is very much in the mind of the Apostle at this point. Here he is, writing to these Philippian people who are surrounded by troubles and problems. Yes, says Paul, many things may happen to you, but your own condition is of greater importance than those things because if your spirit is right, in a sense it does not matter what happens to you. Someone once said, 'It is not life that matters, but the courage that you bring into it.' Now I do not like that man's use of the word 'courage'; I prefer the way in which the Apostle puts it here. What ultimately matters in life is not so much the things that happen to us as the way in which we look at those things, so that if my spirit is right, then I am more or less independent of what is happening around and about me. Now that has been the major theme of the Apostle throughout this epistle. He is in prison, and in a sense everything is against him, but he is above it all because his spirit is right. 'The grace of the Lord Jesus Christ' is controlling his spirit.

We have been looking at that great phrase, 'The peace of God shall keep your hearts and minds' – and it is just the same thing. So that what the Apostle is saying in these last words is, in effect, 'I pray that the grace of the Lord Jesus Christ shall be with your spirit, because if he is there in his full grace, guarding your spirit, then whatever may happen to you, you yourself will be all right.'

Or let me put it like this. Is not a wrong spirit the cause of most of our troubles and problems in life? Look back across your life and consider the causes of unhappiness and pain and distress. Have we not honestly to admit to one another in the sight of God that we ourselves have created most of our problems and troubles? Evil thoughts and imaginations and desires – what havoc they play with us! A sense of wrong or a grudge, jealousy, envy – those are the things which distress and cause us trouble. How much unhappiness and wretchedness we would avoid in this life and world if only our spirits were sweet and pure. That is why the Apostle says, 'The grace of the Lord Jesus Christ be with your spirit.' There will be no evil thoughts, there will be no evil imaginations, there will be no jealousy and envy, there will be no sense of wrong or of grudge, there will be no tendency to complain against God, if your spirit is sweet and wholesome and pure. That is why Paul puts his special emphasis upon our spirits.

Finally, let me emphasise this in a third and last principle. What, then, does the grace of the Lord Jesus Christ do to us and to our spirits? Let me suggest these answers.

Firstly, the grace of the Lord Jesus Christ endues us with every one of the Christian graces. I can best explain this by quoting 2 Corinthians 8:7: 'Therefore, as ye abound in every thing, in faith, and utterance, and knowledge, and in all diligence, and in your love to us, see that ye abound in this grace also.' Paul is referring here to the grace of liberality, so when the grace of the Lord Jesus Christ is with you, you have all the graces of the Christian life, faith, hope, love, knowledge, understanding, and all these things. Now this is another way of saying, 'I pray that all the fruits of the Spirit may be manifested in your spirits.' If the grace of the Lord Jesus Christ is with our spirits, we will have knowledge, as Paul here tells us – knowledge of sins forgiven, knowledge of the gracious purpose of God with respect to us, and, after all, that is the greatest thing a man can ever know. What I am anxious for you to know at all times, says the Apostle to these beloved Philippians, is what God's purposes of grace are with respect to you, so that wherever you are you may always know that God loves you as your Father, that you are a child of God, that you are in the great purpose of God, and, finally, that you are in the plan of salvation and are ultimately destined to the glory which will go on, world without end. The grace of the Lord Jesus Christ endues us with every other grace, so having that, I have faith, I have hope, I have love, I have knowledge and understanding, and I begin to manifest these various fruits of the blessed Holy Spirit.

Then, secondly, the grace of the Lord Jesus Christ always restrains us. Those of you who are interested in the old theologians will remember that they always devoted a section to what they called 'restraining grace', and a vitally important thing it is – this grace of the Lord Jesus Christ that holds us back when we would rush forward into something which is wrong, or when our spirits tend to run away with us. Our Lord never manifested such faults – there was a calmness, a composure, a balance and a perfection of life in him, with the meekness, the humility, and all these things about which we read in the Gospels. So as his grace controls our spirits, he will restrain us in that way.

What else? Well, thirdly, the grace of the Lord Jesus Christ also animates, and stimulates us in our dealings with one another. That is why Paul wrote that great word which I have already quoted, 'For ye know the grace of our Lord Jesus Christ, that, though he was rich, yet for your sakes he became poor, that ye through his poverty might be rich' (2 Cor. 8:9). Paul was writing to those members of the church at Corinth who had not made a collection for the poorer saints. He said, in effect, 'As that is what Christ has done for you, do you not think that you ought to make yourself responsible for the poorer brethren?' The grace of the Lord Jesus Christ thus makes us love one another and consider one another. The Philippians had done it to Paul, and he prays that this grace may continue to lead and guide them.

Finally, the grace of the Lord Jesus Christ strengthens and sustains us, and Paul has written about this in the second chapter. Here were people, members of the church at Philippi, who, in a great trial and affliction, were abounding in joy. How did they manage it? The answer is that the grace of the Lord Jesus Christ strengthened and sustained them. The Philippians were passing through a period of very great trial, but they knew an abundance of joy, and out of their deep poverty, they were extremely liberal. It is the great theme of the New Testament. You find it most perfectly in 2 Corinthians 12, where Paul has been praying about his thorn in the flesh, and, you remember, having prayed three times that it might be removed, he learned this great lesson; Christ said, 'My strength is made perfect in weakness.' And that is what the Apostle is trying to tell these Philippians.

How does the grace of the Lord Jesus Christ strengthen and sustain us? It is by assuring us of his love, giving us perfect peace, enabling us to see beyond our problems to the glory that lies ahead. In Psalm 63 the Psalmist spoke those great words: 'Thy lovingkindness is better than life.' The man who can say that has conquered life. 'I may have trials in life,' he says, 'yes, I know that eventually they have to come, but they are only temporary and passing. But your lovingkindness will never go, will never leave me nor forsake me.' And Paul had proved that, whether in prison, or in shipwreck, or in persecution, the grace of the Lord Jesus Christ was always with him. It is something of which the world can never rob us. 'Thy lovingkindness is better than life.'

Or let me put it like this: the grace of the Lord Jesus Christ is sufficient for all things. Back we come again to Paul: he prayed three times that the thorn in the flesh might be removed, and the Lord answered him and said, 'My grace is sufficient for thee.' It is enough; yes, the thorn shall remain, but it does not matter, his grace will be enough, it will take you through. And that, it seems to me, is the supreme blessing in life. 'The grace of the Lord Jesus Christ be with your spirit.'

My beloved friends, we live in an uncertain world, an uncertain life; no one knows what is going to happen to any one of us. There are an almost infinite number of possibilities. Can we end our consideration of this mighty epistle on a grander note than this? Whatever may happen in life or in death; whatever may take place in any conceivable situation or circumstances, whatever may be your lot, the grace of the Lord Jesus Christ will be sufficient, it will hold you, it will sustain you, it will even enable you to rejoice in tribulation, it will strengthen you, establish you, hold you, keep you, answer your every need and take you through. Ultimately it will present you faultless, perfect, in glory in the presence of God. 'The grace of the Lord Jesus Christ be with your spirit. AMEN.'

D. Martyn Lloyd-Jones (1899–1981) pastored the Westminster Chapel, a Congregational church in London, from 1939 to 1968. The expositions contained in *The Life of Joy and Peace* were originally preached at Westminster in 1947–48. Lloyd-Jones is the author of numerous books, including *The Sermon on the Mount* and *Preaching and Preachers*.